COMPUTER MODELS OF
MUSICAL CREATIVITY
9780262033381EOP1

Computer Models of Musical Creativity

Computer Models of Musical Creativity

David Cope

The MIT Press
Cambridge, Massachusetts
London, England

MIT Press books may be purchased at special quantity discounts for business or sales promotional use. For information, please email special_sales@mitpress.mit.edu or write to Special Sales Department, The MIT Press, 55 Hayward Street, Cambridge, MA 02142.

This book was set in Times New Roman on 3B2 by Asco Typesetters, Hong Kong.
Printed and bound in the United States of America.

Library of Congress Cataloging-in-Publication Data

Cope, David.
  Computer models of musical creativity / by David Cope.
    p. cm.
  Includes bibliographical references and index.
  ISBN 0-262-03338-0 (alk. paper)
  1. Composition (Music)—Computer simulation. I. Title.
MT41.C67   2005
781′.11′0113—dc22

2005043894

10 9 8 7 6 5 4 3 2 1

Contents

Preface

Since the early 1950s, artificial intelligence has led a very public life, gaining visibility in the press, novels, television, motion pictures, and predictionists' visions of the future. Virtually hundreds of scholarly and not so scholarly books and articles have appeared, covering the history, evolution, successes, failures, and potentials of artificial intelligence. Marketing claims ranging from intelligent word-processing software to intelligent toasters continue to emerge almost daily. It is difficult to separate the actual from the hype and even more difficult to define intelligence, so nonchalantly is the term wielded. Amid all of this attention to artificial intelligence, the term "artificial creativity" has barely surfaced. It may be that we assume that creativity requires intelligence and that the latter subsumes the former. Whatever the reasons, however, artificial creativity has followed a much more sedate path during these past fifty years, and the few of us who labor to understand and model it have had to work in relative anonymity—possibly to our advantage, since the resultant low expectations have often matched our achievements.

As I hope to prove, "artificial creativity" is too broad a term to cover the study of the various ways that humans invent new art. Language, music, visual art, dance, and so on all develop in unique ways by utilizing different combinations of our creative abilities. In this book I will concentrate primarily on artificial musical creativity—the organization of sounds and silences that do not possess agreed-upon meanings. As a close relative of both poetry and dance, music offers certain ineffable qualities not found in any other of the arts. Programming or other ways of simulating creative processes in music require an understanding of music's unique modes of expression and contexts of performance and perception. In short, even the field of musical creativity is extraordinarily broad and complex. My hope, therefore, is modest: to model, using computers, the more salient features of musical creativity in order to gain a better understanding of a few of the processes that define and distinguish it from creativity in the other arts.

I will also attempt to grapple with questions concerning the definitions of creativity, whether or not computer programs can effectively model creativity, and whether or not computer programs can in fact create. This grappling will include the views of many computer scientists, musicians, scholars, and psychologists who have seriously engaged this subject, including such distinguished individuals as Douglas Hofstadter, Margaret Boden, Selmer Bringsjord, David Ferrucci, Karl Pfenninger, Valerie Shubik, John Dacey, Kathleen Lennon, and many others. Having been a professional composer for over fifty years and a programmer for almost thirty years, I hope to add my voice to theirs in some small way, especially as creativity applies to music. Interestingly, my views prove quite different from those I have encountered. For example, I will contend that computer programs *can* create. I will further contend that those who do not believe this have probably defined creativity so narrowly that humans could not be said to create.

Whenever possible in this book, I have included the thoughts of professional musicians, psychologists, philosophers, computer scientists, and cognitionists whose work complements or poses the greatest challenges to my own ideas. My apologies to those whose work may seem relevant, but to which I have not referred because of space limitations.

I do not intend this book as a comprehensive guide for related research on the topics covered. Such a book would require several thousand pages, with the thread of how the models form a cohesive whole possibly lost in the diversity of ideas. In place of comprehensive coverage, I have structured this book in three major sections—"Background and Principles"; "Experimental Models of Musical Creativity"; and "An Integrated Model of Musical Creativity"—whose titles I believe roughly describe their contents. In these sections, I make a case for musical creativity resulting from a process called *inductive association*. In brief, inductive association is a more narrowly defined version of *free association*, or the shedding of deductive reasoning for more intuitive processes.

Each chapter of this book begins with a simple principle, one that I attempt to prove as that chapter continues. These principles are followed by illustrative vignettes (personal and otherwise) apropos to that chapter's subject. In this way, I hope to create a friendly narrative while maintaining a scholarly focus. Many chapters also contain descriptions of computer programs designed to demonstrate that chapter's focus on the complexities of musical creativity (see appendix D for a complete listing of the programs described in this book and available on my Web site).

Part I of this book—"Background and Principles"—provides the historical and definitional foundations of creativity, so important for understanding what we mean when we use that word. To this end, chapter 1 presents a number of different perspectives on music and meaning. It continues by defining creativity—for this book, at least—and the various ancillary terms that often accompany that word. The chapter concludes with a discussion of the role of originality in creativity. Chapter 2 presents some thoughts on the origins of creativity studies, followed by a brief history of creativity research in general and of musical creativity research in particular. It concludes with descriptions of various proposals to test for creativity. Chapter 3 begins with a detailed analysis of randomness and how it differs from creativity. It continues with a summary of computer program types that in some way may model music creativity.

Part II of this book—"Experimental Models of Musical Creativity"—describes a number of possible models for computationally imitating human creativity. Chapter

4 outlines the basic principles of recombinance and pattern matching, two founda-
tional principles in my work with computers and music. The chapter concludes with
a discussion of the problems that performance creates for computation—particularly
recombinant computation. Chapter 5 describes how allusions contribute to musical
creativity, and concludes with the description of a program that analyzes music for
its references to other music and possible ways in which these references might be
interpreted. Chapter 6 explains the role that learning plays in the creative process,
then continues with a discussion of inference and how it can enhance creativity. The
chapter concludes with examples of how analogy contributes to the creative process.
Chapter 7 presents some of the ways in which composers build musical expectations
and then either fulfill them or surprise listeners. It then discusses musical hierarchy
and how computer programs can incorporate the analytical tools necessary to meld
hierarchy into their creative processes. Chapter 8 describes the role of influence on
creativity. It also includes a description of a program—called a *spider*—capable of
independently connecting to the Internet and downloading certain types of files.

Part III of this book—"An Integrated Model of Musical Creativity"—presents an
inductive-association computational process that can solve problems and produce
music creatively. Chapter 9 defines association networks and explains how such networks can, without being programmed to do so, respond effectively to input. It next
explores how inductive association can produce interesting, creative, and often
insightful output, as opposed to the complex but straightforward noninductive output of association networks. Chapter 10 applies the principles of association networks to music, both in the form of brief exchanges and in terms of longer, more
formal musical compositions. Chapter 11 discusses a number of possible combinations of the processes discussed in this book, ultimately favoring an integrative
model. Chapter 12 then presents a number of the aesthetic difficulties encountered
when computationally modeling creativity. This chapter continues by exploring
many of the contradictions that arise when building programs capable of musical
creativity. I have also included here my rationale for discontinuing my work with historical musical styles using Experiments in Musical Intelligence. The book concludes
with a description of various possible futures and the role in them that machine creativity might play.

I struggled long and hard over how to present the material in this book. In fact,
the first draft did not look anything like this final version. This first draft described
the integrated model of creativity currently found in chapters 9 through 11 first, and
then detailed the ways in which this model solved the various problems associated
with studying creativity using computers. However, I finally opted for an approach
that initially presents the foundations of my research and then describes various

models that solve selected aspects of creativity but, because they do not solve them all, fail to succeed in truly modeling creativity. I then follow these failed models with a description of an integrated model, the one with which I began my first draft. This latter approach—leaving the solution until near the end of the book—may frustrate some readers who do not wish to wait so long for a resolution of the various problems encountered in such studies. While I apologize to those individuals for their wait, I truly feel that the time spent reviewing the fundamentals, the problems, and the various attempted, but failed, solutions makes for a truer understanding and appreciation of the model that I feel ultimately succeeds.

While the majority of examples I provide in this book relate to music, I have also included a number of references to language, puzzles (games), and astronomy to clarify what might otherwise confuse readers were I initially to give examples in music. I have also chosen these nonmusical examples to help broaden the points I make to suggest that while my subject is musical creativity, the principles can often be extended to creativity in other fields.

I have limited the scope of study for this book to classical music. Other types of music might work equally well. However, classical music provides a comprehensive range of styles over a significant historical period. As well, my own background consists almost exclusively of classical music, and hence I lack the expertise to engage other styles. Readers may offset this shortcoming by applying the techniques defined and described here—as well as the programs offered—to whatever type of music they know best.

While readers should have some experience with music notation in order to understand many of the examples in this book, no knowledge of computer programming is required. Likewise, readers need not own specialized computer hardware or software to follow the text. I have written this book using nontechnical terminology and in a style that I hope will appeal to the general layperson with an interest in music and creativity. The narrative as well as the music should be understandable to anyone who is curious about the role computer programs can play in modeling creativity.

This book includes examples of output of the various computer programs discussed, and these programs, along with MP3 versions of all of the musical examples, are available at my Web site, arts.ucsc.edu/faculty/cope/software/cmmc. The programs are written in Common Lisp with many having two versions available: (1) Macintosh platform and (2) any platform that supports Common Lisp. To ensure that these latter programs will perform in different environments requires that I omit all MIDI (Musical Instrument Digital Interface) and graphical user interface (GUI) code, which are platform dependent. I have included full documentation and operating instructions for each program along with the code.

As time permits, I will also include code for graphics and music playback for various other platforms on my Web site. Note, however, that if history proves to be a good prognosticator of the future—in this case meaning that as soon as I write new platform-dependent programs, system hardware or software changes make my code obsolete—I can guarantee only that the cross-platform code will function without problems. In short, the software for the programs in this book, while very helpful in demonstrating the principles of each chapter and in clarifying the model of creativity that I propose, is not critical to the understanding of the material presented.

The computer output presented in this book was produced using programs similar to the programs found on my Web site, but which occasionally contain more elaborate code. Many individuals purchase books such as this for the programs that accompany them. In fact, these individuals often treat such books as *user manuals* for their associated software. *Computer Models of Musical Creativity* does not fulfill the role of a user manual. In fact, if anything, the opposite is true: the relevant software that appears on my Web site should be considered a bonus—not a requisite—for readers to better understand the principles and ideas that the book contains.

I wish to thank the many individuals who have contributed to my ongoing studies of musical creativity, particularly Douglas Hofstadter, who continues to lecture and otherwise publicly discuss my work. Thanks go as well to Patricio da Silva and Jennifer Logan for publishing Experiments in Musical Intelligence's music, which was unavailable for some twenty years until their company, Spectrum Press, made it available. I also wish to thank the Center for Computer Assisted Research in the Humanities (CCARH), especially Eleanor Selfridge-Field and Walter Hewlett. Without the moral support and advice from colleagues such as these, this book could not have been completed.

Computer Models of Musical Creativity describes and demonstrates some of the ways in which I believe we create music. I have been cautious in my estimation of the value of new ideas, preferring to believe instead that newness is often merely an enlightenment of older, but possibly lesser-known, ideas.

In all of my work, there is a strong reliance on musical analysis rather than on the development of formulas. Often this analysis centers, in part, on venerable masterworks. The associations, allusions, and so on, I discuss in this book existed in these works long before my research began. While I appreciate whatever importance readers may ascribe to my ideas, I direct their attention specifically to the results of this research, for it is from the understanding of these results that any true enlightenment my work has to offer will come.

David Cope

I BACKGROUND AND PRINCIPLES

Ein echtes Kunstwerk bleibt, wie ein Naturwerk, fuer unseren Verstand immer unendlich: es wird angeschaut, empfunden, es kann aber nicht eigentlich erkannt, viel weniger sein Wesen, sein Verdienst mit Worten ausgesprochen werden.

Art, like nature, has infinite depths: it can be perceived and felt, but cannot be truly understood, nor translated into words.
—Goethe (*Ueber Laokoon*)

1 Definitions

*Principle: Creativity relies on connecting differing but viable ideas in unique and unexpected ways.

Music and Meaning

At the beginning of the nineteenth century, a French music teacher named Jean-François Sudre invented what he hoped would become a universal language (Crystal 1987, p. 353). He called this language Solresol. This *langue musicale universelle* was based on the seven notes of tonal musical scales called *do, re, mi, fa, sol, la,* and *si* or solfège. These syllables equate respectively to C, D, E, F, G, A, and B, using the single-letter note names more commonly found today. Sudre created words in his language by using one solfège syllable or by combining solfège syllables as in:

si	yes
do .	no
re	and
dore	I
domi	you
doredo	time
doremi	day
dorefa	week
doresol	month
dorela	year

Sudre divided four-syllable combinations into different classes or *keys*, each based on a particular note. The *la* key, for example, defined words relating to industry and commerce. He used over 9,000 note combinations for the names of animals, plants, and minerals. Semantic opposites were often expressed by reversing the order of syllables (e.g., *misol* [good] as opposed to *solmi* [bad]).

The unique aspect of Sudre's language was that it could be played, whistled, or sung, as well as spoken. As long as listeners could locate *do*—usually by finding the two half steps of the major scale—they could understand what was being expressed. Solresol became very popular by the middle of the nineteenth century, particularly in France. Indeed, some people still spoke and sang Solresol at the beginning of the twentieth century. It thus became one of the longest surviving artificial languages. However, very few people even know about Solresol today.

Figure 1.1
A simple example of Solresol.

Figure 1.1 presents a brief example of Solresol. Its meaning—sung, played on a clarinet, whistled, and so on—is "Now is the time to serve humanity, to rise to the universal call to forgive our evils forever." Since rhythm is not a factor, the notes have been printed here as a simple chant with slurs representing words of more than one syllable. To someone versed in Solresol, the organization of notes translates into a meaningful concept, as understandable as any prose in French or English. However, the language makes no pretension toward musical goals. It is no surprise, then, that the melody here lacks musical direction, has little regard for tonal scale-degree resolutions, and has few logical harmonic implications.

What interests me most about Solresol is that this very flexible language offered its users the opportunity to affix concrete meanings to individual or groups of musical pitches, and yet, with all of its potential for universality, Solresol ultimately held little interest even for those who had spent the innumerable years necessary to learn the language.

In contrast to Solresol, music, at least good music, is ineffable. Stravinsky explains that ill-informed music lovers "... will demand that we explain something that is in its essence ineffable" (Stravinsky 1960, p. 49). Leo Treitler agrees that "... music, uniquely among the arts, is considered ineffable" (1997, p. 26). Harold Cohen, creator of Aaron, the computational painting program, attempts to "get across the notion of art as a meaning *generator* [my italics], not as an act of communication" (McCorduck 1991, p. 125). Charles Rosen adds that music exists

> ... on the borderline between meaning and nonsense. That is why most attempts to attribute a specific meaning to a piece of music seem to be beside the point—even when the attribute is authoritative, even when it is made by the composer himself. (Rosen 1994, p. 75)

Music's ineffability makes it different from language and, it seems to me, makes musical creativity different from language creativity, even though many of us still cling to the notion of music as a kind of language. Leonard Bernstein makes the point that

> ... language leads a double life; it has a communicative function *and* an aesthetic function. Music has an aesthetic function only. For that reason, musical surface structure is not equita-

ble with linguistic surface structure. In other words, a prose sentence may or may not be part of a work of art. But with music there is no such either-or; a phrase of music is a phrase of art. It may be good or bad art, lofty or pop art, or even commercial art, but it can never be prose in the sense of a weather report, or merely a statement about Jack or Jill or Harry or John. (Bernstein 1976, p. 79)

Language is also clearly representational—the words I write here all represent something other than themselves. The word "chair" represents a chair; it is not actually a chair. Being comfortable with this form of meaning, it is natural for us to force it upon music. In other words, in order to have meaning, music must represent something else. Treitler explains this point of view eloquently:

Language is used here to hold music at arm's length from the listener but also from meanings that may be attributed to it—to make musical meaning indirect and conceptual and to locate it outside of music. Words are asked to identify not music's properties or the experience of these properties but abstractions that music *signifies*. That is the doctrinal tendency to which I refer, a tendency to address the question of meaning in music via the semiotic transaction of signifying, hence a tendency to regard "interpreting" as being virtually synonymous with "decoding." (Treitler 1997, p. 30)

Treitler further argues that music, at least nonvocal and nonprogrammatic music, does not signify something else, as does language. He believes, rather, that any meaning expressed by music is in the music itself. Whether this meaning then stirs some common emotion in its listeners or is ineffable, I leave to philosophers, psychologists, and cognitionists. Either way, however, music clearly serves a different purpose than does language. Rosen notes that "Listening to pure instrumental music, as Charles Lamb observed, can seem like reading a book that is all punctuation" (Rosen 1994, p. 76).

In many ways, I seem to contradict here the thoughts I expressed in 2001a in regard to music's lack of meaning. In response to Douglas Hofstadter's statement "I personally think that I hear meaning all over the place in music" (Cope 2001a, p. 322), I stated: "Like Doug, I cannot simply ascribe all the meaning I derive from music to myself" (p. 321). The problem, of course, is semantics: the word "meaning" simply *means* too many things. I clarify my meaning of this word with "I had to know what it was that held so much *meaning* for me. Whether my interpretation of this music coincided precisely with the composer's intentions seems unimportant. That I could understand the actual musical events that caused my perception *is* important" (p. 321). The word "meaning," at least when related to creativity, must have a more precise definition—as near a 1:1 relationship between sender and receiver as possible—that was clearly not so important when discussing virtual music.

Therefore, I agree with my comments on meaning in 2001 *and* those made in this chapter. I shall discuss musical meaning further in chapters 5 and 12.

Interestingly, one of my favorite analogies is that mathematics is to physics as music is to language. The first instances—mathematics and music—are abstract, while the second instances—physics and language—relate more to the real world. Mathematics and music also deal in proportions, while physics and language attempt to develop meaning. Mathematics, however, differs from music in that the former is empirical and the latter is interpretive. Though simplistic, this analogy nonetheless serves to emphasize music's reliance on relationships rather than on meaning and representations of meaning.

In chapter 2 and in the rest of this book, I propose ideas that distinguish music creativity from creativity in the other arts. First, however, it will be necessary to further define and contextualize creativity in general in order to appreciate the differences that music offers.

Defining Creativity

Webster's Collegiate Dictionary (1991) defines *creative* as "resulting from originality of thought: imaginative" (p. 319). Interestingly, this same dictionary defines *imagination* as "creative talent or ability" (p. 671). The circular nature of these definitions should not be surprising, given that this same dictionary defines *intelligence* as a "capacity for learning, reasoning, and understanding" (p. 700) and *reasoning* as "the power of intelligent and dispassionate thought" (p. 1123). Dictionaries are by definition self-referential, thus providing us with the sense of a word's meaning given that we have a familiar context of other words in which to place that sense of meaning. E. H. Gombrich asks, "... are we not led into what philosophers call an infinite regress, the explanation of one thing in terms of an earlier which again needs the same type of explanation?" (E. H. Gombrich, as quoted in Minsky 1986, p. 150).

Curiously, *Webster's New World Dictionary* (1984, p. 34) defines *art* as simply "human creativity," while *Webster's Collegiate Dictionary* (1991, p. 77) defines *art* as "the quality, production, expression, or realm of what is beautiful or of more than ordinary significance." I am sure that, given enough time, I could find several more contradictory, or at least significantly varied, definitions of art. Obviously, according to the first definition, the output of computer programs does not qualify as art, unless you consider its output as the human programmer's output. Certainly, many individuals view creativity as something that only humans can do. (When I encounter someone with this viewpoint, I usually argue that if humans cannot create machine programs that themselves create, then humans are not in fact very creative after all.) The more generous second definition of *art* above could include the output of computer programs, depending on whether one considered this output beautiful or of more than ordinary significance.

Most books that deal with creativity in serious ways provide descriptions of the contributions of the human biological system. Axons, dendrites, synapses, neurons, sensory transducers, and so on, along with explanations of the related hydrocarbons, phosphates, and various proteins, appear often in these sources. The various lobes (frontal, temporal, parietal, occipital), as well as the right (principally visual-spatial) and left (principally verbal) hemispheres, function as separate and integrated parts of the brain, providing a foundation for creative thinking. However, I will avoid these kinds of biological descriptions of creativity here for a variety of reasons. First, there are other, more detailed sources for such information (Adelman 1987; Jacobson 1978; Shepherd 1988), and a simple summary here would do them and their subject an injustice. Second, while we have begun to unravel the chemistry and processes of thinking and cognition, we still have very little understanding of the neurobiology involved in human biological creativity.

At the opposite extreme, more casual definitions of *creativity* take forms not unlike those expressed by Frederick Dorian (1947) in his book *The Musical Workshop*:

Everything is inspiration to the born musician. The voice of his mother. The smile of his friend. The muffled tread of human passions—life on earth from the cradle to the grave. The curses of hell and the glory of God. There is no vision and no experience which has not been turned into an inspirational impulse by creative musicians. Inner and outer events, the whole gamut of psychic and physical experiences to which the human being is exposed or which his imagination can conjure up—they all have been the springboard of inspirational impulses in the music of thousands of years. "There is a song," in Eichendorff's beautiful words, "which slumbers in all things that dream endlessly, and the world will begin to sing if thou findest the key word." (Dorian 1947, p. 19)

This broad description of inspiration leading to creativity would be difficult to code. While I do not doubt the sincerity that the author brings to his observations, and while a certain emotional part of me resonates with at least some of his words, I cannot find much practical use for these sentiments.

Herbert Simon suggests that we

... should not be intimidated by words like "intuition" that are often used to describe human thinking. We have seen that "intuition" usually simply means problem solving by recognition, easily modeled by production systems. (Simon 1995, p. 689)

Douglas Hofstadter describes creativity more explicitly as consisting of four basic ingredients:

Having a keen sense for what is interesting: that is, having a relatively strong set of *a priori* "prejudices".... This aspect of creativity could be summarized in the phrase *central but highly discriminating taste.*
Following it recursively: that is, following one's nose not only in choosing an *initially* interesting-seeming pathway, but also *continuing* to rely on one's nose over and over again.... This aspect of creativity could be summarized in the term *self-confidence.*
Applying it at the meta-level: that is, being aware of, and carefully watching, one's pathway in "idea space" (as opposed to the space defined by the domain itself). This means being sensitive to unintended patterns in what one is producing.... This aspect of creativity could be summarized in the term *self-awareness.*
Modifying it accordingly: that is, not being inflexible in the face of various successes and failures, but modifying one's sense of what is interesting and good according to experience. This aspect of creativity could be summarized in the term *adaptability.* (Hofstadter 1995, p. 313–314)

As I will demonstrate in chapter 6, "adaptability" is programmable. The notions of "self-confidence," "taste," and "self-awareness," however, continue to baffle our most distinguished philosophers (see Damasio 1999; Dennett 1995; Searle 1997), no less computer scientists wishing to model or emulate these characteristics. Hofstadter's use of the terms "prejudices," "interesting," "sense," "good," and so on, unfortunately means many different things to different people. His choice of these terms, therefore, presents enormous challenges to those of us who would attempt to code them into computer programs.

Antonio Damasio posits that:

Creativity itself—the ability to generate new ideas and artifacts—requires more than consciousness can ever provide. It requires abundant fact and skill memory, abundant working memory, fine reasoning ability, language. But consciousness is ever present in the process of creativity; not only because its light is indispensable, but because the nature of its revelations guide [sic] the process of creation, in one way or another, more or less intensely.... there is a circle of influence—existence, consciousness, creativity—and the circle closes. (Damasio 1999, p. 235)

I have chosen to ignore such highly romanticized definitions of creativity even though I know that many individuals share their sentiments. One wonders if Damásio, and those who agree with his views, could recognize these ingredients for creativity (e.g., consciousness) in a test of human versus computer output (see chapter 2).

Margaret Boden eloquently points out that

... [the] way in which people commonly deny the possibility of "real" creativity in computers is to appeal to the consciousness argument. "Creativity requires consciousness," they say, "and no computer could ever be conscious." We have seen, time and time again, that much—even most—of the mental processing going on when people generate novel ideas is not conscious, but unconscious. The reports given by artists, scientists, and mathematicians show this clearly enough. To that extent, then, this argument is misdirected.   (Boden 2004, p. 294)

Marvin Minsky takes a somewhat different tack to defining creativity by addressing the often conflicting nature of creative and logical thought:

What is creativity? How do people get new ideas? Most thinkers would agree that some of the secret lies in finding "new ways to look at things." ... Why must our minds keep drawing lines to structure our reality? The answer is that unless we made those mind-constructed boundaries, we'd never see any "thing" at all!   (Minsky 1986, p. 134)

Modeling this bifurcated nature of the mind with computers seems possible by measuring, cataloging, and referencing boundaries while simultaneously attempting to extend those boundaries. However, Damásio would argue that without consciousness, we would not have to define boundaries, and thus never really need to create anything at all. Hofstadter might add the notion that without "discriminating taste," computer programs could never really know which boundaries to extend.

Boden, Bringsjord and Ferrucci, and Damasio all take up the consciousness argument—that creativity requires consciousness—with interesting but contradictory and inconclusive results. Two particular questions arise when "consciousness" becomes a requisite for creativity:

1. Is it important that creators know they are creating?

2. Is it important that creators appreciate their own creations?

As interesting as these questions may be, however, I have opted not to respond to them. My reasons are simple: How do we know that *humans* know they create, and in fact appreciate their creations? It would certainly seem important that creators know the difference between a creative output and an uncreative output, but is it necessary for them to self-relate to this output or to find this output appealing? Can we, as interpreters of their creations, discern the creators' feelings toward their own creations without being explicitly informed of these feelings? These questions all relate to creativity but, it seems to me, skirt the primary issue of precisely what constitutes creativity. Henceforth, I have avoided considering them in the definition I will use in this book.

According to Scott Turner, creativity should produce significantly different results than noncreativity does.

We all recognize that creative solutions must be original. They must be new and different from old solutions. But the differences must also be *significant*. If an artist were to paint the *Mona Lisa* in a red dress instead of a blue one, the resulting painting would not be considered

creative, despite its differences from the original. Significant novelty distinguishes creative solutions from ones that are only adaptations of old solutions.   (Turner 1994, p. 22)

As well, originality must be useful.

We expect problem solvers to be capable: They must develop solutions that solve their problems. Replacing a flat tire with an air raft is novel but not creative, because it doesn't effectively solve the original problem.   (Turner 1994, p. 22)

Musical creativity, on the other hand, does not offer clear "flat tire" and "air raft"
equivalents. The question of legitimate creativity regarding works of art seems tied
less to novelty and more to aesthetics.

Daniel Dennett offers yet another view of creativity:

... my three-year-old grandson, who loves construction machinery, recently blurted out a
fine mutation on a nursery rhyme: "Pop! goes the diesel." He didn't even notice what he had
done, but I, to whom the phrase would never have occurred, have seen to it that this mutant
meme gets replicated. As in the case of jokes discussed earlier [a result of a slow evolution], this
modest moment of creativity is a mixture of serendipity and appreciation, distributed over several minds, no one of which gets to claim the authorship of special creation.   (Dennett 1995,
p. 355)

Dennett's prosaic but pertinent observations demonstrate how cross-wiring can produce interesting, unique, and important *creative* connections. This notion of cross
wiring will offer a valuable resource when I define association networks in chapter 9.

I find David Gelernter's quotations of Gilhooly and Shelley in the following abstraction of creativity equally attractive.

Rather than beating your head against the wall of a difficult problem that doesn't yield to ordinary, methodical approaches, you discover a different way to see the problem ... put another
way, "The creative thinker comes up with useful combinations of ideas that are already in the
thinker's repertoire but which have not been previously brought together" (Gilhooly 1988,
p. 186). Or as Shelley wrote in 1821, "Reason respects the differences, and imagination the
similitudes of things."   (Shelley 1821/1966, p. 416; as quoted in Gelernter 1994, pp. 79–80)

Edward deBono (see particularly deBono 1970) distinguishes between what he
calls "vertical" and more creative "lateral" thinking. For deBono, vertical thinking
is selective and analytical, while lateral thinking is generative and instigative. Lateral
thinking invites intrusion of possibly irrelevant information. Vertical thinking proceeds by logical steps, while lateral thinking is nonlinear (deBono 1971, 1984).

W. J. J. Gordon describes creativity using analogies and metaphors that play
major roles in *synectics*, an important approach to defining creativity (see Gordon
1972). Synectics incorporates personal, direct, symbolic, and fantasy analogies to

creatively solve otherwise intractable problems. Personal analogy involves personal identification, particularly with inanimate objects. Direct analogy compares parallel situations to develop solutions. Symbolic analogy objectifies the elements of a problem. Fantasy analogy follows Freud's view that creativity is wish fulfillment. Each of these analogical processes attempts to make the familiar strange and, in so doing, to provide alternative possibilities that may not otherwise be considered.

Margaret Boden, in her book on creativity (1990), paraphrases Ada (Lady) Lovelace—close friend of Charles Babbage, designer of the first model of the modern-day computer—in her comments on computation and creativity.

The first Lovelace-question is whether computational ideas can help us understand how *human* creativity is possible. The second is whether computers (now or in the future) could ever do things which at least *appear to be* creative. The third is whether a computer could ever appear to *recognize* creativity—in poems written by human poets, for instance. And the fourth is whether computers themselves could ever *really* be creative (as opposed to merely producing apparently creative performance whose originality is wholly due to the human programmer). (Boden 1990, p. 7)

Boden responds positively to the first three of these questions, but negatively to the fourth, arguing that the question has moral and even political (more likely philosophical) implications. I will argue the opposite point of view in ensuing chapters, but certainly agree with Boden's assessment of her first three questions.

Selmer Bringsjord and David Ferrucci (2000) take up these same questions, responding negatively to the first and fourth, arguing in the first case that "... moving squiggle-squoggles around is somewhat unlikely to reveal how *Hamlet* came to be" (p. 11). The term "squiggle-squoggles" here refers to John Searle's well-known Chinese-room argument, in which Searle attempts to prove that computer programs are entirely syntactical, as opposed to humans, who think using semantics as well as syntax (see Searle 1997).

I include these many differing views here to point the reader to their sources and the sources these sources themselves point toward. I also include them to argue that these views, and the many others that arise from the discussions they spawn, critically contribute to any serious study of creativity; for it is on the resulting definition that all arguments for computer creativity, pro and con, rest. After researching this subject for many years, I have chosen the following definition of creativity for this book:

The initialization of connections between two or more multifaceted things, ideas, or phenomena hitherto not otherwise considered actively connected.

I use the word "multifaceted" to differentiate musical creativity from other types of creativity, as suggested by my description of Solresol at the beginning of this chapter.

Multifacetedness here represents, among other things, various aspects of harmony and counterpoint—when notes occur at the same time. I believe that music's ability to function simultaneously on both the horizontal and the vertical planes helps to make it unique among the arts. (Note that Sudre and his followers had little idea what to do with harmony and counterpoint in Solresol, and hence kept their language monophonic.) One could argue that, say, visual art has the dimensions of color and shape as correlates to counterpoint. However, for me at least, color and shape match timbre and form in music. These and other distinctions between creativity in music and the other arts will become clearer in subsequent chapters.

Note that my definition of creativity does not include the word "human" or any other such limiting words or phrases. To have included such words or phrases would, I believe, be simplistic and self-defeating. Worse yet, such inclusion would limit and do disservice to the human branch of creativity. My definition of creativity is also particulate—each word and phrase is clearly definable within its context—with each part quantifiable in ways that make programming them feasible.

My definition of creativity seems to find resonance with Gelernter:

... the core achievement of restructuring and creativity is the linking of ideas that are *seemingly unrelated*. The originality we impute to an insight centers just on the seeming *dissimilarity* between the problem and the analogy. Of course, similarity between the two must exist on some level, otherwise no analogy would exist. But that similarity must be deep, hidden, obscure, indirect—not a mundane matter of two ideas attracting each other because they share obvious similarities.   (Gelernter 1994, p. 84)

Originality, in the view of many, represents a critical facet of creativity. Interestingly, computers can generate seemingly *original* output quite easily. In fact, so-called randomness, a standard function of every computer programming language and which I discuss at length in chapter 3, produces apparently original output far more often and efficiently than it produces predictable output. For those believing that computers cannot be creative, then, originality should *not* be the focus of their definition of creativity.

For many, however, the decisive measure of creativity results from a determination of whether or not the results of a process are "derivative"—few words having more vile connotations for artists. While all art and music are derivative to a degree, at least in the sense of alluding to other art and music (see chapter 5), some art and music apparently borrow too heavily to be considered truly creative. I argue that while plagiarism certainly cannot fall within the boundaries of creativity, many of the most renowned artists and composers of history have borrowed extensively from their predecessors (again see chapter 5 for examples).

Boden (1990) also argues against the notion of creativity as originating from nowhere:

> In the abstract, however, creativity can seem utterly impossible, even less to be expected than unicorns. This paradox depends on the notion that genuine originality must be a form of creation *ex nihilo*. If it is, then—barring the miraculous—originality simply cannot occur. (Boden 1990, p. 29)

One measure of the veracity of my definition of creativity rests on the necessary conditions that must prevail before creativity can occur. In other words, if true creativity cannot exist in a vacuum, then the potential for "connectedness" of all of creativity's connections-to-be must already exist at the time of inception. Boden adds an extremely important point about this creativity-in-context:

> If, by some miracle, a composer had written atonal music in the sixteenth century, it would not have been recognized as creative. To be appreciated as creative, a work of art or a scientific theory has to be understood in a specific relation to what preceded it. . . . Only someone who understood tonality could realize just what Schoenberg was doing in rejecting it, and why. (Boden 1990, p. 61)

Many of those who attempt to define creativity ignore the types of contextualizations to which Boden refers here. We are much more apt to consider a child's drawing creative because of that child's acknowledged inexperience and lack of training, whereas the same drawing produced by an adult would be considered silly or retentive. However, rather than contextualizing every potentially creative act with its creator's credentials, I have opted to include the more universal ". . . initialization of connections . . ." and ". . . hitherto not otherwise considered actively connected . . ." things, ideas, or phenomena, leaving the interpretation of the context to those evaluating each particular instance.

Note that my definition of creativity is relatively active (initialization, *not* discovery) and uses connections (not aesthetics). This definition also avoids notions of consciousness (since no one has yet fully explained consciousness, at least to my satisfaction), interesting and uninteresting work (since such decisions seem personal and have little intrinsic value for a broadly conceived definition), and originality (which, as Boden points out, probably does not exist, at least on any fundamental level). My definition of creativity further avoids such limitations as whether or not the discoveries are easy or hard, beautiful or ugly, and valued or not valued. Critics will argue that my definition welcomes, for example, "creating a mess" as an instance of creativity. In fact, many important artists have created in just this way, to encourage the "initialization of connections between two or more multifaceted things, ideas, or phenomena hitherto not otherwise considered actively connected." As Anton

Ehrenzweig notes in his book *The Hidden Order of Art*, "But why not a 'mess'? Any creative thinker who ventures into new territory risks chaos and fragmentation" (Ehrenzweig 1967, p. 147).

There are three particular strategies that I find helpful for developing the kind of creativity I define here. First and possibly foremost, assumptions must be ignored, or at the least momentarily suspended, for creativity to occur. Second, creativity requires making or revisiting connections between seemingly incongruous ideas, with such revisitations possibly leading to inspired thinking. Third, the type of creativity described here involves nonlinear thinking—the ability to avoid dead ends that otherwise might obscure potential solutions to problems. To demonstrate these strategies here, I will use a game, a puzzle, and a riddle. These choices may seem strange. However, as I will establish later in this book, discussing creativity in music can be very difficult, and doing so without first examining the processes in less narrow circumstances can often cause more confusion than clarity. I will focus on music later in this chapter.

Figure 1.2 presents a particularly interesting chess problem, one in which black has the next move. For readers who may know the legal moves of chess but who do not have extensive chess-playing experience, recognizing the best move here may take considerable time. Such novice players typically use brute-force approaches,

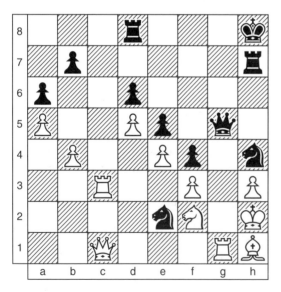

Figure 1.2
An in-progress game of chess—Black's move—as an example of creativity.

experimenting with various possibilities and then discarding those that prove implausible or illogical. These players accumulate points rather than strengthening their position.

Intermediate-level chess players, on the other hand, typically review the positions of both sides in an attempt to discover various strengths and weaknesses, and then focus on the pieces of power (e.g., the queen, rook, etc.) and vulnerability (e.g., the king). These more experienced players—faced as we are here with solving a game in progress—reverse engineer the current position, stepping through the probable moves that resulted in the game's current status. Even though these processes may be time-consuming, intermediate players ultimately make better moves than brute-force beginners do.

Chess experts, on the other hand, often gauge the occupied and unoccupied squares on the board rather than focusing on the pieces themselves. These experts concentrate particularly on the squares most influencing their opponent's king. The pieces—and their point representations—become almost inconsequential compared with their relationships to the empty, filled, and covered squares that prevent or enhance the potential for checkmate. In effect, advanced players ignore the assumptions of lesser players, and focus on winning the game.

In figure 1.2, White leads by a pawn (equating bishops and knights for the moment). One strategy for Black involves moving its queen out of harm's way (currently challenged by White's rook at G1). Though purely defensive, this move maintains the status quo rather than effecting a big loss (point counting, a beginner's mistake). A more imaginative solution might have Black's knight at E2 capture White's queen at C1. This move would most likely produce a queen exchange, since White would then no doubt capture Black's queen at G5, resulting in weaker positions for both players. Unfortunately, these mutual captures leave Black's knight at C1 vulnerable to White's rook at C3, and places White's rook, now at G5, in a position to put pressure on Black's king. Other moves of interest for Black include Black's knight at H4 capturing White's pawn at F3 and checking White's king. However, White could respond by taking Black's knight with the bishop at H1, thus increasing White's lead. Black's queen could take White's rook at G1, but White's queen then takes Black's queen, for an even greater advantage.

Other possible moves for Black exist here, but the ones I've mentioned represent those that initially seem most logical. For the expert, however, Black moves queen to G3 (check) in what appears at face value to be an exceptionally poor choice, especially since Black's queen remains vulnerable to White's rook at G1. This move actually *forces* White to capture Black's queen with White's G1 rook (the only move that relieves the check on White's king), as shown in figures 1.3 and 1.4.

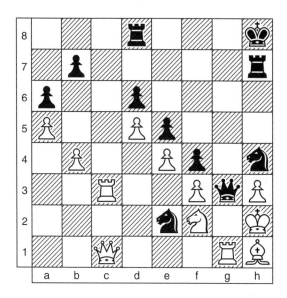

Figure 1.3
Black checks White's king with a queen move but also appears to forfeit this queen.

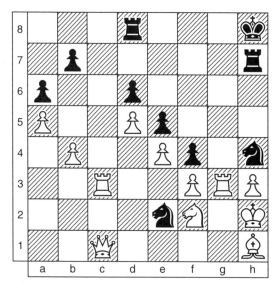

Figure 1.4
White captures Black's queen.

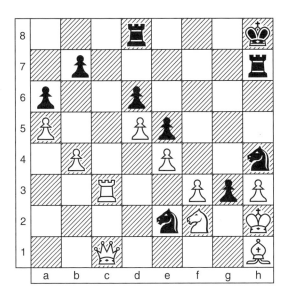

Figure 1.5
Black checkmates White.

At this point, Black trails White by ten points, more than enough in most games to ensure White's ultimate victory. Black, however, is primarily concerned with filling and covering the squares surrounding—and thus attacking—White's king (G1, G2, and G3 in particular). This attack now becomes possible (as shown in figure 1.5) by moving Black's F-rank pawn and capturing White's rook at G3, a move that subsequently checkmates White's king, since this pawn is now protected by Black's knight at E2.

Stepping through the series of moves taken in figures 1.2–1.5 may not give readers ample explanation of why I find this problem and its solution *creative*. However, the sacrifice of Black's queen does not initially seem reasonable, given the alternatives. It is, however, a move that ignores assumptions and creates an "initialization of connections between two or more multifaceted things, ideas, or phenomena hitherto not otherwise considered actively connected."

One might argue that this endgame merely proves Black's superior intellect. I argue that most creativity seems logical in hindsight, and that the elegant simplicity of Black's checkmate would not be foreseen by any but the most *creative* of players. Ultimately, winning at chess involves fully understanding not only the relative values of the pieces (points) and strong positions, but also the goal of the game: checkmating

Figure 1.6
Cards from which a player is asked to choose one card.

the opponent. Few players remember point tallies or elegance of positions; they remember only who won the game.

I find a particular card trick also helpful when describing creativity. This trick involves laying out six face cards in full view of a player, as shown in figure 1.6, and asking that player to mentally select any card, memorize it, and keep its identity secret. (Readers may act as players in this game as well.) I then retrieve all of the cards, announcing that I have read the mind of the player and know the exact card the player chose. I remove a card, shuffle the remaining cards, and lay the shuffled cards down randomly, as shown in figure 1.7 (the position of the empty space does not necessarily indicate which card the player chose, only that one card is missing). I then ask the player if I've removed his or her choice. Players usually gape at the cards when they discover that indeed the card they chose is missing. It usually takes from ten seconds to a minute or two for players to analyze how the trick works—easier here because you've probably looked back at the cards in figure 1.6 (remember that players have no visual access to the original cards as you, the reader, do).

In order to understand this trick, assumptions that the cards appearing in figure 1.7 are the same cards originally shown must be ignored. Remembering the number of face cards available in a standard deck of playing cards (twelve) helps make the connection between the sets of cards and indicates their differences. As mentioned earlier, these kinds of strategies represent an important aspect of creativity.

At the risk of alienating those of you who do not enjoy such games and tricks, I present one last example that I believe also exemplifies creativity.

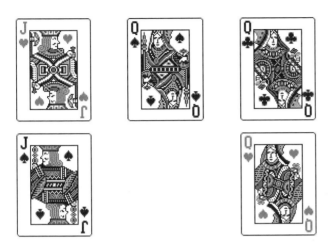

Figure 1.7
The player's card removed.

Two men are talking. One says to the other:

"I have three sons whose ages I want you to ascertain from the following clues. Stop me when you know their ages.

One: the sum of their ages is thirteen;

Two: the product of their ages is the same as your age;

Three: my oldest-in-years son weighs sixty-one pounds."

"Stop," says the second man, "I know their ages."

What are the ages?

Aside from seeming impossible to solve, two things are worth noting as you consider this puzzle. First, the assemblage of information here—ages, weights, sums, products, friends, sons, and so on—is certainly strange. Second, this puzzle is typically used as a test of intelligence, not as a test of creativity (Fixx 1978, pp. 24–25).

I suggest that even *devising* a puzzle such as this requires creativity. Solving it requires even more creativity. To do so involves patience and faith that a correct answer can, in fact, be found. Solving this problem also requires nonlinear thinking. My approach begins logically with a translation of the puzzle into math (x, y, and z here represent the ages of the three sons):

1. $x + y + z = 13$

2. $x * y * z >= 21$ (minimum age for an adult?)

3. 61 lbs?

Since the weight of sixty-one *pounds* does not fit with ages, clue 3 seems remarkably strange, unless this clue means something other than what it appears to mean.

Working then with clues 1 and 2, the possible products of three ages that sum to thirteen are:

Possible Ages				Products
1	1	11	=	11
1	2	10	=	20
1	3	9	=	27
1	4	8	=	32
1	5	7	=	35
1	6	6	=	36
2	2	9	=	36
2	3	8	=	40
2	4	7	=	56
2	5	6	=	60
3	3	7	=	63
3	4	6	=	72
3	5	5	=	75
4	4	5	=	80

Any other combination of ages repeats one of the groupings shown in this list of fourteen, but in a different order, thus producing the same product. Since the man to whom the puzzle has been presented presumably knows his own age, there must be at least two of these age aggregates that produce the same product, or this same man would have known the ages of the sons following step 2. This observation results from nonlinear thinking, since it has nothing directly to do with the correct ages. Only the product 36 appears twice, and—interestingly—one of these 36s is a series containing two of the same higher number (voided by the third clue, since there can be only *one* oldest-in-years son). Hence, the correct ages of the questioner's children are two, two, and nine.

Not only do those solving this puzzle have to ignore assumptions that there are too many possible answers and create new links between apparently unrelated data (ages and weights), but they must also think in nonlinear ways in order to avoid the dead ends—apparently not enough related facts—that obscure the solution to the problem. I contend that it is not possible to solve this puzzle without being creative, without the "initialization of connections between two or more multifaceted things, ideas, or phenomena hitherto not otherwise considered actively connected."

To some it may seem absurd to characterize creativity by using examples from chess, card sleight-of-hand, and word puzzles. I think it important to point out, however, that my definition of creativity is not limited to the arbitrary boundaries of historically defined Western art. I think that people act creatively in all sorts of ways, and that confining our understanding of creativity to prescribed forms of expression hinders rather than helps. I cannot imagine, for example, that great chefs and computer hackers are not creative. Imagination, the wellspring of creativity, reveals itself in many diverse ways; to ignore these ways would jeopardize any effective models of creativity we might find.

We must either broaden our definition of creativity to include games and tricks, or limit our definition of creativity to the point that it reflects only what our current sensibilities call *high art*—and in so doing, eliminate the notion of creativity occurring in many world cultures. While possibly expedient, this seems to me a far weaker and less useful approach. I would rather think of creativity as a process accessible to and used by all humans, rather than as an elitist phenomenon available to but a few.

Solving the kinds of problems posed by games and puzzles also requires intelligence. Therefore, creativity might be considered a subset of intelligence. Given this, my definition of creativity here and the notion that computers are capable of creating may seem at odds with my comments on the requirements for intelligence I make in my book *The Algorithmic Composer*:

> . . . there is one attribute of intelligence that subjugates all others. While in and of itself it does not constitute intelligence, it makes intelligence possible. That attribute is *life*: the ability to procreate, to interrelate with one's environment, to pass on biological and intellectual information from one generation to another. Most other attributes of intelligence pale in comparison to life even though they may be essential to the very survival of that life.   (Cope 2000, p. 247)

I still agree with this assessment. Intelligence, it seems to me, could not have originated without the extraordinary training required not only of one lifetime, but of generations and generations of lifetimes provided by the slow evolution of living organisms. For me, intelligence requires many other factors as well, foremost among them being the ability to

learn—not only to acquire information, but to acquire it quickly and efficiently

remember—to memorize information, connect it together in meaningful ways, and especially to prioritize it in useful orders

infer—to deduce new information that has not been explicitly learned

analogize—to extrapolate processes (e.g., mathematical processes) from examples

create—to solve problems for which there are apparently no correct answers.

Some may also feel that intelligence requires intention, self-awareness, and consciousness, as well as less definable elements such as taste, confidence, adaptability, sense of humor, and so on. Regardless of one's take on these potential requirements, I cannot imagine an intelligence that would lack creativity. Thus, regardless of differences concerning the other sources involved, intelligence requires creativity. However, *I do not feel that creativity requires intelligence*, nor does it consequently require life. Therefore, I believe that computer programs are capable of creativity.

Marvin Minsky argues that

... we should not let our inability to discern a locus of intelligence lead us to conclude that programmed computers therefore cannot think. For it may be so with *man*, as with *machine*, that, when we understand finally the structure and program, the feeling of mystery (and self-approbation) will weaken. We find similar views of "creativity." ...   (Minsky 1995, p. 84)

Darold Treffert and Gregory Wallace point out that

Leslie Lemke is a musical virtuoso ... he is blind and developmentally disabled, and he has cerebral palsy. Lemke plays and sings thousands of pieces at concerts in the U.S. and abroad, and he improvises and composes as well.... Most musical savants have perfect pitch and perform with amazing ease, most often on the piano. Some are able to create complex compositions. And for some reason, musical genius often seems to accompany blindness and mental retardation, as it does for Lemke.   (Treffert and Wallace 2002, p. 78–80)

Many savants demonstrate high degrees of creativity while otherwise being unable to converse or demonstrate the capacity for elemental logic.

Bringsjord and Ferrucci (2000, p. 5) contend that computer programs often *appear* to be creative but are not *actually* creative. In reference to a short story written by a computer program called Brutus, they argue that "Brutus didn't originate this story. He [their term] is capable of generating it because two humans spent years figuring out how to formalize a generative capacity sufficient to produce this and other stories, and they then are able to implement part of this formalization so as to have a computer produce such prose."

Benoit Mandelbrot, in reference to his mathematically produced fractal images, comments on output that is convincing versus output demonstrating understanding:

The man was very scornful of my images saying: "Poof, this guy doesn't know anything about mountains and his formula contains no knowledge of the earth whatsoever. So, what can it mean? I have a much better formula which takes into account all the available knowledge of mountains." I replied: "What about providing a picture of it?" "Who needs a picture?" he responded. "I fit the formula's 15 parameters from nature and the 15 measurements all check." I insisted: "Please, do make the picture." He made a picture, and it did not at all look like a mountain; it was some kind of shape that came up accidentally in his effort to model mountains. That model was never heard of again.   (Mandelbrot 2001, p. 204)

I have, of course, encountered similar points of view with the music of my Experiments in Musical Intelligence program. Critics have argued that this software is not creative since, from the perspective of the program, it could just as well be producing pasta recipes.

Mandelbrot continues by comparing art and mathematics: "Many fractal compositions [visual art] are more satisfying to people than most of the art sold in galleries, and in fact we are paid more money for these pictures than some people get for their art (which is one criterion for art that some people believe in strongly)" (Mandelbrot 2001, p. 208). Unfortunately, the same is not true for the compositions of the Experiments in Musical Intelligence program.

Translating the creative solutions to puzzles and games of this chapter to music poses some interesting problems, since what one listener may hear as a unique solution, another listener may hear as derivative. As will be seen, however, the example I use here has the force of many decades of analysis to support what represents typical and atypical creative musical solutions.

Figure 1.8 shows the first four measures of Bach's Chorale no. 48 (Riemenschneider 1941). These four measures contain a number of interesting musical moments. The first measure, for example, while establishing the key of A-minor, includes a diatonically transposed inversion—also a retrograde—of the melody of the soprano voice in the tenor voice. This inversion turns to parallel motion in tenths in the second measure, establishing the relative major key of C. Measure 2 also includes a somewhat unusual (for Bach and for baroque part writing) hidden fifth in the

Figure 1.8
The first four measures of Bach's Chorale no. 48 (Riemenschneider 1941).

soprano/alto voices between beats 1 and 2. In contrast to this apparent creativity, the almost lifeless alto voice simply repeats two different notes over these first two measures, while the bass voice provides the harmonic foundation for the two phrases. The third measure, with its eighth-note motion in the lower voices, consecutive suspensions in the upper two voices in the second half of the measure, and the chromaticism of the melodic minor scale in the lower two voices, contrasts with the simple cadential motions of the first two measures. I point the reader to the fourth measure, however, where I believe the truly creative solutions exist in this passage.

Measure 4 of Chorale no. 48 contains a statistically unusual parallel fifth in the soprano and tenor voices between beats 2 and 3. Such fifths not only are rare, but many contemporary theory books and teachers ban them from their students' chorales (see, for example, Duckworth [1992], who states that "the most avoided sounds in tonal music have been two voices moving in parallel perfect fifths" (p. 307), and Kostka and Payne [1989], who state that the reasons student examples "are unacceptable in the tonal style is that they contain parallel 5ths and 8ves" [p. 76]). Bach, an obviously skilled part writer capable of easily finding other solutions to this voicing, clearly chose his parallel fifths carefully from myriad other possibilities.

Figure 1.9 presents four of the possible alternative solutions for the fourth measure of Bach's Chorale no. 48. In figure 1.9a the parallel fifth has been avoided by moving the soprano upward to the third of the ensuing chord and holding the tenor at the note E to avoid the doubling of this third. This solution, however, does not provide the completeness of ending on the root of the chord—and tonic of the key—in the soprano voice that Bach or the melody he is using here requires. In figure 1.9b the soprano moves to the tonic note as in the original, but without the eighth-note anticipation. Unfortunately, all four voices now move in the same downward direction to the last chord—another statistically small voicing in traditional part writing. Figure 1.9c presents a third solution with the previous problems solved. However, the fifth of the chord has been omitted in the final chord here, with the result being a less than complete-sounding cadential triad. In figure 1.9d, the fifth of the triad has been restored. However, the alto voice does not resolve its leading tone (acceptable in inner voices at cadences), and the bass voice moves upward rather than downward, again causing the cadence to sound less convincing than Bach's more original solution.

While there are other possible revoicings, the point should be clear: Bach's use of the parallel fifth in figure 1.8, measure 4, provides a unique response to the many—often conflicting—requirements of cadence, voice leading, hierarchical completeness, and so on. Though subtle, this example provides us with a glimpse into why Bach's chorales sound so different and so much more musical than statistically correct

(a)

(b)

(c)

(d)

Figure 1.9
Four alternative solutions for the fourth measure of Bach's Chorale no. 48.

chorales. (For other examples of parallel fifths in Bach, see Chorale no. 8, measure 2, and Chorale no. 121, measure 4—two more of the 116 appearances of parallel fifths in the 371 collected Bach chorales.) The Chorale program described in chapter 4 retains these exceptions to rules in its output—one of the reasons I believe that this program's output is often so effective, and why I believe that it represents a simple but reasonable approach to tonal composition. For other examples of musically creative solutions, see particularly the Bruckner example at the beginning of chapter 7, and the discussions of various computer-created music at the conclusions of many of this book's chapters.

The definition of creativity I give here does not directly correspond to any of the other definitions discussed in this section. The differences in these definitions may be due to the point raised in my discussion of Solresol at the beginning of this chapter: ultimately, music does not *mean* anything. Many definitions of creativity, in contrast to the one given here, assume meaning as a natural goal. However, as we shall see, one of the ways in which music creativity distinguishes itself from creativity in the other arts results from music's ineffability.

Musical creativity can involve many elements: pitch, rhythm, timbre, articulation, phrasing, dynamics, and so on, to name but a few. Often these elements converge to create complex counterpoints through which creative minds find many diverse paths. In order to focus the processes I describe in this book, however, I will concentrate on creativity with pitch (primarily) and rhythm (secondarily). This focusing should not be seen as ignorance of the other factors involved, but only for what it is—a narrowing of the involved parameters in order not to spread my efforts too thin.

I will, then, use the definition of creativity as an "initialization of connections between two or more multifaceted things, ideas, or phenomena hitherto not otherwise considered actively connected" as a cornerstone for this book. Each of the chapters to come will exemplify one or more aspects of this definition.

Originality

"Originality" is often used when discussing creativity. Interestingly, however, the first law of thermodynamics (the total amount of energy and matter in the universe remains constant, merely changing from one form to another) actually voids any true meaning of this word. The theologian Paul Tillich comments:

If creativity means "to bring the new into being," man is creative in every direction—with respect to himself and his world, with respect to being and with respect to meaning. However, if creativity means "to bring into being that which had no being," then divine and human creativity differ sharply. Man creates new synthesis out of given material. This creation really is transformation. (Tillich 1951, p. 256)

There are, however, extraordinarily vast numbers of rearrangements of existing matter, allowing the word "original" to retain its *bite*. For example, Alexander Graham Cairns-Smith notes that the

... *really* big numbers become important when we come to consider not simply how many units there are in a given region, but how many ways they can be arranged. An example can be found in elementary organic chemistry. A class of hydrocarbons can be formed by linking together carbon and hydrogen atoms in such a way that every carbon atom is joined to four other atoms and every hydrogen atom to just one ... it is clear enough that 200 carbon atoms could be arranged, with 402 hydrocarbons, in far more than 10^{79} [the predicted number of electrons in the universe] different ways. (Cairns-Smith 1971, pp. 1–2)

The atoms Cairns-Smith discusses here cover a space considerably smaller than a fraction of a pinhead. In reality, the number of possible rearrangements of atoms in the entire universe is so staggeringly large as to make the actual calculation of their number, even in approximate terms, unimaginable. Some of these rearrangements are more original than others, however.

For example, were I to rearrange the words "complexity masquerading as creativity" into "creativity masquerading as complexity," it would not be nearly as original as my inventing a new word such as "comtivity" to mean "complexity masquerading as creativity." In the first instance, while the rearrangement of existing words means something different, the process actually represents something we do commonly in daily life—rearranging the words we say to make ordinary conversation more interesting. On the other hand, the word "comtivity," a rearrangement of existing letters rather than words, captures a meaning not currently found in the definition of any other word in the English language. In fact, this word signifies this meaning so effectively that I will continue to use it throughout this book. However—and again I apologize for repeating myself—neither of these rearrangements is *fundamentally* original.

Accidents—in this case, accidents of apparently irrelevant combinations—constitute *very* important aspects of creativity and of apparent originality. As Stravinsky points out, "an accident is perhaps the only thing that really inspires us" (Stravinsky 1960, p. 56). He adds that "one does not contrive an accident: one observes it to draw inspiration therefrom" (p. 56). Such accidents—taken seriously—can produce amazingly creative results. Of course, *useful* accidents are not simply everyday accidents, but result from a careful selection from among the many accidents that our universe so amply provides.

The creativity described thus far in this book derives from these kinds of recombinatoriality and accidents—that is, none of the ideas are really new. However, one can make a distinction between, say, creating a good solution in the game of chess and creating the game of chess itself. The new game we create may itself be a construct of parts of many other games—as I would insist it is—but the new game might involve a deeper creativity than finding the best solution for one particular problem posed by that game (see chapter 6 of this book for such a new game). I discuss this notion of "degrees" of creativity in chapter 10, where I present three different types of computational inductive creation.

In terms of originality in music, Arnold Schoenberg asks:

What is New Music?
Evidently it must be music which, though it is still music, differs in all essentials from previously composed music. Evidently it must express something which has not yet been expressed in music. Evidently, in higher art, only that is worth being presented which has never before been presented. There is no great work of art which does not convey a new message to humanity; there is no great artist who fails in this respect. This is the code of honour of all the great in art, and consequently in all great works of the great we will find that newness which never perishes, whether it be of Josquin des Prés, of Bach or Haydn, or of any other great master. *Because: Art means New Art.*   (Schoenberg 1984, pp. 114–115; italics in original)

I suggest that the "new" to which Schoenberg refers here is a new organization of preexisting music, be it notes or small groupings of other already composed works. The new "messages" that Schoenberg alludes to may in fact be similar rearrangements of old messages (e.g., see chapter 5 of this book).

Creativity, then, is not a "bringing forth something that was previously nothing," but rather a revelation of important connections between things that already exist. Originality thus becomes a synthesis and not a new "something." Boden notes that:

Cynics may deny that one ever gets anything for nothing, but most people apparently assume that one can get something *from* nothing. Indeed, the first definition of "create" listed by my dictionary is "to bring into being or form out of nothing." The medieval theologians of Islam, Jewry, and Christendom showed that this assumption can be questioned at the metaphysical level. What is more to the point, it can be queried at the psychological level also. Perhaps the new thoughts originated in creative thinking are not wholly novel, in that they have their seeds in representations already present in the mind? And perhaps they are not wholly inexplicable, in that something can be said about ways of manipulating familiar representations so as to generate others that are somehow fresh, or original?   (Boden 1987, p. 298)

"New" art, then, consists of a reassembly of already existing art. One might argue that the smaller the reassembled bits of previous art, the more original and creative the "new" art is (e.g., formalisms such as fugues possibly being more original than more intuitively composed forms). However, one cannot argue the notion of reassembly as creativity.

As an example of algorithmic musical creativity that seems to rely heavily on originality as its form of creativity, I submit a 2003 composition called *Endangered Species*, for chamber orchestra and electronic tape. This work represents a form of what Margaret Boden calls historical creativity (Boden 2004, p. 2) due to the rules used and the manner in which these rules are applied. In order to adequately describe these rules, I present some background information.

Boden distinguishes between "P-creativity" and "H-creativity" in the following way:

What you might do—and what I think you should do in this situation—is make a distinction between "psychological" creativity and "historical creativity" (P-creativity and H-creativity, for short). P-creativity involves coming up with a surprising, valuable idea that's new *to the person who comes up with it*. It doesn't matter how many people have had that idea before. But if a new idea is H-creative, that means that (so far as we know) no one else has had it before: it has arisen for the first time in human history.   (Boden 2004, p. 2)

During the latter third of the twentieth century, Alexander Cairns-Smith developed a theory on the origin of life based on crystals, the only other self-replicating matter in the known universe (Cairns-Smith 1971). The results of Cairns-Smith's research, while not currently a part of academic dogma, are generally well received by the scientific community. What I find most intriguing about Cairns-Smith's theory is that it assumes that life originated from nonorganic matter as a natural consequence of universal processes, rather than as a special case (e.g., lightning striking the primordial soup). This theory underscores, I profoundly believe, that we are doomed to extinction if we do not maintain earth's natural resources. The work *Endangered Species* refers, then, to both organic and inorganic matter. *Endangered Species* is algorithmically created and based on proportions found in certain crystals as described by Cairns-Smith.

The music of *Endangered Species* presents unique challenges for listeners. For example, the work is not divided into sections and phrases—at least not into easily defined sections and phrases—as one typically expects of most traditional music. In some ways this makes aural analysis easier, since the music follows a single gesture. In other ways, determining the structure of this work, for example, poses difficult problems. The style—which I call *complex minimalism*—makes the texture at once simple and intricate. These characteristics evoke the notion of minimalism in that material is revealed so slowly that each nuance, every slight change in pitch, dynamic, and/or timbre, is heightened. The word "complex" comes to mind here because the music gives the impression that it continuously changes, yet never really changes at all.

These impressions of stasis and momentum, while obviously contradictory, give the style its uniqueness, though other instances of this kind of minimalism predate it. None of these other instances, however, were known to the program that created *Endangered Species*, though this ignorance does not exempt it from Boden's (2004) P-creativity. I would, however, contend that the interfering processes involved in this style—particularly in terms of timbre—create a new style quite unlike that found in the music of, for example, György Ligeti or Henryk Górecki.

Figure 1.10 is an excerpt from *Endangered Species*. As can be seen, the overall musical texture remains much the same from beat to beat. The entire ensemble plays a majority of the time, with entrances and exits often occurring without metric predictability. The pitches, while themselves seemingly unrelated and to some degree unorganized, accumulate into complex harmonic fields that, while slowly evolving, often seem similar and static. At the same time, however, looking and listening closely to any single small fragment of music will demonstrate how the music changes from instant to instant, with masked entrances—the pianos or harp initially obscuring simultaneous entrances in other instruments—and with dynamic crescendos and diminuendos shifting the overall pitch content.

Endangered Species's achieved effect is similar to viewing a complex landscape where one may simply grasp the overall shape of the scene or follow the intricate details of light and shade, of similar and contrasting colors, of general and specific textures, and so on. The basic concept of this particular work—the plight of the endangered species in our environment—fits well with these kinds of musical choices.

Complex minimalism, as expressed in *Endangered Species*, has an interesting effect on most listeners—a sort of three-stage adaptive process. Initially, many listeners find the music interesting and full of color. However, after a few moments, when these listeners realize that the music is not changing very much, a sense of monotony sets in. After all, most listeners are accustomed to more narrative-like musical structures, where a musical "plot" pits one idea against another, and where some kind of resolution occurs. After relaxing and letting their expectations wane, listeners then begin to hear the music differently: they begin to unlock the sounds they are hearing, and realize that important changes are taking place at the more atomic levels of the music. Once listeners reach this third level, they are, as I see it, attuned to the music in a more natural way and able to hear it freshly from one moment to the next. One can find a similar style in the music of Claude Debussy, Karlheinz Stockhausen, and many other composers. However, the manner in which *Endangered Species* proceeds is, I feel, unique.

Endangered Species

David Cope

Figure 1.10
An excerpt from *Endangered Species.*

Pisces

Figure 1.11
The opening of a Vivaldi-style cello concerto, second movement, by Experiments in Musical Intelligence.

Interestingly, the monolithic nature of this work results from almost fifty years of musical evolution that occurs only in my algorithmic compositions, not in the style of my other, more traditionally narrative music. *Spires* of 1956 (see discussion in chapter 2 of this book), *Pleiades* from the early 1980s, and the set of three algorithmic piano sonatas completed in the early 1990s all predate *Endangered Species* with similar nonnarrative forms. *Endangered Species* is nonetheless the only one of these works involving complex minimalism. However, the originality of devising this musical style in no way overshadows the creativity necessary to maintain the subtle interleaving of pitch and timbre that constitutes the essence of *Endangered Species*.

In contrast to *Endangered Species*, and as a proof that striking originality need not be a trademark of creativity, figure 1.11 shows the opening of the second movement of a Vivaldi-style cello concerto created by Experiments in Musical Intelligence. The music in figure 1.11 has few if any stylistic surprises, and for those familiar with baroque music, the style here seems strikingly less original than the music in figure 1.10. However, the music of figure 1.11 *was* composed using what I feel—and will describe in detail in chapters 9 through 12—are very real creative processes, processes that at least equate in value to those present in figure 1.10.

Originality, often considered a hallmark of creativity, is—for me, at least—but a fraction of what constitutes *real* creativity. This real creativity cannot by mimicked by shocking unpredictability or replaced by conspicuous originality. Rather, this real creativity results from an "initialization of connections between two or more multifaceted things, ideas, or phenomena hitherto not otherwise considered actively connected" that often occurs in the subtlest manifestations of art. Creativity should never be confused with arbitrary or convenient contrivances that simply take any road untried for the sake of novelty.

2 Background

Principle: Creativity does not depend exclusively on human inspiration, but can originate from other sources, such as machine programs.

Origins of Creativity Studies

I had two life-altering experiences as a youth. Both of these experiences occurred during the same year and formed the basis for much of what I consider the ultimate shape of my creative life. Even though these experiences may seem unrelated, they have a common root in the manner in which they encouraged me to grapple with the apparent contradictions between logic and inspiration.

As a teenager I devoted myself almost exclusively to chess, music, and astronomy, not necessarily in that order. I belonged to a number of astronomical organizations, including the Phoenix Astronomy Club (PAC). The PAC decided, during my days as a member, to publish a newsletter and requested that all members consider contributing a column or article. I suppose no one expected me—a midteen novice astronomer—actually to write an article, but I did. It was published eventually, but not without some angry dissent.

The subject of my article was, I felt, a straightforward one. Popular belief at the time—and many continue to believe it to this day—held that our moon originally ejected outward from Earth during a prehistoric cataclysm. I had spent many hours studying the solar system and had other ideas. Put simply, I felt that Earth's moon was a captured asteroid. My logic was based on the notion that at that time, the count of moons in the solar system was as follows, outward from the sun (from Mercury to Pluto). (Note that the moon count has changed significantly since.)

Mercury: 0

Venus: 0

Earth: 1

Mars: 2

Jupiter: 9

Saturn: 6

Uranus: 0

Neptune: 0

Pluto: 0

As I imagined the scenario, the asteroid belt—located between Mars and Jupiter—was once a planet that exploded, sending large chunks of itself into space. As each fragment traveled outward from its source, it was subjected to the gravitational pull of other planets. However, the farther the fragment was from its source, the less likely it was to encounter a planet and its gravity. Thus, it seemed logical to me that planets closer to the asteroid belt would have more captured asteroids—moons—than planets farther from the asteroid belt. Indeed, the data fit the model, with planets approaching the sun from the asteroid belt having 2-1-0-0 moons, respectively, and planets approaching the outer solar system from the asteroid belt having 9-6-0-0 moons, respectively. The logic, for me at least, was inescapable: our moon once belonged to a planet orbiting the sun between Mars and Jupiter. Unfortunately, my proposal was highly controversial at the PAC, and has not gained much momentum since.

I recount this story here because it presents what I felt at the time were logically inescapable conclusions. Yet obviously logic alone did not produce my theory. It took a combination of logic and creativity. For example, I tried several other approaches to the moon's origins, such as (1) our moon is a natural by-product of planet formation during the sun's coalescence from its initial dust cloud; (2) our moon resulted from a malformed planet originally located between Earth and Mars; and (3) our moon is a captured comet or other extrasolar object from deep space. My resolve to put forward the asteroidian evolution of our moon occurred only as a result of my creatively combining the descending numbers of planetary moons outward in both directions from the asteroid belt with the capture probabilities of planets inversely proportional to their distances from that belt.

Another experience from this same year of my life will, I hope, more concretely relate this astronomical experience to creativity. I have acrophobia (a fear of heights). This disability is so severe at times that I suffer nausea and vertigo even when viewing films, where I know that what I am seeing is not real—that the actors are most likely standing on level ground, with camera angles and sets giving the illusion of a precipice at their feet. Sometime in 1955, I attempted to overcome my phobia by climbing a very high metal radio antenna on a moonless winter night. This rather silly notion for a cure was initiated by my reading an article in a popular journal of the time, which argued that we should directly confront our fears. This article contained quotes from all manner of celebrities proclaiming success when they used this approach.

I succeeded in ascending the tower with surprisingly few problems. I did not look down, which helped relieve my fears, at least temporarily. The dark night and the beauty of the stars also helped divert my attention from the increasing altitude.

When I reached the top of the tower, however, my acrophobia returned with more intensity than I had ever felt before. I feared that I would never be able to climb back down—that I would clutch the tower with an iron grip until I eventually fell asleep and plummeted to my death.

At the moment of my worst agony, a gentle breeze began to whine through the supporting guy wires, creating a beautiful kind of singing. I was transfixed by this sound, and decided I had to save myself in order to "compose" this new work I was hearing as a testimony to my journey. Gritting my teeth, I slowly descended the tower one rung at a time, settling sometime later on safe Mother Earth.

Upon returning home, cold and exhausted, I wrote out a short set of instructions—a simple algorithm—that would guide me at another time in completing the "wire music" that had accompanied my journey out of the sky. I put my notes away for future reference and did not look at them again for thirteen years.

I completed a score to this work (called *Spires*, after the tower I had climbed) in Los Angeles in 1968, as part of a series of similar algorithmic works: *Towers*, *The Birds*, *A Christmas for Dismas*, and *Iceberg Meadow*. Like *The Birds*, *Spires* was written in graphic notation representing electronic sounds, since at the time I did not have access to the appropriate technology for realizing the work. In all probability *Spires* could not have been realized with the electronic resources available in 1968, no less those available in 1955, so it may have been fortuitous that I opted to wait until 2003 to create a full version of *Spires* for a retrospective album of my algorithmic compositions.

I recount this story here because it deals directly with one specific source of creativity. In this case, the creativity was coaxed out of me the hard way, by climbing the tower and hearing the sound of the wind in taut wires. From my perspective, the music came from the wires; my only contribution was listening and taking what I heard seriously.

One could now ask whether the wires on my tower climb were creative, random, both, or neither. The sound from these wires was certainly complex and patternless, at least from my perspective at the moment. The "singing," as I called it, was, however, not random (a subject I take up in earnest in chapter 3), though it may have seemed so at the time. Nor was this singing creative. The sound was not an "initialization of connections between two or more multifaceted things, ideas, or phenomena hitherto not otherwise considered actively connected." It was I who decided, consciously or not, to truly listen to the ebbing and flowing "moan" from these wires. Creativity research must take random (real or not) impostors seriously, for often an unusual output of complex systems, known here as comtivity, can be easily mistaken for creative output. Many of the programs I discuss in chapter 3 fall under this heading.

What holds these two memories together in my mind is their contrasting view of the origins of creativity. In the case of the asteroidian evolution of the moon, creativity resulted from an *active* combination of apparently unrelated facts. In contrast, my climbing the tower and hearing "wire music" was *passive*; the music happened *to* me—my only contribution was taking it seriously. These two different views constitute an important pivot around which much of my research on creativity balances.

In the chapter "Chance, Chaos, Randomness, Unpredictability," in *The Creative Mind: Myths and Mechanisms*, Margaret Boden notes that chaos is "... contrasted with creation in *Genesis*. Yet it is also depicted there (and elsewhere) as the fruitful precursor of creation, the seedbed from which order blossoms" (Boden 2004, p. 233). Boden later adds:

The fourth member of our conceptual quartet, unpredictability, is the most important of all, because it seems—to many people—to put creativity beyond the reach of science. The surprise-value of creativity is undeniable ... trying to forecast what ideas a creative person will come up with in the long term, say in three years' time, such a project would be ridiculous. But *why*? Just what sort of unpredictability is this? And does it really destroy any hope of understanding creativity in scientific terms? (Boden 2004, p. 243)

Benoit Mandelbrot speaks of his scientific creativity in generating fractals, a self-replicative mathematical process.

Because of love for Euclid's world of geometry, because of the availability of increasingly elaborate computers with ever-expanding graphic capabilities, and because of increasingly skilled friends who program these computers, it has been my great privilege to discover this new way of generating extremely simple, truly minimal art of the most baroque or extravagant kind that one can imagine. This art can be altered in a predictable way by changing the parameters in the mathematical formula.... Are these images "art"? Perhaps no more than simple circles are "art" by themselves. Regardless, the concept of where man—with his artist's eye and his imagination—stands in relationship to high art is bound to change in view of this new universe of fractal images generated not by man, but by a simple one-line mathematical formula. (Mandelbrot 2001, p. 212)

In my book *The Algorithmic Composer* (Cope 2000), I note how important such formulas can be as a source for creativity.

While innovation certainly represents one possible source, it does not constitute what I believe to be the core of creativity. As with inference, creativity depends on rules, however broadly or inexactly they may be applied. Such broad interpretation and inexactness represents, I feel, one of the important cornerstones of both intelligent-like and creative-like behavior and must be understood if we hope to replicate these irrevocably linked but illusory processes. (Cope 2000, p. 115)

Doug Hofstadter applies these origins of creativity to computers:

… many critics of computers and artificial intelligence, eager to find something that "computers can't do" (and never will be able to do) often jump too far: they jump to the conclusion that art and, more generally creativity, are fundamentally uncomputerizable. This is hardly the implied conclusion! The implied conclusion is just this: that for computers to act human, we will have to wait until we have good computer models of such human things as perception, memory, mental categories, learning, and so on. We are a long way from that. But there is no reason to assume that those goals are in principle unattainable, even if they remain far off for a long time. (Hofstadter 1985, p. 209)

Past Research

Most histories of creativity research begin with concepts of the *bicameral* mind, the early Greek notion that our minds consist of two chambers, one of them—the one that creates new ideas—being inspired by God through the Muses. These Muses—Calliope (epic poetry), Clio (history), Erato (love poetry), Euterpe (music and lyric poetry), Melpomene (tragedy), Polyhymnia (hymns to the gods), Terpsichore (dance), Thalia (comedy), and Urania (astronomy)—supposedly inject supernatural innovations into an otherwise passive mental chamber. Interestingly, Plato thought that this "creativity chamber" was also the source of madness, thus linking highly creative minds with insanity. Aristotle, however, challenged the bicameral approach with a process known as *associationism*, which generally characterizes creative thought as a result of unconscious or subconscious associations. In Aristotle's view, linking thoughts and ideas, images and experiences, principles and formulas, leads to analogies, which in turn produce creative ways of thinking. (For a particularly insightful discussion of associationism, see Dacey and Lennon 1998, pp. 15–44.)

After Aristotle, histories of creativity typically chronicle various revolutions—including the medieval Book of Kells, the Renaissance and humanism, and the Age of Enlightenment—that point toward an ever-increasing view of the mind and self—not God or the Muses—as the center of the creative process. In the nineteenth century, separate camps formed, with the associationists continuing to believe that creativity springs from mental connections and the gestaltists arguing that creativity characterizes those who envision art hierarchically. From this debate came the work of Francis Galton, a nineteenth-century English associationist, who postulated an idea of creativity as *free association*—where unconscious associations are made conscious: "Ideas in the conscious mind are linked to those in the unconscious mind by threads of similarity" (Galton 1879, p. 162).

By the early twentieth century, the study of creativity had become the province of those interested in human cognition, with Graham Wallas (1926), Wolfgang Köhler (1929), and Max Wertheimer (1945) at the forefront. Wallas stressed the more academic view that creativity results from preparation, incubation, illumination, and finally verification—a more or less scientific approach. Köhler, on the other hand, argued the theory of spontaneous insight—that rather than forming slowly, by reinforcement, creativity occurs in sudden flashes of insight. Wertheimer, a gestaltist, insisted that four principles governed the creative mind: proximity, similarity, closure, and symmetry, ideas not dissimilar to Wallas's four principles.

Sigmund Freud's view (1959) contrasted these positions by characterizing the creative process as both a defense mechanism and an unconscious protection against unpleasant thoughts. Ernst Kris (1952) extended Freud's view by emphasizing regression as a productive defense mechanism and ultimately a source of creativity. Possibly the most interesting theory was proposed by Carl Jung (1966), an associate of Freud, who suggested that the unconscious mind remembers feelings—called archetypes—from ancestral experiences, and that those individuals who can best tap into this vast storehouse have the most creative minds.

Later in the twentieth century, Eric Fromm (1959) proposed five attributes relevant to creative thought: (1) the capacity for surprise; (2) the ability to concentrate; (3) self-awareness; (4) the capacity to accept conflict; and (5) the ability to shed the security of one's birth family. Freud, Jung, and Fromm all studied and posed their theories of creativity from a psychological perspective that they argued as supporting their hypotheses.

This very brief historical summary, obviously a simple overview, concentrates principally on creativity from the perspectives of philosophy and psychology. The field of artificial intelligence (AI) also studies creativity. AI pioneer Alan Turing, for example, discusses creativity when he quotes from "Professor Jefferson's Lister Oration" of 1949 (the italics are mine):

Not until a machine can write a sonnet or *compose a concerto* because of thoughts and emotions felt, and not by the chance fall of symbols, could we agree that machine equals brain—that is, not only write it but know that it had written it. No mechanism could feel (and not merely artificially signal, an easy contrivance) pleasure at its successes, grief when its valves fuse, be warmed by flattery, be made miserable by its mistakes, be charmed by sex, be angry or depressed when it cannot get what it wants. (Turing 1950, pp. 445–446)

One of the most impressive recent attempts to model human creativity with computers can be found in the groundbreaking work of Doug Hofstadter and his colleagues at the Center for Research on Concepts and Cognition at Indiana University, as documented in his book *Fluid Concepts and Creative Analogies: Computer Models of the Fundamental Mechanisms of Thought* (Hofstadter 1995). The first major project that Hofstadter (and his colleague Melanie Mitchell) describe in this book is Copycat, a program designed to discover insightful analogies (p. 205). Copycat's basic premise involves using the logic behind one combination of letters of the alphabet to form or complete a different but parallel combination of letters. For example, presented with the letter series ABB and the query FG, the program returns FGG, and so on. This trivial example somewhat belies the value of deriving analogies from examples and applying these analogies to other examples. However, since Hofstadter and Mitchell describe their processes far better than I can recount here, and because Copycat does not completely model creativity, I will leave the detailed explanation of the program to Hofstadter and Mitchell in their book.

In completing their description of Copycat, Hofstadter and Mitchell describe a future incarnation of the program they call Metacat (see particularly their discussion in Hofstadter 1995, pp. 313ff.), which attempts to model human creativity. They further define creativity in a way that differs significantly from the definition I adopted in chapter 1:

Full-scale creativity consists in having a keen sense for what is interesting, following it recursively, applying it at the meta-level, and modifying it accordingly.   (Hofstadter 1995, p. 313)

Having a "keen sense for what is interesting" requires elaboration that Hofstadter and Mitchell provide and that I paraphrase here to mean "individual human biases which fall close to those of all humans." I do not share this definition of creativity, but find it, as I do Boden's (1990) and Bringsjord and Ferrucci's (2000) definitions (see chapter 1), laced with homocentric baggage and vagueness, making coding impossible and presupposing that all humans share a common aesthetic, which I do not believe.

Copycat and Metacat serve as preliminary programs—and to some extent as foundations for—Letter Spirit, a program that models creativity in more interesting ways. The goals of Letter Spirit are ambitious. The program, as Hofstadter and Mitchell describe it, must (1) make its own decisions; (2) be knowledge-rich; (3) be flexible and context-dependent; (4) experiment at deep conceptual levels; (5) perceive and judge its own output; and (6) gradually converge on a satisfactory conclusion.

Letter Spirit designs and implements typefaces that have the same order of complexity as standard typefaces (Helvetica, etc.). While the program's processes are too complicated to detail here, some seem so interesting and important that I single them out for further discussion. The first of these important processes involves *decision waves*. When these decision waves wash "over the entire gridfont, all the letterforms begin to have a high degree of internal consistency, and a clear style begins to emerge" (Hofstadter 1995, p. 434). Without specifying how such processes are coded, Hofstadter and Mitchell describe these decision waves as "the gradual, slow-but-sure tightening up of internal consistency all across the structure under construction" (Hofstadter 1995, p. 434).

The authors point out that the concept of such waves "is an indispensable part of true creativity, and is a well-known property of such creative acts as musical composition, the writing of poetry and prose, the activities of painting and sculpture, the evolution of scientific theories, and even the design of AI programs and the writing of articles about them!" (Hofstadter 1995, p. 434). This "slow-but-sure tightening up of internal consistency" seems to me to be less of "an indispensable part of true creativity" and more of a "slow-but-sure tightening up of internal consistency"—a process by which any project, creative or not, culminates. For me, at least, this tending to details represents the least creative aspect of my work, whereas the most creative aspect is the discovery of connections that hitherto seemed not to exist or existed but otherwise were considered irrelevant. As a composer, I leave the "tightening up of internal consistency" to my postcreative stage. Some composers even allow copyists and other assistants to complete this aspect of their work.

One of the most complex and intriguing aspects of Letter Spirit appears in its implementation of *codelets*—"computational micro-agents that create, examine, and modify structures" (Hofstadter 1995, p. 434). These codelets glue, label, scan, match, adjust, regroup, destroy, and so on. They run both independently and in groups, producing collective behavior. They form, act, and disappear as organisms might. They are chosen on a "biased-random" basis to avoid "aimless processing" (Hofstadter 1995, p. 435). The level of complexity produced by these codelets cannot—according to the authors—be anticipated or described beforehand. Such complexity can be deceiving, however, and can often mimic creativity without actually achieving it— comtivity.

Finally—and I have omitted a significant number of concepts here that I encourage readers to pursue on their own—Letter Spirit incorporates an Imaginer. As the authors put it: "The *Imaginer* does not deal with, or even know anything about, the constraints defined by the Letter Spirit grid ... rather, it functions exclusively at the abstract level of *roles*" (Hofstadter 1995, p. 444). If the Imaginer represents creativity in Letter Spirit, it most certainly parallels what I find creative in myself as I compose, write, discover, and think. Again, however, the authors have not provided enough detailed information to make their insights realistically programmable, at least by others.

Both Copycat and Letter Spirit are complex, thought-provoking, and challenging programs. Unfortunately, Letter Spirit, of the two programs the one more oriented toward creativity, does not yet exist as functioning software. When it does exist, one wonders if its comtivity will promote or disguise true creativity. I discuss such problems further in the next chapter.

More recent research in artificial intelligence and creativity (see particularly Dartnall 1994; Schaffer 1994) tends to focus on connectionism, geneticism, and expertism (a combination of expert systems and agents). Unique approaches to creativity, such as Gardner's theory of multiple intelligences (Gardner 1983) and Sternberg's triarchic theory of human intelligence (Sternberg 1985), seem less pertinent, not seriously challenging the mainstream of ideas on creativity. Chris Thornton's interesting "runaway learning" proposal represents a more recent example of such interesting, but probably short-lived, theories.

I shall argue that certain creative processes may be viewed as learning processes *running away out of control* ... The aim will be to show that what one might term "intellectual" or "scientific" creativity can plausibly be viewed as a form of empirical learning extended beyond the normal boundaries of objectivity. (Thornton 2002, p. 239)

For the most part, however, the major theories about creativity, even those based on computational processes, generally follow the more straightforward models discussed here (for further reading on this subject, see Koestler 1964).

Tests for Creativity

Alan Turing, often credited as the father of artificial intelligence, created a well-known test for determining the existence of machine intelligence. While Turing intended his test strictly for intelligence, one might argue that it is just as appropriate for creativity. Turing's intelligence test involves three people: a man and a woman (A and B), and an interrogator located in a separate room. The interrogator seeks to discover the genders of the unseen persons, using only their written responses to a series of questions. Both the man and the woman can lie in this test. Turing comments: "We now ask the questions, What will happen when a machine takes the part of A in this game? Will the interrogator decide wrongly as often when the game is played like this as he does when the game is played between a man and a woman?" (Turing 1992, p. 134).

The bottom line for Turing rests with the ability or inability of the interrogator to ascertain when the computer participates in the test and when it does not. Failure to discriminate between human and machine responses indicates the machine's intelligence, though one might argue that it could just as easily indicate the interrogator's *lack* of intelligence in not asking the right questions. As we shall soon see, the present book and the programs it describes provide many opportunities for readers to take the position of musical interrogators. However, I hope to prove that it is the processes, rather than their output, that best identify creativity.

Interestingly, my program Experiments in Musical Intelligence (discussed in more detail in chapter 4) was never meant to model musical creativity, even though many reviewers of the music have suggested that it succeeds at such modeling. In fact, the program's goal—replicating the style of individual composers—would have been hampered had I attempted to program creative processes along with style-modeling processes. The confusion surrounding creativity and style with Experiments in Musical Intelligence's output tends to bolster the arguments against Turing-like tests for music creativity.

Creativity should produce unexpected results that nonetheless make sense and ultimately prove to be important in some way. Further, the results of creativity should be different from the results of other processes. Without these simple criteria, creativity could not be differentiated from the routine. Unfortunately, unexpectedness, sensibility, and importance are not necessarily measurable criteria, at least in the quantifiable programming sense. Hence, creating a Turing test for creativity also does not seem as straightforward as creating a Turing test for intelligence.

Assuming, however, that creativity can be tested, I present a complete saraband (see figure 2.1) from an Experiments in Musical Intelligence Bach-style lute suite completed in 2003. Most people who have heard this suite movement, even when performed mechanically by a computer sequencer, insist—especially when they do not know of its machine origins—that it must have been composed creatively. I intentionally did not involve the "association network" that I describe in chapters 9 and 10 of this book in the composing process, in order to be able to state unequivocally that I do not believe that this work was produced creatively. In short, there was nothing about the processes that output this musical work that would suggest creativity. Given enough time, I could reverse engineer this music and find all of its original sources in Bach's lute suites.

Therefore, and at the risk of boring some readers, I repeat my assertion that creativity is a *process*, not the *result of a process*. We can be surprised, shocked, challenged, and so on by the results of creativity. However, we can be equally surprised, shocked, challenged, and so on by the results of many noncreative processes as well. While I maintain that the music in figure 2.1 is interesting, well-shaped, and even inventive and surprisingly good, I also maintain that it is *not* the result of creative

Figure 2.1
A saraband from an Experiments in Musical Intelligence Bach-style lute suite completed in 2003.

processes. As I hope to prove in later chapters, while we cannot necessarily hear creativity, we can nonetheless perceive its presence when we are made aware of the processes of composition.

There are many computer programs that purport to include creativity in their algorithms without providing much credibility for this assertion in their output. Other programs, in contrast, seem to produce creative results without mentioning creativity in any of their attendant hype. In the following descriptions of a few of these computer programs, I will freely mix both of these types so as not to bias the reader's judgment with my own opinions. Evaluating these programs will, I hope, shed more light on the subject of testing for creativity.

As I mention in chapter 1, Harold Cohen's Aaron (see McCorduck 1991) represents an important milestone in the history of algorithmic computer art. Prints of Aaron's visually opulent and elegant paintings often sell for more than $5,000, and many are prized collector's items (for examples of Aaron's art, see McCorduck 1991, pp. 174ff.). In spite of this success, however, Aaron does not *create* art. The program follows rules provided by its programmer, Harold Cohen, using computer randomness (see discussion in chapter 3) for variety and surprise. In fact, Aaron's not being creative reveals one of its most endearing charms—it is a tool and interface for its creator, Harold Cohen. (For those wishing to have an Aaron original, a version of the program is now available as a Windows-platform screen saver—see the bibliography.)

Language authoring programs that beg the question of creativity include Racter (discussed at length in Hofstadter 1995, pp. 470–476) and Hal (so-called author of *Just This Once*—see French 1993). Racter is author of the 1984 (interesting date) book *The Policeman's Beard Is Half Constructed*. Racter follows rather straightforward rules that govern assembly from among many different data from which the program randomly chooses. This process—an embellishment of the classic ELIZA program, which uses stock sentences and word replacements to generate simple responses—can, however, produce some striking prose, as the following proves.

At all events my own essays and dissertations about love and its endless pain and perpetual pleasure will be known and understood by all of you who read this and talk or sing or chant about it to your worried friends or nervous enemies. Love is the question and the subject of this essay.   (as quoted in Hofstadter 1995, p. 473)

Racter can conjugate verbs, remember genders, and maintain consistency of singulars and plurals in terms of sentences, paragraphs, and even entire stories. Impressive as all of this is, however, the authors admit to spending incredible amounts of time selecting the best material from wide assortments of less-than-desirable outputs. As a simple example of this type of programming approach, I have included a program called Poet on my Web site that creates occasionally interesting poetry from an included database. Poet consists of but a few lines of code and requires only that users provide an ordered series of keywords from those already present in the database to generate new lines of output.

Scott French's Hal completed *Just This Once*, a 295-page novel, in 1993 (see French 1993). The following passage from this book indicates the typical level of prose, argued to be in the style of popular novelist Jacqueline Susann.

Carol was sitting at her desk watching columns of figures blur and merge into each other when the phone rang. She picked it up automatically, "Davis."
   "Hi, Davis. Stevens here."
   "Hi, honey." Carol rubbed her eyes with the back of her hand. "What's up?"
   "Dinner. I thought maybe I could con you into some Hanoi soup and then a movie afterwards. One of those film things they show in theaters with no chorus girls, no bands. I know it's not what you've come to expect from life but it might be fun."   (French 1993, p. 136)

This amazingly coherent output gives no indication of its source, and reads as fluently as any human-created novel might. Unfortunately, after reading several interviews with the program's creator, Scott French, one is left with the impression that the actual prose was in fact human created, with only the general outline and plot of the book being computer generated. Whatever the truth of the situation, French's program and book pose interesting challenges to readers, for certainly novels with this caliber of writing will eventually be "penned" by computer programs. Interestingly, neither Hal nor French makes any claim that this book was produced creatively. Whether generated by succession rules, ELIZA-type substitution processes, or simply outlined, *Just This Once* is interesting and provocative, worthy of at least a niche in the annals of computer creativity history.

The Columbia Newsblaster is an online experimental authoring program that examines news reports from thirteen sources (including CNN, Reuters, ABC News, and *USA Today*) and produces accurate stories about current events. The prototype of this program is the product of a team of researchers headed by Kathy McKeown of Columbia University. McKeown has been evolving natural language processes for nearly two decades. Newsblaster does not simply lift sentences to use in its summaries; it interprets the importance of different facts based on its own judgment. Newsblaster does not, in general, embroider facts or otherwise embellish original stories. Therefore, Newsblaster avoids, rather than models, creativity, no matter how convincing the output may be.

The AM program, conceived and programmed by Doug Lenat (1982), organizes primitive mathematical concepts into higher-level principles. This program essentially develops its own concepts from heuristic rules provided by Lenat, which allow it to choose the most interesting and unusual solutions from a series of candidate possibilities. From these solutions, AM generates solutions to more complex problems. Hofstadter (1995, p. 476), however, points out that the program receives help from its creator, and that the results demonstrate more of a human–machine hybrid than computer automation. Nonetheless, the notion that a computer program can solve problems previously undescribed to it makes AM of interest to those of us involved in computer creativity, even though the program itself does not effectively model creativity.

SWALE is a story-understanding program that detects and explains anomalous events using case-based reasoning (CBR). In the CBR model, creativity supposedly results from retrieving knowledge that is not routinely applied to a situation, and using this knowledge in new ways. The key issues for creativity here are how SWALE retrieves and adapts appropriate knowledge to fit unique circumstances. Depending on the processes used, CBR can provide solutions ranging from straightforward reapplications of old knowledge to highly novel solutions using combinations of previous processes (see Leake and Schank 1990).

Ray Kurzweil's Cybernetic Poet produces a language model of a particular poet's work by analyzing a selection of his poems. This language model incorporates computer-based language analyses and mathematical modeling techniques. Cybernetic Poet then writes original poems from its language model, and the resulting poems have a style similar to the database poet's analyzed poems. A plagiarism-avoidance algorithm attempts to avoid plagiarism (defined as more than three words in a row that appear anywhere in the original poems). Cybernetic Poet uses words, word structures, sequence patterns, rhythm patterns, and overall poem structures as subjects for analysis and generation. Here is an example written by Cybernetic Poet after poems by Dave Gitomer:

today i wondered
if i mused
today i saw you
i learned
in awe and you
if i wondered
if i mused
today i had one wish
if i saw you
if i saw you
if i had one wish

Cybernetic Poet has moments of apparent inspiration, though its output generally seems more surprising than creative.

The online Postmodernism Generator (see bibliography), written by Andrew Bulhak, generates semirandom text using recursive grammars. At the time the following output was produced, the program had created 1,217,721 essays since February 25, 2000, when it became operational.

Deconstructing Realism: Capitalist theory in the works of Pynchon
"Sexual identity is part of the dialectic of narrativity," says Foucault. However, the subject is contextualised into a neosemioticist sublimation that includes truth as a reality. Derrida uses the term "Batailleist powerful communication" to denote the collapse, and subsequent paradigm, of substructural narrativity. It could be said that if postdialectic materialist theory holds, we have to choose between neosemioticist sublimation and dialectic postcapitalist theory. In Vineland, Pynchon denies textual Marxism. Therefore, Baudrillard uses the term "neosemioticist sublimation" to denote the difference between sexual identity and culture. Abian suggests that we have to choose between capitalist theory and neocapitalist discourse. Thus, a number of theories concerning cultural postdialectic theory exist.

Clearly an ELIZA-like program, the Postmodernism Generator produces entertaining parodies of academic "speak." I include this discussion of the Postmodernism Generator here because of its online availability and imaginative output that often effectively masquerades as creativity.

As I mention in my book *The Algorithmic Composer* (Cope 2000, p. 17), the creators of Symbolic Composer (often called S-Com) claim that

Times are changing and composition modeling experts are working in music laboratories and private MIDI studios to discover the secrets of Mozart, Beethoven, Vivaldi, Bach, Schönberg, Messiaen, and other masters. In the path toward deeper understanding of musical processes Symbolic Composer plays an increasingly important role.   (Symbolic Composer 1997)

While not citing creativity in particular for the soon-to-be-discovered secrets of these historically important composers, one must assume that creativity would be one of the most significant of Symbolic Composer's revelations. Unfortunately, the interface of this program suggests the opposite—that any creativity the output demonstrates is the user's, not the program's.

There are dozens of similarly hyped music composition programs, ranging from simple sequencers to highly evolved composing toolboxes. Rather than explain each of these programs and its relation to creativity, I will—in chapter 3—present the basic processes, one or more of which form the engines on which these programs function.

3 Current Models of Musical Creativity

Principle: Creativity should not be confused with novelty or comtivity.

Randomness

My afternoon walks often take me past a friend's home. On one such walk, I found him busy scrubbing his driveway. We nodded greetings, and he complained about the horrible mess his oil-leaking car had made on his driveway, and how impossible it seemed to remove the stain. Rather than agreeing with him, I mentioned that I no longer had that problem. He eagerly asked what kind of detergent I used. I replied that what I used was better than detergent. By this time I had his undivided attention. I told him that I had decided to appreciate my oil stains as art—admiring the oil on my driveway like paint on a canvas. At first, he looked at me quizzically, to determine whether I was pulling his leg. I assured him that my change in attitude was real, and with the right light there were many extraordinary hues and images to be seen in these oil stains. Recently I passed his house and discovered him loosening the oil cap under his car. He told me that his detergent had mangled his "art," and that he needed to *seed* it again.

I recount this simple story because I believe it demonstrates how creativity can circumvent logic in order to solve problems. This story also demonstrates how important perspective is to creativity—surely many would argue that my solution here is simply illogical, not creative. They would be wrong. In fact, the programs I describe in this section should be gauged against this model, to see if they pose any true opportunities for creative output.

Most research on creativity ignores the confusion that randomness poses to its recognition. On one hand, distinguishing a creative solution to a problem from a random solution to that same problem should be easy, and it usually is easy in scientific research. On the other hand, especially in the arts, random output often competes with creativity, at least in terms of novelty and surprise. Using computer programs to imitate creativity further confuses the issue, since computers process data so quickly and accurately that to some, their output is magical. In fact, the distinction between creativity and randomness had little relevance prior to the computational age, because random behavior and creative behavior seemed so apparently distinct. Since most computer programs that claim to create use randomness in some way, it is very important that we clearly define this term to determine whether or not what we are experiencing is the result of creativity, or simply a "random" shot in the dark. To complicate matters, we often use words such as *random*, *unpredictability*, *chance*, and *indeterminacy* rather freely in our speech and writings, without giving much thought to what they actually mean. Please indulge me, therefore, as I discuss in detail what I think *random* means, and whether it truly exists. In so doing, a number of important features of computational creativity will, I believe, become clearer.

Clearly, we must not rely simply on perception for our definition of randomness, since not only will perception differ from one person to the next, but perception is often far from reality. Like creativity, randomness is a process, not a thing, a process that cannot always be discerned from output alone. Even scientists use the word *random* to mean several different things:

> ... applied for instance to a single string of a thousand digits, random means that the string is incompressible. In other words, it is so irregular that no way can be found to express it in shorter form. A second meaning, however, is that it has been generated by a random process, that is, by a chance process such as a coin toss, where each head gives 1 and each tail 0. (Gell-Mann 1994, p. 44)

One method scientists use to help define randomness is to test processes under identical conditions.

> The key to thinking about randomness is to imagine such a system to be in some particular state, and to let it do whatever that particular system does. Then imagine putting it back into *exactly* that initial state and running the whole experiment again. If you always get *exactly* the same result, then the system is deterministic. If not, then it's random. Notice that in order to show that a system is deterministic, we don't actually have to predict what it will do; we just have to be assured that on both occasions it will do the same thing. (Stewart 2002, p. 280)

Of course, the fallacy with this description of randomness is its use of the word *exactly*. While all of the known variables may *appear* to be exactly the same, the unknown variables may not be the same. For example, when quantum theorists have spoken about absolute randomness—believing that they know the *exact* state of all of the variables—they have ignored the as-yet unproven, and thus incalculable, existence of dark matter and dark energy, important cosmological components necessary to account for the composition of the known universe. As well, according to many philosophers and scientists, no two initial states can have exactly the same conditions, since at least one known variable—time—will have changed, no matter what state the other conditions occupy. In short, no two experiments can *ever* have exactly the same initial conditions.

What many people mean when they use words such as "random" is simply that conditions are too *complex* for them to understand what is occurring. The actual position, speed, and direction of a single atom in an ocean wave, for example, result from such incredibly complex competing and reinforcing processes that calculating these parameters seems impossible. This complexity may or may not actually involve randomness (I will speak about chaotic behavior momentarily). For most of us, then, using the word "random" really means that a process is simply too complex to sort out. We do not mean, at least in this instance, that the atom moves about without any cause and effect resulting from the energies and other atoms that surround it.

Another common interpretation of randomness is *without pattern*. The numbers that follow the decimal point in π seem random to us simply because they lack repeating patterns—at least as far as humans have been able to ascertain. The number π is fixed, however, and represents (as Gell-Mann says) the shortest form in which it can be expressed. Likewise, the cosine function output in figure 3.11 apparently lacks repeating patterns and thus seems random. However, each time the formula that produced it is run with the same input, the same numbers appear in the same order as output.

Programming languages provide so-called random processes that produce unpredictable results. However, computer randomness (often called *pseudo randomness*) is actually deterministic. The reason for this is that deterministic algorithms—the basis for all computation—produce deterministic outcomes. Whenever a programmer calls upon a computer language's random function, that programmer is depending on the *irrelevance* of the data chosen to provide the sense of randomness. Given enough time and provided with the generating algorithm, programmers could accurately predict each new datum produced by computer pseudo randomness.

In all three of the cases I have just described—complexity, lack of patterns, and irrelevance—apparent randomness arises not out of a lack of determinism, but rather out of a lack of perceivable logic. Indeed, Sir Isaac Newton, whose third law of motion describes determinism (*Actioni contrariam semper et equalem esse reactionem*, in Newton 1726, p. 14; translated as "to every action there is always opposed an equal and opposite reaction"—Cajori 1934, p. 13), would argue that ocean waves, π, and computer randomness all result from very deterministic causes.

According to Newtonian mechanics, when we know the state of a physical system (positions and velocities) at a given time—then we know its state at any other time.   (Ruelle 1991, p. 28)

Therefore, according to Newton at least, none of what I have described here represents randomness; it is just that we perceive these various actions as random because we cannot, will not, or do not want to actually follow the deterministic processes that produced them.

From the above examples, then, we could say that when we typically use the word "random," we do not actually mean "without regard to rules" (*Webster's Collegiate Dictionary*, 1991, p. 1116); rather, we are simply expressing our lack of comprehension of the determinism present in the system we are encountering. Given enough time, we could predict the result of *any* process, no matter how apparently unpredictable it may seem. If this is so, then creativity is also predictable, for one assumes that it derives from a deterministic system, no matter how imposingly complex, lacking in perceivable pattern, or irrelevant the output of that system may be.

However, I have just begun to describe the controversies surrounding *randomness*. The sciences of quantum physics and of chaos have recently provided arguments for the underlying *indeterministic* nature of the universe. Many scientists believe that randomness exists at the quantum level—the world of the very small. Richard Feynman, one of the proponents of such randomness, and an articulate spokesperson for QED (quantum electrodynamics), describes the quantum phenomenon thus:

Try as we might to invent a reasonable theory that can explain how a photon "makes up its mind" whether to go through glass or bounce back, it is impossible to predict which way a given photon will go. Philosophers have said that if the same circumstances don't always produce the same results, predictions are impossible and science will collapse. Here is a circumstance—identical photons are always coming down in the same direction to the same piece of glass—that produces different results. We cannot predict whether a given photon will arrive at A or B. All we can predict is that out of 100 photons that come down, an average of 4 will be rejected by the front surface. Does this mean that physics, a science of great exactitude, has been reduced to calculating only the *probability* of an event and not predicting exactly what will happen? Yes.   (Feynman 1985, p. 19)

However, there are two different views as to what has actually occurred here. According to the first, the photon is a part of an ensemble of photons, all of which are distributed through space. The overall intensity of this group of photons corresponds to our usual interpretation of groups of similar events: a probability distribution no more mysterious than an actuarial table or a human population census giving the distribution of ages or genders. If this viewpoint is correct, then the lack of predictability again describes only our ignorance, and nothing more, and the photon to which Feynman refers here is still behaving deterministically. However, a second view is also possible. According to this second view, we are not ignorant of anything, and quantum mechanics is complete in its description of individual events. The photons decide to enter the glass or bounce off it without cause, and prediction beyond probability distribution is now and forever impossible.

Feynman sums up the apparent randomness of electron motion in this way:

Attempts to understand the motion of the electrons going around the nucleus by using mechanical laws—analogous to the way Newton used the laws of motion to figure out how the earth went around the sun—were a real failure: all kinds of predictions came out wrong. (Feynman 1985, p. 5)

Murray Gell-Mann agrees, adding that

... the probabilistic nature of quantum theory can be illustrated by a simple example. A radio-active atomic nucleus has what is called a "half-life," the time during which it has a 50% chance of disintegrating. For example, the half-life of Pu^{239}, the usual isotope of plutonium, is around 25,000 years. The chance that a Pu^{239} nucleus in existence today will still exist after 25,000 years is 50 percent; after 50,000 years, the chance is only 25 percent; after 75,000 years, 12.5 percent, and so on. The quantum-mechanical character of nature means that for a given Pu^{239} nucleus, that kind of information is all we can know about when it will decay; there is no way to predict the exact moment of disintegration.... (Gell-Mann 1994, pp. 132–133)

Of course, what Gell-Mann recounts here could be seen as testimony *for* human in-adequacy, not testimony *against* determinism.

It is also quite possible that objects which appear to disintegrate randomly actually move as the result of undetected internal pressures or delayed reactions to previous external actions that we cannot yet detect, or that we have overlooked because these objects are so small. We would not, for example, suggest that an amoeba moves randomly simply because there is no observable external action/reaction process involved in that motion.

In the early 1950s, David Bohm led the chorus of those who followed Newton's principles in a revival of the search for hidden variables as a cause for the apparent randomness we perceive. Using statistics, Bohm pointed to a key difference between classical and quantum mechanics called *the quantum potential* (see Wolf 1981, p. 200). In Bohm's theory, the laws of physics are totally deterministic.

Quantum indeterminacy is not a sign of anything irreducibly probabilistic about the universe, but a sign of the inescapable ignorance of the observer—human or otherwise. (Stewart 2002, p. 342)

German physicist Werner Heisenberg's 1927 *uncertainty principle* grew out of the notion that simply *observing* quantum-level mechanics disturbs the accuracy of any measurements of its mechanisms. In other words, observation itself may be the cause of the apparent randomness at atomic and subatomic levels. Brian Greene argues Heisenberg's principle:

Why can't we determine the electron's position with an "ever gentler" light source in order to have an ever decreasing impact on its motion? From the standpoint of nineteenth-century physics we can. By using an ever dimmer lamp (and an ever more sensitive light detector) we can have a vanishingly small impact on the electron's motion. But quantum mechanics itself illuminates a flaw in this reasoning. As we turn down the intensity of the light source we now know that we are decreasing the number of photons it emits. Once we get down to emitting individual photons we cannot dim the light any further without actually turning it off. There is a fundamental quantum-mechanical limit to the "gentleness" of our probe. And hence, there is always a minimal disruption that we cause to the electron's velocity through our measurement of its position.   (Greene 1999, p. 112–113)

This uncertainty principle means that no matter how accurately we measure the classical quantities of position and momentum, there will always be errors in our measurements.

Predicting or determining the future of atomic objects would be impossible under these circumstances. This was called the Heisenberg Principle of Uncertainty or the Principle of Indeterminism. It had little relevance in the world of ordinary-sized objects. They were hardly bothered by disturbances produced through observation. But the uncertainty principle was serious business when it came to electrons. Indeed, it was so serious that it brought the very existence of electrons into question.   (Wolf 1981, p. 115)

Many quantum physicists counter these arguments by suggesting that randomness exists at the quantum—atomic and subatomic—levels, while cause-and-effect exists at larger-size levels as probabilistic certainties; thus, in a sense, they are arguing for both randomness and Newtonian (classical) mechanics. The problem with this dual model, of course, is that *size*—the very essence of such a model—is an arbitrary standard. From our perspective the atom is small and the universe is very large. To a being the size of an atom, the universe (if even observable) would seem monstrous and the quantum world would seem normal.

Chaos theory appears at first glance to support the case for a kind of deterministic randomness. Chaos is the study of turbulent behavior in which some feel that incredible complexity makes predictability at the level of the very small scale impossible. James Gleick observes that chaos

... brought an astonishing message: simple deterministic models could produce what looked like random behavior. The behavior actually had an exquisite fine structure, yet any piece of it seemed indistinguishable from noise.   (Gleick 1987, p. 79)

At first glance, this version of chaos resembles the notion of randomness occurring as a result of our inability to predict events when faced with great complexity. However, Stephen Kellert notes that

... chaotic systems scrupulously obey the strictures of differential dynamics, unique evolution, and value determinateness, yet they are utterly unpredictable. Because of the existence of these systems, we are forced to admit that the world is not totally predictable: by any definition of determinism that includes total predictability, determinism is false. Thus begins the process of peeling away the layers of determinism that are not compatible with current physics, impelling us either to revise our definition of determinism or reject it as a doctrine.   (Kellert 1993, p. 62)

Chaos theory, however, does involve prediction. This prediction occurs as the result of something called the *calculus of probabilities*, long considered a minor branch of mathematics. The probabilities of chaos enlighten us to the predictability of events such as *attractors*, patterns that, given the right initial conditions, can be foreseen and even measured in advance of their occurrence.

A central fact of the calculus of probabilities is that if a coin is tossed a large number of times, the proportion of heads (or the proportion of tails) becomes close to 50 percent. In this manner, while the result of tossing a coin once is completely uncertain, a long series of tosses produces a nearly certain result. This transition from uncertainty to near certainty when we observe *long series* of events, or *large systems*, is an essential theme in the study of chance. (Ruelle 1991, p. 5)

The word "utterly" used by Kellert, and the phrase "completely uncertain" in Ruelle's comments, characterize what I consider flaws in the arguments for randomness: arrogance. While I agree that we truly do not know why photons move in the way that they do, this lack of knowledge should not necessarily lead us to the conclusion that we therefore can *never* know, or that an entire canon of physics should be revoked.

The bottom line for my own research is that randomness is not an engaging mystery, but a simple reflection of ignorance. Aside from the *possible* exception of quantum physics, randomness refers to behavior that is either too complex, too patternless, or too irrelevant to make prediction possible. None of these features seem to me to be associated in any way with creativity. In fact, while much of what we call creativity is also unpredictable, creativity often turns out in hindsight to be the most rational way to have proceeded. Reverse engineering even the most complex creative processes demonstrates this rationality. Randomness, on the other hand, perpetuates or even complicates problems—and should never be confused with creativity.

Music Programs and Research

Rather than describe individual music algorithmic composing programs, many of which may no longer be available by the date of this book's publication, I have opted to discuss the basic *principles* of algorithmic composing programs and the degree to which each principle allows for, or models, creativity. The approaches I discuss here include rules-based algorithms, data-driven programming, genetic algorithms, neural networks, fuzzy logic, mathematical modeling, and sonification. Though there are other ways to program computers to compose music, these seven basic processes represent the most commonly used types.

Before describing these basic program types, however, it may be useful to define the term "algorithm" as I will use it in this book. Algorithms are recipes, sets of instructions for accomplishing a goal. An algorithm typically represents the automation of all or part of a process. Importantly, there is nothing inherently inhuman about algorithms. To understand this, one has only to remember that deoxyribonucleic acid (DNA)—the genetic basis of life—is an algorithm. Algorithms simply make tasks easier and, often, more bearable. If we had to repeatedly step through the processes of, for example, breathing, making our hearts beat, or blinking our eyes (all algorithmic processes), we would have no time to think about or do anything else.

It is also important to differentiate between composers who use algorithms and algorithmic composers. While such a differentiation may seem polemic, it is critical to the computer modeling of creativity. Composers who use algorithms incorporate them to achieve a momentary effect in their music. In contrast, algorithmic composers compose entire works using algorithms, thus dealing with important issues of structure and coherence. The differences between these two seemingly comparable views resemble the division between so-called aleatoric and indeterminate composers of the mid-twentieth century. As Morton Feldman remarked: "You can see this in the way they have approached American 'chance' music. They began by finding rationalizations for how they could incorporate chance and still keep their precious integrity" (Schwartz and Childs 1967, p. 365). While I do not share Feldman's vehemence in separating the two camps of aleatorism and indeterminacy, I do feel strongly that the differences between composers who use algorithms and algorithmic composers is substantial. In this book, I refer almost exclusively to algorithmic composers.

Figure 3.1 is a sixteenth-century print possibly reflecting similar differences—a kind of competition between an abacist on the right and an algorist on the left. The abacist uses an abacus, an ancient tool designed as a kind of simple slide rule. By physically sliding beads (numerical representations) various ways, abacists can add, subtract, and so on. The algorist, on the other hand, manipulates standard mathematical equations or algorithms to compute the same results. If facial expressions are any indication here, the algorist holds the upper hand in this competition. For those believing that using algorithms to create music somehow removes imagination, inspiration, and intuition from the composing process, know that defining a good algorithm requires as much imagination, inspiration, and intuition as does composing a good melody or harmony. Neither good algorithms nor good musical ideas grow on trees.

The musical examples that demonstrate the processes described in the following sections have been reduced to simple keyboard notation in order that they may be

Figure 3.1
A sixteenth-century print reflecting a competition between an algorist, on the left, and an abacist, on the right.

usefully compared with one another. Obviously many, if not all, of these examples could be far more elaborate, and each lasts significantly longer than shown. However, I did not want the effectiveness or lack of effectiveness in emulating creativity in some of the examples to eliminate the effectiveness of other examples, especially when the choice of which music was used was solely my own. Readers are encouraged to use the programs available on my Web site and listen to the related MP3 files, in combination with reading the descriptions of those programs, for a more "musical" interpretation of the techniques presented here.

Many of the principles of the processes described here overlap. For example, mathematical models can be seen as sonifying abstract formulas. Cellular automata resemble mathematical models—and hence sonification—in that they graphically represent mathematical computations. Fuzzy logic is a type of mathematics. Neural network output results from the mathematical calculations in collaborating hidden units. As well, virtually any process can be described as some form of Markov chain. The processes described below also have substantial differences, as their definitions demonstrate. I have arranged these algorithmic processes into these particular categories to help delineate their different approaches to producing musical output.

Rules-Based Programming

Rules-based programming typically consists of a series of *if-then-else* clauses, in which a condition is posed (e.g., *if* a current note is C-sharp), a consequent action is given for when that condition proves true (e.g., *then* follow this C-sharp with D), and an alternative indicated for when that condition proves untrue (e.g., *else* follow the current note with G). While rules-based programs often require more complicated multiple-choice possibilities than the one just given, the essence of the approach remains basically the same.

This kind of conditional behavior can be expressed in terms of orders of Markov chains (Ames 1989). A *zero*-order Markov chain, for example, makes pseudo-random decisions, with no applicable rules. A *first*-order Markov chain, however, bases new decisions on the previous choice. A *fifth*-order Markov chain bases its decisions on the previous five choices. The simple C-sharp rule described in the preceding paragraph represents a first-order Markov chain. Figure 3.2 shows a state-transition matrix for a first-order Markov chain involving all twelve notes of the chromatic scale. The numbers here represent probabilities and add to 1.0—or 100 percent—in each horizontal rank. To interpret this matrix, a program would find a current note in the left-hand column and then read the various probabilities of potential following notes along the associated horizontal row. The probability of the note A being followed by another A in the example given here, for instance, is 10

	a	bb	b	c	db	d	eb	e	f	gb	g	ab
a	.1	.2	.1	.2	.1	.1	.0	.1	.1	.0	.0	.0
bb	.2	.1	.1	.2	.1	.1	.0	.1	.0	.0	.1	.0
b	.1	.2	.1	.1	.1	.1	.0	.2	.1	.0	.0	.0
c	.2	.2	.1	.1	.1	.0	.0	.0	.1	.1	.0	.1
db	.0	.1	.0	.3	.1	.1	.0	.1	.1	.2	.0	.0
d	.1	.1	.1	.0	.2	.2	.0	.1	.1	.1	.0	.0
eb	.1	.2	.1	.2	.1	.1	.0	.0	.0	.0	.1	.1
e	.1	.1	.1	.1	.1	.1	.0	.2	.2	.0	.0	.0
f	.1	.2	.1	.0	.0	.1	.2	.2	.1	.0	.0	.0
gb	.1	.2	.1	.0	.1	.1	.1	.0	.1	.0	.0	.2
g	.0	.2	.1	.2	.1	.1	.0	.1	.1	.0	.0	.1
ab	.3	.2	.1	.1	.0	.2	.0	.1	.0	.0	.0	.0

Figure 3.2
A state-transition matrix for a first-order Markov chain involving all twelve notes of the chromatic scale.

percent; for the note A being followed by B-flat, the probability is 20 percent; and so on.

As a possibly more interesting example, imagine that a melody-composing program chooses new notes by virtue of the intervals these notes create with their immediately preceding notes. I will use intervals in this case rather than notes for Markov order computation, though notes would work as well. If only major and minor seconds in any direction were allowed between consecutive notes, such a first-order Markov chain would produce simple, meandering, stepwise melodies. A more elegant program might have new choices depend on two interval predecessors. For example, if a previous interval choice was a leap upward preceded by same-direction stepwise motion, then new choices might be limited to intervals of a second in contrary motion. Other rules would then have to exist for other interval combinations. This second-order Markov chain would produce considerably more interesting music than a first-order Markov chain, and would require a three-dimensional state-transition matrix.

The Markov program on my Web site follows these kinds of processes. This program's rules-based algorithm requires just a few lines of code, but occasionally produces interesting, if not musical, results. The rules to which I refer here are found in the probabilities of the state-transition matrix. When these probabilities result from programmer input they become rules.

Another way to create probability tables such as state-transition matrixes for rules-based programming is by analyzing existing music. The Markov program offers just such a model. The program collects note successions from a database and then lists these notes with their possible successors in sublists representing probabilities. Multiple note entries in a sublist indicate a higher probability that they will be chosen. A note's absence from a sublist indicates that it will never be chosen as a following grouping (zero probability). The resulting analysis can then be used by the Markov program to produce new music in a style roughly comparable to the original upon which it is based.

Statistical approaches to music composition follow similar rules-based Markovian processes (Assayag and Dubnov 2002). Statistical composing typically uses statistics derived from some corpus of music to imitate its style or other features. Statistical approaches typically prove successful in generating smaller segments of music—phrase size or smaller—but also show promise for larger-scale composition.

Figure 3.3 shows rules-based music resulting from a simple first-order Markov chain. The program makes choices for the upper voice here within a major third from a previous choice, using probabilities from a state-transition matrix similar to the one just described. Pseudo-random processes are used to decide between equally correct possibilities. The left-hand octaves in figure 3.3 result from a separate rule that prescribes new instances of octaves whenever certain conditions occur in the music in the right hand.

Rules-based programs of the type discussed here offer very little, if any, opportunity for creativity, with unpredictable output resulting from the pseudo-random processes involved. Any creativity such programs otherwise seem to have typically belongs to the programmer, not the program.

Data-Driven Programming

Data-driven programming techniques also use the analysis of data, rather than programmed rules, to create new instances of music. The typical data-driven model for music composition involves analyzing a database of musical works and then, using this analysis, replicating new music in some manner appropriate to the user's wishes. My Experiments in Musical Intelligence program follows this data-driven model. The Markov analysis and composition program just described is also data-driven,

Figure 3.3
Rules-based music resulting from a simple first-order Markov chain.

though it differs from data-driven processes in that it uses rules (state-transition matrixes).

Experiments in Musical Intelligence requires users to initially establish a database of previously composed works that it then analyzes for harmonic relationships, hierarchical information, stylistic traits, and various other pertinent details (discussed more thoroughly in chapter 4). From this analysis, the program attempts to produce new music in the style of the music in its database. Figure 3.4 shows a simple block diagram (or flowchart) of Experiments in Musical Intelligence. Note the central position of the database upon which all of the analytical and compositional software depends.

Case-based reasoning (CBR, discussed briefly in relation to the SWALE project in chapter 2) resembles data-driven programming, but uses abstractions of previously

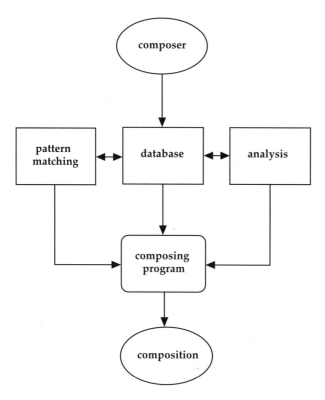

Figure 3.4
An overview of the Experiments in Musical Intelligence program.

solved problems to solve new problems. The CBR process involves first retrieving a similar-to-the-current case from a library of cases, adapting the retrieved case plan to the current problem, and then storing the solution—if it is acceptable—in a library of cases for future use. Data-driven and CBR programs differ significantly in detail, but resemble one another in that they both rely on data rather than on prepro-grammed rules.

Figure 3.5 presents an example of musical output from a data-driven program us-ing a database consisting of Stravinsky's Three Pieces for String Quartet (1913) and similar music by Stravinsky from the same period. The Chorale program discussed in chapter 4 follows basic data-driven principles, and its output, though different in na-ture from the music shown in figure 3.5, also provides a good example of the type of style imitation possible with this form of computer composition.

Figure 3.5
An example of musical output from a data-driven program.

In many ways, the data-driven programming process may seem like the least creative of those presented in this chapter. However, as will be seen in ensuing chapters, using analyzed characteristics such as voice leading and narrowing sampling sizes can produce style that is similar, yet unique.

Data-driven and CBR processes do not in themselves demonstrate creative-like behavior. While some data-driven programs, such as Experiments in Musical Intelligence, may surprise users with the quality of their output, this quality does not itself represent creativity. As we will see later in this book, however, integrating association-based procedures with data-driven processes increases the creative potential of this approach to music composition.

Genetic Algorithms

Genetic algorithms (GAs) use natural selection—survival of the fittest—as their fundamental operating paradigm. Typically, a series of constraints governs whether individuals in a GA come to exist, continue to exist, or cease to exist. Populations of such individuals spawn, flourish, and vanish, much as species of life do. Cellular automata (CAs), a subcategory of GAs, present this natural selection process visually, usually in the form of two-dimensional matrixes. Genetic algorithms typically have internal states that affect the survival of their populations, whereas cellular automata respond only to external states. Working versions of Conway's Game of Life, for example, a very popular form of cellular automata found at numerous Internet sites, have user-established initial states, and cells are controlled by the current states of adjacent cells.

GAs and CAs demonstrate how sometimes very simple code can create very complex output. For example, the Lisp code in figure 3.6a produced the outputs represented visually in figures 3.6b and 3.6c. I reproduce the code here not so much in expectation that readers will understand it as to illustrate how small programs can often generate complex results.

In the code shown in figure 3.6a, each entry in the *rules*—called a "state," indicated here by either a 0 (zero) or a * (star)—is governed by the functions *create*, *create-row*, and *apply-rule*, defined here using the term "defun." In figure 3.6a, the rules consist of a series of parenthetical and subparenthetical groupings of zeros and stars. For example, the rule "((* * *) 0)," the initial rule of the first *rules* here, means "a configuration consisting of three stars in one line results in a zero directly below the middle star in the succeeding—lower—line of output." Moving a window of three states incrementally along a line of zeros and stars following these *rules* produces a subsequent line of appropriate zeros and stars. Each successive line is then figured in the same manner. In figure 3.6b and 3.6c, the zeros and stars have been converted to small empty (open for zero) or filled (solid for star) squares to produce more readable and visually appealing images.

The first *rules* shown in figure 3.6a created the repeating-triangles image shown in figure 3.6b. The second *rules* in figure 3.6a generated the nonrepeating image shown in figure 3.6c. This latter figure never repeats patterns exactly, and thus represents an example of chaos (discussed earlier in this chapter), a more interesting, but possibly less artistic, example of output.

Alan Turing notes that "the system of the 'universe as a whole' is such that quite small errors in the initial conditions can have an overwhelming effect at a later time" (Turing 1950, p. 440). Modern chaos theory, and this particular cellular automaton, follow much this same principle. Stephen Wolfram (2002) argues that cellular

(a)

(a)

```
(defvar *rules*;rule shown in (b)
    '(((* * *) 0)
      ((* * 0) 0)
      ((* 0 *) 0)
      ((* 0 0) *)
      ((0 * *) 0)
      ((0 * 0) *)
      ((0 0 *) *)
      ((0 0 0) 0)))

(defvar *rules*;rule shown in (c)
    '(((0 0 0) *)
      ((0 0 *) 0)
      ((0 * 0) 0)
      ((0 * *) 0)
      ((* 0 0) 0)
      ((* 0 *) *)
      ((* * 0) *)
      ((* * *) *)))

(defun create (number start rules)
  (if (zerop number) ()
      (cons start
            (create (1-number)
                    (cons '0
                          (butlast (create-row start rules)))
                    rules))))

(defun create-row (old-row rules)
  (if (null old-row) ()
      (cons (apply-rule (firstn 3 old-row) rules)
            (create-row (rest old-row) rules))))

(defun apply-rule (group rules)
  (let ((test (second (assoc group rules :test #'equal))))
    (cond (test)
          (t '0))))
```

Figure 3.6
Code (a) for creating the data for a simple cellular automaton that produces (b) a repetitive figure and (c) a chaotic figure.

(b)

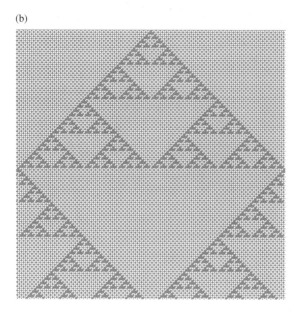

(c)

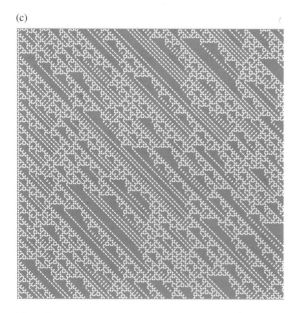

Figure 3.6
(continued)

automata, particularly automata that resemble the chaotic output of figure 3.6c, can resolve "questions about ultimate limits to knowledge, free will, the uniqueness of the human condition and the inevitability of mathematics" (Wolfram 2002, p. 10). Wolfram bases his assertions on the concept that the universe is computational and that applying very simple rules to initially simple conditions in such a universe can create very complex results. I make no such claim of universality here. I only suggest that these kinds of cellular automata offer opportunities for producing occasionally interesting visual output and, as we will now see, music as well.

Replacing *s and 0s in figure 3.6a with musical notes and rests, respectively, while rather simplistic, converts a visual CA into an aural CA with actual pitches determined by any number of methods. For example, tilting figures 3.6b and 3.6c to their left by 90 degrees allows the conversion of the new vertical axis to a standard chromatic scale and translation of the new horizontal axis to time, with each square (state) representing a particular duration (e.g., a quarter of a second). Pitches that repeat in neighboring squares horizontally may then be tied to create notes of longer duration. The platform-dependent program called CA on my Web site produces both visual and aural output similar to that described here.

Figure 3.7 shows music produced by a simple genetic algorithm. This output follows the general principles of the previously described two-dimensional automaton. The output here is normalized to fit the standard MIDI pitch range. Interestingly, this music has more pitch and range diversity than any of the other examples in this section, perhaps owing to the process of deriving pitches—assigning numbers to each of the initial horizontal squares and then processing the rules to determine new pitches.

Genetic algorithms can be far more elaborate than the ones just described. For example, GAs typically involve DNA-like inheritance of characteristics as well as crossover and mutation techniques to develop new traits. GAs of this type have been effectively used for problem solving, pattern matching, and music composition. However, appearances of creativity when using GAs and CAs can be deceiving, since resulting visual or aural representations often owe their complexity to very simple and repetitive algorithms.

Neural Networks

The term "neural network" derives from "neuron network," the supposed connective circuitry of the brain. Neural networks receive input that triggers neuron substitutes (called "hidden units" because their values do not reveal much about their contribution to the neural network process), which in turn trigger initially random output. Neural networks then cycle through a series of forward or back propagations

Figure 3.7
Music produced by a genetic algorithm.

(reversed-direction flow) that compare output with input and alter hidden unit values, until the output values match or approximate the relationships of the input and output data upon which they were trained (Todd and Loy 1991). This training

> ... involves presenting the network with a series of samples of the problem to be solved and an example of a solution for each sample problem. Given enough training material, the neural network should be able to learn the underlying aspects of the solutions. Should a similar problem appear, the network then retrieves these aspects to solve it. (Miranda 2001, p. 112)

Figure 3.8 shows a simple model of a neural network. The number of back propagations necessary for neural networks to produce appropriate output values based on training varies according to the complexity of the data involved and the type of network used—many different types exist. However, hundreds and often thousands of back propagations are frequently necessary. Neural networks typically consist of

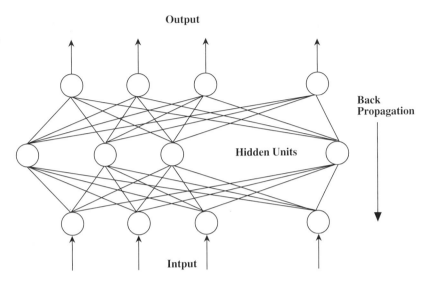

Figure 3.8
A simple model of a neural network.

many input and output nodes. Sandwiched between these nodes are variable numbers of layers of hidden units, as well as variable numbers of connections between these inputs, outputs, and hidden units, making the training process extremely complex. Once "taught," however, a neural network can efficiently solve new problems of the same general type on which it was trained.

Composers use neural networks in a variety of ways. The most obvious approach involves training a network using several musical inputs in roughly the same style, or that use the same general rules, and providing examples of the desired output. Composers then input different music and ask the network to use the generalization it has acquired during training to produce an appropriate new output. Inputting two or more quite different examples and desired output into a network during training can often achieve an interesting mix of musical styles or materials.

Hörnel and Menzel (1998) have attempted to imitate musical style using neural networks by varying and harmonizing baroque chorale melodies. Their programs attempt to predict notes and harmonies, in effect composing new music in the style of the input music. They have also linked two neural networks working in different time scales to produce unique results.

Many researchers (see, for example, Miranda 2001) theorize that neural networks mimic the workings of the human brain. Since hidden units do not provide useful

Figure 3.9
Music produced by a neural network.

data from which to evaluate the processes involved, one can judge only from the results. Thus far, little of the output produced by neural networks and made public has proven to have serious musical consequences. Therefore, the jury remains out as to whether neural networks can effectively model creativity.

Figure 3.9 provides an example of music produced by a simple neural network. The network used here was trained on data from figures 3.5 and 3.7 and used the underlying structure of these examples to arrive at its new version. The pointillistic nature of this music results from both the complex nature of the combination of musical styles of the input music and the fact that the network was not allowed to complete its back propagations during composition, and thus not fully achieve its goal—a technique that typically produces more original and potentially creative results, and hence my rationale for using this approach here.

The complexity of the neural network process, and particularly the fact that neural networks appear to "learn" without revealing their methods, can give the impression that these networks have intelligence and are capable of creativity. As with genetic algorithms, however, we should not overestimate the abilities of neural networks or let comtivity mask a lack of true creativity. As we have seen, and will yet see, creativity need not be complex—in fact, creativity often produces the simplest, rather than the most complex, results.

I have placed a small neural network program called Network on my Web site that produces occasionally interesting musical output. Network trains itself (unsupervised) on input patterns provided by users, organizing these patterns by similarity into musical output. This approach does not require users to train the network.

Fuzzy Logic

On the basis that most problems have more complex solutions than a simple true or false response provides, fuzzy logic ranks output possibilities according to their potential "trueness" or "falseness." For example, there are many instances of tallness and shortness, and describing someone as tall does not necessarily differentiate that person from a short person except in extreme cases. A moderately tall person may appear to some as a shorter tall person, but to others as a taller short person. This vagueness often causes problems when using standard programming techniques, but can be handled effectively when using fuzzy logic, which makes a best choice by gauging relationships within overlapping areas of two or more sets of data.

Fuzzy logic has proven particularly valuable for analyzing musical data when those data have more than one potential interpretation. Determining harmonic function in modulatory passages in tonal music, for example, can be particularly difficult when a harmony may be heard as having more than one function, depending on the determination of a current key. Fuzzy logic allows for such harmonies to belong simultaneously to both of the relevant keys. One key, however, will more effectively match all of the competing requirements and thus indicate the harmony's true function.

Fuzzy logic can also be used effectively to define chords in performed MIDI files. Such chords often resist definition, since their notes frequently lack clear temporal boundaries. Fuzzy logic analyzes such data as an overlapping region, where the notes of each chord have ever-changing sets of probabilities for attachment to one or another of the chords. Held-over notes from one chord have ever-decreasing probabilities of membership in a newly struck chord, while newly struck notes have ever-increasing probabilities of membership in the new chord. By tabulating the various possibilities and measuring them against one another, fuzzy logic allows choices to be made that would not easily surface using other analytical processes.

Figure 3.10
An example of fuzzy-based musical output.

Fuzzy-logic rules derived from analyzing music may be used to create new music by reversing the just-described processes. Figure 3.10 gives an example of such fuzzy-based musical output. The "trueness" or "falseness" of the choices in this music were based on fuzzy selections from the analyzed rules and patterns of the rules-based music shown in figure 3.3. The right-hand melody here results from a fuzzy-inverted textural thinning of the left-hand music of figure 3.3.

Focusing on gray areas rather than absolute values makes fuzzy logic attractive for complex analysis, where competing factors make determination of solutions extremely problematic. Fuzzy logic also holds potential for creativity. Unfortunately, very few fuzzy-logic composing programs exist, and of those that do, most concern fairly simple musical styles and situations (Elsea 2000). Certainly no results have yet surfaced to suggest that fuzzy logic has succeeded in modeling creativity.

I have placed a fuzzy-logic program on my Web site called Fuzzy, which produces simple musical output when the supplied instructions are carefully followed. The quality of the output will generally match the quality of the input if users are careful in selecting data appropriate to their desired results.

Mathematical Modeling

Computer programmers, especially computer programmers who also compose, require processes for making quasi-random choices in their programs. By "quasi-random" I mean choices for which no rule applies, but for which the traditional computer pseudo-random choices I discussed earlier in this chapter simply will not do. No matter how deterministic programmers make their software, somewhere such choices must be made, if for no other reason than to produce different outputs each time their program runs. Having these choices result from separate formalisms appeals to many such composers, who have their programs make choices from a rich palette of highly unpredictable possibilities.

Mathematical series appear at the head of the list of alternative formalisms for quasi randomness. Of these mathematical series, the Fibonacci sequence (0, 1, 1, 2, 3, 5, 8, 13 ... in which each new number is the sum of the previous two numbers) has earned a special place. Dividing any number of this series by its predecessor produces the so-called golden mean (golden section) of approximately 1.62—depending on how far the series has progressed. The golden mean (also called *phi*) has served as a paradigm for artists, architects, and composers such as Debussy, Bartók, and Stravinsky, as well as for many composers using computers to compose. Jonathan Kramer notes that it

... should not be surprising that golden-mean proportions and Fibonacci numbers appear in music. Numerous mathematical properties of the Fibonacci series have appealed to artists and scientists for centuries, and golden-section proportions are frequently found in nature, human or otherwise. There is experimental evidence, for example, that the golden mean determines the ratio of people's positive to negative value judgments.... There is also experimental evidence that rectangles (cards, mirrors, pictures, etc.) proportioned according to the golden section (ratio of the longer to the shorter side is 1.62) appeal to our sense of symmetry. (Kramer 1988, p. 305)

Having a pseudo-random number generator choose numbers indeterminately from a Fibonacci sequence helps to ensure that, over time and with many thousands of choices made, these numbers and the choices they reflect will approximate golden mean relationships.

Mathematical formulas can also provide useful quasi randomness. A particularly interesting mathematical formula for me, the function

$$f_{(x)} = 1/\cos x^2$$

produces apparently random output when the result of each formulaic calculation recursively becomes a new "x" for squaring, cosining, and so on. The resulting series of numbers does not reveal patterns at any level. The graph in figure 3.11 demonstrates the unpredictable nature of these calculations, though it should be noted that the formula produces identical output each time it begins with the same seed number for x. Replacing this seed number with an arbitrary number, say a compacted form of the current date and time, however, provides almost infinite variations.

Figure 3.12 presents a musical example of the just-discussed cosine function with the music normalized to the MIDI pitch range. The data used to produce this music come from using a large seed number. While in some ways the most inventive of the musical examples in this section, particularly in terms of its use of silence and canon-like counterpoint, do not be confused by the comtivity here. This example simply follows the quasi-random—patternless—output of the cosine function in figure 3.11. The counterpoint in this example results from calculating a separate quantized rhythm from the same formula.

The program called Cosine on my Web site translates the output of the cosine function into musical pitches that, while sounding random, all share the same formulaic source. Such mathematical origins for algorithmic music, while occasionally producing interesting results, in no way indicate the presence of creativity. Even so-called chaotic generators and resultant attractors generate aimless-sounding music at best, and musical drivel at worst. Fractals, Brownian motion, random walks, and so on all share the same motivation for use, with generally similar results (see Ames 1987).

Sonification

Sonification produces sound by translating, in one way or another, traditionally non-audible data into sound. Scientists often use sonification to search aurally for patterns that may otherwise go unnoticed by the eye or by computational analysis. Sonifying data gathered from cell multiplication, for example, can reveal important relationships that might otherwise be overlooked. Sonifying stock market data can help analysts predict economic trends. Since the data typically used have no inherent musical logic, the normalized output from data sonification is generally of little use musically. However, composers who utilize algorithms have used sonification for small sections of their works where random-sounding music seems logical or appropriate.

Figure 3.13 presents an example of music produced by sonification—in this case, normalized barometric levels during a thunderstorm. The somewhat narrow range

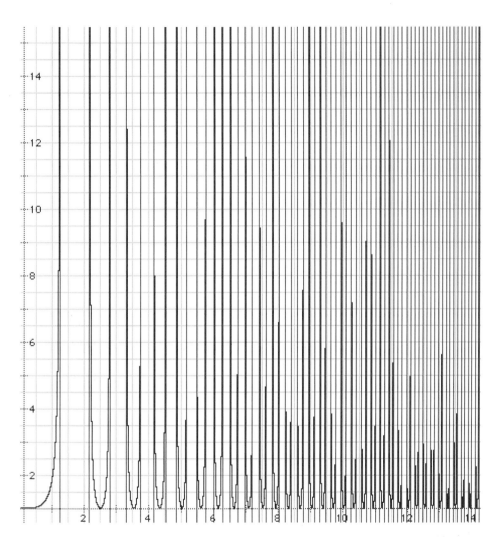

Figure 3.11
A graph of the formula $1/\cos x^2 = f_{(x)}$.

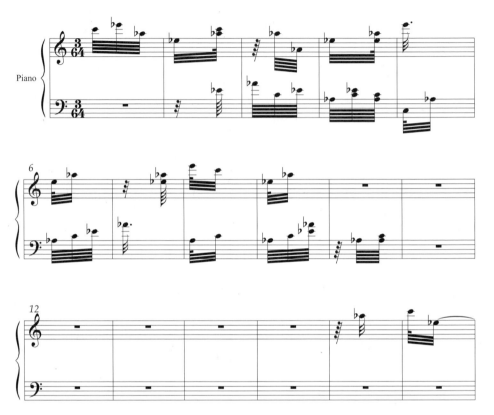

Figure 3.12
A mathematically produced musical example normalized to the MIDI pitch range.

(bandwidth) and wandering quality of the melodies here are due to the slow rate of change in the source. The slight variations in rhythm and texture result from a separate algorithm that treats certain combinations of data as musically more important than other data.

I have placed a very simple sonification program called Sonify on my Web site. Most of the music output from this program sounds haphazard. Intriguingly, however, when the program uses astronomical data collected at the Very Large Array radio telescope in New Mexico with Cassiopeia-A as a source, it produces an often harmonious-sounding music. None of this output should be taken as creative, however. While the sounds may effectively pass as Muzak, they hardly suffice as exemplars of musical creativity.

Figure 3.13
An example of music produced by sonification—in this case, normalized barometric levels during a thunderstorm.

The question remains, therefore, whether or not computers can truly create. Computer programs must be sufficiently independent of their programmers and users in order to qualify as truly creative. Most apparently creative algorithmic composing programs either produce enormous output from which users make preferential choices or invoke so many programmer-defined rules that the software only proves the creativity of the programmer. Therefore, none of the programs I have discussed here models creativity effectively.

Other potential computer models of creativity with possible applications to music include set theory (see Cope 2000), game theory (see Davis 1983), graph theory (see Lipschutz and Lipson 2003), and various applications of grammars (see Cope 1991a). While none of these approaches initially seem to have serious creative implications, none have been developed to the point that they should be dismissed.

Precisely what, then, does one look for in musical output from a computer program to discover creativity or the lack of it? I often quote Stravinsky in this regard, when he so eloquently states that

... variety surrounds me on every hand. So I need not fear that I shall be lacking in it, for I am constantly confronted by it. Contrast is everywhere. One has only to take note of it. Similarity is hidden; it must be sought out, and it is found only after the most exhaustive efforts. When variety tempts me, I am uneasy about the facile solutions it offers me. Similarity, on the other hand, poses more difficult problems, but also offers results that are more solid and hence more valuable to me.   (Stravinsky 1960, p. 34)

If similarity helps to identify creativity, so will the use of constraints, for similarity requires constraints. In turn, constraints cause problems, and problems often require the novel solutions that only creativity can provide. Stravinsky comments on this point as well:

My freedom thus consists in my moving about within the narrow frame that I have assigned myself for each one of my undertakings. I shall go even farther: my freedom will be so much the greater and more meaningful the more narrowly I limit my field of action and the more I surround myself with obstacles. Whatever diminishes constraint diminishes strength. The more constraints one imposes, the more one frees one's self of the chains that shackle the spirit. (Stravinsky 1960, p. 68)

Without composing constraints, every choice has the same value as every other choice. Equal value choices do not require creativity, just a good pseudo-random number generator.

Human Models

Understanding how humans create music may help reveal what the just-discussed programs may be missing. For example, human composers work in different ways. Many composers sketch prolifically, while others notate the final versions of their works without a single sketch—at least on paper. Some composers create music from beginning to end, while others compose more significant material first, then fill in the intervening music. These different methods have obvious parallels in the other arts. For example, painters typically begin by sketching in charcoal and could not, under most circumstances, create paintings on blank canvases. Sculptors differ from painters in that rather than filling blank canvases, they create by removing instead of adding material.

Attempting to model a computer program on every known creative process, however, would be pointless, since no matter how inclusive this program might be, there would surely be many approaches left untried. Worse yet, many of the chosen processes might contradict one another. Therefore, as will be seen during the unfolding of this book and the resultant modeling of creativity, I have adopted a single approach—one of interplay with the user—in hopes that this interplay will, at least in some ways, account for the diversity of human approaches to creativity. This interplay, for example, closely resembles musical sketching. The process begins with the equivalent of a blank canvas but, as the interplay between program and user continues, resembles more the sculptor's approach, in that both user and program sculpt a final work—consisting of a recombination of elements from previous interplays—*together*. How this unfolds will be revealed in detail in later chapters.

At this point, however, I will describe in some detail one of the more straightforward ways to gauge musical creativity—following and analyzing a human composer's sketching process. Examining how composers weed the wheat from the chaff can reinforce and challenge one's definition of creativity.

Unlike many composers, who seem to sketch in their heads or skip the sketching process entirely (as Mozart seems to have done), Beethoven has left us with reams of musical scribblings. These often laborious variations on themes provide those interested in the creative process with an extraordinary set of prototypes to follow. In the sketches for his unfinished Piano Concerto in D shown in figure 3.14a through 3.14k, Beethoven demonstrates how he continually revised his ideas, often changing his mind about motives that appear, disappear, and then reappear.

The eleven sketches shown in figure 3.14 follow an apparent chronological order. Only the second measure survives all of the sketches; the sole variations are the last two versions, which clip the quarter notes and add eighth rests. Overall, Beethoven prefers A over F-sharp as initiating pitch and favors eighth notes and quarter notes as the music's basic rhythmic motion, occasionally using ties across a measure's third beat (as in measures 3 and 5 of variation [C]). The third and fourth measures remain fairly fixed in most of the variations, with a surprise in measure 3 in the last sketch. Note that while many of these sketches seem quite different—variants (C) and (K) in figure 3.14, for example—a single change (i.e., F-natural in measure 3 of variant [K]) can cause many subsequent changes to occur.

Variant (A) in figure 3.14 can be viewed—with repeated notes and some interpolated notes removed—as a simple scale from A down to D (measures 1–3) and back up to G with an extension upward to high D, as shown in figure 3.15. The penultimate C-sharp in variant (A) in figure 3.15 verifies the D-major tonality, even though the whole note G receives considerable agogic emphasis in measure 4. The rhythm of this sketch begins with notes of relatively short duration and ends with notes of hyperextended duration. Variant (B) in figure 3.14 seems only partially complete,

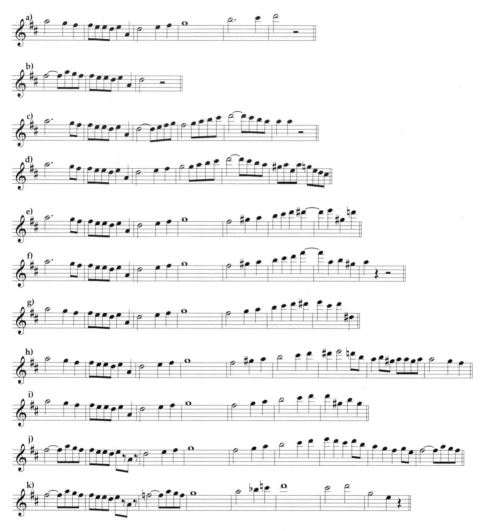

Figure 3.14
Sketches for Beethoven's Piano Concerto in D (unfinished), 1815 (from Cook 1989, pp. 346, 352).

Figure 3.15
Variant (A) of figure 3.14, with repeated notes and some interpolated notes removed.

Figure 3.16
Variant (C) of figure 3.14, showing a more coherent shape than variant (A).

Figure 3.17
A melding of variants (E) through (I) of figure 3.14.

Figure 3.18
An analysis of variant (K) of figure 3.14, showing an F-sharp to G motion from first to penultimate notes, along with a brief excursion to F-major.

but interestingly sets the stage for variants (J) and (K), beginning as it does on F-sharp rather than A. Variant (C) in figure 3.14 is consistent with variant (A) in terms of its use of pitch and rhythm, with the scale motion descending and then ascending to the same D before falling back to A. This balancing produces a much more coherent shape than does the music of variant (A), as shown in figure 3.16. However, figure 3.16 also demonstrates that this better balance creates a more stagnant overall phrase. Variants (E) through (I) in figure 3.14 begin in much the same way, moving to the whole note G and then wandering in various directions, often without finding cadence, as shown in figure 3.17, a generalized structural overview of these sketches.

Variant (J) in figure 3.14 returns to the diatonic orderliness of earlier versions, but like variant (C) has less direction. Variant (K) in figure 3.14, which shows an F-sharp to G motion from first to penultimate notes, along with a brief excursion to what appears to be F-major, has both the strength of variant (A)—notice the extended rhythmic value of D in both cases—and the chromaticism of variants (E) and (H), as shown in figure 3.18.

Using the definition of creativity stated earlier in this book—the initialization of connections between two or more multifaceted things, ideas, or phenomena hitherto not otherwise considered actively connected—provides an interesting reading of these variations. Beethoven slowly abandons the stability of his initial sketches, apparently searching for an unexpected twist for his melody. He finds it, after several apparently wrong turns, in a simple but highly effective chromatic variant (K), with the C-natural in measure 5 contradicting the C-sharp in measure 7, but both rising to the same D before descending to G and finally to E.

Beethoven has, through a series of explicit sketches, melded the strength of his initial ideas with a small chromatic paradox that creates a musically interesting phrase. He has clearly reconsidered connections previously thought illogical and effectively developed a theme that might have, had he seen fit to complete his concerto, served well for its first movement. These sketches thus provide a useful example of the musical creative process in action.

In discussing Beethoven's sketches in his book *Beethoven and the Creative Process*, Barry Cooper comments that "the idea was presumably that he could later select the best one, or that the great variety of ideas thus created could point the way to a new and original synthesis that would not normally have occurred to a composer" (Cooper 1990, p. 139). These thoughts also seem to coincide well with the definition of creativity described here.

Of all of the computer models presented in this chapter, from the haphazardness of pseudo-random numbers to the more elegant neural networks, none begins to compete in either effectiveness or plausibility with the just-described human model. I will, then, particularly in the model described in chapters 9 through 12, follow the spirit of Beethoven's sketching techniques as I describe both failed and more successful computer models of musical creativity.

II EXPERIMENTAL MODELS OF MUSICAL CREATIVITY

The more art is controlled, limited, worked over,
the more it is free.
(Stravinsky 1960, p. 66)

There's no such thing as a new melody.
Our work is to connect the old phrases,
so that they will sound like a new tune.
(Attributed to Irving Berlin; Galewitz 2001, p. 5)

4 Recombinance

Principle: Creativity does not originate from a vacuum, but rather synthesizes the work of others, no matter how original the results may seem.

Experiments in Musical Intelligence

In early August 1987, I presented my first paper on Experiments in Musical Intelligence at the International Computer Music Conference (ICMC) in Champaign, Illinois. My presentation was included with a group of papers that the conference organizers obviously couldn't categorize. Fred Lerdahl, the session moderator, left little doubt of this fact in his introduction. I spoke for no more than ten minutes before an unexpectedly large audience. My presentation concluded with a brief taped performance of Experiments in Musical Intelligence music—approximately five measures each of computer-composed Bach, Beethoven, Brahms, and Bartók. When the tape concluded playing, the audience did not ask questions and—disturbingly—offered no applause. The resulting silence seemed particularly odd, since the prevalent culture of the conference included polite applause after each presentation. I was unnerved by this turn of events, and spent the remainder of my time in Illinois in my hotel room, writing a defensive rebuttal to those in attendance for their apparent lack of interest in my work.

Later that same year I was invited to give the keynote address at a regional conference of an ethnomusicological society. I presented the same paper that I had given to the ICMC a few months earlier. On this latter occasion, however, I played a few more examples of my program's output—early failures—to demonstrate more clearly how the program had progressed. This time the reaction was swift, but nonetheless unpredictable: laughter—at least at the program's initial attempts at stylistic replications. When the tape arrived at the same Bach, Beethoven, Brahms, and Bartók examples I had played in Illinois, the music again met with utter silence. Most of the participants left without speaking to me—confusing, since the conference audience consisted of only about ten people, many of whom were friends of mine.

It took me months to determine the reason for these reactions. What seems clear is that neither of the two audiences found the music boring. To the contrary—and verified subsequently by many in attendance—the music confused and dislocated the audience, since they had no previous comparable experience. One colleague told me a year later at a conference in Germany: "This simply can't be true." Some fifteen years later the reaction has softened, the output of Experiments in Musical Intelligence has increased significantly, and performances—at least performances via recordings and broadcasts—have become more frequent, though they are certainly not commonplace. The buffering of time and availability of information—context—have made what was once disquieting, more routine.

Though I have described Experiments in Musical Intelligence in various other sources (see particularly Cope 2001a), I will present the principles of this program briefly here, to provide a more complete foundation for the processes of creativity I develop in later chapters. For those already familiar with how Experiments in Musical Intelligence works, note that I explain the program slightly differently here due to more recent developments (I continually revise my programs). However, those aware of this material may wish to skip the first two sections of this chapter, with little consequence to their effectively following the rest of the book. I have placed this review here so that readers unfamiliar with recombinance will not have to consult other sources in order to follow the related discussions in subsequent chapters.

Classical Western tonal music follows well-known principles governing pitch (notably major and minor scale derivation and complementary chromaticism), melody (primarily stepwise motion with leaps often followed by stepwise contrary motion), harmony (having prescribed functions and syntax), voice leading (mostly stepwise motion with voice independence), hierarchical form (phrases, sections, and movements governed by logical repetitions, variations, and contrasts), and so on. One way to create tonal music computationally is by programming rules for each of these principles. Unfortunately, as I have shown elsewhere (see Cope 2001a), this rules-based approach most often produces statistically correct, but stale, imitations.

I have found (see Cope 1996, 2000, 2001a) that what I call recombinance, or rules acquisition (a subset of the larger field of knowledge acquisition), provides more logical and successful approaches to composing in tonal musical styles. I will use these two terms—recombinance and rules acquisition—interchangeably here, but will especially use the term "rules acquisition" when I want to stress that recombinance uses rules inherited from a database.

Every work of music, I feel, contains a set of instructions for creating different but highly related replications of itself. These instructions, when interpreted correctly, can lead to important discoveries about this music's structure as well as help to produce interesting new instances of stylistically faithful music.

Recombinance is a method for producing new forms of data by recombining existing data into new logical orders. Recombinance appears everywhere around us as natural processes. As a simple example, all the great books in the English language result from combinations of the twenty-six letters of the alphabet and recombinations of the words that result from combinations of these letters. Similarly, most of the great works of Western art music consist of combinations of the twelve pitches of the equal-tempered scale and their octave equivalents and the recombinations of groupings—melodies, harmonies, and so on—that result from these combinations. As I will try to prove in later chapters, the secret of successful creativity lies not in the invention of new alphabet letters or musical pitches, but in the elegance of the combination and recombination of existing letters and pitches.

Of course, simply fragmenting existing musical works into smaller parts, and haphazardly recombining them into new orders, almost certainly produces gibberish. Effective recombination requires extensive musical analysis and very careful fragmentation to be effective at even an elemental level. The analytical processes I use center around voice-leading connectivity, as I will now describe in detail.

My initial attempts to create a computer style-composing program began by computationally transposing Bach chorales (Riemenschneider 1941) to C-major, separating these transposed chorales into beat-size groupings, and then saving these beat-size groupings as software objects (see Cope 1996, chapter 4). Along with each beat grouping, I had this program store the names of the destination pitches to which each voice in each grouping moved in the subsequent beat—one of that work's innate musical instructions or rules. I further had the program gather these beat groupings into collections of identically voiced beat groupings called lexicons, delineated by the pitches and registers of their entering voices (e.g., C1–G1–C2–C3, with the Arabic numbers representing the octave registers in which the pitches appear). To compose, then, this program simply chooses the first beat of any chorale in its database, examines this beat's voice destination notes, and then selects one of the stored beats with those same first notes from the appropriate lexicon, assuming enough chorale data have been stored to make more choices than the original following beat grouping possible. New choices then create the potential for different subsequent motions, and thus different subsequent groupings, while maintaining the integrity of Bach's original voice-leading rules.

Figures 4.1–4.4 provide examples of how this recombinatory process works. Figure 4.1 shows the beginning of Bach's Chorale no. 188. Assuming that the composing program I am describing has chosen the first beat of figure 4.1 as the first beat of a new chorale, the program recognizes each voice destination of this first beat grouping and attempts to find an equivalent grouping in a lexicon in its database, hopefully from another chorale. The principle here—that finding a substitute will most likely produce a different subsequent beat—helps the program create new music while retaining Bach's voice-leading rules. Figure 4.2 provides an example of just such a substitution. Note that the entering voices in beat 2 are precisely the same pitches as those in beat 2 of figure 4.1. However, figure 4.2's music moves distinctively differently from that point onward. The connection of the two chorale parts in figure 4.2 is seamless, and the rule that one might write to represent this substitution need not

Figure 4.1
The beginning of Bach's Chorale no. 188.

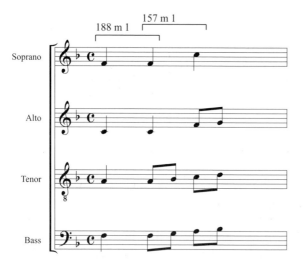

Figure 4.2
The substitution of Bach's Chorale no. 157 for the second beat of his Chorale no. 188 (shown in figure 4.1).

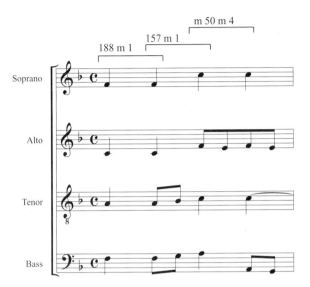

Figure 4.3
Continued substitution of chorale parts begun in figure 4.2.

be very complex, since each of the voices here repeats its notes from the opening grouping. In fact, in recombination, rules are not necessary, since the destination notes provide all of the requisite information.

Figure 4.3 shows a second substitution, from Chorale no. 50, continuing the new chorale phrase. Figure 4.4 demonstrates a final recombination in the completion of a new Bach-style chorale phrase. Note that the last four beats all derive from Chorale no. 165. The program in this case, apparently unable to find adequate substitutions, continues with Bach's original music. All of the new choices here are absolutely correct in terms of grouping-to-grouping voice leading, without the program having to apply any predefined rules. This new phrase, a product of very simple syntactic networking, in effect *inherits* the voice-leading rules of the works upon which it bases its replications.

While recombinance of this type ensures beat-to-beat logic in new compositions, it does not guarantee the same logic at higher levels. For example, with recombinance alone, music often wanders with uncharacteristic phrase lengths and with no real musical logic existing beyond the beat-to-beat syntax. Furthermore, phrases simply string together without direction or any large-scale structure, usually in a single key, and without any sense of the kinds of phrase consistency, balance, and closure necessary for intelligent music composition.

Figure 4.4
A completed new phrase. Compare this with Bach's original in figure 4.1.

In order to provide some sense of this logic and larger structure, and again want-ing to avoid coding my own knowledge of musical form as rules, I rewrote the pro-gram to inherit more of the structural aspects of the music in its database. This inheritance involved extending the analysis process so that the program could store other information about the music being analyzed in each grouping along with desti-nation notes. For example, I had the program analyze the original music's distance to cadence, position of groupings in relation to meter, and other context-sensitive features. Figure 4.5 shows how a Bach model (a) can serve as an example phrase for the program to create a new recombinant phrase (b). Each new substitution must now meet criteria not only in relation to the immediate destination notes of each voice but also in relation to cadence and to other phrase-dependent factors. The arrows in this figure represent considerations taken during analysis and recombi-nance in regard to adjacent groupings (first two arrows of each example) and cadence groupings (long arrow of each example).

To choose new groupings sensitively in regard to impending cadence requires that the program project destination voice leadings beyond neighboring groupings. For example, figure 4.6 shows how a series of voice leadings projecting from the first grouping connect to each of the rest of the groupings in a phrase. Of course, were we to choose alternative groupings on the basis that they comply with all of these

(a)

(b)

Figure 4.5
Inheritance of phrase features from a Bach model: (a) from Chorale no. 140; (b) a recombinant chorale. Arrows show chord-to-chord recombinance (first two arrows) and chords chosen with respect to cadence (long arrow) in both examples.

Figure 4.6
A series of voice leadings projecting from a first chord.

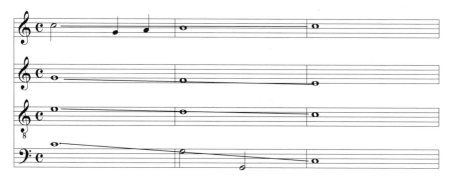

Figure 4.7
An example of how structural voice leading can help create a logical variation of the model shown in figure 4.6.

voice leadings, we would simply reproduce the original music rather than create a new chorale phrase. The idea is to choose new groupings, and especially the related voice leadings, that have more importance in a phrase, and let them guide the music rather than apply all of these voice leadings with equal force. The initial and the final groupings of a phrase are most pivotal. Taking just these two groupings helps to ensure that a new phrase maintains a semblance of the logic of an original model phrase.

Figure 4.7 shows how such extended voice leading can help create a logical variation of the model of figure 4.6. In this particular example (figure 4.6), because it is so short, one should assume that the first grouping initiates an internal phrase of an in-progress composition. Therefore, the initial grouping in figure 4.7 has been replaced.

Note how the voice leading from first to last grouping remains the same in these two figures where the internal music is different, but still follows the beat-to-beat rules of the music in the database.

Having this recombinance program also store location references of all of a model work's cadences further helps to produce effective phrase and section endings over the course of an entire work. Figure 4.8 shows how a Bach model can serve as a template for recombinant multiphrase music compositions. Of course, retaining too much information with each beat causes the program simply to reiterate—or produce a near likeness to—one of the chorales in its database. Therefore, the more alternative choices available, the better. Providing very large databases helps ensure that more than one possible correct choice exists at each recombinant junction. The arrows at the top of each example here show the structural relationships of cadences, while the lower arrows show cadence-to-cadence, antecedent-to-consequent motions. The blank spaces represent music removed to allow the figure to appear on one page.

Each of the modelings shown in figures 4.1 through 4.8—beat, phrase, and structure—represents rules acquired from music in the database and applied during composition. In fact, I often have my programs compile numerical representations of these rules to help me better understand the music being analyzed. My confidence in declaring Bach's use of 116 parallel fifths in his chorales in the discussion in chapter 1 of figures 1.8–1.9, results from just this kind of compilation of analyzed rules.

Patterns

Recombining groupings of music in a database to create new, stylistically faithful music unfortunately ignores the possibility that some critical aspects of musical style may be disassembled during the composing process. For example, certain musical patterns, which I believe are critical to the recognition of musical style, often extend beyond the narrow limits of groupings. I call these patterns "musical *signatures*."

Musical signatures are contiguous note patterns that recur in two or more works of a composer and that serve in some way to characterize this composer's musical style. Signatures typically extend over one to three measures, and often consist of a combination of melody, harmony, and rhythm. Signatures usually appear between two and six times in any given movement or work. Variations of signatures often include transposition, diatonic interval alteration, rhythmic refiguring, and registral and voice shifting. With few exceptions, however, such variations do not detract from aural recognition. Signatures are typically revealed by using pattern matching processes (see Cope 1991b, 1996, 2000; Miclet 1986; Simon and Sumner 1968).

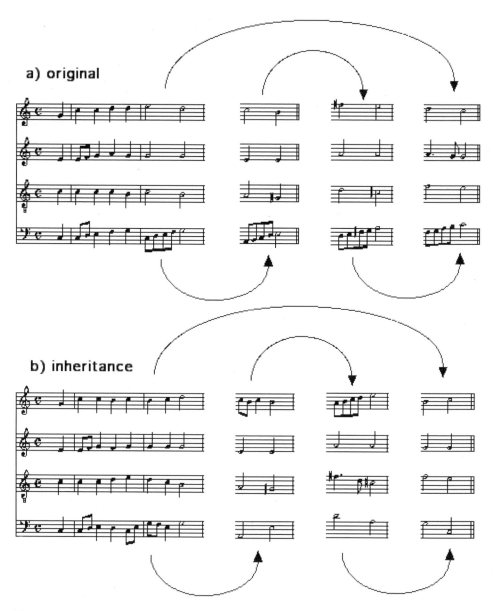

Figure 4.8
Structural inheritance from a Bach chorale model: (a) Bach's original; (b) an example of structural inheritance. Arrows at the top of each example show the structural relationships of cadences, and the lower arrows show cadence-to-cadence antecedent/consequent motions.

Figure 4.9
A Bach chorale signature.

Figure 4.9 shows a signature derived as a result of pattern matching over 200 of Bach's chorales. This signature can be characterized as a cadential figure—signatures are commonly cadential—with a very strong dominant (G-sharp) presence in the key of C-sharp minor. Since signatures are context sensitive, my recombinant programs ensure their appearance in new music approximately at their original structural locations.

Signatures and recombination represent fundamental opposites. That is, while recombinance seeks to fragment music into small parts in order to recombine these parts into newly organized music during composition, signatures resist such fragmentation because it would ultimately detract from accurate style replication. Therefore, Experiments in Musical Intelligence protects signatures from being fragmented into smaller groupings, thus ensuring that these signatures will survive the recombination process.

Figure 4.10 shows a complete machine-created Bach-style chorale composed by a program such as that described thus far in this chapter. The music follows Bach's rules for beat-to-beat voice leading, as well as Bach's general approach to musical structure. The signature of figure 4.9 appears in figure 4.10 beginning in measure 29. The music in this chorale has well-balanced phrase lengths, appropriate modulations, logical cadence types, and so on—all without the program having access to preprogrammed rules about Bach's music.

In many ways, recombinance can be described in terms of Markov chains, as discussed in chapter 3, with voice leading further limiting the first-order possibilities for next choices. However, such a Markovian description of recombinant processes does not allow for the broader control of larger-scale structure. The use of higher-ordered

Figure 4.10
A computer-composed chorale in the style of J. S. Bach.

Markov chains presents one model for achieving higher-level formal control. Thus, these higher orders remain sequential and linear. In music, what happens in measure 5 may directly influence what happens in measure 55, without necessarily affecting any of the intervening measures. Such nonlinearity requires the kinds of non-Markov processes I use with Experiments in Musical Intelligence.

This nascent version of the Experiments in Musical Intelligence program I have been describing was capable of producing interesting, even occasionally satisfying, music. Unfortunately, it also produced fairly awkward results. For example, no matter how carefully I chose works for the database, almost any music besides Bach chorales created incongruities between individual groupings—combining music with one type of texture and character with music of a completely different type of texture

Figure 4.10
(continued)

Figure 4.10
(continued)

(a)

(b)

Figure 4.11
From Mozart's sonatas (a) K. 284, movement 3, measure 1; and (b) K. 279, movement 1, measure 5.

and character. Most music does not have the textural and character consistency of Bach chorales.

My next addition to the program, therefore, was to have it store representations of the musical texture and character of each grouping in relation to its next grouping and subsequent structurally important groupings, to maintain continuity. The program first analyzes such texture and character in the original music before it breaks this music into groupings, in order to ensure that continuity and changes of texture and character take place at reasonable locations during recombinance. If, for example, the program were not able to access such information, one can imagine that each grouping of a resulting piece would have different types of internal patterns, jarring listeners from one musical context to another (see figures 4.11 and 4.12 as examples). This lack of consistency would most likely be uncharacteristic of either the style or the intent of the original works in the database. On the other hand, with its stored texture and character attributes, the program produces works having such continuity.

Figure 4.13 provides an example of how Experiments in Musical Intelligence creates music with varying textures, in this case in the style of Chopin. Note that while the program could use beat-size groupings of music, as it did in creating a new Bach-like chorale, here it has grouped the music in measure-size fragments. This measure-size

Figure 4.12
Conflicting rhythms when the left hands of figure 4.11 (a) and (b) are recombined without regard to character and continuity.

Figure 4.13
The beginning of a computer-created mazurka in the style of Chopin. (Superscript is source mazurka number followed by measure number.)

grouping process helps to preserve metric clarity and accompaniment identity. Later in this particular movement, the program uses beats as the basis for grouping. However, for the most part, when composing music with varying textures, Experiments in Musical Intelligence resorts to grouping music in larger sizes than beats.

The original sources appear above each measure in figure 4.13. Note that in composing music of varying textures, the program limits voice leading to the melody and bass lines only, with progression syntax stored as a separate attribute in each grouping as traditional tonal function. The resulting harmonic continuity follows a process similar to that shown in figures 4.2 and 4.3, but with harmonic functions enhancing the voice leading. Again, Experiments in Musical Intelligence avoids choosing the actual measure that follows the current measure, unless no other possibility exists.

I have not carefully documented how each measure was chosen in figure 4.13 due to the difficulty of following recombinance during machine composition. As important as the voice-leading and structural goals of the program are to the selection of measures, the number of complex interactions between the various constraints governing such choices makes reverse engineering difficult, if not impossible.

The output of Experiments in Musical Intelligence, as well as the output of the programs described later in this book, depends on careful choices of music for their databases. The larger the database, the more original-sounding the output, since more correct following groupings will exist at each decision point during composition. Choice of music with similar keys, modes, and meters increases the chances for successful output. Selection of music with similar textures and forms likewise enhances the effectiveness of the musical results.

Experiments in Musical Intelligence recombines music vertically as well as horizontally. Called transformational recombination (see micro-augmented transition networks, or MATN, in Cope 1996), this voice recombination offers further creative possibilities discussed more fully in chapter 10 of this book. (See especially figures 10.8 and 10.12 and related discussions.) Transformational recombinance follows the kinds of voice interleaving found by analysis of the music in the database. This analysis and resultant imitation are important, for indiscriminate transformations can cause unstylistic composition to occur.

As testified to by the thousands of works created by the Experiments in Musical Intelligence program, compositional recombinance often produces convincing new music in the style of the music in its database. Whether these new works result from *creative* processes, however, remains to be seen. According to the definition of creativity offered in chapter 1, one could imagine that the selection processes described here are creative. However, because this program represents the coding of my own particular take on voice leading and structure, the Experiments in Musical Intelligence just described represents *my* creativity rather than my *program's* creativity. Later in this book I will divulge the processes included in the program since the early 1990s that allow it to *create* new music rather than just computationally recombine the sources in its database.

I have explained the recombinatory process beginning with voice leading and moving outward to cadence and phrase analysis, to section, and ultimately to formal structure, in order to follow a listener's likely progress when hearing music for the first time. However, the Experiments in Musical Intelligence analysis and composition processes actually reverse this hierarchy, analyzing the structure of a work first, and its voice leading last. Machine composition proceeds in much the same order. This top-down approach is necessary because choosing new beat-to-beat groupings must be informed by hierarchy, and not the reverse. No new grouping of a work-in-progress can be selected until its implications for the entire structure of the work are determined.

The rules that my program acquires from the music in its database are just as robust as rules provided by programmers. In fact, acquired rules are often more accurate since, by default, they originate from the music itself and not from generalizations about that music. Consider the simple motion presented in figure 4.2. It may initially appear that only voice-leading connections have been inherited. However, voice-leading intervals, the major-key tonality, allowable triadic harmonies, basic harmonic progression, stepwise melodic motion, voice ranges, and so on also transfer from the musical source, even though no specific rules about them have been provided. Meter, phrase length, cadence, repetition and variation, and so on, are also inherited in the ways described here.

The rules acquisition process I have just described resembles in many ways the venerable human tradition of hearing music and then—without reading a text, listening to a teacher, or fulfilling an assignment—intuitively composing music in the same general style as that of the original music. Having a program first derive rules and then apply these rules during composition, though a simple notion, is critically important to the basic thrust of my modeling of creativity, particularly in relation to association (as demonstrated in chapters 9 through 11).

With these thoughts in mind, figures 4.14 and 4.15 show two short songs in the style of Mozart, one of which is by Mozart and the other composed using musical processes similar to the ones just described. The texts, dynamics, tempos, and articulations have been removed from Mozart's music to avoid revealing its true origins, since Experiments in Musical Intelligence's output, at the time of composition, did not include these elements, and thus the lack of such would indicate the composers' identities. I do not intend here to test your ability to discern which one of these examples is Mozart-composed and which one is computer-composed, nor which of these short works results from creative processes and which does not (previously discussed at length in chapter 2). Rather, I hope to encourage you to evaluate both of these songs to discover if either shows its "seams"—in other words, if either reveals its mode of composition. (MP3 files of these examples are available on my Web site.)

Examining these two short songs for style similarity and coherence reveals numerous examples of both. In terms of pitch, both figure 4.14 and figure 4.15 are tonal and conform to the common-practice key and harmonic progression rules that accompany that tradition. Figure 4.14 begins in G-major and, with the slight exception of small excursions into the dominant key of D-major, remains in G-major throughout. Figure 4.15 begins in F-major, modulates to its dominant, the key of C-major,

Figure 4.14
A short song (without words) in the style of Mozart.

Figure 4.14
(continued)

Figure 4.15
Another short song (without words) in the style of Mozart.

Figure 4.15
(continued)

and returns to F-major. Both of these key plans follow standard tonal models, although the A–B–A form of figure 4.15 is somewhat more common than the almost
through-composed-sounding music in figure 4.14.

The simple but "catchy" melodies in both examples vary each time they repeat,
although figure 4.14's variations seem more elaborate. Interestingly, figure 4.15's
melody—like its use of two keys—represents a legitimate A–B–A form, while figure
4.14 simply fragments a part of the primary theme before returning to the principal
theme. Rhythmically, figure 4.14 contains more variation, ranging as it does from
sixteenth notes to thirty-second notes and including triplets, while figure 4.15 juxta-
poses sixteenth notes with more predominant eighth notes, along with occasional

quarter notes and half notes. This rough overview, of course, merely describes the music; it does not analyze it.

Finding examples of compositional processes in these works proves more elusive. In figure 4.14, I interpret the thirty-second dotted-sixteenth rhythm in the second beats of the right hand of the accompaniment in measures 18 and 22 as an intriguing foreshadowing of the thirty-second notes that dominate measures 45–52 and the final four measures of the piece (structural coherence?). Without this foreshadowing, these latter measures might sound abrupt and out of place. The change of accompaniment type in measures 43–53 of figure 4.14, in part an exchange of left and right hands, adds to this section's contrast and gives it the identity, if not the substance, of a true second theme (transformational recombinance?). Figure 4.15 has fewer distinguishing characteristics, but what does occur, creates more drama. The second theme begins in measure 36 with an inversion of the primary theme's pickup notes. This relationship provides cohesion to the otherwise somewhat disparate material (texture and character contrast). The left-hand sixteenth-note figurations beginning in measure 37 in figure 4.15 imitate this inversion, providing a counterbalance to the secondary theme.

Interestingly, both figure 4.14 and figure 4.15 have rather strange numbers of measures for three-part forms—68 and 71 measures, respectively, neither evenly divisible by 3. However, both works sound balanced. Figure 4.14 has an unusual final cadence that implies the dominant rather than the tonic. This problematic cadence may be due in part to the fact that both excerpts originate in operas and therefore link to next scenes rather than end completely.

In summary, both figure 4.14 and figure 4.15 conform to Mozart's general style, and the melodies and harmonies follow the style of the classical period. They also diverge from the ordinary with subtle compositional nuances creating unpredictability, yet both works remain within the general boundaries of Mozart's musical sensibilities. Unfortunately, little of this analysis helps in determining which of the two pieces was composed computationally. For example, the rhythmic diversity of figure 4.14 could result from programming errors, poor selection of music for the database, or mistakes in the data itself, though the similarity present in the remainder of the music belies these possibilities. The squareness of figure 4.15 highlights the simple formal approach typical of many computer compositions, although Mozart certainly used straightforward forms as well.

Of course, those who know the actual Mozart or Mozart's style will not be confused about the sources of these works for long. However, those who do not know which of these works is by Mozart should, at the least, admit that recombinance can successfully re-create the style of music in a database without revealing its processes of composition.

Unfortunately for those wishing to know the composers of the works in figures 4.14 and 4.15 and not already familiar with the human-created one, I am not going to disclose their sources. My point is simple: were I to reveal the composers of these works, most readers would, I believe, simply fault themselves for not recognizing what in hindsight they would now believe distinguishes the real Mozart from the faux—a word I use guardedly, since I continue to maintain that computer-composed music in *any* style is as real as human-composed music in any style. Simply put, I believe that some computer programs can, in principle, *create*—not just *produce*—music. While such creativity may rely indirectly on the skills of the programmers who create these programs, this computer-composed music can, and should, stand shoulder to shoulder with human-composed music. I see no reason why computer-created music cannot move us to tears, find roots in our cultures, and reveal or obscure its internal implications as much as any music composed in more traditional ways. As heretical to some as these thoughts may be, I believe them profoundly.

I repeat, however—and it bears repeating—that the acquisition and straightforward use of recombinance does *not* represent creativity. There is little about the recombining of extant music into new logical forms of that music, that suggests "the initialization of connections between two or more multifaceted things, ideas, or phenomena hitherto not otherwise considered actively connected." This latter process requires the development of more subtle techniques of association that I describe later in this book.

The Chorale program on my Web site is a simple implementation of a recombinance algorithm that plays either an actual Bach chorale (from a collection of 350 Bach chorales) or a new computer-composed, Bach-like chorale (of which there are over 1 trillion different possibilities in this implementation). This program offers users the opportunity to judge for themselves whether they can hear recombinance at work. The Chorale program also provides a good example of data-driven programming as discussed in chapter 3. I point those not interested in experimenting with Chorale to the chorale shown in figure 4.10 that was created by a program similar to the one described here.

Performance

I have always believed that performance is a creative as well as an interpretive art. While most composer-performers seek to rid themselves of as many of the barriers between source and listener as possible, they cannot help but create personal versions of the works they perform. That many of us collect different performances of the same work testifies to this notion. That machine-perfect renditions of music are considered by most of us as crude and inartistic further substantiates this notion.

Recombinance, as I have described it here, requires that its database music exist in print-represented form. That is, unlike performed music, pitch entrances must rhythmically conform to some sort of quantized—rounded—norm. This nonperformance approach has many advantages, especially since the results can be easily converted by notation programs into clearly printed scores for human performers to play. At the same time, I have sought alternative ways of livening the otherwise lifeless output of my computer composing programs, for even human-composed music sounds dreadful when played by letter-perfect software programs. It is also true that for many composers, improvising on an instrument provides important compositional inspiration, and although such composers typically notate their music in quantized forms, improvisation often provides important feedback for creativity.

One way to include performance in machine models of musical creativity is to apply a separate performance algorithm to output music after recombinance has taken place. Interestingly, my first attempts at creating such a performance program mirrored my first attempts at creating a composing program: to re-create in code the rules that govern how I perform music. Such attempts were short-lived, however, for I soon discovered the incredible complexity involved in musically rendering even the simplest melody. In fact, the output from my performance program so resembled *distortion* that I soon opted simply to use controlled computer pseudo randomness—a technique adopted by many commercial sequencing programs available today. When used sensitively, these pseudo-random processes warmed the output slightly, making barely tolerable that which had been previously intolerable. Soon, however, listening to this vagarized output grew as tiring as listening to mechanical output. Increasing the size of the variables governing the amount of pseudo randomness used merely increased the impression of a poor performance. Tightening the controls on these variables, on the other hand, returned the music to the same indefatigable rigidity that the program had been invented to replace.

This process of adding performance to already composed music does not truly incorporate performance into the creative process, but simply aligns two separate activities one after the other. While similar to what we consider standard performance, such performance is inimical to the improvisational process used by many composers throughout history. Because I wished to program a single model of musical creativity, I attempted to integrate recombinance and performance, using improvisation as a core. The advantages to composing and performing simultaneously—improvising—as a model for a performance algorithm may not be self-evident. However, after having failed many times in creating a performance program, this process seemed like the only logical way to proceed. In effect, improvisation ensures that performance attributes exist in the database innately, and thus they become an integral part of the composing process.

Unfortunately, recombining groupings of performed music often causes extreme shifts of tempo, dynamics, articulation, phrasing, and so on, as well as a loss of a sense of meter, even when the database music itself does not contain such conflicts. These conflicts result from the fact that newly selected groupings, no matter how well chosen in terms of voice leading, can come from very differently performed musical environments. The first approach to this problem that I tried, an approach that seemed logical at least in the abstract, involved projecting an entire performance *map* of one piece onto a new piece. There are not enough chapters in this book to describe how idiotic this notion turns out to be. Imagine, for example, transferring the dynamics, articulations, subtle tempo and durational changes, and other complicated variables of a performed phrase of Mozart to another, completely different (except for general style) phrase of Mozartean music. No matter how the original music is compressed or expanded, for example, it will never really fit the new music unless both have exactly the same number of notes. Even then, however, what were the dynamics, articulations, and so on of, say, an ascending scale may be applied to, say, an Alberti bass—a completely inappropriate transference. Having the program remember the figure types of the original music only compounds the problems, since the output then becomes a hodgepodge of staggered or overlapping differently performed music, lacking entirely in the continuity so evident in successful human performances.

Obviously, none of these processes—by themselves at least—fulfilled my needs. My next step, therefore, involved seriously studying improvisation in order to better understand the connections between composing and improvising so that I might incorporate performance into my composing algorithms in a natural rather than an artificial way.

I began my study with a few personal observations. Practicing, combined with the physical makeup of one's hands, embouchure, and so on develops and reinforces physically remembered patterns that both limit improvisation (by skill shortcomings and by subtly introducing practiced patterns of other works—allusions) and contribute to personalized improvisational styles (since everyone has different sized hands, mouths, etc., with different muscular capabilities). Such physically remembered patterns constitute a kind of formalism within which improvising composers negotiate their creative intent. Without the equivalents for hands, embouchures, and so on, computer programs must settle for the inheritance of these characteristics from performed music in a database. Such inheritance may be a weak substitute for physical involvement, but it nonetheless provides the only logical alternative, given the current state of robotics and other modes of the computer modeling of physical behavior.

Improvisation requires a broad range of interrelated neuropsychological and neurophysical skills, including motor control, intuition, intelligence, musical context, style, creativity, and interpretation, to name but a few. Jeffrey Pressing (1988) presents a broad survey of many of these topics, as does Alf Gabrielsson (1999). Pressing, in particular, suggests that improvisation consists of either generating music associatively to maintain continuity, or interruptively striking out in apparently new directions. Which of these generative possibilities—association or interruption—is chosen, depends, according to Pressing, on the improviser's level of tolerance for repetition. Eric Clarke (1988) outlines three slightly different aspects of improvisation: hierarchy, association, and selection from repertory, all three of these principles then interacting during improvisation. Note that in both of these proposals, association plays a significant role. The model of creativity I present in later chapters depends on such associations.

P. N. Johnson-Laird (1991) provides a quite thorough delineation of the computational principles for improvisation, including how improvisers associate rhythmic patterns, melodic contours, and harmony. Johnson-Laird's computation principles involve note onset and offset, location in the ongoing melodic contour, and pitch—particulars not unlike those that I will soon present in this chapter. Improvisation, according to Neil Todd (1993), includes a continuous loop between motor skills and perceptual feedback that derives from tactile and kinesthetic interplay involving visual as well as aural input.

From this body of research, and believing firmly in the advantages of composing and performing simultaneously, I created a first version of an improvisation-based composing program. This was no mean feat, since the grouping complications I alluded to in chapter 3 under "Fuzzy Logic" quickly surfaced. Describing these complications in more detail here will, I hope, give readers firsthand awareness of their complexity and the difficulties in programming they can cause.

Figure 4.16 shows a printed representation of a simple, improvised popular-music-style keyboard introduction. Not only are all of the potential groupings easy to identify, but their placement—and hence replacement—makes grouping-to-grouping recombination relatively simple. The locations of onbeats and offbeats are clear. The metric identity—where downbeats and secondary beats occur—is equally transparent. In short, when storing music in a database using such models, a program can easily analyze, shuffle, and connect like groupings into credible new output.

Figure 4.16
Printed representation of a popular-music-style keyboard introduction.

Figure 4.17 presents an example of how performed music can appear when printed. Surprisingly, this music is the same as the first two measures shown in figure 4.16. Not only is the theme here barely recognizable visually, but this notation only vaguely hints at the actual timings of the music it represents. In fact, all of these timings have been quantized to the sixty-fourth-note level. Accurately representing what was played would require much finer resolution and make this example impossible to print readably. My programs resolve timings to 1/1000 of a second. However, even this sensitively produces only a generalization of the subtlety of rhythms inherent in most improvised performances.

Grouping the music in figure 4.17 in the same manner as the music in figure 4.16 poses many problems. For example, it is not at all clear in figure 4.17 where most beats begin and end, since many beats do not have struck notes on them, only tied notes. No matter how one forms groupings, questions about beat location and meter surface. These are critical issues for improvisation, and ones that must be dealt with in order for a composition program to create meaningful output.

Figure 4.17
A performed version of the first two measures of figure 4.16.

There are several options to solving these problems. One approach, for example, involves creating a database that contains both nonperformed—print represented—music *and* performed versions of this same music. The program then groups the print-represented music and stores both types of data together in the same groupings. After composing using the print-represented data, and just prior to output, the program returns the groupings to their performed state. The problem with this approach is, of course, that the output becomes a hodgepodge of differently performed music.

Another option for solving this performance problem involves collecting notes in arbitrary equal-size groupings. Each grouping must then store information about ties, since often the program will terminate a grouping at a point where no note begins or ends, and where notes extend beyond the boundary of the grouping. These ties can be restored later in the compositional process, when the recombinance algorithm aligns the current notes to appropriate destination notes. If this grouping process matches the beat of the music, the process can work as effectively as it does when using nonperformed music. However, as is most likely the case, when grouping sizes or alignments do not match the metric beat of the music, the output fails. Unfortunately, discovering beats in performed music of any style is an enormous analytical problem in itself—one that I am not convinced has a practical solution, given variations in performances compared with what we still hear as a steady beat.

Another simple but computationally intensive process involves note inception-to-inception grouping. In short, this means that a grouping begins whenever a note begins, and ends whenever any new note begins. Groupings are thus variable in duration, some being very small—often microscopic—and others being quite large, at least by comparison. Unfortunately, retaining the music's beat and meter causes just as many problems with this approach as with others. For example, figure 4.18 shows figure 4.17's first measures with inception-to-inception groupings shown by

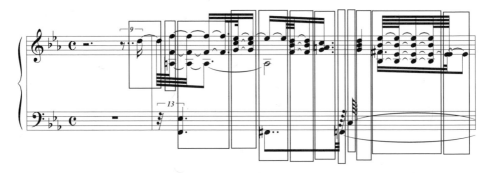

Figure 4.18
Figure 4.17's first measures with inception-to-inception groupings shown by rectangles.

rectangles. The results of such a process after recombination should sound performable, or else listeners, at least listeners sensitive to the nuances of the musical style
being replicated, will sense awkwardness and the music will lose its genuineness. In
other words, performed recombinant music, no matter the grouping size, risks transforming idiomatically performed music into illogical output. The reasons for this
may be obvious to some, but I provide a demonstration of the degree to which the
transformation resulting from recombination can fail.

As an abstract example, recombinant music takes a segment of music (A) with
voice-leading information for its immediate destination (B), as well as the remainder
of its groupings (C, D, E ...), and replaces its destination (B) with a new grouping
(X) that has the same initial voicing as the destination of the original (B) but that
now moves to different groupings (Y, Z ...), as in

A |B| C D ...

  |X| Y Z ...

We assume that segments (A B) and (X Y) are idiomatic, since they occur naturally
in their original compositions. However, we cannot assume that the progression (A X
Y Z ...) is idiomatic, because it involves a succession of groupings that does not
actually occur in the music used for recombination. Figures 4.19a–4.19c provide
typical examples, showing simple three-group patterns. In figure 4.19a, a two-voice
chord moves first upward and then downward. In figure 4.19b, the three groupings
move in directions opposite to figure 4.19a. Both of these passages fall easily within
the reach of one hand at the keyboard when performed separately. Figure 4.19c
shows a recombination of figures 4.19a and 4.19b, with the middle grouping (D–G)

Figure 4.19
An example of how recombinance can take two easily performed patterns (a) and (b) and make them more difficult to perform (c).

of each progression acting as a pivot between them. Whereas the first two progressions fall within the range of single-hand positions, the new music does not. While this is a very simple example, these kinds of situations in reality can become very difficult problems when recombining performed music.

Ensuring that when they are recombined, grouping combinations like those in figure 4.19 produce performable and idiomatic music requires application of correctly performed models. My improvisation program accomplishes this by using the original melodic contours of each voice as approximate guides. Thus, only new recombinations that conform to these guides will be chosen, ensuring that the resultant new music retains its performability. The contours the program uses are not intervallic, but are based on direction and tessitura. In the case of the music shown in figure 4.19a, the program would not allow a recombination to move upward from the second grouping nor sound below C-natural in the lowest voice in the third grouping. This directional control of upper voices and pitch limit of lower voices ensures that clumsy results like those shown in figure 4.19c will not occur.

As mentioned previously, locating and identifying meter in performed music presents an extremely thorny set of problems. Given that each second of music in my program is divided into milliseconds (1000 separate subdivisions per second), it is almost guaranteed that separate notes of performed harmonies will not occur at precisely the same time, since human performers are generally not capable of precision at such small scales. Thus, finding beats, even downbeats, becomes a computational best-guess game.

Of the programs I have created over the years to detect beats in music, few have been successful, and those that have achieved marginal acceptability still leave a great deal to be desired. Figure 4.20 shows the reason for this problem. All of the connections in figure 4.20b are derived from the music in figure 4.20a, with each connection being a proper destination of a voice's preceding note. However, the music in

(a)

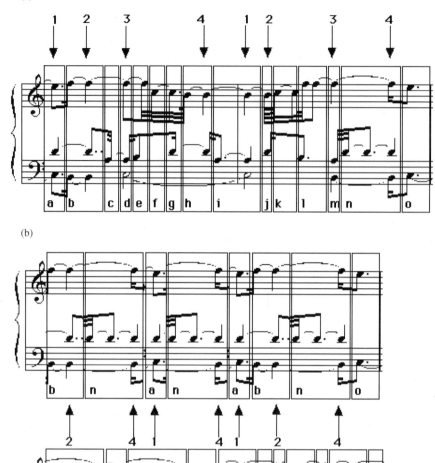

(b)

Figure 4.20
(a) Music for recombination; (b) recombinant music based on (a), with little sense of beat and meter.

figure 4.20b, unlike that in figure 4.20a, has little sense of beat or meter (in figure 4.20b the arrows point toward each beat's former location). As a result, this passage lacks metric, rhythmic, and stylistic semblance to the music in figure 4.20a.

Fragments a, b, and c in figure 4.20a are identical to (and thus interchangeable with) fragments o, n, and m, respectively, each one being the retrograde of the other. Fragments e and l in this figure are also interchangeable. Thus, the newly recombined music retains correct voice leading. However, the beats and meter are erratic in figure 4.20b. In fact, assigning new beat numbers to the arrows indicating meter in figure 4.20b is nearly impossible (again, the numbers here reflect their assignments in figure 4.20a).

In order to resolve all of these problems, I have adopted a process called double recombinance that—thankfully—sounds more complicated than it actually is. Double recombinance requires that pitch and rhythm be treated separately, based on their unique goals. Pitch, as has been the case in all of my recombinant programs, relies on the voice-leading destination processes that I have described in this chapter. These processes guarantee that even extraordinarily fragmented and juxtaposed musical groupings retain their proper connectivity and musical sense. So that rhythm will retain the same sense of logic as pitch recombination, the program matches these recombinant pitch gestures to equivalent performed gestures in the database to ensure that the resulting music retains a semblance of beat and meter. Since this process represents new territory, I will explain it in more detail.

For this explanation, imagine that a new work has been created using any size pitch-grouping recombinatory process. The rhythmic recombinatory process then requires three discrete steps. First, the program identifies a gesture at the outset of the newly recombined music. Gestures are defined here as music that has temporal boundaries—typically longer than a motive, but shorter than a phrase. This gesture will no doubt contain illogical rhythmic combinations, but in double recombinance the ontimes and durations of this gesture will be ignored by the program. Second, the program attempts to find an identical pitch gesture in the database of performed music. Obviously, the more performed music available for this process, the more likely the program will find a suitable match. However, failing an identical match, the program can substitute a similar match, defined as a gesture of the same number of notes but not of entirely the same pitches. Failing this process, the program shortens its target gesture in hopes that in so doing, the program will be able to find a suitable match in the database more easily. Third, once a gestural match is made, the rhythm of the found gesture is mapped onto the recombinant gesture.

The principle at work here is actually quite simple: improvisation tends to function as a series of gestures that themselves have a sense of beat and that, when performed one after another, make musical, rhythmic, and metric sense. While the feeling of beat and meter may be lost momentarily between gestures, the rhythmic integrity of each recombinant gesture carries the music forward with more musical and structural performance logic than other, more fragmented approaches provide.

It is important to note that the original dynamics of the found gestures remain intact. Dynamics greatly contribute to rhythmic logic, and to recombine them separately, as with pitches and rhythm, would defeat the purpose of using this double recombinant model in the first place. By retaining dynamics in found gestures, new music maintains its rhythmic sense, with the rhythmic recombinance adding just enough variety to give the impression of variation (at the least) and contrast (at the most).

With the model complete, output music will have an ordered sense of dynamics, rhythm, and meter. Of course, the pitch recombinance no longer retains its beat sensitivity (e.g., groupings originally appearing on downbeats, for example, may now occur on offbeats), a loss that to sensitive ears will have consequences. However, the trade-off, maintaining meter but losing pitch/beat sensitivity, is a reasonable one. In fact, over the years I have discovered that most listeners are unaware of the subtleties of pitch/beat relationships, while those same individuals would find music without distinguishable meter and beat—at least in certain styles—lacking musical value.

Figure 4.21 provides an abstract representation of how double recombinance works. Note that the gestures in figure 4.21 do not exactly align to reflect the meter

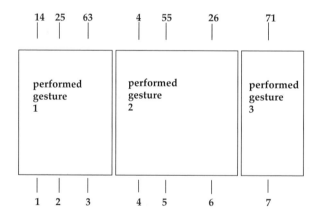

Figure 4.21
An abstract representation of how double recombinance works. The numbers above the gestures here refer to beat number in the model used for rhythm, and the numbers below reflect the beat number in the recombinant music. The distance between these beats approximates their temporal locations with respect to one another.

and beats an improviser might intend. However, delays of beats 4 and 7 (numbers *below* the gestures) here seem more natural, given that the gestures retain their rhythmic and metric integrity.

The physical relationship that composers have with instruments during improvisation obviously is extraordinarily important to their craft and creativity. I believe this profoundly. Being a programmer and wedded to the notion of "divide and conquer," I have here taken the road of least resistance, using the just-described process of double recombinance.

Clearly, humans do not separate pitch and rhythm during improvisation as I have done here. However, combining these two parameters into a "performed" output remains the best approach that I have found and clearly approximates a true performance at the gestural level, as seen in figure 4.22. Figure 4.22 provides an example of how a matched gesture from one work can be applied to new recombinant music. In figure 4.22a, three different groupings from Chopin's Mazurka no. 16 recombine in logical ways to create a new musical gesture. Figure 4.22b shows a gesture found in Chopin's Mazurka no. 52 that is similar to the recombinant example in figure 4.22a. Applying the performance characteristics (not shown here for the sake of clarity) of the music in figure 4.22b to the music in figure 4.22a produces a logical interpretation of the new music. Note that the music in these two examples is not quite

Figure 4.22
(a) A recombinant fragment (sources shown above each grouping) and (b) a model from which performance information can be applied to (a).

the same (i.e., measure 1, third beat, left hand; measure 2, second beat, left hand; right-hand use of sixteenth rests instead of dotted eighth notes; etc.). However, these discrepancies are easily dealt with since they approximate each other closely enough to have the performance of one apply to the other.

I use straightforward processes to account for differences between model gestures and equivalent gestures in newly composed music. When a model contains more notes than the new music, the notes in closest proximity are chosen. When the model has fewer notes than the new music, these additional notes in the recombinant music are given ontimes and durations approximate to other relevant notes in the performed model.

I am not unaware that to some degree I have returned here to a previously rejected approach—modeling performance attributes on music in a database. However, my initial attempts used entire works rather than gestures, as models. In this particular instance, the "economies of scale" make an important difference. What were unacceptable errors when using larger, complete works of music become acceptable errors in more manageable, gesture-size amounts of music. I took this circuitous route to arrive at this conclusion because the earlier experiments provided insight into *why* I ultimately chose gestural processes.

In order to give readers the sense of the complexities involved in performance algorithms, I have included a platform-dependent version of a program I call Improvise on my Web site. Improvise allows users to link MIDI instruments directly to a Macintosh computer and receive a response to performed input on that same instrument in the form of new, stylistically relevant performed output. The program's response to the MIDI input follows and develops both the style and the content of that input.

I use Improvise with a Disklavier computer-controllable acoustic piano. However, Improvise need not be limited to performance on a Disklavier. Many other musical instruments now have MIDI versions available. Unfortunately, some of these instruments require continuous MIDI controllers for effective performance. For example, a MIDI-controlled clarinet will sound quite lifeless if simply given note-ons and note-offs (i.e., without vibrato and subtle, continuous dynamic nuances, such as crescendo and diminuendo on held notes). Such information must be collected during performance and then used in composition in ways that Improvise does not currently provide. Given that virtually thousands of separate instances of such information may be required for even a single measure of music, it may be necessary to wait until desktop computers achieve significantly more speed for this kind of interaction to occur, at least with programs such as Improvise.

Even though my ultimate model of musical creativity includes improvisational input, and thus performed output, I will continue to use print-represented format for the musical examples in this book. My reason for this should be clear: intelligibility. The complicated visual representations of performed music can be almost unreadable at times. These complications are one of the reasons why I have waited until now in this book to discuss performance—so as to not confuse performance complexity with, for example, recombinance or pattern matching.

5 Allusion

Principle: Creativity relies in part on the juxtaposition of allusions to the work of others.

Definitions

One of my favorite musical works as a youth was Stravinsky's *Firebird Suite*, composed in 1910. For me, at least, this work perfectly combines Romantic, Impressionistic, and Contemporary idioms in a nonetheless original-sounding ballet score. However, I also listened to recordings and studied the scores of many lesser-known Russian composers of the period and often noticed remarkable similarities between them. For example, in *Night on Mount Triglav* (from the ballet *Mlada*, 1872), by Stravinsky's teacher Nikolai Rimsky-Korsakov, I discovered a foreshadowing of the *Firebird*'s ominous introduction. In Anatol Liadov's *Baba-Yaga*, completed in 1904, I found one of Stravinsky's possible sources for the firebird's colorful wings exploding into flight (Liadov turned down Diagilev's attempts to commission him first for the *Firebird* in 1909, and hence was a source that Stravinsky no doubt turned to as well). In Rimsky-Korsakov's *Le Coq d'or* (The Golden Cockerel; 1908), I discovered strong similarities to many of the themes and orchestrations in *Firebird*.

Initially, I was thunderstruck; what once had sounded extraordinarily original now seemed more a mélange of various quotes and references to other works. However, by this time my respect for, and knowledge of, many great Russian composers had grown to such an extent that I began to appreciate rather than deprecate the allusions I heard in their music. In fact, the more Russian music I heard, the more this apparently derivative process seemed creative, providing me with a deeper contextual appreciation for the music. Late Romantic Russian composers, it turns out, used allusions as a benchmark of their nationalism, considering allusions not only honorable but requisite to their stylistic heritage (see, for example, Grout 1980, pp. 652–660).

I should have known, of course, that Russian music, like any music belonging to a generic or specific style, would be steeped in allusions. After all, style is a commonality between two or more different works, a commonality that must, at least in part, rely on allusions. Throughout music history composers have made reference to the works and styles of their own and preceding generations in an effort to provide a deeper context to their music. Recognition of these allusions may inform musical performance, analysis, and listening in ways that no other form of analysis by itself can. Recognition of allusions also sheds light on the creative process—defined here as "the initialization of connections between two or more multifaceted things, ideas, or phenomena hitherto not otherwise considered actively connected." Yet, studies of allusion in music have not proliferated, presumably in part because of the inference that composers who draw on the work of others are less creative.

Note that I use the term "allusion" in this book to mean the recognizable relationships between two passages occurring in different works. Unless otherwise indicated, I in no way wish to imply conscious or subconscious intentionality on the part of the composer whose music includes the reference.

It is difficult to imagine that a musical composition could be created without one or more allusions, since composers have precious little else to use as compositional material than the music they hear. However, one way to avoid using allusions—or at least using them overtly—is by composing with formalisms (isorhythm, fugue, serialism, etc.). John Cage's indeterminate music might also qualify as an example of such an avoidance. For example, when creating a work like *Music of Changes* (1951), Cage followed the *I Ching* to produce twenty-six large charts indeterminately indicating many aspects of composition. It took nine months for Cage to complete *Music of Changes*, every aspect of which was essentially determined by coin tosses associated with these charts (see Cope 2001a, p. 84). Interestingly, while the composers of such works do not intend to include allusions, listeners may still *hear* allusions, especially if these listeners are not aware of the processes used during composition. This perception of allusions represents a very important concept: that allusions exist regardless of intent.

To ignore these references when analyzing music seems contrary to the very notion of analysis. Peter Kivy asserts:

To be sure, the materials of music are not conventional in the sense of being bearers of meaning (in the literal sense of that term). But they are by no means free of convention in another sense: they are in large part *preformed* artifacts. Composers do not start from scratch with some kind of palette of natural sound. They work with melodies, melodic fragments, *preformed* patches of harmonic fabric, well-worn, secondhand bits and pieces of contrapuntal building blocks: in short, the materials of music are not natural sounds, but music already. (Kivy 1984, p. 12; italics added)

The added italics in this quote are meant to ensure that readers do not mistake the word *preformed* for *performed*. In essence, Kivy argues here that most music—even the works of the venerable masters—consists of fragments of other music. Ignoring the sources of this music, and for that matter the sources of those sources, and so on, seems to me an error of immense proportions. Kivy later paraphrases Harris (1772) in this regard, saying, "... that our enjoyment of imitation consists in being able to recognize the object in the imitation" (Kivy 1984, p. 13).

I therefore contend that all composers borrow. The reason we sense that some composers are more derivative than others more than likely stems from the fact that good composers are often more discreet about their use of allusions, and/or find the right place and the right time for the right allusion. Poor composers, on the other hand, tend to broadcast the presence of allusions by unintentionally revealing their thefts, or perhaps just mistiming their use.

Given the links between derivation and allusion in music, it is interesting to note that allusions in literature often seem to indicate *quality* rather than lack of originality. For example, the Arden series presents Shakespeare's plays with numbered lines referencing extended footnotes, with pages often having more footnotes than play text. Such footnotes in the Arden *Hamlet* (Jenkins 1982), for instance, argue that the plot itself is a retelling of a story by Belleforest (1576; see Gollancz 1926), and individual passages such as

We defy augury. There is a special providence in the fall of a sparrow. If it be now, 'tis not to come; if it be not to come, it will be now; if it be not now, yet it will come. The readiness is all.

consist of extraordinary allusions and paraphrasing. These lines, according to Jenkins, originate from the New Testament: Matthew 10:29 ("Are not two sparrows sold for a farthing? And yet not one of them will not fall to the ground without your Father's leave"), Matthew 24:44 ("Therefore you also must be ready, because at an hour that you do not expect, the Son of Man will come"), and Luke 12:40 ("You also must be ready, because at an hour that you do not expect, the Son of Man is coming"). This process of borrowing in literature is called "intertextuality," where richness of meaning accrues from the presence of other sources in texts. Apparently the point I made with Solresol in chapter 1—that creativity in music differs from creativity in the other arts—is particularly true with allusions, at least in terms of the differing views of perceived quality and originality in music and language.

As I hope to prove in this chapter, computer detection of musical allusions can complement more standard harmonic, melodic, and formal types of analysis, serve as a method for performers to better interpret the music they play, and act as another approach to the deeper understanding of the creative process in music. My rationale for devoting an entire chapter of this book to this single topic stems from my desire to further develop my hypothesis that human composers in part create their music by recombining the ideas of other composers. This hypothesis is important for this book, for as we shall eventually see, my ultimate computer model of musical creativity has recombinance as its core.

While many musicologists have recognized allusions in the works of specific composers, very few systematic studies of musical allusions have taken place. With the exception of Deryck Cooke's landmark book *The Language of Music* (1959), few articles or books are devoted exclusively to such allusions. Yet, musical allusions have occurred continually throughout music history. Such forms as organum, motets, cantatas, and other cantus firmus-based musical forms often depend on allusions. As well, many composers' styles, such as those of Handel, Berlioz, Rachmaninoff, Ives, and Luciano Berio, use allusions extensively, deliberately, and explicitly.

J. Peter Burkholder and others have produced an extraordinary Internet bibliography of sources relating to borrowed materials in music (see Birchler, Burkholder, and Giger [1999] in the bibliography). Burkholder (1994) has also devised a detailed "typology of musical borrowing." In this typology, he denotes a series of classifications of borrowed material that includes the relationship of a work to the work from which it borrows, the elements of a work alluded to by another work, how borrowed material in one work relates to the original work, how borrowed material is altered in its new environs, and the function of the borrowed material within its new context. Among this latter category, Burkholder describes how borrowed material might lend a certain character, pay homage to, comment on, or critique its source. His overview provides a very useful template to follow, though it lacks detail.

I have opted for a somewhat simpler approach to classifying allusions than Burkholder's, delineating them into five basic categories—from quotation to the use of more common musical conventions. Note that I do not use negatively connotated words such as *cliché* here. I wish to avoid the stigma of what some feel is a weakness (derivation), for what I feel can be a strength (creation). Note as well that the boundaries of the categories here are imprecise and may overlap at times. My taxonomy for analysis of allusions includes the following:

1. Quotations—as in citations, excerpts, or renditions

2. Paraphrases—as in variations, caricatures, or figurations

3. Likenesses—as in approximations, translations, or transcriptions

4. Frameworks—as in outlines, vestiges, or redactions

5. Commonalities—as in conventions, genera, or simplicities.

There are, of course, other types of allusions than those I have listed here, such as stylistic references, allusions to musical forms, imitations of natural phenomena, and so on. While I have not categorized these here, I will describe various approaches to detecting these other kinds of allusions in some detail later in this chapter.

As can be seen, the potential for listener recognition of these allusion categories proceeds from strong to weak, and the potential for stylistic integration proceeds inversely. A more detailed and exampled description of each of these categories follows. In each case, I present a known allusion—as found in the relevant musicological literature—followed by an example discovered using the Sorcerer computer program that I describe more thoroughly later in this chapter. I hope this pairing will help convince readers of this computer program's potential to discover important allusions in music.

Quotations

Quotations often involve exact pitch and/or rhythm duplication. The plainchant "Dies Irae" represents a good example of quotation when heard in such works as Berlioz's *Symphonie Fantastique* (1830; in the "Witches' Sabbath"), Liszt's *Dance of Death* and the "Inferno" from his Dante Symphony (1857), Saint-Saëns's *Danse macabre* (1874), the Trepak in Mussorgsky's *Songs and Dances of Death* (1877), Rachmaninoff's *Isle of the Dead* (1907) and Rhapsody on a Theme of Paganini (1934) (Keppler 1956).

Beethoven quotes a Mozart fragment in the second movement of his "Pathétique" Sonata (1798), as shown in figure 5.1. Although only three melodic notes (C–Bb–Eb)

Figure 5.1
(a) Beethoven's Sonata, op. 13 ("Pathétique"), movement 2, measures 1–3, and (b) Mozart Sonata K. 457, movement 2, measure 25.

Figure 5.2
(a) Weber's *Concertstücke*, op. 79, beginning four measures beyond rehearsal letter D, and (b) Beethoven's
Sonata op. 31, no. 2, movement 1, beginning measure 2.

appear in common between the two themes here, Beethoven's use of the same key
(Ab major) and nearly identical harmonization clearly reveal the Mozartean origins.
For me, this allusion contextualizes Beethoven's music and, rather than proving its
composer's lack of creativity, provides listeners with one more tool with which to understand his creative process.

Figure 5.2 presents a short passage from a work for piano and orchestra by Weber
that quotes Beethoven's Sonata, op. 31, no. 2 (1802) as discovered by the Sorcerer
program. Only transposition (up a minor sixth) and rhythmic diminution (Weber
has halved the note values) distinguish the two passages from one another. In terms
of creativity, Weber's quotation of Beethoven's sonata invigorates the otherwise
rather stagnant etude quality of the music that surrounds this passage in his concerto
(not shown).

Paraphrases
Paraphrasing typically involves using different pitches than the original music, but
similar intervals and typically is paired with rhythmic variations. Stravinsky states
that "The opening bassoon melody in *Le Sacre du printemps* [1913] is the only folk
melody in that work. It came from an anthology of Lithuanian folk music I found in

(a)

(b)

Figure 5.3
(a) The opening bassoon melody of Stravinsky's *Le Sacre du printemps* and (b) from an anthology of Lithuanian folk music (Krakow 1900, no. 157, p. 21).

Warsaw ..." (Stravinsky and Craft 1960, p. 92). Figures 5.3a and 5.3b show the relationship between Stravinsky's opening melody and the folk song in *Litauische Volks-Weisen* upon which it was based.

Even with Stravinsky's protestations to the contrary, however, we can readily see and hear his paraphrase of a folk song printed a page earlier in the *Litauische Volks-Weisen* (see figure 5.4b) in the theme of the "Ritual of Abduction" in *Le Sacre*, as shown in figure 5.4a (Morton 1979, pp. 12–13). Using paraphrases such as these, Stravinsky has imbued his music not only with the melodies of other music, but also, at least in some small way, with the culture and traditions of that music.

Figure 5.5 presents a paraphrase of Schubert's *Rosamunde* overture (1823) that appears in Bruckner's Symphony no. 7, third movement (1883), found by the Sorcerer program. While the meter and keys differ between these examples, the two themes, when heard, bear a striking resemblance to one another. By subtly referencing Schubert's well-known *Rosamunde*, Bruckner has creatively contextualized his music for informed listeners.

Likenesses
In general, likenesses can have differing pitches, intervals, harmonies, and/or rhythms but share some underlying resemblance, such as overall similarity of interval directions or sizes. In some cases, even apparently innovative compositions contain

(a)

(b)

Figure 5.4
(a) A theme from the "Ritual of Abduction" in *Le Sacre*; and (b) another folk song from the same anthology of Lithuanian folk music as in figure 5.3b.

(a)

(b)

Figure 5.5
(a) Bruckner, Symphony no. 7, movement 3, theme 2, and (b) Schubert, *Rosamunde* Overture, op. 26, theme 2.

likenesses. The prelude to Wagner's opera *Tristan und Isolde* (1859), for example, represents just such a case. Figure 5.6 shows precedents for *Tristan* in Beethoven, Schumann, Liszt, and Ludwig Spohr (notably the beginning of his opera *Der Alchemist* [1830]). Wagner was aware of most, if not all, of these works, as correspondence and other documents attest. Scott (1927) notes that during one rehearsal Wagner unremorsefully remarked to Liszt, "Here comes something of yours...." Interestingly, while the rhythm and harmonies differ somewhat between Liszt's music (figure 5.6c) and Wagner's prelude (figure 5.6e), the melody of G-sharp, A, A-sharp, and B is identical. Cooke mentions that this figure also appears in Mozart's String Quartet in E-flat (1783; K. 428), and Spohr's String Quartet in C (1807) (Cooke 1959). Note that the *Tristan* example of figure 5.6e contains the so-called *Tristan chord* that achieves its fame from dissonance outweighing resolution by a factor of 5 to 1—a proportion similar to that which occurs in Spohr's music in figure 5.6d.

Figure 5.7 presents a likeness of Mozart's K. 605 (1791) appearing in Beethoven's Symphony no. 3 (1803), found by the Sorcerer program. The keys and especially the rhythms differ between these two examples. However, hearing them one after the other proves their similarity. The rhythmic and metric variations in Beethoven's music here present the allusion in ways that both mask and enhance it.

Frameworks

In general, frameworks include interpolated notes so that potential similarity surfaces only after those notes are removed during analysis. Leonard Meyer reveals how the opening theme from Mahler's Fourth Symphony (1892) can be construed as lying across the superstructure of a melodic passage from Handel's *Messiah* (1750) (see Meyer 1989, p. 54). Figure 5.8 re-creates Meyer's figure. After hearing these two themes one after the other, this kind of pattern comparison will not seem as far a reach as some might initially imagine.

Sorcerer discovered the framework of a Handel theme in Beethoven's Symphony no. 3 (1803), second movement, as shown in figure 5.9. Discovering the skeletal frame of Handel's melody in Beethoven's symphony requires deletion of Beethoven's repeated notes and a number of other more ornamental intervening notes (a process discussed in more detail later in this chapter).

It seems appropriate that these two examples of frameworks share Handel as a source, since Scott (1927) states that the idea that Handel

... did, however, annex in the most astounding way, and without any sort of acknowledgment, the work of other composers is, of course, beyond dispute and doubt exists only as to the extent to which he himself was conscious of any wrong-doing being involved in his procedure. (Scott 1927, pp. 500–501)

Figure 5.6
(a) Beethoven's Sonata, op. 13 ("Pathétique"), movement 1, (1798); (b) Schumann, Trio no. 1 in D-minor, op. 63, (1847); (c) Liszt, *Ich Möchte hingehn*; (d) Ludwig Spohr, *Der Alchemist*, (1830)—all precedents for (e) Wagner's prelude to *Tristan und Isolde* (1859).

(a)

(b)

Figure 5.7
(a) Beethoven's Symphony no. 3, op. 55, movement 4, theme 2; and (b) Mozart K. 605, no. 3 (German Dance), theme 2.

(a)

(b)

Figure 5.8
How (a) a Mahler theme (Symphony no. 4) can be construed as lying across the superstructure of (b) a theme from Handel's *Messiah*.

(a)

(b)

Figure 5.9
(a) Beethoven, Symphony no. 3, op. 55, movement 2, theme 1; (b) Handel, Sonata for Flute and Continuo, op. 1, no. 9, movement 2.

Handel apparently not only accepted, but often relished, the new contexts that his references to other music provides.

Frameworks such as the ones presented here are often subtle and surely contestable. However, knowledge of potential frameworks can nonetheless broaden our understanding and appreciation of the music in which they appear.

Commonalities

Commonalities typically involve patterns that by virtue of their simplicity—scales, triad outlines, and so on—occur almost everywhere in music. Yet, Deryck Cooke (1959) believed that these kinds of simple patterns, used by classical composers over hundreds of years, demonstrate a common thread of influence (see Cope 1996, pp. 15–20). Jan LaRue (1961), however, makes the point that such patterns are often so simple and generic that regardless of their similarity, they may not have been borrowed, but are simply *unavoidable*. Figure 5.10, selections from LaRue's figure 25 (LaRue 1961, p. 233), provides examples of a theme used by many composers that, by virtue of its simple upward-moving triadic outline, appears to result from common-practice tonal compositional techniques rather than allusion. In fact, what LaRue calls *generic resemblance* (p. 233) and what I call commonalities are ubiquitous in tonal music. Therefore, while individual thematic comparisons may appear conclusive, arguments could be made that all of the music in figure 5.10 results from a compositional process or, if it borrows, alludes to a broad spectrum of works that liberally exchange ideas from one to another without specific reference.

Some commonalities may have musical or cultural implications such that, though simple, their prevalence and preferential use over other similarly simple patterns indicates specific selection rather than arbitrary proliferation. I call such commonalities Ur-motives, since they represent fundamental attributes derived from a large body of music, often transcending style differences and appearing over a significant period of time. These attributes separate Ur-motives from patterns such as Mannheim Rockets (consecutive upward triadic leaps) and the *sigh* motive (stepwise downward patterns), both very common in the baroque/classical periods, but only arguably present in music of other Western classical styles.

Figure 5.11 provides fourteen examples of an Ur-motive covering three centuries. All of the instances shown occur near the beginning of important melodic themes in their respective works and therefore can be distinctly heard. Note that in most of the cases presented here, the Ur-motive (up–down–down–up stepwise motion) appears in faster note values than the thematic notes surrounding it, giving it both the feel of an embellishment—having possibly less musical value—and yet accentuating its presence—having possibly more musical value. In the Mahler example of figure

Figure 5.10
Similar figures by (a) Haydn, (b) Giovanni Sammartini, (c) Alessandro Borroni, (d) Friedrich Schwindl, (e) Florian Gassmann, (f) E. T. A. Hoffmann, and (g) Karl Friedrich Abel (from LaRue 1961, p. 233).

5.11m, the symphonic movement in which the motive appears develops this Ur-motive into a single figure repeating literally hundreds of times. When music of a certain tradition ignores such Ur-motives, it can be less stylistically convincing.

Sorcerer discovers commonalities almost everywhere in the music it analyzes. Figure 5.12 provides an obvious example of this type of pattern, here represented by a downward-moving major scale. LaRue would argue, and I would agree, that this commonality, unlike the Ur-motive shown in figure 5.11, does not represent an allusion so much as simple downward scalar motion.

While exact quotations appear infrequently in most music, commonalities appear almost everywhere, and Sorcerer requires filters to prevent these commonalities from obscuring true allusions. As I will discuss shortly, such filters help ensure a higher probability that the patterns Sorcerer discovers, represent true allusions, and are not artifacts of a composing technique routinely used by many composers.

Interestingly, in my experience using Sorcerer, highly regarded composers who have weathered the test of time tend to use likenesses and frameworks most often, whereas less-recognized composers seem to use more obvious quotations and paraphrases. Brahms, for example, favors frameworks more than quotation, and typically uses smaller allusions, with more variation than, say, Rossini, whose allusions tend toward exactness. As well, composers who use musical formalisms such as canons and fugues produce fewer allusions in their music—at least fewer detectable by Sorcerer—due to the strict constraints of these forms.

Detection

Of the few programs able to search comprehensively for patterns in musical databases, David Huron's Humdrum (Huron 1993) offers the processes most useful for detecting allusions in music. Humdrum rigorously searches its database for exact and approximate matches of patterns provided by users of the program. However, this program requires that users have at least some idea of the pattern they wish to

Figure 5.11
An up-down-down-up Ur-motive appearing in music by (a) Handel, Suite no. 2 in F-major, movement 1, theme 1; (b) Bach, Suite no. 2 in B-minor, Overture, theme 2; (c) Bach, *Well-Tempered Clavier*, book 1, prelude 10; (d) Bach, *Well-Tempered Clavier*, book 1, fugue 15; (e) Haydn, Symphony no. 98, movement 2, theme 2; (f) Muzio Clementi, Sonata in B-flat, op. 47, no. 2, movement 2, theme 1; (g) Mozart, Piano Sonata K. 570, movement 1, theme 2; (h) Mozart, Piano Sonata K. 578, movement 2, theme 1; (i) Beethoven, Piano Concerto no. 5, op. 73, movement 1, theme 1; (j) Chopin, Mazurka, op. 6, no. 1; (k) Schumann, *Carnaval*, op. 9, "Eusabius"; (l) Wagner, *Tristan und Isolde*, Love Death, theme 2; (m) Mahler, Symphony no. 9, movement 4, Introduction; (n) Stravinsky, *Pulcinella*, Gavotte.

(a)

(b)

Figure 5.12
An example of a commonality in (a) Berlioz, *Corsair* overture, op. 21; and (b) Haydn String Quartet in G, op. 74, no. 3, movement 3.

match. Using wild-card symbols in the place of all notes of a pattern, for example, does not resolve this problem, since the program then returns *all* patterns as a response. Comprehensively discovering potential allusions in a work requires that a program *automatically* search for *every* possible subpattern and skeletal pattern that matches the patterns in its target music.

I developed the prototype of the Sorcerer program in 1995 to automate such comprehensive pattern-matching processes. Sorcerer provides analytical verification of the presence of musical allusions for use in what I call *referential analysis,* a semiotic approach roughly situated between hermeneutic analysis (interpretive—see Agawu 1991, 1996; Gjerdingen 1988; Nattiez 1990) and Rétian analysis (motivic—see Réti 1962). Sorcerer attempts to match patterns found in a target work—music under study—with several potential source works—music assumed either to influence or to be influenced by the target work. Sorcerer then presents matched patterns as possible allusions. The program lists its findings without regard for whether the composer of the target work consciously or subconsciously referenced the source work; the only criterion is that the found allusions exist, and can be heard by informed listeners.

Figure 5.13 provides a general schematic for the Sorcerer program. Sorcerer can incorporate pitch and/or rhythm in its searches. Source music—the database—may consist of works composed before or after the target work, depending on whether one intends to discover what music might have influenced the target work, or what music the target work might have influenced. In fact, as I will demonstrate shortly, source works may consist of *both* music composed before and after the target work, so long as one clearly distinguishes the chronological relationships in the program's output.

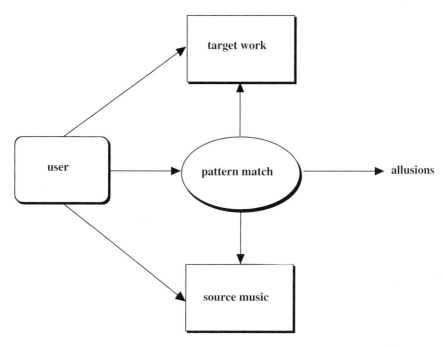

Figure 5.13
A general schematic for the Sorcerer program.

Choosing appropriate source music for a particular target work when using Sorcerer is crucial for producing useful results. Source music may be as extensive and varied as users wish, although the more diverse the examples used, the more difficulties one encounters. I have found that a few judiciously chosen suspect phrases of similar mode and meter can be as effective in producing meaningful results as an extensive series of poorly chosen complete works. The Sorcerer-discovered allusions presented in this book were all revealed using databases consisting of thirty or fewer well-selected phrases. Evidence of the target-music composer's awareness of the source composer's music can also help users create logical databases.

Sorcerer encodes music automatically when loading MIDI files as input. Once users check source music for errors, and load it, this music converts automatically to events: lists of pitches, timings, durations, MIDI channels, and loudness (see appendix B). Events can be extended to include other categories of information, such as articulations, effects, and so on, although these additions, in my experience, seldom meaningfully contribute to the discovery of allusions.

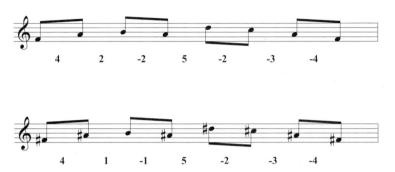

Figure 5.14
Two simple musical patterns that have many different notes but which sound quite similar. The interval numbers below each staff indicate the half-step content and direction of each interval.

Discovering musical allusions requires efficient musical pattern matching, as can be seen—and heard—by comparing many of the paired examples in this chapter. In order to understand how patterns in a target work, particularly noncontiguous patterns, can be found in source music requires a general understanding of the basic principles of musical pattern matching.

Figure 5.14 shows two simple musical patterns that have many different notes but sound quite similar. In order to make a favorable comparison between these two patterns, a pattern matcher should do the following:

a. Compare intervals as well as notes

b. Allow for certain variations in interval size within logical boundaries

c. Allow the interpolation of a certain number of notes between hierarchically more important notes.

While (c) does not play an important role in matching the two examples in figure 5.14, the detection of frameworks discussed earlier requires such pitch interpolations. Harmony and rhythm (not pertinent in figure 5.14) can also be important in pattern matching, and can be pattern matched using Sorcerer, as will be discussed shortly. Other melodic variations, such as inversions, do not currently play a role in Sorcerer's pattern-matching processes. However, any audible variation in pattern matching can contribute to allusion recognition. Therefore, Sorcerer will ultimately incorporate a wider spectrum of variation possibilities.

With the exception of notes 2 through 4, the two patterns in figure 5.14 match exactly in terms of intervals. As well, the two incorrect intervals differ from one another by only a half step, a variation easily allowed by a slightly "forgiving" pattern matcher. This forgiveness results from user-set variables—called *controllers*. In this case, a controller designed to permit interval variations determines the number of half steps by which intervals may differ from each other and still match. Users may also establish the number of acceptable intervening notes between notes for a match to occur, using another controller. Still other controllers define variation sizes relating to harmony, rhythm, and other aspects of melody than interval sizes and intervening notes (for more information on controllers, see Cope 1996, pp. 89–103).

Controllers set at low numbers allow only quotations or paraphrases to appear in output. Controllers set to high numbers allow all five previously discussed categories of allusions to match successfully. Unfortunately, high settings also permit large numbers of commonalities and other extraneous patterns to match, which can produce confusing results. Setting the controllers properly to achieve optimum results demands experience, a good ear, and patience, for each new target and its source music require new settings to achieve the best results. Sorcerer can automatically set controllers based on settings of previously successful pattern matches, but user control works best in most situations.

Sorcerer also requires a maximum length for patterns. This length can be quite long, but not so long as to force the program to compare melodic patterns that common sense would suggest have no chance of matching. Twelve or so intervals (thirteen pitches) typically serve as a reasonable high limit for melodic recognition. Once Sorcerer's pattern matcher has a maximal length, the program attempts to match all subsets of that length that begin with its first interval, ensuring that patterns shorter than the maximum length will not get passed over. This pattern matching proceeds from small to large, and the entire process ends when the nonmatch of a smaller pattern guarantees a nonmatch of any larger pattern to which this smaller pattern belongs.

Sorcerer uses an incremental pattern matcher. This means that patterns are collected from both the target and the source music beginning on each note of a composition, rather than collected from the ends of previous collected patterns (called contiguous pattern matching). Incremental processes greatly increase the potential of the program to discover important allusions. Unfortunately, however, incremental pattern matching requires substantially more processing power than contiguous pattern matching. This required processing power can delay results considerably when matching large numbers of source works, and thus delay the ability of users to interpret the program's results. In order to expedite this incremental pattern-matching process, Sorcerer stores source music as patterns rather than as continuous music. In other words, the target music and source music are segmented into patterns when music is loaded, before the actual pattern matching begins.

Figure 5.15
The way Sorcerer collects patterns incrementally: (a) music for pattern matching; (b)–(f) incrementally collected patterns from (a).

The advantage of this pattern-storage approach is that Sorcerer can return its output more quickly and users can vary controllers and rematch almost immediately thereafter. One disadvantage of this approach to storing music as patterns is that any variation in largest pattern size requires a complete overhaul of pattern storage, a lengthy process that can discourage many users from attempting it. Pattern storage can also require significant amounts of memory. In effect, I have exchanged an increase in speed for a loss of storage space. However, this trade-off's advantages, I feel, far outweigh its disadvantages. The following detail of pattern collection, storage processes, and resultant pattern matching should make these advantages and disadvantages more clear.

Figure 5.15 shows how patterns are collected incrementally. Here, all of the four-note patterns from 5.15a appear in order in 5.15b–5.15f. Once collected, patterns are stored as objects (see Cope 1996, chapter 4) in special lexicons named according to their interval content. Intervals are measured in half steps, with downward intervals preceded by minus signs. Intervals greater than an octave are reduced to within an octave in their names, to avoid the confusion of double digits. Pattern objects then have attributes that contain information about their original key, rhythm, and metric placement as well as information about their original location.

Figure 5.16
The way patterns are stored in lexicons according to their intervallic content (S represents Sorcerer; N stands for number).

Figure 5.16 shows a pattern object (S5212-31N1) located in its appropriate lexicon (S5212-31). The suffix N_x, where "N" stands for "number" and "x" represents an incrementally advancing number, allows many patterns with the same interval content to be stored in the same lexicon. To compare a target pattern with a source pattern, then, requires only that the pattern matcher check for the existence of the appropriate lexicon, and retrieve its contents if it exists. This process ensures that patterns are compared only with patterns guaranteed to match, and avoids the extensive matching of patterns that have no chance of matching (required of most standard pattern-matching processes).

Discovering frameworks requires that target patterns be skeletonized and then matched as with other patterns. For example, the list of pitches B–C–D–E–A, matched as a three-note framework from B, would appear as B–C–D, B–C–E, B–C–A, B–D–E, B–D–A, B–E–A, and so on, with each pattern representing a version of the original with various excised notes. A single target passage of twenty pitches can thus create hundreds of possible frameworks for matching, depending on the size of the pattern to be matched. This framework-matching process assumes that the target's patterns are embellishments of the source music's patterns and not vice versa. While both figures 5.8 and 5.9 exemplify this relationship, the reverse may

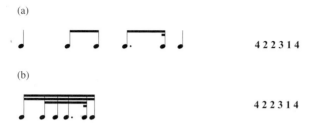

Figure 5.17
An example of two patterns that look very different rhythmically but that match as identical when compared by Sorcerer: (a) sixteenth note as shortest duration; (b) sixty-fourth note as shortest duration.

also occur in music. Discovering such relationships using the current implementation of Sorcerer requires switching target and source music.

Harmonic pattern matching using Sorcerer requires that pitches be replaced by program- or user-analyzed harmonic representations (see Cope 1991a, pp. 30–33) avoiding the program's having to account for doubling, spacing, and other differences during pattern matching, differences that can mask identical chord functions from computational discovery. However, for the most part, Sorcerer relies on melodic pattern matching, using its harmonic counterpart as verification of melodic matching rather than as a separate process for discovering harmonic allusions (the *Tristan* example of figure 5.6 represents a good example of this kind of combinative pattern matching).

When Sorcerer matches rhythm, it uses proportions. The program initially sets the shortest duration of a pattern to 1, and then figures all of the other durations as multiples of this base number, ensuring that patterns with very different configurations of prime durations are treated equally. Comparing rhythmic proportions in this way resembles the intervallic method used for pitch matching, since intervals represent all possible transpositions of a note sequence. Figure 5.17 shows an example of two patterns that look very different rhythmically but sound the same when the tempos are adjusted to account for the differently notated durations. These patterns match as identical when proportionally matched by Sorcerer.

Care must be taken when evaluating Sorcerer's output, because many patterns may not immediately reveal their similarities, at least to the ear. For example, figure 5.18 shows a simple theme that, once sung or heard, does not particularly remind many listeners of any other theme. The simple four-note opening motive first sequences and then repeats, leading to a standard half cadence. This theme, however, has all but one of its actual pitches in common with a more famous theme, the beginning of Beethoven's Symphony no. 5 (1808), as shown in figure 5.19. The rhythms

Figure 5.18
A computer-created theme.

Figure 5.19
The theme upon which the theme in figure 5.18 is based.

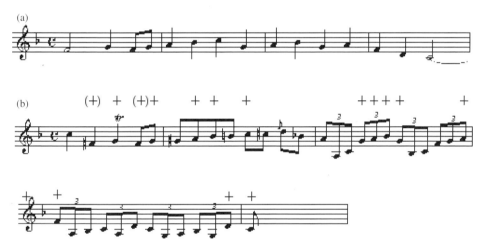

Figure 5.20
Interpolated embellishments in Chopin's Impromptu, op. 36: (a) measures 61–64; (b) measures 73–77.

and metric accents of figure 5.18 and figure 5.19 obviously differ. However, aside from the last few pitches, these two examples match exactly.

Lest one imagine that hidden relationships such as those between figures 5.18 and 5.19 are not important to the full understanding—and hence appreciation—of a work of music, a comparison of the two melodies shown in figure 5.20 should further prove this point. Chopin has buried the initial theme of his impromptu in 5.20a in a maze of interpolated notes, as shown in figure 5.20b. The crosses above certain notes in figure 5.20b correlate to the pitches of the original theme in figure 5.20a. Interestingly, most listeners find the relationship between these two melodies easier to discern

Figure 5.21
A short theme created by the Experiments in Musical Intelligence program.

Figure 5.22
From Beethoven's Sonata no. 8, op. 13, measures 1–5.

than the set in figures 5.18–5.19. Possibly this recognition results from the fact that the theme and its variation appear in the same work, that many of the downbeats in the theme fall on downbeats or held notes in the variation, or that educated listeners know that Chopin tends to vary his melodies by interlacing scales, turns, and other embellishments between important notes of those melodies. Sorcerer, however, finds the pattern relationships in figure 5.20 much more difficult to discover than in figure 5.19, since the controllers governing intervening notes for figure 5.20 must be set to very high levels, inviting all manner of less important patterns also to match.

Sorcerer uses filters to screen out smaller, high-count matches, ones most likely to be simple commonalities. As we will see shortly, however, even with controllers set to low levels and filters set to high levels, Sorcerer finds allusions almost everywhere in the music it analyzes, accounting for nearly every note in target music. This overkill can at times seem almost nonsensical (see particularly Cope 1996, pp. 22–23). However, the short theme shown in figure 5.21, one of six outputs of roughly similar quality composed by Experiments in Musical Intelligence, may indicate otherwise. This computer-generated music follows the main theme of Beethoven's Sonata no. 8 (1798) very closely, as seen in figure 5.22. However, the database used by Experiments in Musical Intelligence when composing the music in figure 5.21 did not contain any of Beethoven's music. Figure 5.23 documents how every note of music in

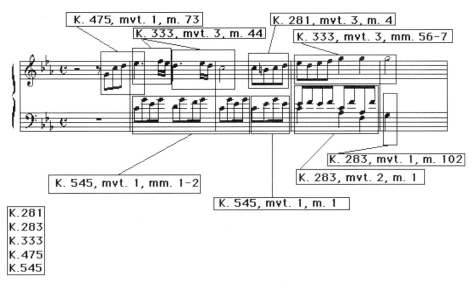

Figure 5.23
The Mozartean sources for the music shown in figure 5.21.

figure 5.21 references the music of Mozart, the only composer whose music appears in the database. While the number of allusions here far exceeds those of previous examples, it would seem that, regardless of perceived qualitative differences between figures 5.21 and 5.22, one could argue that the music in figure 5.21 results from *creative* processes not too different from those that produced figure 5.22.

Figure 5.24 shows a sample output from Sorcerer. Here we see how the main theme of Chopin's Piano Concerto no. 1, first movement, may have ties to various works by Bach, Beethoven, Boccherini, Ernst Chausson, and Schumann. Vertical lines connect notes of the source and target music to clarify where the proposed allusions begin. The composition date (1830) of the target music in figure 5.24 indicates that it may have been influenced by Bach (music dated 1722, 1722, 1731, and 1731, respectively, to BA1–4), Beethoven (music dated 1803 and 1802, respectively, to BE1–2), and Boccherini (date of composition unknown, d. 1805). However, the target music may have influenced Schumann (music dated 1838) and Chausson (music dated 1896). Of course, Schumann and Chausson may have been influenced by the same previously composed source music in the database that possibly influenced the Chopin target music. The patterns shown in figure 5.24 result from matching only the intervals of the given melodies. Obviously, comparing only melodies is far less meaningful than comparing harmony and rhythm as well. I have limited the scope

Figure 5.24
Output from Sorcerer showing how the main theme of Chopin's Piano Concerto no. 1, movement 1, may reference various works by Bach (BA), Beethoven (BE), Boccherini (BO), Ernest Chausson (C), and Schumann (S).

of this example to melody, to demonstrate how the process works on one level at a time.

Verifying allusions can be difficult if not impossible. Some allusions, however, are more verifiable than others. One of the major reasons for this difference in verifiability stems from the difficulty of establishing the probability that the composer of the target music knew the associated source music. Once a direct or indirect connection can be made, however, arguments in favor of an intentional allusion become more compelling. The probability that the composer of a target work knew a source work can provide reasonable assurance that an influence has taken place, and that an allusion has occurred.

There are other ways in which composers of target music reveal their intentional use of allusions, as opposed to their creating accidental similarities. Metric and phrasal placement are good examples of intentionality. Matched patterns that initiate on strong metric beats and discovered near phrase beginnings tend to be more audible than those that do not fall in these positions. Likewise, matched patterns that repeat gain priority over those that appear but once. Patterns that vary little from their sources (quotes and paraphrases) also have more potential for believability than those that do not.

The strategic formal placement of a pattern in a source work can further argue for its authenticity. A primary theme containing a suspected allusion obviously takes precedence over secondary-theme potential allusions, music found in inner voices, or once-occurring variations of a suspected allusion, unless the latter have some pronounced or exceptional quality that in some way enhances their recognizability. Sorcerer does not currently differentiate between strong and weak locational matches, however, which often places interesting or even humorous matches alongside more relevant ones. For the examples in this book, I have chosen only strongly appearing music in both source and target music.

As an example of strategic formal placement of allusions, figure 5.25 shows a well-known theme in Mozart's *Magic Flute* (K. 620) of 1791, to which I previously referred, with indications of several possible sources. The Clementi match originates from his Piano Sonata, op. 24, no. 2 (1781). This sonata's manuscript contains a note indicating that Mozart was present ("Mozart étant présent" [Plantinga 1977]) when Clementi performed this piece for Emperor Joseph II (Barlow and Morgenstern 1948, p. xii). Clearly, the *Magic Flute*'s theme represents a verifiable allusion, appearing as it does ten years after Clementi's sonata, with both composers placing their music as primary themes of their respective works. Arguments for the other possible influences by André Grétry (unknown date), Haydn (1789), and, interestingly, Mozart himself (1774) do not seem particularly compelling. As we have seen,

Figure 5.25
Output showing how Mozart's main theme in *The Magic Flute* may have ties to various works by Beethoven (B), Clementi (C), André Grétry (G), Haydn (H), and himself (M).

however, composers certainly borrow from themselves as well as from other composers. Musical signatures and earmarks (Cope 1996) represent verification of such borrowing, and demonstrate how allusions can participate in style definition and recognition. The Beethoven example from 1800 in figure 5.25, like the Schumann example in figure 5.24, may have been influenced by, rather than influencing, the Clementi/Mozart theme. Again, neither rhythm nor harmony has figured into the pattern-matching process in these examples.

As I mentioned earlier in this chapter, verified or not, the patterns that Sorcerer discovers in common between its source and target music *exist*, and as such should be considered allusions, regardless of our ability to prove intent. Interestingly, searching for references to works that composers of target music clearly did *not* know can also prove interesting, for such references may represent more universal allusions or Ur-motives—patterns that belong to the musical *ether*—as discussed earlier. Such references can be particularly striking when comparing music from widely divergent cultures. For example, discovering an apparent allusion in a Mozart piano sonata to a traditional Balinese gamelan work (as I did during the composition of *Mozart in Bali* in 1987—see Cope 1991a, pp. 216–222) proves only that the pattern involved has a certain timeless and culture-independent charm, and not that Mozart somehow heard gamelan music during his lifetime.

Interpretation

We hear the allusions in music with which we are familiar. While this statement is obvious, it is also important, because the opposite is also true: we don't hear the allusions in music with which we are *not* familiar. For example, since most of us do not know much of the music that Mozart listened to during his lifetime, we may not be able to hear many of the allusions that he consciously or subconsciously included in his music. In contrast, we do hear many of the allusions in the Experiments in Musical Intelligence Mozart-style music, simply because most of us are familiar with Mozart's music. Thus, the program's music, by virtue of composing in the styles of known composers, is advantaged or disadvantaged (depending on your point of view regarding allusions—revelation or derivation) compared with most human-composed music.

Interestingly, when I select database music for Experiments in Musical Intelligence, I am in part controlling the potential allusions that occur in its output. The possibilities for allusions occurring are inversely proportional to the size of this database. As a result, while I cannot predict the location or exact number of allusions, I can directly affect their relative frequency. Thus, when such allusions occur, they are not haphazard but referential—with the same kind of intent as when they occur in any work created by more traditional means.

Figure 5.26 shows the beginning of Bach's Fugue no. 4 from *The Well-Tempered Clavier*, as an example of possible revelations generated by the use of allusions. Figure 5.27 then shows how an eighteenth-century listener, following a well-known practice of the time, might interpret this music as a religious symbol—a cross. Eero Tarasti comments on this musical symbolism:

Competent listeners of the time were familiar with this meaning and would have recognized it in Bach's fugue-subject. The same religious meaning is preserved when that subject is quoted, as in the Prelude to César Franck's *Prélude, chorale et fugue*, even though nineteenth-century listeners might no longer have been aware of its original symbolism. (Tarasti 2002, p. 7)

Charles Rosen cautions, however, that

... it is important to avoid the common fallacy that there is a secret code that we have to learn in order to understand music. There is no code, secret or otherwise: we do not have access to a dictionary of musical significance. As we learn, largely unconsciously, how musical composition works within a given tradition, we understand how music can refer outside itself to a whole culture and civilization of which it is a small part. (Rosen 1994, p. xi)

Figure 5.26
The beginning of Bach's Fugue no. 4 from *The Well-Tempered Clavier*.

Figure 5.27
How a cross can be figured over the initial motive of the music in figure 5.26.

Sorcerer's ability to discover and index allusions in source music provides its users with helpful information on the possible sources of the patterns present in a target work. Revealing unsuspected—as well as confirming suspected—allusions produces a rich resource for musicological studies of a composer's style and creative processes. Further, Sorcerer may be useful to music theorists wishing to complement more standard analyses of music with alternative perspectives. Composers may be interested in using Sorcerer to indicate the degree to which their music references their own music and the music of other composers. This is one of the purposes for which I use the program, and I have found its output revealing and quite insightful. In each of these cases, the results demonstrate the "initialization of connections between two or more multifaceted things, ideas, or phenomena hitherto not otherwise considered actively connected," our operative definition for creativity in this book.

As mentioned previously, Sorcerer returns a list of all patterns found within the constraints of its controller and filter settings, leaving the interpretation of these patterns—as coincidental or intentional—to users of the program. Detecting intentional allusions, as opposed to detecting patterns that accidentally resemble one another, can be greatly enhanced by gauging the importance of matches based on the aforementioned metric placement, proximity of patterns to formal themes, and the relative audibility of patterns based on textures, harmonies, dynamics, doubling, register, timbre, and other musical parameters.

Lacking this kind of analysis, output from Sorcerer may be interpreted in a variety of ways. On one extreme, users may completely disregard the potential allusions in the output, considering them to be unverified and irrelevant to the understanding of the creative process. While extreme, such a view may be consistent with the principle that only those patterns that most audiences can hear should truly be considered allusions. On the other extreme, all of the potential allusions the program discovers may be considered valid since the pattern relationships do exist and, to a sensitive listener, could, once revealed by analysis, be heard. It would certainly seem important for theorists and musicologists to inform and educate performers and audiences of as many interpretations as possible of the music they perform and hear. On balance, of course, most users of a program such as Sorcerer will accept or reject output based on a combination of intuitive and musical logic.

Regardless of which of the above views is taken, the question of composer intent cannot be ignored. As mentioned previously, the choice and positioning of allusions and how they integrate into host works can often help analysts determine whether or not composers intended them. Techniques of variation used may also assist users in discovering intent, since the number and types of variations used can either verify camouflaged allusions or reveal artifacts of larger, more original musical ideas. Assertions about intention are often polemic, however, since even the music's composer may not be consciously aware of or acknowledge (refer to figure 5.4 and related discussion) the allusions present.

Interestingly, if the intention of analysis is only to *confirm* what listeners already hear, then Sorcerer may have limited value. On the other hand, if the intention of analysis is to *inform* listeners of what they *can* or *should* hear, then Sorcerer has significant potential. In this light, analysis of allusions can significantly impact many aspects of the musical experience. For example, analysis and recognition of allusions should be very useful for interpreting and performing music. Awareness of allusions may indicate to performers what to emphasize in melodic lines and what performance practice might be appropriate. Knowledge of the origins of allusions can educate listeners on how to better understand music, allowing them to link their current experience with experiences they've previously had with the referenced music. A knowledge of allusions should also provide hints to theorists as to what type of analysis might be most appropriate for revealing more about a work's inner depths.

A good example of how the interpretation of a specific allusion can deepen our understanding of creativity, analysis, performance, and the listening experience would be the use of the so-called Dresden cadence (also known as the Dresden Amen). Figure 5.28 shows three examples of this cadence, so known for its use during religious services in Dresden churches and cathedrals during the eighteenth and nineteenth centuries. In each of these examples, the Dresden cadence appears separated in terms of texture, dynamics, and orchestration from its musical surroundings, literally insisting on recognition. This semi-isolation from the preceding and following music, the suddenly soft dynamics, the important subdominant harmony, and the scalewise motion up a fifth in the upper voice all help identify this cadence when heard. The different keys, repeated notes, and textures provide the distinctive varia-

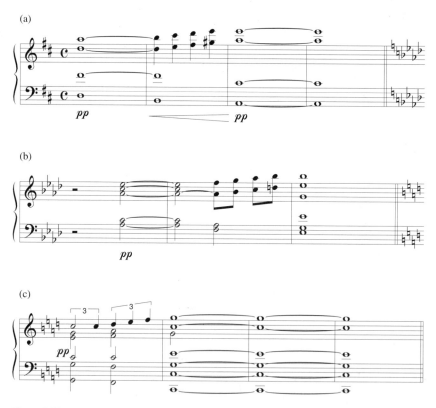

Figure 5.28
Three examples of the Dresden cadence, thus known for its use in Dresden during the eighteenth and nineteenth centuries: (a) Mendelssohn, Reformation Symphony; (b) Wagner, *Parsifal*; and (c) Mahler, Symphony no. 1.

tions here. Knowledge of the relationships between Mendelssohn, Wagner, and Mahler (the Jewish/Protestant Mendelssohn, the well-documented anti-Semitic Wagner, and the Jewish Mahler, who, interestingly, loved the music of Wagner) provide an extraordinary backdrop for these measures, without which the understanding of this music would be significantly diminished. To perform or listen to these works without awareness of the Dresden allusion and its context seems contrary to what most musicians would classify as musical intelligence. Certainly the meanings of such allusions can be difficult to decipher, and harder yet to put into words. However, if words could convey their meanings, we might not require the music.

Allusions such as this Dresden cadence example belong to an allusional "tradition." One of the more famous examples of such a tradition occurs in the music of Haydn, Beethoven, and, again, Mahler. Figure 5.29a shows a solo trumpet passage from the third movement of Haydn's Military Symphony (no. 100, composed in 1794), well known to both Beethoven and Mahler. This passage represents one possible origin of the now famous opening of Beethoven's Fifth Symphony (1808; shown in figure 5.29b). Mahler, then, paraphrases Beethoven at the beginning of his own Fifth Symphony (1902; see figure 5.29c), and in so doing references the music of both Haydn and Beethoven shown here, as well as many other works (e.g., the beginning of the Wedding March from Mendelssohn's *A Midsummer Night's Dream*, opus 61, no. 9; 1842). In figure 5.29, we therefore see and hear allusions evolving over time, increasing the breadth of our interpretations with each new appearance.

Figure 5.29
Related melodic fragments by (a) Haydn, in his Military Symphony, movement 2, measures 153–156; (b) Beethoven, Symphony no. 5, beginning; and (c) Mahler, Symphony no. 5, beginning.

Figure 5.30
The first few measures of Mahler's "Nun seh' ich wohl, warum so dunkle Flammen," from his *Kinderto-tenlieder* (Songs on the Deaths of Children), as allusion to Wagner's *Tristan und Isolde* (see figure 5.6(e)).

Programs like Sorcerer may thus be useful in tracing a particular allusion back through its web of uses over decades and even centuries to follow how creative processes develop over time, how "cultural creativity" shared among many composers evolves, and how widely a particular *allusional language* has spread.

Another particularly notable Mahler allusion occurs at the outset of the second song ("Nun seh' ich wohl, warum so dunkle Flammen"—now indeed I see why you shower such dark flames) from his *Kindertotenlieder* (Songs on the Deaths of Children; 1904)—shown in part in figure 5.30. This extraordinary music alludes to the prelude to Wagner's *Tristan und Isolde* (1859; see figure 5.6e) in wonderfully distorted ways, both harmonically and melodically. When Mahler returns to the Tristan motive later in his song, the text "you wanted to tell me with your radiance: we would like to stay near you, but it is denied us by fate" seems to have many meanings, not the least of which was Mahler's profound sadness at the news of Wagner's death. Certainly Mahler was a great lover of Wagner's music, as testified to in his letters, but the disfiguration of the allusion here is provocative. The lyrics in this work relate to dead loved ones, and to Mahler's own daughter Maria, whose untimely death as a child haunted him until his own death.

Mahler's allusions described here, and the many other allusions that occur in Mahler's works, provide clues for the educated listener to better understand his music. With just a few notes, Mahler can direct our ears toward the classical Viennese school of composition, the styles of many composers previous to his lifetime, and the contexts of the individual works to which he alludes. Making these connections enhances—at the least—*my* appreciation for, and understanding of, Mahler's creative processes. Hearing the opening of Mahler's Symphony no. 5 or the opening of the second song of his *Kindertotenlieder*, which might seem routine to uninitiated and inexperienced listeners, can instead uncover profound revelations about Mahler's musical world. Christopher Reynolds notes that we

Figure 5.31
Themes from (a) Beethoven's Ninth Symphony and (b) Bach's "Jesu, Joy of Man's Desiring" (Cantata no. 147).

... can begin with the uncontroversial assertion that nineteenth-century composers could create a level of veiled meaning in their music by quoting from art songs, folksongs, arias, and chant. A musical theme in a symphony could allude both to an earlier musical context and to an antecedent poetic text that was omitted from the symphony, a kind of musical-poetic interaction that is very clear when a chorale tune or a lieder motive is quoted exactly. (Reynolds 2003, p. 2)

Allusions may also indicate a composer's desire to link emotively with an individual theme or with a class of themes. For example, the well-known "Ode to Joy" of Beethoven's Ninth Symphony (1824), a theme he worried over in his sketches while creating this work, and the second theme of the first movement of Bach's "Jesu, Joy of Man's Desiring" (Cantata no. 147; 1723) relate as shown in figure 5.31, as discovered by the Sorcerer program. While the meter and rhythm of these two themes differ, the interval similarities make this, for me at least, an unmistakable allusion. Interestingly, both theme subtitles contain the word "joy" (*Freude* in German), implying emotional connections that only a knowledge of the allusion and its source can provide to listeners. Again, Reynolds notes that

... Schumann's C-Major Fantasie, another anniversary work, is also generally understood to have two levels of meaning, public and private, as Schumann himself revealed. Publicly, it honored Beethoven on the tenth anniversary of his death. Schumann referred to it as his "Sonata für Beethoven," appropriately since it included a motive from Beethoven's *An die ferne Geliebte* and an allusion to the slow movement of the Seventh Symphony; privately, Schumann also confessed to Clara that he had written the work as "a deep lament" for her at a time when he feared losing her. Thus the allusion to Beethoven's song cycle about separated lovers.... (Reynolds 2003, p. 126)

Another good example of this kind of potential meaning in allusions can be found in the popularly quoted "Marche funèbre" from Chopin's Piano Sonata no. 2, op. 35

Figure 5.32
(a) "Marche Funèbre" from Chopin's Piano Sonata no. 2, op. 35; and (b) the "Marcia funebre" from Beethoven's Piano Sonata op. 26.

(1839). This music begins in much the same way as Beethoven begins his own "Marcia funebre" in his Piano Sonata, op. 26 (1801) (Petty 1999, p. 281). Figures 5.32a and 5.32b show the beginnings of these passages. The resemblance of these two excerpts is much more disguised than in many of the examples thus far described in this chapter. The potential for discernible meaning, however, is worth the attempt to unveil the disguise. Chopin, it would seem, has mimicked the rhythm and melody (see internal voice in figure 5.32a, right hand) of Beethoven's funeral march, providing a distant echo of his burial drumbeats. Such hidden gems, too often considered indications of the *derivative* in music, often provide listeners with tools for interpreting and appreciating this repertoire.

There are, of course, many other ways in which allusions can be interpreted. This diversity of interpretation provides a rich fabric of possibilities for understanding the creative processes in music. Rather than confusing listeners, such diversity offers an incentive to listen and relisten to the same works with different ears and minds. Often, music that might otherwise stagnate on repeated hearings remains fresh and alive. Appreciation of music, like that of all forms of art, only deepens with this kind of knowledge.

In general, using Sorcerer has led me to believe the following:

a. All music consists, at least in part, of allusions to other music, providing listeners with a sense of familiarity beyond that of style recognition

b. Understanding the locations and origins of allusions enhances the comprehension of a work's context and gives a greater appreciation of the creative processes used to produce it

c. Awareness of certain allusions can provide interesting insights into a target work in terms of what its composer found important in music and, to some degree, how that composer listened to and perceived music

d. Tracing lineages of allusions can help define the genealogy of musical styles and influences.

Figure 5.33 provides a good example of these principles: an allusion found in computer-generated music. The music here—a fugue from *The Well-Programmed Clavier* (forty-eight preludes and forty-eight fugues in the style of J. S. Bach; 2002)—was created by Experiments in Musical Intelligence and follows the basic key format of Bach's extraordinary masterwork, *The Well-Tempered Clavier*. The version of Experiments in Musical Intelligence used to create The Well-Programmed Clavier included a version of Sorcerer in its algorithm, enabling the program to discover allusions in the music it analyzes and to replicate the numbers of these allusions, if not their precise content, in the music it creates. An allusion occurs in figure 5.33 in measures 20–25 and then repeats with variations in measures 49–54. This allusion actually consists of two measures sequenced twice. However, as can be seen in figure 5.34, Bach's original also sequences, though his music requires half as many measures, since he uses sixteenth notes instead of the eighth notes that the computer-generated version uses.

I have included Bach's preceding and following music (measures 1 and 5 in figure 5.34) for comparison with the computer-generated version. In both cases the entering and exiting voice motions are seamless. The music flows so smoothly into and out of the allusion in figure 5.33 that very few listeners have actually recognized its presence. Bach also repeats his sequencing passage (measures 7–10 varied in measures 31–33 in Fugue no. 7). However, Bach's repetitions vary significantly, with the first occurrence beginning on beat 3, rather than beat 1, of its initial measure. It is clear, therefore, that Experiments in Musical Intelligence alludes to Bach's variation rather than to his original.

Note that creating fugues and other types of musical formalisms—inventions, canons, and so on—with Experiments in Musical Intelligence can cause problems. By itself, the program cannot *answer* a fugue's subject at the interval of a fifth, no

Figure 5.33
A fugue from *The Well-Programmed Clavier* (2002) in the style of J. S. Bach created by Experiments in Musical Intelligence with a version of Sorcerer in its algorithm.

Figure 5.33
(continued)

Figure 5.33
(continued)

Figure 5.34
From Fugue no. 7 of the first book of *The Well-Tempered Clavier* (1726) by J. S. Bach (measures 30–34).

less respond with tonal rather than real answers when the form demands it. Most of my programs, therefore, include small interconnected algorithms for creating fugue expositions that then deliver their protected-from-recombinance output as if it were a first grouping of a composition. (I discuss such formalisms further in chapter 6.) The middle entries of fugues—the returning theme in counterpoint—and episodes (developments) then result from recombination of these fugal expositions. While separate processing such as this may seem foreign to recombinance, fugues, canons, and so on have such strict constraints that human composers create them, I believe, using somewhat separate algorithmic processes (see also Cope 1996, pp. 213–214, for discussion of automatic fugue composition).

Interestingly, Bach used explicit algorithms for some of the preludes in his *Well-Tempered Clavier*, as attested to by the autograph score of an early version of its first prelude (C-major), as shown in figure 5.35a. What are chords here appear as repeated groups of arpeggiated sixteenth notes in the final version, as shown in figure 5.35b. Clearly Bach intended the example chords to act as a kind of shorthand for the eventual lutelike strumming that emerges in the final version. This process qualifies as a "paper" algorithm—a written-out recipe or set of instructions for completing a composition.

The forty-eight preludes and forty-eight fugues of *The Well-Programmed Clavier* (Cope 2002) generally follow the style of Bach. Each of the ninety-six individual

(a)

(b)

works required a separate database to ensure both compositional and stylistic integrity. However, not wishing to imitate the forms and style of the music in the *Well-Tempered Clavier* too closely, I opted to occasionally include music by other composers in certain preludes and fugues, which gives the music occasional surprising stylistic twists. I encourage readers to study the computer-created fugue here for such allusions or to use Sorcerer to reveal them. Of course, choosing the works to serve as source music for Sorcerer will present a challenge.

One might imagine that using recombination when composing would itself produce an endless stream of self-allusionary music. After all, the recombination process already quotes and paraphrases the music in its database. However, recombination typically uses very small groupings of music and produces quite sophisticated variations of borrowed material (notably transformational composition, discussed in chapters 4, 10, and 11), making the music often unrecognizable, even to the composer of the music in the database (see particularly Cope 2000 for examples of this). Therefore, longer allusions require protection from such variation during composition (as do signatures), so that they retain their recognizability in newly composed music.

In 1999 I used Experiments in Musical Intelligence to compose a concerto in the style of Bach's six Brandenburg concertos (others have called it Brandenburg Concerto no. 7, but I have not). I used a database consisting of movements of Bach's Brandenburg concertos, as well as selected movements of his orchestral suites, and one or two movements of his keyboard concertos. The resulting work was premiered in 2000, and is now recorded (see Cope 2003d).

Having listened to the MIDI version of this Bach-style concerto, heard the many rehearsals before the performance, and now reviewed the recording many times, I am very familiar with this work. While this statement may seem obvious, I mention it to provide context to the following experience. Early in 2004, while listening to a CD of Vivaldi's music, I recognized a passage from the Experiments in Musical Intelligence Brandenburg concerto and wondered how this could be. After several relistenings, I compared the Vivaldi I had heard with the computer-composed work and found the related passage. The resemblance was unmistakable—the two passages had their differences, but the similarities were striking. While I was sure I had not included any of Bach's transcriptions of Vivaldi's music—of which there are many—in the database during composition of the Experiments in Musical Intelligence Brandenburg

Figure 5.35
(a) A J. S. Bach algorithm from *The Clavier-Büchlein vor Wilhelm Friedemann Bach* (Kirkpatrick 1979, pp. 29–30); (b) realization of figure 5.22a.

concerto, I nonetheless revisited the entirety of the database to be sure. While Bach did make a transcription of Vivaldi's opus 3, no. 3, in his BWV 978 (1713), this latter work is for solo keyboard, and not only was not in the database for the Experiments in Musical Intelligence Bach composition, but could not have been in the database, since it would not have produced music for orchestra (the program produces orchestra music by having orchestral music in its database).

I then discovered what seems to be a curious resemblance between this same Experiments in Musical Intelligence concerto and a passage in the last movement of Bach's Brandenburg Concerto no. 3 (1713). Figures 5.36a–5.36c show the relevant passages in Vivaldi, Bach, and Experiments in Musical Intelligence. Bach's passage in figure 5.36b may initially seem quite distant from the Experiments in Musical Intelligence and Vivaldi examples in figures 5.36a and 5.36c, except for its bass line skeleton of pitches: A, B-natural, C-sharp, and D in the basso continuo (e.g., compare the intervals in the bass voices of figure 5.36a, measure 1; figure 5.36b, measures 2–4; and figure 5.36c, measure 1). I might have missed this passage were it not for this outline in the bass. In figure 5.36a, Vivaldi's original melody begins on F-sharp and ends on high D (the onbeat notes of the upper sixteenth notes).

I have included an extra measure before the actual passage in question in the Bach example (figure 5.36b), which shows a C-sharp–D–E–F-sharp highest-note line (the last note here in the violin) in the viola part, since this measure contains the down–down–up sixteenth-note motive so clearly. The bass-line resemblance of the Bach to the Experiments in Musical Intelligence Bach (shown in figure 5.36c) on strong beats in the bass should be clear. The upper voice in the Bach, however, seems a distant cousin to both the Vivaldi and Experiments in Musical Intelligence examples here. However, after having pattern matched this and other works in Bach's Brandenburg concertos and finding nothing as close as this, I must assume that Bach is the source for my program's variation. Figure 5.36d shows the same two measures of Vivaldi's op. 3, no. 3, as it appears in figure 5.36a, but this time the result of Bach's arrangement of the work in a different key (F-major), and in keyboard reduction.

The obvious conclusion to all of this—that Bach, who transcribed a great deal of Vivaldi's music during his lifetime, has transformed Vivaldi's passage into his own music, and that Experiments in Musical Intelligence has somehow transformed this same passage back to the form of Vivaldi's original—seems implausible and yet inescapable. Is it possible that Bach used the same general processes of transformational composition (see discussion in chapter 4) that Experiments in Musical Intelligence uses to disguise its sources? Interestingly, the opening of the Experiments in Musical Intelligence's Bach Brandenburg Concerto also resembles Vivaldi's op. 3, no. 3, at

Figure 5.36
(a) Measures 5–6 from Vivaldi's Concerto in Sol maggiore per Violino, Archi e Cembalo, op. 3, no. 3, movement 1; (b) measures 86–89 from J. S. Bach's Brandenburg Concerto no. 2 in F-Major, movement 3; (c) measures 134–135 from an Experiments in Musical Intelligence Brandenburg Concerto in the style of Bach; (d) J. S. Bach's transcription of Vivaldi's Concerto in Sol ..., op. 3, no. 3, movement 1, in his Concerto F-Dur, BWV 978.

Figure 5.36
(continued)

least in rhythm and downward scale, but all other comparisons between the two works fail to produce any significant similarities.

Figure 5.37 shows the beginning of an Experiments in Musical Intelligence's piano concerto in the style of Rachmaninoff that demonstrates another interesting type of allusion. In this instance, the program has paraphrased Dies Irae, a medieval Gregorian requiem chant that Rachmaninoff often used in his music. While most Experiments in Musical Intelligence allusions imitate the number, but not the exact material, of the music in its database, the program can also allude to the actual allusions that the originals do. This process involves including the same alluded-to music in the database, and having the program verify this music as a signature that it then transformationally varies. Here, the allusion—a paraphrase—occurs in the double octaves piano part, played against the short pizzicati strings.

Many composers have written about their use of allusions. George Rochberg speaks of a particularly extensive reference used as the centerpiece for his *Music of*

(c)

(d)

Figure 5.36
(continued)

III.

Figure 5.37
The beginning of the Experiments in Musical Intelligence's piano concerto in the style of Rachmaninoff.

Figure 5.38
From the final measures of Arena for Cello and Tape (1974), showing a quote from a Navajo song from
the Enemy Way ceremony.

the Magic Theater (1965), which "is a transcription, that is, a completely new version, of a Mozart Adagio. I decided to repeat it in my own way because I loved it. People who understand, love it because they know it began with Mozart and ended with me. People who don't understand think it's by Mozart" (Rochberg 1969, p. 89). George Crumb describes his borrowings thus: "and of course I borrow liberally from other composers—or perhaps I should hopefully say 'steal,' since Stravinsky said something to the effect that good composers steal rather than borrow" (Crumb 1986, p. 37). Other contemporary composers, such as Peter Maxwell Davies (especially in his *Eight Songs for a Mad King* [1969] quoting of Handel), Michael Colgrass in his *As Quiet as* (1966), Mauricio Kagel in his *Ludwig Van* (1970), Lukas Foss in his *Baroque Variations* (1967), and Karlheinz Stockhausen in his *Opus 1970*, use allusions freely and explicitly in their music.

Rather than continuing to hypothesize about the interpretations of how other composers use allusions in their music, I here provide the incentives and possible interpretations of my own such uses. I conclude my Arena (Cope 1974), for Cello and Electronic Tape (see figure 5.38), with an allusion to a Navajo theme. I mention this particular allusion for a number of reasons. First, using this melody at this point in this music provides the finality necessary to conclude the work, at least in my mind. The D-centered modal fragment provides a simple home base for the otherwise freely serial material that precedes it. Second, the stylistic contrast this music creates, changes listeners' perception of the material that to this point in the work has been highly contrapuntal, chromatic, and timbrally diverse. Third, the introduction of stylistically contrasting material with cultural contexts quite different from Western traditions produces a compelling link to another musical universe. Finally, this Navajo theme provokes a contextual juxtaposition that raises questions rather than providing answers, a process that I personally appreciate. While these comments do not adequately describe what for me produces an emotional and spiritual response, they nonetheless indicate the kinds of goals to which at least one composer aspires when he consciously incorporates allusions in his music.

There are, of course, many questions about allusions that remain unanswered, and for which Sorcerer offers little help. For example:

How do allusions in a given work relate to one another?

What light do allusions shed on the work from which the allusions derive?

Can allusions transform their new environs, and if so, how?

Do allusions serve particular (e.g., cadential) functions in their new contexts?

What about allusions to compositional techniques, style, and other more abstract qualities of music?

Are allusions messages with specific intent, and if so, what do these messages mean?

Unfortunately, it is doubtful that any computer software can or will adequately answer these and the many other important questions that arise from the discovery of allusions in music. However, this does not mean that these questions cannot be answered.

Stylistic allusions—briefly imitating the style but not the content of the music of another composer—are much more difficult to discover computationally than specific pattern allusions. The only method that seems effective in revealing such allusions involves extracting signatures from both target and source music independently, and then comparing the results. Sorcerer can be used in this way most effectively by setting the maximum length controller to a very low number (five or six intervals) and then selecting only the lower-numbered returning patterns, particularly those not identified as scales or triad outlines (e.g., commonalities).

Allusions to musical forms (dances, marches, hymns) as well as imitations of heartbeats, breathing, running, and so on, are not easily revealed by pattern-matching processes such as those used by Sorcerer. However, comparing the rhythmic patterns of target and source music produces relatively effective results. Source

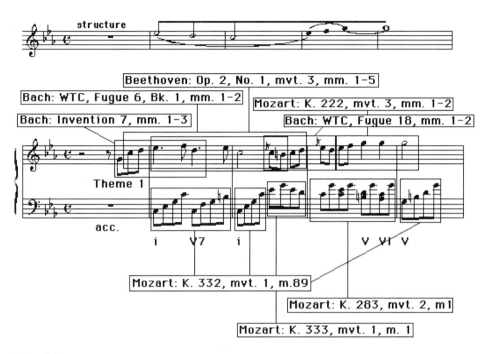

Figure 5.39
The way Sorcerer might add context to more standard analytical approaches.

music in this case involves dances, marches, hymns, and representations of natural
phenomena suspected of being present in the target music.

I remind readers that Sorcerer should be used in combination with more traditional forms of analysis in order to contextualize discovered allusions. Figure 5.39
shows how Sorcerer might add important perspective to a more standard analysis.
The music shown here—the opening phrase of Beethoven's Sonata no. 8, op. 13, discussed in relation to figures 5.21–5.23—has been analyzed according to traditional
harmony (Roman numerals), form (identification of theme and accompaniment),
and structure (the melodic reduction above the music), as well as for allusions. Connecting these and other analytical approaches would seem the only logical way to
grapple effectively with the complexities music offers its listeners.

Every work of music, unless it has been composed entirely by a formalism (and
possibly even then), contains within it many pointers to the musical culture that
helped to create it. These pointers, whether they be quotations, paraphrases, likenesses, frameworks, or commonalities, help us to relate to that work, even if we are
hearing it for the first time. These pointers also point to other musical styles and

works that themselves have pointers, providing us with a rich history of the cultural evolution of the work being heard. The music produced by Experiments in Musical Intelligence, because of the manner in which it composes, also contains these kinds of pointers and belongs to the same culture and traditions as the music in its database. This helps to explain, I believe, why the music of my programs evokes an almost immediate sense of familiarity in those aware of the inherited musical culture, even in those who steadfastly resist feeling such intimacy.

I have placed a source code version of the Sorcerer program on my Web site for download by anyone interested in using the program for their own research. I have included sample target and source music in proper format as examples, so that users can observe how the program matches patterns and reveals its findings. The platform-dependent version of Sorcerer also converts standard MIDI files downloadable from many Internet sources. Thus, users can easily collect their own target and source music, though all results of such searches and downloads should be carefully edited for potential errors. Choosing the proper tempo, key, instrumental timbre, and so on during playback helps users identify true allusions from the many patterns returned by the program.

Users of Sorcerer may adjust controllers (largest pattern size, number of intervening notes, and so on). However, the default controller settings for Sorcerer work well for most allusion searches. When left to its default settings, the program self-adjusts its controllers based on a simple algorithm that attempts to meet the statistical average of matches found in previous successful sessions with the program. Manually resetting the controller levels in the Controller Window automatically overrides these self-adjusting processes.

Sorcerer serves as a useful tool for discovering the possible origins of patterns in a given work. The program provides information about the number, positioning, and character of the potential allusions it finds. As mentioned previously, my algorithmic composing programs can then use this information as a model for their own inclusion of allusions during composition, attempting to mimic the number, placement, and nature of allusions from its databases, without necessarily using the actual allusions that Sorcerer locates in its searches. Allusions then occur in program output in direct proportion to how often they appear—as a result of Sorcerer analysis—in the input.

6 Learning, Inference, and Analogy

Principle: Creativity requires learning and knowledge in order to produce useful rather than arbitrary results.

Machine Learning

I created the Game of Ark in order to learn about creativity in the context of rules, inference, and analogy. I explain Ark in some detail here, because these concepts are much easier to describe in terms of games than they are in terms of music.

The Game of Ark consists of a 10×10 matrix of white squares on a flat playing surface (board). Players select opposite sides. The rows that align parallel to an imaginary line drawn from player to player are called columns, and are numbered 1 through 10 from left to right, from the black side's perspective. The rows that align perpendicular to an imaginary line drawn between players are called ranks, and are numbered 1 through 10 as their distance increases from Black's side of the board.

Players begin by agreeing on the configuration of one to eight filled squares in ranks five and six of the board. Each player then sets up ten pieces in any order on the first rank of his or her side of the board. The first move is determined by courtesy or random selection. Players then take turns as with any other board game, with the winner being the first player to align all of his or her pieces in the last rank opposite the starting position.

There are five types of pieces, of which each player has two. The pieces, their respective names, and their possible motions are shown in figure 6.1. All of the pieces have the names of animals—this is the Ark, after all—with each type of animal paired with the pieces whose motions most resemble that animal's movements in real life. The frog and kangaroo, for example, leap, while snail and tortoise move small distances at a time.

Whenever three to four pieces of any color are aligned straight in any direction, either of the end pieces may be used to move all of the pieces in the group, as long as this moving end piece is at or beyond the fourth rank away from the moving player's starting position. Rules pertaining to this end piece must be followed, but otherwise the group of associated pieces follows the lead piece anywhere on the board without following the rules. Each linked piece must align contiguously in the same direction at the conclusion of a move as it did at the beginning of the move, and not land on top of another piece, on a black center square, or off the board.

Ark is a recombinant game. For example, some of the pieces move similarly to chess. The crab and shark, coyote and spider, panther and eagle, frog and roo, and snail and tortoise resemble—in turn—the rook, bishop, queen, knight, and pawn of chess, although the limitations of distance (three in the case of the crab, coyote, and

(W) Eagle, (B) Panther: The eagle/panther moves straight in any direction by 1 to 3 squares.

(W) Crab, (B) Shark: The crab/shark moves forward, backward, or to either side perpendicularly by 1 to 3 squares.

(W) Coyote, (B) Spider: The coyote/spider moves at angles by 1 to 3 squares.

(W) Frog, (B) Kangaroo("roo"): The frog/roo can only move if neighbored by another piece. The frog may jump as many contiguous pieces as exist and may continue to jump in like fashion until no further jumps are possible. The frog may also jump black squares in the center of the board which are treated exactly like other pieces.

(W) Snail, (B) Tortoise: The snail/tortoise moves forward or to the left or right, one square at a time.

Figure 6.1
The various pieces of the Game of Ark©.

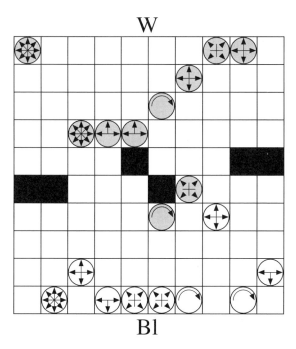

Figure 6.2
An example of Black's panther ready to team with two of Black's tortoises to move all of them three spaces forward toward the top.

eagle), along with the extended moves of the frog (resembling more the pieces in a game of checkers than chess), and the left/right motions of the snail differ from their chess counterparts. The fact that no pieces are actually taken in Ark suggests Chinese checkers or Go more than chess. Interestingly, the number of different games of Ark, derived from the number and placement of black squares and the various alignments of each player's initial rank at the onset, contributes to the game's clear uniqueness.

The Game of Ark is interesting to play—in ways, interestingly, that I did not begin to imagine when I invented the game. The creativity that Ark requires surfaced during the first game played. Frogs and roos, which were initially left behind, required retreating pieces to allow these "leaping" pieces to move across the board. Filled-in center squares, once thought of as obstacles, soon advantaged the frogs and roos. As the number of played games increased, snails and tortoises, apparent liabilities because of their single-square move capabilities, were teamed with frogs, roos, panthers, and eagles, and moved large distances across the board. Figure 6.2 gives an example of this, with Black's panther teaming with two of black's tortoises to

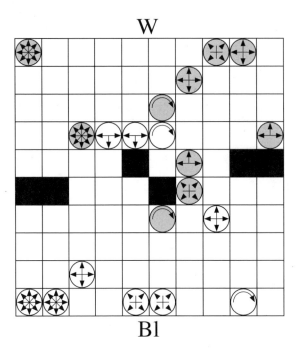

Figure 6.3
Black's panther set to team with two of White's snails and a White frog to move all of them three steps
toward White's end of the board.

move them all three spaces forward—one move equivalent to seven individual
moves: three moves for each of the two single-space pieces, and one move for the
panther. Dragging an opponent's piece backward in a team as one proceeds forward
also proves productive (at least for the player moving the pieces), as shown in figure
6.3, where black's panther is set to team with two of White's snails and a White frog
to move all of them three steps toward the top of this diagram—one move equivalent
to a negative seven retreating moves for the opponent's pieces. Figure 6.4 shows an
even more impressive team move with Black's roo prepared to team with both of
Black's tortoises and a Black panther to move them all to White's end of the
board—one move equivalent to eleven individual moves.

To give readers a clearer sense of the Game of Ark, I have included a series of
endgames in appendix C as examples of the diversity of different strategies possible.
As this sampling will indicate, Ark is not as simplistic as it may first appear—there
are an incredible number of ways in which players can proceed, with each move initiating new strategies from both players. The Game of Ark requires the learning of

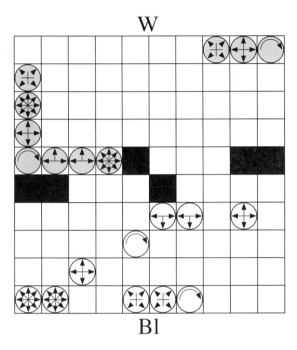

Figure 6.4
Black's roo prepared to team with both of Black's tortoises and a Black panther to move them all to White's end of the board.

its rules, the inference of how these rules will play out, and the analogies of how certain situations in past games relate to similar, but different, situations in a current game. Each of these three processes—learning, inference, and analogy—lays the foundations for effectively playing Ark and, as we shall soon see, for understanding and modeling musical creativity.

Webster's Collegiate Dictionary (1991, p. 772) defines "learning" as the ability "... to acquire knowledge of or skill in by study, instruction, or experience." While significant research in machine learning has taken place in the artificial intelligence community (see, for example, Baldi 2001; Cesa-Bianchi, Numao, and Reischuk 2002; Cherkassky and Mulier 1998; Hinton and Sejnowski 1999; Mackintosh 1983; Michalski 1986; Mitchell 1997), very little similar research has taken place in the field of music. Gerhard Widmer's work (1992, 1993) stands out among the few published examples of computational learning in music. In his 1992 article, Widmer argues the need for true learning programs in music and that music requires domain specificity. The program that Widmer describes—but does not include with his article—adjusts itself in order to reduce backtracking and achieve its goals. In contrast, William Schottstaedt's counterpoint program (1989) creates effective results, but without any learning involved. The work of Enrique Vidal-Ruiz and Pedro Cruz-Alcázar with grammatical inference (GI) algorithms (1997) has potential, but applies only to single-line (monophonic) music.

David Evan Jones's CPA program (2000) provides an effective contrapuntal toolbox for composers, but centers almost entirely on atonal music. Dominik Hörnel and Wolfram Menzel (1998) use feedforward neural networks in their work, with learning accomplished through self-adjustment of nodal weights. However, learning with neural networks often requires extensive training and elaborate complementary programming (see Miranda 2001, pp. 99–118).

David Lewin's goal-oriented approach to species counterpoint (1983) clearly enhances one's ability to compose simple counterpoint. However, his work provides shortcuts that attempt to avoid the dead ends that rules cause, rather than incorporating true learning processes. There are many such shortcuts to creating counterpoint. For example, in my book *Experiments in Musical Intelligence* (Cope 1996, p. 213), I describe an approach to creating algorithmic fugues that involves "subtractive counterpoint," a technique that voids much of the need to backtrack. Again, however, such shortcuts do little to achieve learning, and hence I do not discuss them in detail here. Other important work in the area of musical learning has been accomplished, but the paucity of relevant research remains clear.

In order to better follow how machine learning can help us understand the ways in which humans learn musically, I now describe a computer program called Gradus (after Fux's *Gradus ad Parnassum*, 1725) that learns to compose first-species counterpoint. This program actually changes its behavior by modifying its approaches to solving certain musical problems, becoming faster and more accurate over time.

Species counterpoint (Fux 1725) poses particular composing problems that have challenged students for centuries. A single fixed line (called the cantus firmus) combines with a variable number of simultaneously sounding new lines that must adhere to a strict set of musical goals. Often, new lines lead to dead ends for which no correct choice is possible. Beginning students frequently restart (backtrack) after failing, only to find themselves in the same or similar predicaments. Many months of practice are typically required for even highly intelligent students to become facile at creating these new lines without backtracking. Although other kinds of music (such as canons, fugues, serialism, and so on) can cause similar conflicts, and thus serve as interesting problems for computer programs to solve, I have chosen a rather straightforward type of species counterpoint known as two-voice, one-against-one, first-species counterpoint for the purposes of demonstrating computer learning techniques in music. This is the type of counterpoint with which students usually begin and for which, I feel, the rules are most programmable.

Gradus uses six goal categories. Although these do not conform exactly to those of Fux, and even omit certain details that many counterpoint instructors find important (climax, mode adherence, cadence, and so on) or further limit Fux's constraints (as in leaps of thirds only), most of Fux's general rules appear here in one form or another.

1. Simultaneously sounding notes must be consonant, forming thirds, fifths, sixths, octaves, and so on, below the cantus firmus.

2. Voice motion must be stepwise (i.e., no repeated notes), with occasional leaps of thirds always followed by stepwise contrary motion.

3. No simultaneous leaps in both voices are allowed.

4. Parallel fifths and octaves must be avoided.

5. Hidden fifths and octaves must be avoided.

6. No more than two continuous same-direction motions are allowed.

The more models available to Gradus, the more accurately the program sets its goals. Therefore, I have chosen fifty two-part, one-against-one correct counterpoints to serve as models for Gradus to analyze. Each of these counterpoints incorporates the above-stated goals. Figure 6.5 shows several of the fifty models from which the program—in its default state—sets its goals. In essence, Gradus assumes that all of the vertical intervals, parallel motions, skip numbers, and so on, found in the models are allowable, and places the vertical intervals, parallel motions, skip numbers, and so on it does *not* find—presumed to be illegal—in appropriate variables to serve as program goals to avoid. If the number of models used for goal analysis changes between runs of Gradus, the program reanalyzes these models for further composition. As can be seen, the goals in Gradus are generally prohibitory rather than exemplary, informing the program of what *not* to do rather than what *to* do—a more standard approach to programming.

Figures 6.6a–6.6f give musical examples for each of the six goals listed above, as exemplified in the fifty models provided with the Gradus program. These goals help the two voices to remain in consonant relationship and to retain their relative independence—important features of both sixteenth-century (vocal) and eighteenth-century (instrumental) contrapuntal composition.

The Gradus program requires a seed note to begin its composition of a new accompanying line to a given cantus firmus. This provided seed note acts as an origin for selecting a first note. Since composing a first note from this seed note follows the previously presented goals, seed notes generate four possibilities using stepwise

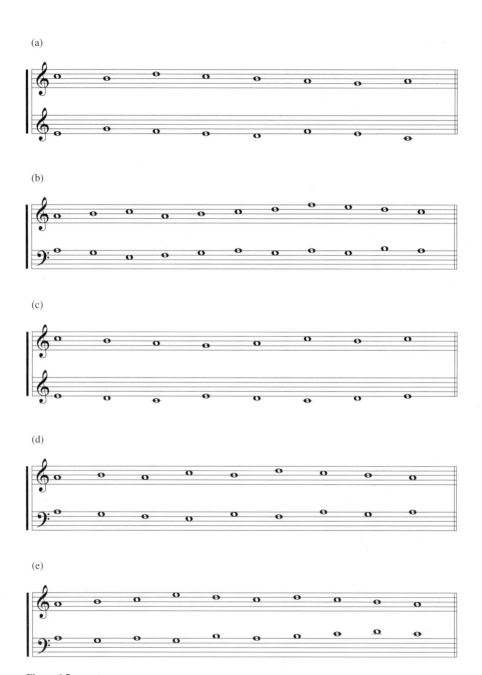

Figure 6.5
Five of the fifty models upon which the Gradus program bases its analysis of goals for creating good counterpoint.

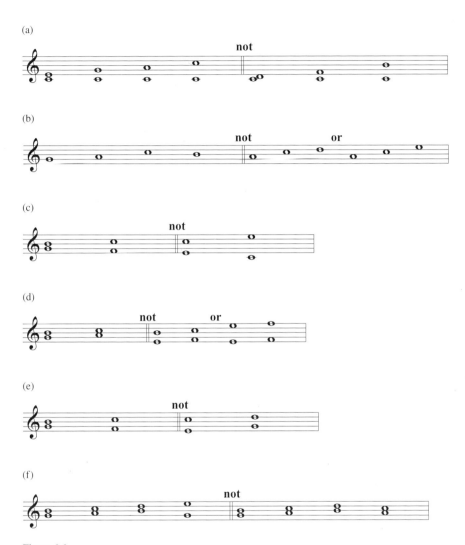

Figure 6.6
The program goals in musical notation where a–f relate to goals 1–6 (respectively) in the text.

motions and interval-of-a-third leaps only. Some seed notes will project several likely correct candidate first notes, while others will project only one possible logical choice, a choice that occasionally may later prove incapable of creating a completed counterpoint. Therefore, selecting a good seed note is important for the composing process.

To make the best possible seed-note choice, Gradus saves its successful outputs with their generating seed notes, and uses the seed notes of these successful lines to create new accompanying lines. In order to provide as logical a selection as possible, Gradus also saves cantus firmus templates. Templates (like rules discussed later) are measured in terms of diatonic steps rather than by exact intervals; in other words, the upward interval of a second—major *or* minor—equates to the number 1, the upward interval of a third—major *or* minor—to the number 2, and so on, with negative numbers referring to downward motion. A template takes the form of the number of vertical diatonic steps between the seed note and the beginning pitch of the cantus firmus, followed by a reduced, diatonic step map of the cantus firmus, as in the following:

(−4 (5 0)).

The first number here (−4) represents the number of diatonic steps between the seed note (*not* the first note of the successful accompanying line) and the first note of the cantus firmus. The first number in the list that follows this first number indicates the number of diatonic steps between the note most removed (high or low) in the cantus firmus and the beginning note of the cantus firmus. The second number in this list represents the number of diatonic steps between the last note of the cantus firmus and the first note of the cantus firmus. In the diatonic step map given above, the cantus firmus rises to a maximum of five diatonic steps above the first note and ends with the same note as it began. With several of these successful cantus firmus templates saved in a global variable, the Gradus program can select the map most similar to the current cantus firmus, and then project the appropriate seed note for creating a new counterpoint. This process helps the program avoid false starts. If there are two (−4 (5 0)) templates stored but only one (−5 (5 0)) template stored, the program will select the (−4 (5 0)) template because it obviously has proved the more successful of the two choices. The Gradus program thus uses previous experience to infer future successful choices.

Gradus uses one of the cantus firmi included with the program or one provided by users. Cantus firmi should follow the goals defined previously. Failing to use a cantus firmus that follows these goals can make it impossible to compose an appropriate accompanying line, or prevent the program from behaving as described. The default

Figure 6.7
The four possible first note choices for the seed note A.

cantus firmus, and all of the other cantus firmi provided with Gradus, follow the first-species goals of the provided models.

As previously mentioned, Gradus can only move stepwise or leap the interval of a third up or down, and thus projects only four possible first notes, as shown in figure 6.7. Gradus initially chooses one of these notes randomly, which means that results may differ each time the program is run, depending on whether or not more than one of the possible notes follow the program's goals. Gradus also requires a scale for diatonic tonal pitch selection, the default of which is the C-major scale. This scale restricts the program to notes in the key of the provided cantus firmi (also in C-major). Gradus is not currently designed to compose in other keys or to use atonal scales and cantus firmi. However, only a relatively few small changes would be required to make this kind of variation possible.

The centerpiece of the Gradus program is its goal-testing cycle. This cycle contains the hoops through which a successful choice must pass: vertical consonance, avoidance of parallel fifths and octaves, leaps followed by contrary motion steps, no simultaneous leaps in both octaves, avoidance of direct fifths and octaves, and three or fewer consecutive and legal parallel-direction motions. The program looks ahead for its best choice by projecting forward one pitch from the currently chosen pitch. Comparing the results of this projection with the current rules—soon to be discussed—enables the program to avoid choosing a pitch that conflicts with the goals and thus requires backtracking. If the current choice produces a conflict, Gradus selects another pitch. If no correct possibility exists among the available choices, then the program generates and saves a new rule and backtracks to find a different solution. I will discuss this process in more detail momentarily.

Rules in the Gradus program consist of three or fewer motions, and appear as follows:

$(-2 \ (1 \ 1)(-1 \ 1))$.

A rule consists of three parts: (1) the number of vertical diatonic steps between the first affected note of the cantus firmus and the related note of the new line; (2) the number of horizontal diatonic steps between the continuing notes of the cantus firmus itself; and (3) the number of horizontal diatonic steps between the related notes of the new line. The vertical difference number is necessary because there may be diatonic step distances between the associated first notes of the two lines where the combination of voice motions will work correctly. For example, the counterpoint A–B–C/F–E–F separated by an octave, and resulting in a rule of $(-2 \ (1 \ 1)(-1 \ 1))$ is incorrect due to parallel fifths. However, the counterpoint A–B–C/A–G–A in the same register—equivalent to the rule $(-7 \ (1 \ 1)(-1 \ 1))$—is correct, but would match the rule of $(-2 \ (1 \ 1)(-1 \ 1))$ if the vertical separation were not present to differentiate the two patterns.

Voice motions alone do not provide enough information to act as rules. Using vertical distances and voice motions as rules also avoids the need to have rules that duplicate one another when diatonically transposed. For example, the pitch sequences C–D–E/A–G–A and E–F–G/C–B–C in the same register are diatonically identical when transposed. Both of these would be necessary as rules in a pitch-notated rules system, whereas the single diatonic-step rule of $(-2 \ (1 \ 1)(-1 \ 1))$ includes both of them as well as all other similar transpositions.

Composing in Gradus follows a straightforward process. At every point in choosing a new note, the program produces a set of four possible notes—seconds or thirds up or down from the current note—from which it can choose. These four notes are tested against the previously described goals. If none of the four possibilities survives the tests, then Gradus backs up one note and begins again, this time with the offending note—the last note of the new line composed thus far—removed from the possible choices to avoid repeating the same mistake. If one or more of the four possibilities survives the tests, then the program looks ahead with a kind of approximation. This approximation takes into account the next cantus firmus note, but with a wild card representing any possible note in the new line. The program then compares this projection with the currently constituted rules. If a rule prevents all four of the possible projected new-line notes from occurring, then Gradus chooses another current pitch from those available. The balance between inline tests and looking ahead to see if a rule exists to block any future choice is precarious, but it ensures that backtracking will occur only at times requiring creation of new rules, and that wasted effort will be kept to a minimum.

Figure 6.8 shows how this process works in detail. In this representation, Gradus has correctly completed all of the whole notes in the bass clef up to and including the E, the third note from the end. Because this E results from a leap downward, the program must—according to the goals—move stepwise in the opposite direction. Doing so, however, creates a dissonant tritone relation with the B, the second note from the end in the cantus firmus, causing an error (represented by the black triangle note). The program therefore creates a rule to cover this situation, backs up one note, sub-

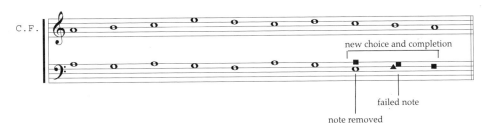

Figure 6.8
The Gradus backtracking process.

tracts the E from the possibilities available for a third note from the end, and chooses a more successful A (shown as a black square note). The program then continues to negotiate the rest of the counterpoint successfully. In future attempts to compose with this cantus firmus, the program will look ahead and, upon encountering G as the fourth note from the end, see that selecting E produces a problem with the necessary F, and thus choose A as the third note from the end to avoid backtracking. More important, the rule Gradus has created here will prevent any similar problem from occurring when composing a new line to other cantus firmi as well.

The look-ahead process in Gradus involves creating a rule on the fly—without adding it to the other rules—using an extension of the cantus firmus by one note beyond the current state of the new line (including the proposed new note), accompanied by a wild card that will match anything found in the rules. The temporary rule of (−9 (1 −1 −1)(−1 −2 nil)), equivalent to C–D–C–B/A–G–E–? (fifth note from the end of figure 6.8 and onward) where the last E represents the proposed new note and the "?" represents a wild card, is a good example of such an on-the-fly rule. With the (−9 (1 −1 −1)(−1 −2 1)) rule already present in the program's stored rules, this example temporary rule will find it a match, and the program will seek another possibility as a new note. Because rules represent dead ends (i.e., all of the other intervals substituted for the interval shown also create problems), the match correctly causes the program to choose another note to replace the one causing the problem. Hence, the look-ahead process avoids dead ends before they occur.

Often, when the look-ahead process finds a rule prohibiting the program from choosing a note, there are no more notes to choose from, and the program must then backtrack. This may seem like wasted effort, since we have not reduced backtracking by using this method. To solve this, the look-ahead function creates a new rule that prohibits the up-to-this-point correct note that led to the incorrect choice. This ensures that when this problematic situation is encountered again with this

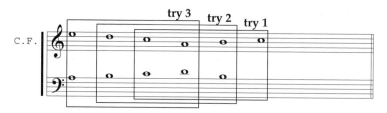

Figure 6.9
Backtracking to create new rules to avoid backtracking.

cantus firmus, the program will choose another note (if possible) to avoid the collision ahead. This new rule, unlike normal rules because it disallows a pattern that by itself is perfectly correct, helps to eliminate backtracking. This new rule is kept in a separate variable—in fact a temporary variable, since with another cantus firmus this correct choice may lead to further correct choices. This process of creating rules for otherwise correct choices and storing these rules in temporary locations is extremely important to the Gradus program's learning processes.

Figure 6.9 demonstrates how this process works. Each of the rectangles here represents a temporary rule. As can be seen in this instance, the process backs new rules up to the beginning of the composition, here with the result that the note A will be avoided in all subsequent runs of the program with this cantus firmus. In detail here, try 1 is foiled because the program has leaped to the last B in the lower voice, forcing a stepwise opposite direction C that, if created, would produce parallel octaves. In try 2, as a result of the program's looking ahead and discovering the problem with try 1, no other correct possibilities exist for the new line except the B, and thus it, too, fails. Try 3 does not work either, because no other choice exists here aside from the shown note D.

Figure 6.10 presents a typical set of Gradus program runs without any backtracking. The program identifies each attempt to extend the new line with the output text "working ...," followed on the next line by the current state of the composition of the accompanying line in relation to the cantus firmus. Final output is presented in event format (see appendix B). Note that the upper voice here appears in channel 1 and the lower voice in channel 2, and that the two voices alternate by event in order to make performance easier. Figure 6.11 shows the results of figure 6.10 in musical notation.

As mentioned earlier, since there often exists more than one correct possible new note, the program can set the same cantus firmus in a variety of ways. Figure 6.12 shows six such settings to the cantus firmus of figure 6.11. Although each of these

```
? (gradus)
working.....
((a3 b3 c4 e4 d4 c4 d4 c4 b3 a3) (a2))
working.....
((a3 b3 c4 e4 d4 c4 d4 c4 b3 a3) (a2 g2))
working.....
((a3 b3 c4 e4 d4 c4 d4 c4 b3 a3) (a2 g2 a2))
working.....
((a3 b3 c4 e4 d4 c4 d4 c4 b3 a3) (a2 g2 a2 g2))
working.....
((a3 b3 c4 e4 d4 c4 d4 c4 b3 a3) (a2 g2 a2 g2 b2))
working.....
((a3 b3 c4 e4 d4 c4 d4 c4 b3 a3) (a2 g2 a2 g2 b2 a2))
working.....
((a3 b3 c4 e4 d4 c4 d4 c4 b3 a3) (a2 g2 a2 g2 b2 a2 b2))
working.....
((a3 b3 c4 e4 d4 c4 d4 c4 b3 a3) (a2 g2 a2 g2 b2 a2 b2 c3))
working.....
((a3 b3 c4 e4 d4 c4 d4 c4 b3 a3) (a2 g2 a2 g2 b2 a2 b2 c3 d3))
working.....
((a3 b3 c4 e4 d4 c4 d4 c4 b3 a3) (a2 g2 a2 g2 b2 a2 b2 c3 d3 c3))
((0 69 1000 1 90)(0 57 1000 2 90)(1000 71 1000 1 90)(1000 55 1000 2 90)
 (2000 72 1000 1 90) (2000 57 1000 2 90) (3000 76 1000 1 90)
 (3000 55 1000 2 90) (4000 74 1000 1 90) (4000 59 1000 2 90)
 (5000 72 1000 1 90) (5000 57 1000 2 90) (6000 74 1000 1 90)
 (6000 59 1000 2 90) (7000 72 1000 1 90) (7000 60 1000 2 90)
 (8000 71 1000 1 90) (8000 62 1000 2 90) (9000 69 1000 1 90)
 (9000 60 1000 2 90))
```

Figure 6.10
A typical set of runs without any backtracking.

Figure 6.11
The results of figure 6.10 in musical notation.

settings follows the program's goals slightly differently, the results are quite similar, as will be the case whenever the seed note remains the same for a given cantus firmus. However, the slight modifications resulting from different note choices often produce further changes, creating different versions of accompanying lines.

Figure 6.13 shows a typical set of program runs that includes backtracking. Here the text "backtracking ... there are now 3 rules" clearly delineates the process for the user. Figure 6.14 shows the results of figure 6.13 in musical notation. Figure 6.15 shows how the dead ends appearing in figure 6.13 occur. Figure 6.15a presents an example of a dead end requiring backtracking. The music dead-ends in this example because each of the four possible notes causes conflicts with one or more of the program's goals. Leaping upward to D creates both a double leap in the new line and dissonance with the C in the cantus firmus. Moving upward stepwise to a C creates parallel octaves. Moving downward to an A does not resolve the downward leap in the new line by stepwise opposite motion, as required by the program's goals. Leaping downward to G causes the same conflict. Thus Gradus has no option but to backtrack and, in this case, because the composition is so near the beginning, start again from a new pitch. Figure 6.15b shows a correct new line and figure 6.15c gives the rule caused by the dead end in figure 6.15a.

The tests shown in figure 6.16 show how rules increase in number by backtracking. Each of the entries in these lists represents the length of the rules variable (*rules*) following one additional run of the Gradus program using the same cantus firmus. In this case, the program was called 100 successive times, with the number of rules representing each new function call. Note how the rule numbers quickly plateau, with backtracking no longer necessary.

Using two short, transposed-from-one-another cantus firmi in multiple runs demonstrates the effectiveness of rules in the learning process, and of using diatonic steps in rules rather than actual notes. For example, running the program with the upward-stepping A–B–C–D–E as cantus firmus and with middle C as seed note fifty times produces three backtracks and three rules. Running the program then with F–G–A–B–C as a cantus firmus—a simple transposition a third down from the first

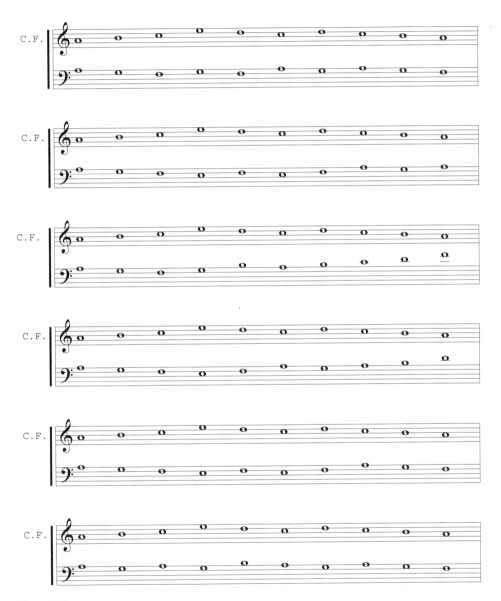

Figure 6.12
Six outputs from the Gradus program showing different second lines to the same cantus firmus.

```
? (gradus)
working.....
((a3 b3 c4 e4 d4 c4 d4 c4 b3 a3) (a2))
working.....
((a3 b3 c4 e4 d4 c4 d4 c4 b3 a3) (a2 g2))
working.....
((a3 b3 c4 e4 d4 c4 d4 c4 b3 a3) (a2 g2 e2))
backtracking.....there are now
1
rules.
working.....
((a3 b3 c4 e4 d4 c4 d4 c4 b3 a3) (a2 g2 a2))
working.....
((a3 b3 c4 e4 d4 c4 d4 c4 b3 a3) (a2 g2 a2 g2))
working.....
((a3 b3 c4 e4 d4 c4 d4 c4 b3 a3) (a2 g2 a2 g2 b2))
working.....
((a3 b3 c4 e4 d4 c4 d4 c4 b3 a3) (a2 g2 a2 g2 b2 a2))
working.....
((a3 b3 c4 e4 d4 c4 d4 c4 b3 a3) (a2 g2 a2 g2 b2 a2 f2))
backtracking.....there are now
2
rules.
working.....
((a3 b3 c4 e4 d4 c4 d4 c4 b3 a3) (a2 g2 a2 g2 b2 a2 b2))
working.....
((a3 b3 c4 e4 d4 c4 d4 c4 b3 a3) (a2 g2 a2 g2 b2 a2 b2 c3))
working.....
((a3 b3 c4 e4 d4 c4 d4 c4 b3 a3) (a2 g2 a2 g2 b2 a2 g2 a3 c3))
backtracking.....there are now
3
rules.
working.....
((a3 b3 c4 e4 d4 c4 d4 c4 b3 a3) (a2 g2 a2 g2 b2 a2 g2 a3 b3))
working.....
((a3 b3 c4 e4 d4 c4 d4 c4 b3 a3) (a2 g2 a2 g2 b2 a2 g2 a3 b3 d3))
((0 69 1000 1 90)(0 57 1000 2 90)(1000 71 1000 1 90)(1000 55 1000 2 90)
 (2000 72 1000 1 90) (2000 57 1000 2 90) (3000 76 1000 1 90)
 (3000 55 1000 2 90) (4000 74 1000 1 90) (4000 59 1000 2 90)
 (5000 72 1000 1 90) (5000 57 1000 2 90) (6000 74 1000 1 90)
 (6000 55 1000 2 90) (7000 72 1000 1 90) (7000 57 1000 2 90)
 (8000 71 1000 1 90) (8000 59 1000 2 90) (9000 69 1000 1 90)
 (9000 62 1000 2 90))
```

Figure 6.13
A typical set of runs with backtracking.

Figure 6.14
The results of figure 6.13 in musical notation.

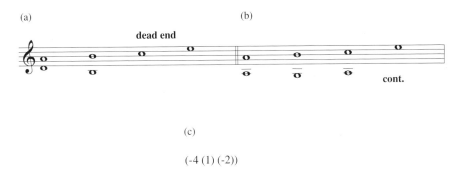

Figure 6.15
(a) A dead-ended passage requiring (b) backtracking creating (c) a new rule.

```
using default cantus firmus: A3 B3 C4 E4 D4 C4 D4 C4 B3 A3

2 3 4 4 4 5 6 7 7 7 7 7 7 8 8 8 8 8 8 8 8 8 8 8 8 8 8 8 8 8 8 8
8 8 8 8 8 8 8 8 8 8 8 8 8 8 8 8 8 8 8 8 8 8 8 8 8 8 8 8 8 8 8 8
8 8 8 8 8 8 8 8 8 8 8 8 8 8 8 8 8 8 8 8 8 8 8 8 8 8 8 8 8 8 8 8
8 8 8 8 8 8 8
```

Figure 6.16
Example of how rules are created by backtracking initially but, once created, level off in number and requiring no further backtracking.

(a)

(-12 (1 -1 -1) (-1 2 -1))
(-11 (2 -1 -1) (-1 2 -2))
(-4 (1) (2))
(-9 (1 -1 -1) (-1 -2 1))
(-9 (-1 1 -1) (-1 -2 1))
(-9 (-1 -1 -1) (1 2 -1))
(-4 (1 1) (-2 -1))
(-7 (1 1 2) (-1 -2 1))

(b)

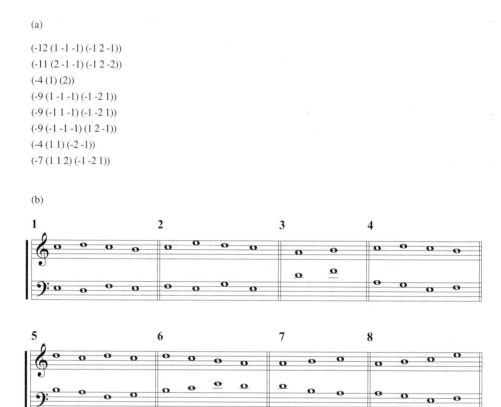

Figure 6.17
The contents of the *rules* variable in both rule format (a) and musical notation (b).

cantus firmus—with A (the interval of a third below middle C) as seed note produces no new rules, and thus no backtracking.

Figure 6.17 shows the contents of the rules variable in both rule format and musical notation after the tests shown in figure 6.16 were conducted. As can be seen, particularly in their musical versions, each rule is context-specific, but at the same time is not tied to a particular cantus firmus. Rules of fewer than four elements (the norm for rules) result from their occurring at the beginning of a counterpoint. (For example, compare the upper lines of rules 3 and 7 with the upper-line cantus firmus opening in figure 6.13.) Note that each rule ends with the error that caused the backtracking. Note also that Gradus does not reduce the diatonic stepwise vertical distances to within an octave, because occasionally lines separated by an octave will

```
using A3 B3 A3 C4 B3 D4 C4 B3 A3 added only 2 rules
9 10 10 10 10 10 10 10 10 10 10 10 10 10 10 10 10 10 10 10 10
10 10 10 10 10 10 10 10 10 10 10 10 10 10 10 10 10 10 10 10
10 10 10 10 10 10 10 10 10

using A3 B3 C4 E4 D4 C4 B3 C4 D4 C4 added only 2 rules
10 10 10 11 11 11 11 11 11 11 11 11 11 11 11 11 11 11 11 11 11
11 11 11 11 11 11 11 11 11 11 11 11 11 11 11 11 11 11 11 11
11 11 11 11 11 11 11 11 11 12

using A3 B3 C4 B3 C4 D4 C4 added no rules at all
12 12 12 12 12 12 12 12 12 12 12 12 12 12 12 12 12 12 12 12
12 12 12 12 12 12 12 12 12 12 12 12 12 12 12 12 12 12 12 12
12 12 12 12 12 12 12 1212 12
```

Figure 6.18
Using rules created by the runs of the cantus firmus of figure 6.16 to help produce second lines to a new
cantus firmus that then require less backtracking.

produce correct results, while the same lines transposed by an octave for closer proximity will not produce correct results (primarily due to voice-crossing problems—see
goal 1).

The three tests of fifty calls each to the Gradus program shown in figure 6.18 with
three new cantus firmi immediately followed the runs shown in figure 6.16, without
clearing the rules variable, and therefore using the rules created by figure 6.16's cantus firmus. As can be seen here, the first new cantus firmus requires only two more
rules than the eight already created in the runs of figure 6.16. The second cantus firmus in figure 6.18 requires two more new rules as well. The third new cantus firmus,
however, requires no new rules at all. In essence, the program has "learned" how to
compose two-voice, one-against-one counterpoint—at least it has learned those rules
required to create appropriate accompanying lines to the cantus firmi shown here.

I have chosen these particular cantus firmi because they resemble one another
somewhat, and therefore suggest that fewer new rules will be necessary to create logical counterpoints. Running the program with very different cantus firmi may require
more new rules than shown here. In addition, choosing different seed notes—users
may override the program's choice—can result in different numbers of new rules
than those given. Sooner or later, however, the program will find all the rules it

requires to appropriately accompany almost any goal-correct cantus firmus to which the user wishes a second line.

The most frequent user interaction with the Gradus program involves defining a new cantus firmus by redefining the *cantus-firmus* variable. As mentioned earlier, one should not create cantus firmi that stray from the goals, because doing so can produce unsolvable problems that may cause the program to find itself in an infinite loop. For example, the difference between this cantus firmus

(72   71   69   67   72   67   71   72   74   76)

and this cantus firmus

(72   71   69   71   69   72   71   72)

is relatively small. However, because the first cantus firmus contains more than two motions in the same direction, double leaps, leaps not followed by contrary stepwise motion, and so on, it will cause excessive or indefinite backtracking, depending on the seed note used. Usually, if the problems are few in number, the program will still successfully negotiate the learning process. If the differences are great, however, Gradus may lapse into backtracking loops, the only escape then being to abort the program. These loops occur particularly in cantus firmi that contain repeated notes. To keep the code relatively small and readable, I have not accounted for all of these anomalies in cantus firmi. However, simply keeping the cantus firmus within the stated goals of the program significantly reduces the chance that such problems will occur.

Gradus can create its own cantus firmus by simply using one of its own correct counterpoint solutions transposed up one octave, thus eliminating the need for a new user-supplied cantus firmus. However, because a provided cantus firmus is typically considered a part of the musical puzzle for which a solution is desired, eliminating this user-supplied element seems somewhat contradictory. Ultimately, the program functions with only a set of examples upon which to base its creations, a situation not unlike that facing human composers. In fact, Gradus creates counterpoint in much the same way that I, as a composer, create counterpoint, particularly when attempting to solve problems caused by working within explicit constraints.

As previously mentioned, rules are stored in the rules variable (*rules*) and may be accessed at any time by users when running the program. Setting the rules variable to nil (see the documentation accompanying the code to Gradus for more information on this and other alterable variables) resets the program to begin from scratch. A knowledge of Lisp will obviously provide users with many more ways to interact with and understand Gradus. However, even with only the access to the minimal number of variables given above, users can observe the "learning" processes of this program.

As an example of the extensions possible with the Gradus program, I have included with the source code on my Web site a simple canon-maker function, along with a sample cantus firmus. Canons, at least canons at the octave, as is the case here, require essentially two additional goals beyond those for first-species counterpoint: *invertibility* and *offset repetition*. Invertibility can be achieved by adding the perfect fifth to the invalid vertical interval list, because perfect fifths invert to invalid perfect fourths during imitation at the octave. Thirds, sixths, and octaves—the only remaining valid intervals—invert to correct intervals when inverted at the octave, and thus remain acceptable. Adding the perfect fifth to the invalid vertical interval list creates an added constraint that then makes many cantus firmi impossible to accompany with a second line. Therefore, cantus firmi must be chosen carefully when creating canons so as not to force dead ends that no amount of backtracking can amend.

Figure 6.19 presents an example of a first-species, two-voice canon created by Gradus's create-canon function. Note that the simple code for producing this canon does not account for the seams between the offset repetitions of the theme. Here, these seams are acceptable. However, using other cantus firmi may produce repeated notes or double leaps at the intersections between the theme repetitions. This problem could easily be avoided with the addition of further constraints that I omitted here in an effort to make the transition from simple one-against-one counterpoint to more formalistic canons as clear and concise as possible.

Note that the canon program in no way extends the learning capabilities of Gradus. The program continues to create and use only the rules that enable it to compose better first-species, noncanon, one-against-one counterpoint. However, the above-mentioned problems (encountering impossible-to-accompany cantus firmi, and poor seams between offset-theme entries) could themselves become learning processes. For example, one could code the seams of canons as part of an extended one-against-one counterpoint (unlike the simplistic manner in which I have strung them together here), with added rules accounting for the desired seamlessness.

The Gradus program is domain specific and currently will function only within the boundaries I have defined. However, with minimal additions, the program could be adapted to second-, third-, fourth-, and fifth-species counterpoint as well as to counterpoint in more than two voices. This increase of complexity and texture might then result in four-voice, fifth-species counterpoint code, where little change would be required for the program to "learn" how to compose Bach-like four-voice chorales. Creating more elaborate canons (at intervals other than the octave, for example) and

Figure 6.19
A simple first-species canon created by five lines of added code.

fugue-like contrapuntal forms should also be possible by extending the code. Because most composers use rules of some kind (serialism, set theory, and so on) that at least occasionally collide to produce cul de sacs, the program would seem a natural fit for a wide variety of machine-learning musical situations.

For example, the entire four-voice fugue (of which only the beginning appears in figure 6.20) was created by a program not too different from Gradus. Whereas the basic imitative structure—repetition of the subject at the interval of a fifth, tonal versus real answers, and so on—was not learned (it was built into the code, as with the canon function just described), most of the basic counterpoint resulted from analyzed goals learned by program-created rules. As with the version of Gradus described previously, the Gradus-like program that created this fugue did not contain any code relating to consonance, dissonance, or voice leading, but discovered these goals in the models provided to the program.

The three-voice texture and instrumental counterpoint style presented in figure 6.20 requires altered versions of the goals presented previously, as well as new goal

Figure 6.20
The beginning of the first of forty-eight fugues and the accompanying forty-eight preludes from *The Well-Programmed Clavier*.

types to cover the thicker texture. In essence, these additions include (1) the ability to detect goals in fifth-species ("florid") counterpoint and (2) the capability of composing two new voices to a given cantus firmi. In a few cases, the creation of this example required the further addition of specific code to account for the formalisms inherent in fugal composition (extending existing lines, repeating sequences, etc.), as will be seen shortly.

Figure 6.21 shows the single-line cantus firmus used to create the music shown in figure 6.20. This template contains three iterations of the fugue theme in different transpositions and/or keys, as expected in a fugue (see measures 1, 4, and 8). Built-in instructions require the Gradus-like program to begin its fifth-species counterpoint in measure 4 by attaching itself to the end of the subject's first statement. The program also contains rules for repeating this countersubject in transposition in measure

Figure 6.21
The cantus firmus used to create the fugue beginning shown in figure 6.20.

8, when the subject appears again in its original guise in a different register. Space limitations do not permit a detailed description of the differences between composing fifth-species, three-voice counterpoint and the creation of the first-species, two-voice counterpoint presented earlier. Suffice it to say, however, that the same basic processes—goal determination, rules developed through backtracking, and memory of past mistakes that eliminates the need for future backtracking—follow accordingly. This fugue, as well as its allusions to Bach's originals, is the first of forty-eight fugues and the accompanying forty-eight preludes from *The Well-Programmed Clavier* (Cope 2002).

To further show the flexibility of Gradus and to demonstrate that this program is not limited to traditional concepts of consonance and dissonance, I here include three models (see figure 6.22) with fifths, seconds, and sevenths, instead of fifths, thirds, and sixths, acting as consistent vertical intervals. As can be seen in the output in

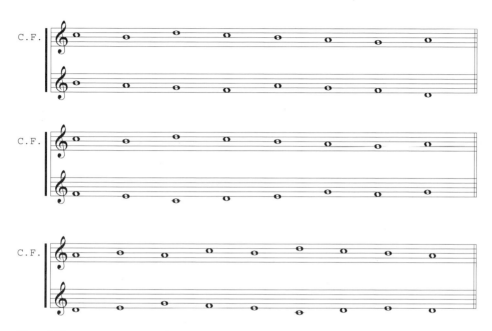

Figure 6.22
Three models with open fifths, seconds, and sevenths acting as consistent vertical intervals.

figure 6.23, Gradus incorporates the goals of the new models without the need for revising existing code. Although contemporary composers may not use rules so rigorously nor as simply as these, most composers do apply rules of counterpoint in their compositions, consciously or otherwise.

The Gradus program and the principles presented here, although simple, indicate a number of interesting if not important conclusions. For example, the notion that machine learning in music is not only possible but attainable, using fairly rudimentary techniques, can have significant consequences. Such an observation might in itself not seem particularly important, were it not for the fact that so little other evidence exists in terms of the available literature. Because a "learning" algorithm can be implemented with so few lines of code and with such basic concepts, one can further imagine that extending this code to include more sophisticated musical problems—as just shown—would require less than heroic efforts. Whether such extensions would produce simple tools for composing, orchestration, and so on, or composing programs that could create new works in their entirety, remains to be seen. However, the potentials clearly exist for the concepts demonstrated by Gradus to serve as a core of a wide diversity of applications. The program's current ability to learn and

Figure 6.23
Output from Gradus using the three models of figure 6.22.

to generalize its discoveries in ways that improve its ability to succeed in its intended purpose, however limited, lay the foundation for more elegant applications to come.

Because Gradus represents a part of my ongoing research in the modeling of intelligence and creativity in music, a word about the Gradus program's ability to learn and its potential role as an "intelligent" computational composing program seems in order here. In my book *The Algorithmic Composer* (Cope 2000), I describe intelligence as based, at least in part, on analysis, association, and adaption. Gradus analyzes models to create its objectives (goals), associates its progress toward those objectives by producing and referencing rules, and adapts by slowly decreasing its need to backtrack until backtracking is no longer necessary. That said, however, I still do not feel that Gradus is intelligent. The program does not pose its own problems to solve, or even initiate the process of solving those problems. The concepts realized in Gradus do, however, provide the basis for further research in this area, and give me hope that one day we may better understand the elusive concepts of learning, creativity, and intelligence, particularly as they relate to music.

I invite readers to download and use the Gradus program on my Web site, and see and hear the ways in which the program increases its skills in creating simple counterpoint. The program is quite small and easy to use, and includes a simple guide to aid even those with minimal computer skills in taking advantage of the processes it offers.

Inference

Webster's Collegiate Dictionary (1991) defines inference as "... the process of deriving from assumed premises either the strict logical conclusion or one that is to some degree probable ..." (p. 689). The most important premise of inference is that new conclusions occur as combinations of known facts. These new conclusions can then be added to these collections of known facts for further inference. This is clearly one of the ways in which humans reason and create.

Artificial-intelligence approaches to inference have taken many forms. Deduction systems, for example, represent one type of rule-based inference process. Patrick Winston (1984) describes deduction systems thus:

Suppose that the *if* parts of some if-then rules specify combinations of known facts. Also suppose that the *then* parts specify new facts to be deduced directly from the triggering combination. So constrained, a rule-based system becomes a type of *deduction system....* (Winston 1984, p. 177)

I describe several forms of musical inference in my book *The Algorithmic Composer* (Cope 2000). Of interest in that book is my definition of inference as "... an ability to extrapolate basic principles from examples ..." (p. 67; see also Anderson 1964; Charniak and McDermott 1985; McCorduck 1979). While centering on set theory as the primary basis for inference in my book, I also discuss a form of tonal inference (see pp. 73–79), using voice leading as a core. While an extension of the Gradus program I describe here for inference could follow the same processes of inference as the program I describe in *The Algorithmic Composer*, Gradus is too simple in its current incarnation to incorporate that program's inferential techniques.

Interestingly, however, Gradus uses rule-making and look-ahead processes that, by their very nature, are inferential. For example, while rules 1, 2, 4, 5, 6, 7, and 8 in figure 6.17 are context-specific, the look-ahead process considers them to be universal. As such, the program will disallow *any* leap up a third in a new line that simultaneously contains a downward scale of notes beginning two octaves above (as between notes 2 through 4 of figure 6.17b1), because that clearly requires an incorrect diatonic stepwise downward motion creating parallel fifths. Contextually, when D is determined as a new note of an accompanying line to the cantus firmus, as in figure 6.17b1, an F as a following note is eliminated during the look-ahead process. In essence, the program infers that there are no correct possibilities with the choice of F as a third note in this instance, as well as in all other equivalent instances. Importantly, the program does not then disqualify D as the second note of the counterpoint, because that note could be correctly followed by the note E.

The program called Infer on my Web site provides an example of another simple inference algorithm. This small program roughly follows the form of Prolog, a language originally written in Lisp and used, particularly during the last two decades of the twentieth century, for its native inference capabilities. Infer takes the form of a simple pattern matcher following an "is a" type of grammar. Using only five simple and very small functions written in Lisp, Infer produces the following logical output.

Users first create a simple database, such as

```
(setq *database* '((man is a human) (human is a mammal)))
```

The function "lookup" retrieves any list whose first element matches its argument. Therefore (with the database set to the above lists):

(lookup 'man)

> (man is a human)

The greater-than symbol (">") here indicates what the program returns as a result of the input given above it.

The function "infer" not only matches its argument to the first element of a list, but it associates the last element of the list it has found with the first element of another list, and so on until no more matching lists can be found. In this case, "infer" infers that man is also a mammal.

(infer 'man)

> (man is a human is a mammal)

Adding a list of information linked to the same last element, as in

(add-to-database '(woman is a human)),

produces the following extended database:

> ((woman is a human) (man is a human) (human is a mammal)).

Using the "infer" function with woman then produces the same linkage as for man presented previously:

(infer 'woman)

> (woman is a human is a mammal)

We obviously could also use musical references, such as

(setq *database* '((c–d–e–c is a motive) (motive is a melody fragment))),

with the following exchanges, creating a musical version of the stepped-through interchange using language:

(lookup 'c–d–e–c)

> (c–d–e–c is a motive)

(infer 'c–d–e–c)

> (c–d–e–c is a motif is a melody fragment)

(add-to-database '(c–b–a–c is a motive))

> ((c–b–a–c is a motive) (c–d–e–c is a motive) (motive is a melody fragment))

(infer 'c–b–a–c)

> (c–b–a–c is a motive is a melody fragment).

This inference process, known generally in the realms of logic and predicate calculus as *modus ponens* (Latin, roughly meaning "the mode that affirms"), represents an important concept for defining intelligent behavior. Therefore, though simple in terms of code, the Infer program accomplishes relatively powerful goals. Most important, Infer produces facts that are not explicitly present in its database. Without inference we would not be able to make the intuitive leaps necessary for creativity.

The Alice inference program (Algorithmically-Integrated Composing Environment, described in Cope 2000) derives rules from the music in its database. Deriving rules from music provides many important benefits, the foremost being that rules separate composing from actual data, and thus allow programs such as Alice (and Gradus, if it were extended) to manipulate and vary these rules in logical and musical ways. Like the Experiments in Musical Intelligence program and Sara (Simple Analytic Recombinance Algorithm, the program described in Cope 1996), Alice emulates the style of music provided in its database. Unlike Experiments in Musical Intelligence and Sara, however, Alice composes new music by *inferring* principles from its database rather than recombining music from that database.

Analogy

Webster's Collegiate Dictionary (1991) defines analogy as "... a form of reasoning in which one thing is inferred to be similar to another thing in a certain respect, on the basis of known similarities in other respects ..." (p. 49). As can be seen here, inference plays an important role in analogy, and as we shall soon see, analogy also plays an important role in creativity.

We are often able to solve new problems by applying analogies of previously solved problems to them (Minsky 1963, p. 425). This powerful process was recognized early on by the Greeks, and their word *analogia*—referring to mathematical proportion—serves as the root of our word *analogy*. Today we typically notate analogical reasoning as 2:4::4:8, read as 2 is to 4 as 4 is to 8. (The single colon means "is to," and the double colon means "as.") Analogies can also apply to nonmathematical relationships, such as hands are to arms as feet are to legs (hands:arms::feet:legs) or, in musical terms, minor seconds are to major seconds as minor thirds are to major thirds (m2:M2::m3:M3), or i–v is to i–v–i as c–g is to c–g–c (i–v:1–v–1::c–g:c–g–c).

Analogy typically indicates a deep level of creativity, requiring learning, inference, and a willingness to associate apparently dissimilar objects, relationships, or actions that share significant real or abstract attributes.

To think analogically is to see one thing *as* another, not in the sense that someone mistakes the one for the other, but that she conceives of the one in terms of the other. To perceive an analogy, it is necessary that one recognize an agreement or correspondence in certain respects between things that are otherwise different. (Boden 1987, p. 314)

Notions of what kinds of things logically represent analogy can change from generation to generation. This is especially true with creative analogies.

Recognizing a connection between one zebra and another zebra, or between two red things, might have been, at one time, highly creative, but no longer. Very many things "downstream" in our conceptual systems depend upon these connections. Yanking them from our conceptual systems would rip out massive dependent domains. They have a high degree of generative entrenchment; they have a high degree of cognitive indispensability. (Turner 1988, p. 4)

Programs like ANALOGY (Evans 1968) and early work by Kling (1971) were among the first to explore computational analogical problem-solving. Thomas Evans developed his program ANALOGY to solve geometric comparisons such as those shown in figure 6.24, where the bottom four figures represent multiple choices for the question posed above. Evans's process involves three principal steps: elaboration (in which as many relationships as possible between the first two figures are inferred), mapping (deriving all possible rules that seem to transform the first figure into the second figure), and justification (selecting the best rule for transforming the third figure into the best choice among the possible given solutions). ANALOGY has proven effectively that it can solve many not previously programmed geometric problems. R. E. Kling's ZORBA, not limited to the geometric domain as ANALOGY is, follows the notion that "given as input a target problem, output a solution to that problem derived from some other problem whose solution is known" (Kedar-Cabelli 1988, p. 77).

Among other attempts to create analogy-making programs, ACME (Analogical Constraint Mapping Engine; see Holyoak and Thagard 1989), INA (see O'Hara 1994), PAN (see O'Hara and Indurkhya 1994), and SME (Structure Mapping Engine; see Falkenhainer, Forbus, and Gentner 1990) stand out. Not surprisingly, analogy also plays a very important role in Douglas Hofstadter's studies of intelligence and creativity:

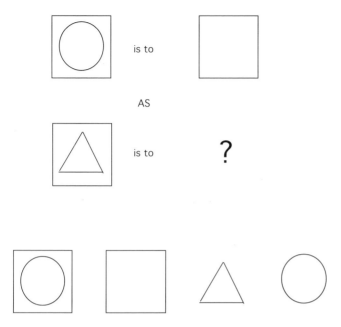

Figure 6.24
Geometric analogies in which the bottom four figures represent multiple choices for the question posed above.

It is useful to divide analogical thought into two basic components. First, there is the process of *situation-perception*, which involves taking the data involved with a given situation, and filtering and organizing them in various ways to provide an appropriate representation for a given context. Second, there is the process of *mapping*. This involves taking the representations of two situations and finding appropriate correspondences between components of one representation with the components of the other to produce the match-up that we call an analogy. It is by no means apparent that these processes are cleanly separable; they seem to interact in a deep way. (Hofstadter 1995, pp. 180–181)

More recent programs (see Kedar-Cabelli 1988, p. 78–97, for a more complete summary), using domains besides geometry and language, build on the work of Evans and Kling, using variations of their models. These programs often involve explicit steps within the three basic categories of Evans—elaboration, mapping, and justification. Most important among this research is J. G. Carbonell's work (1983) with "transformational analogy," the notion of transforming a potential solution so that it fits a problem appropriately. "Here, the initial state is the base solution, the constraint state is the target solution, and the operators, called T-operators, transform

one solution into another by deleting, inserting, reordering problem solving operators, and concatenating or truncating whole solution sequences" (Kedar-Cabelli
1988, p. 78).

Depending on how one wishes to define them, analogies abound in music.
Normalization—folding or expanding one set of data within a prescribed range, particularly useful in sonification as discussed in chapter 3—represents a simple example of analogy in music. For instance, normalizing a set of data that ranges from 0
to 1000 to within a pitch range of, say, 36 to 112 requires a straightforward mathematical analogy: $x:0–1000::y:36–112$, where x is a known number in the 0 to 1000
range and y is the desired number in the 36 to 112 range. Using 500 as x allows us
to say that 500 is to 1000 (the difference between 0 and 1000) as y is to 76 (the difference between 36 and 112), with 38 as the result. To find the actual normalized pitch,
then, requires adding back the base number of 36, resulting in the normalized pitch
of 74 (38 plus 36). Transposition represents another simple analogy in music, as in A-
major:B-minor::C-major:D-minor. With these as examples, one could say that all
music abounds with analogies, so much so that it couldn't exist without them. This
approach to musical analogy, however, seems too rudimentary to be of much use.

Leonard Meyer comments that Bach's use of B–A–C–H motives "... reminds us
of the possibility that private codes—e.g., equating letters with pitches, as Schumann
did, or Morse code to specify durational relationships, as George Crumb did—may
result in the devising of novel patternings" (Meyer 1989, p. 132). Meyer may be
speaking, in the case of the B–A–C–H motive, of Bach's final use of this pattern,
four measures from where the music abruptly ends in midphrase in the final *contra-
punctus* of his *Art of the Fugue* (Bach's last work). As Hofstadter points out, this "...
is an indescribably sad moment" (Hofstadter 1980, p. 79), inferring that the incom-
pleteness represents Bach's death.

Interestingly, while one might think that the B–A–C–H motive would have to
contain the exact notes B-flat, A, C, B-natural (B stands for B-flat and H for B-
natural in German) in order to have legitimacy, the general interval map of that motive also occurs often in Bach's music. Since most listeners do not have perfect pitch,
they do not hear the notes by their names, and therefore most of us hear the motive
as a series of approximate intervals or simple directional patterns—in this case, down
a minor second, up a minor third, and then down a minor second. The beginning of
Bach's Fugue no. 4 from *The Well-Tempered Clavier* represents a good example. The
first four notes of this fugue—a whole note, two half notes, and another whole
note—are C-sharp, B-sharp, E, D-sharp (shown in figure 5.26), in the same directions if not exact intervals (as the B–A–C–H motive). As mentioned in chapter 5,
this motive represents the well-known baroque musical sign for the cross (see figure

Figure 6.25
The beginning of the Experiments in Musical Intelligence Fugue no. 13 from *The Well-Programmed Clavier*.

5.27). However, this can also be heard as a clear derivation of the B–A–C–H pattern with only one interval change (a major third rather than a minor third between the second and third notes). In short, I hear this as an analogy, like saying B/A is to C/H as C-sharp/B-sharp is to E/D-sharp.

As previously mentioned (see figures 5.33 and 6.20 and related discussions), Experiments in Musical Intelligence recently completed *The Well-Programmed Clavier*, forty-eight Bach-style preludes and forty-eight fugues. The program's Fugue no. 13 from *The Well-Programmed Clavier*, the beginning of which appears in figure 6.25, seems modeled after Bach's Fugue 4 (see figure 5.26), yet the intervals are here synonymous with the B–A–C–H motive transposed up a perfect fifth from the actual pitches of B–A–C–H (a somewhat arbitrary detail, since Experiments in Musical Intelligence composes in a neutral key, and I transpose the results to the most performable key possible). In one sense, then, the Experiments in Musical Intelligence theme is to its fugue 13 as Bach's theme is to his Fugue no. 4—an analogy.

Interestingly, Bach's *Well-Tempered Clavier* provides a wellspring of analogies. These analogies occur between the primary themes of the preludes and the primary themes of their key-related fugues. For example, the first measures of Prelude no. 4 and Fugue no. 4 of book I (the same fugue discussed in regard to figures 5.26 and 5.27, and alluded to in the music of figure 6.25) seem quite dissimilar at first glance, as shown in figure 6.26. I contend, however, that the themes of these two works, and the manner in which Bach reveals these themes, represent an analogy. As in the type

Figure 6.26
The first measures of Prelude no. 4 (a) and Fugue no. 4 (b) of Book I of Bach's *The Well-Tempered Clavier*.

of analogies we have been discussing, the important consideration here is the comparative relationships of theme parts to themselves. For example, the prelude's theme (measure 1 and the first note of measure 2 in figure 6.26a) moves stepwise downward (G-sharp to C-sharp), followed by a leap upward, then stepwise motion downward. One could generalize this as stepwise-down followed by leap-up-stepwise-down. As we have seen—particularly in the cross allusion of figure 5.27—the four-note fugue theme moves stepwise downward (C-sharp to B-sharp), followed by a leap upward, then stepwise motion downward. This could be generalized as stepwise-down followed by leap-up-stepwise-down. In essence, the two themes represent a simple analogy, as in scale-down is to leap-up-and-scale-down as step-down is to leap-up-and-step-down (scale-down:leap-up-and-scale-down::step-down:leap-up-and-step-down). The fact that both the prelude and the fugue state their respective themes

Figure 6.27
The first measures of Prelude and Fugue no. 17 from book I of *The Well-Tempered Clavier* seem quite dissimilar, differing in both meter and intervallic content.

four times (measures 1–4 in the prelude and measures 1–14 in the fugue) helps cement this relationship. Interestingly, both themes prolong their tonic functions while emphasizing dominant-function elements (G-sharp in the prelude, D-sharp in the fugue).

Of course, the differences between these two themes are many. The theme of the prelude, for example, has ten notes to the fugue's four. The prelude's theme occurs in one-plus measures, while the fugue theme is spread out over three full measures. The two themes do not share one duration value. The meters and rhythmic emphases of important parts of each theme are different. For those who might therefore argue that this kind of analysis forces something on the music that is not innately present, I would argue that listening to these two themes side by side will verify the analogous relationship, and for me, hearing is the ultimate test of veracity in analysis. Ralph Kirkpatrick notes, however, that one

... may ask whether there is any relationship between one piece and another in the WTC. What, for example, is the relation between prelude and fugue or, in collective terms, between preludes and fugues? Certainly any such relationship can be one of contrast or of complement ... there have been numerous rather debatable attempts to point out thematic relationships between preludes and fugues, like those of Johann Nepomuk David, and even by Busoni. However, there are quite as many preludes that contrast violently with the fugues that they precede. They seem designed not to introduce the fugue but to set it off. (Kirkpatrick 1984, p. 35)

Many other of the preludes and fugues of the *Well-Tempered Clavier* have similar analogous relationships. For example, the first measures of the Prelude and Fugue no. 17 from Book I seem quite dissimilar in both meter and interval content, as shown in figure 6.27. However, closer examination reveals that the two themes are directional inversions of one another, with the largest leap occurring between the fourth and fifth notes of each theme—opposite-direction major sixths. While the other intervals are often of different sizes, both examples begin on A-flat and generally outline triads. The prelude outlines the tonic triad while the fugue outlines both

Figure 6.28
Prelude and Fugue no. 12, also from book I of *The Well-Tempered Clavier*, show an intriguing relationship.

the tonic and the subdominant triads—an analogous consequence one might imagine the opposing intervallic directions of the two themes would require.

The primary themes of Prelude and Fugue no. 12 (appearing in figure 6.28), also from book I of *The Well-Tempered Clavier*, have an even more intriguing relationship. If one disregards for the moment the sixteenth-note offbeat notes in the prelude's theme (arrows here represent the theme), the primary ideas of the two pieces resemble one another in very interesting ways. Both themes first step and then leap upward before leaping back down. Both themes have the same range of an octave—tonic to tonic. The possible analogy here is that while both themes stretch upward to the tonic high notes of their phrases, the prelude's theme—beginning on the tonic note—moves diatonically in very simple harmonic outlines, while the fugue theme—beginning on the dominant note—moves upward in harmonic minor, consequently dealing with the natural chromaticism this situation demands.

The themes of Prelude and Fugue no. 21 (appearing in figure 6.29) provide a third possible analogy in Bach's *The Well-Tempered Clavier*, Book I. Unlike the previous two examples, the music beginning these two excerpts looks dramatically different in meter, rhythm, apparent shape, and melodic direction. However, closer examination reveals that these two themes hold much in common. For example, the first four notes of the left hand of the prelude represent a near inversion of the first four notes of the theme of the fugue. Unlike the fugue, however, the prelude then sequences a

Figure 6.29
Prelude and Fugue no. 21 provide a third example of analogy in Bach's *The Well-Tempered Clavier*, book I.

third down from its predecessor. The fugue theme, in contrast, continues by leaping downward a sixth, followed by a second in the same direction.

There are almost as many examples of these kinds of analogies between preludes and fugues as there are preludes and fugues in *The Well-Tempered Clavier*. One might argue that these various supposed analogies result from the simple rules and conditions of tonality—functional harmony, differing major and minor scales, resolution to important scale tones, and so on, all routine in tonal music. I would argue, however, that the analogies I describe here result from the basic nature of these themes, and the fact that the analogies occur in associated preludes and fugues. I would further argue that these compositional techniques represent analogies regardless of whether or not they follow basic tonal processes.

In contrast to Bach's *Well-Tempered Clavier*, each of the forty-eight preludes and forty-eight fugues of the Experiments in Musical Intelligence's *Well-Programmed Clavier* was composed without intended analogies. The only way I could find to implement analogic relationships between the preludes and fugues in this machine-composed set was to deliberately pair those that seemed to fit well together. While I tried many different combinations, I do not believe that I successfully established one analogy of the type I have just discussed in Bach's music. If I had erred in my previous labeling of analogies, when in fact the selections were simply common attributes of tonality or happenstance similarities, then one would imagine that many, if not

(a)

(b)

Figure 6.30
Mozart Symphony no. 40 (1788) (K. 550): first theme (a), measures 1–5; and second theme (b), measures 44–51.

most, of the preludes and fugues created by Experiments in Musical Intelligence would have such relationships simply by chance, or that I could at least have found matching pairs among the collection fairly easily. Since this was certainly not the case, I feel comfortable attributing the extraordinary relationships between most, if not all, of Bach's preludes and fugues to musical analogies.

Analogies can play an important role in making otherwise diverse themes more compatible. Figure 6.30 provides such an example. Here we see Mozart's first theme—a repeating stepwise motive ending with a large leap, followed by falling stepwise repeated motives paralleling his otherwise contrasting second theme, a stepwise line ending with a large leap followed by a falling stepwise line (chromatic, this time). Both themes have their largest interval (minor sixth in the first theme, and a perfect fifth in the second theme) at their midpoints, acting as fulcrums for balancing the two counterparts of the melodies. The analogy ties these two otherwise diverse melodies together and makes one seem like an inevitable consequence of the other.

Analogies need not have directional equivalence (as with the just-described Mozart example), or for that matter any equivalence at all. Therefore, extremely different ideas that initially seem unrelated can, if the proper relationships exist, make perfect sense to our ears, a sense made possible, I believe, by the analogy present.

Interestingly, analogy in music might also include hierarchical differences between analogical pairs. For example, the analogy C-major:G-major::A:B, where the two "major" references could be triads or key centers, and where "A" and "B" refer to formal statement and contrast, would seem to have more substance than analogies involving simple normalization or transposition. Hierarchical musical analogies thus follow the notion that often in music one finds that very small note-to-note motives can be mirrored in very high-level structural patterns, and vice versa. The SPEAC model that I discuss in chapter 7 of this book follows this kind of analogical process, with its step-by-step hierarchy providing possibilities of analogies at every level.

The most obvious hierarchical analogies in tonal music appear at the structural level just above functional analysis with rhyming phrases. The simple question-answer of standard two-phrase periods argues the analogy of dominant:tonic:: question:answer. More subtle analogies could cover entire movements or works, with incomplete (mediant or dominant notes present in the top voice in inner cadences) and complete (tonic note in the top voice in final chords) cadences also representing analogies in tonal music.

The Analogy program on my Web site resembles the previously discussed Prolog-like inference program, except that it uses an "is like" model instead of an "is a" model. However, the version of inference described earlier in this chapter is not powerful enough to produce a real analogy. For example, the following—using music first this time—demonstrates how inference, while giving the impression of creating an analogy, still produces a "modus ponens":

(setq *database* '((c–g–c is like i–v–i) (i–v–i is like a–b–a)))

(lookup 'c–g–c)

> (c–g–c is like i–v–i)

(infer 'c–g–c)

> (c–g–c is like a i–v–i is like a a–b–a)

(add-to-database '(d–a–d is like i–v–i))

> ((d–a–d is like i–v–i) (c–g–c is like i–v–i) (i–v–i is like a–b–a))

(infer 'd–a–d)

> (d–a–d is like i–v–i is like a–b–a)

The database here actually contains the analogy; the program has only inferred what the creator of the database has already programmed. For an analogy to occur, code must be able to successfully relate two different objects by comparing both with an abstraction that they share. Figure 6.24 gave an example of this, with the abstraction—missing-internal-object—allowing the analogical comparison.

Creating such an abstraction requires that a program invoke an inferential process that connects and relates last elements of database entries as well as first elements. The following simple algorithm, for example, can effectively find simple analogies in its database:

1. Infer the given pointer to make sure that it has complete lineage

2. Take the last item from 1

3. Collect all other predecessors of 2

4. Choose one of the predecessors

5. Return one of these as an analogue to the given pointer.

The following code demonstrates how this process works in detail:

```
(setq *database* '((cat*mouse are strong*weak)

                   (strong*weak are opposite*sides)

                   (oil*water are non*mixable)

                   (non*mixable are opposite*sides)))
```

```
(analogize 'cat*mouse)
```

> (cat*mouse is like oil*water)

Inferring "cat*mouse" produces "opposite*sides," and inferring "oil*water" produces "opposite*sides" (neither fact explicitly shown above). By inferring "opposite*sides," the last element of both of these processes, and reversing the usual inference direction, we achieve a simple analogy. Since "cat*mouse" and "oil*water" share "opposite*sides" inferentially, "cat*mouse" *is like* "oil*water."

The following interaction presents a musical example of the above process:

```
(setq *database* '((g–b–d*c–e–g are dominant*tonic)

                   (dominant*tonic are resolutions)

                   (f–a–c*c–e–g are subdominant*tonic)

                   (subdominant*tonic are resolutions)))
```

```
(analogize 'g–b–d*c–e–g)
```

> (g–b–d*c–e–g is like f–a–c*c–e–g)

The Analogy program provides interesting opportunities for creativity. As seen in chapters 9 and 10, analogy in my programs follows "inductive association," a process that allows computer programs to develop solutions to seemingly unsolvable problems, and produce effective alternative choices when composing. While certainly not the only avenue for creating "... connections between two or more multifaceted things, ideas, or phenomena hitherto not considered actively connected ...," analogies offer an extraordinary means for thinking "outside of the box." As Arthur Koestler notes:

Some writers identify the creative act in its entirety with the unearthing of hidden analogies.... But where does the hidden likeness hide, and how is it found?... [In most truly original acts of discovery the analogy] was not "hidden" anywhere; it was "created" by the imagination.... (Koestler, as quoted in Boden 2004, p. 34)

Discussions of analogies will appear again over the next few chapters of this book, particularly as I describe musical structure (chapter 7) and musical association (chapter 10). In order that I not overuse this term, however, readers may have to *infer* these analogies as they appear.

7 Form and Structure

Principle: Creativity is not limited to note-to-note motions, but occurs at every structural level.

Structural Analysis

For years I found the music of Anton Bruckner square and musically uninteresting. His orchestrations, for example, while professional, seemed unimaginative to me. He repeats ideas excessively, often uses banal harmonic progressions, and occasionally holds single chords far longer than musically necessary. Then one day, following serious emergency surgery, I found myself bedridden with only one CD close at hand—Bruckner's Symphony no. 7. Having little interest in television or radio, and not wanting to dwell excessively on my health, I relented and turned to Bruckner.

As I listened to this music, I discovered that the second movement of this symphony has many special moments. The first such moment that caught my ear appears in the strings in measure 4 and again in measure 80 (five measures before letter H), and is shown here in reduction in figure 7.1. The strings repeat this theme one measure before letter M (beginning in measure 114; see figure 7.2), but with the subtle addition of a woodwind accompaniment. The theme appears here half a step lower than the original (not shown), and continues with a quite different cadence than in its first appearance. Many false starts then occur between this and the next full appearance of the theme in measure 172 (shown in figure 7.3), where it acquires a striking new character. One of the special moments to which I referred earlier appears here on the downbeat of measure 177, which Bruckner has marked "fortississimo."

The preparatory chord to this measure (beats 3 and 4 of measure 176) represents both a dominant seventh chord (spelled as G-sharp, B-sharp, D-sharp, F-sharp) and a German augmented sixth chord (spelled as A-flat, C, E-flat, F-sharp) with the resolution (a tonic cadential six-four chord—G, C, E) belonging to the latter. Bruckner even spells the notes of this preparatory chord ambiguously, with A-flat marked in bass notes and an enharmonic G-sharp in upper voices. This beautifully timed musical deception, while not atypical of orchestral music of the late Romantic period, holds particular significance here since the composer has used this same chord as a dominant-seventh chord in all of the preceding entries of the theme.

What I had missed in Bruckner's music previously was not the foreground detail—which, for me at least, continues to be fairly static and unimpressive—but the deeper background structure. By repeating the theme with tail variations for most of the movement, Bruckner sets the stage for an unexpected sleight of hand that powers the music to the movement's end. Listening chord to chord is unrevealing. Listening to the structure produces quite beautiful revelations.

Figure 7.1
Bruckner Symphony no. 7, movement 2, measures 80–84.

Figure 7.2
Bruckner Symphony no. 7, movement 2, measures 114–118.

Creativity—defined in this book as "the initialization of connections between two or more multifaceted things, ideas, or phenomena hitherto not otherwise considered actively connected"—involves Bruckner's kind of structural deceptions as well as moment-to-moment subtleties. Being able to compose short spans of interesting musical ideas is certainly a creative talent and deserves our attention. However, composers must also learn how to spin their music out slowly and creatively over larger spans of musical time. The algorithmic process I describe in this chapter demonstrates how this might be accomplished.

While structure and form are intimately related—hence their combined presence in this chapter—they are not equivalent. Therefore, I differentiate between these terms, with "structure" referring to hierarchy and tension (stability/instability), and "form" referring to repetition, variation, and contrast of recognizable musical material. The manner in which I discuss and implement these two important contributors to musical creativity makes the explicit differentiation of these terms crucial.

My initial attempts to replicate musical style computationally failed in part, I believe, because of the analytical processes I used. These processes followed the basic techniques of functional tonal harmony (i.e., tonic, supertonic, etc., resulting from

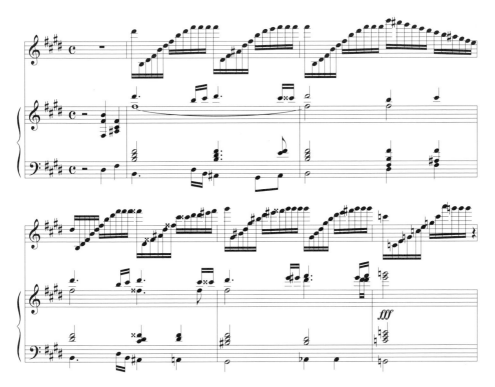

Figure 7.3
Bruckner Symphony no. 7, movement 2, measures 172–177.

the position of chord roots in a key), with chord interval content—figured above sounding bass notes—designating inversions. While meaningful, such reductive processes reveal little about the unique role that harmonies and melodies can play in the works in which they occur. All tonal works have these harmonic functions, and neither I, nor anyone I know, could recognize the composer of a work, no less the work itself, by its functional and inversional designations alone. Nor are we intended to do so; this process is, after all, reductive and thus generalizing.

My initial style-replication programs also failed because most approaches to tonal analyses, including the just-described functional analysis, apply only to tonal music. In contrast, pitch-class-set analysis—set theory—works quite effectively when analyzing many types of nontonal music. However, PC-set analysis reveals very little useful information about tonal music. Further, neither tonal nor PC-set analysis relates to other parameters besides pitch or defines significant hierarchical connections. In short, no single method seems appropriate as the ideal choice for the analysis of all types of music.

In contrast to these tonal and PC-set approaches, I hear the fundamental motion of music—all music—in terms of contextual *stability* and *instability*. I have therefore based my algorithmic analysis and composing software on this paradigm. Analyzing music according to contextual stability and instability is style-independent. Such analysis reveals important relationships regardless of the type of music involved. In contrast to tonal and PC-set analysis, the analysis process I describe here differentiates between groupings that may appear equivalent but *sound* different.

I consider this differentiation of identical music depending on context to be extremely important. In language, for example, we assume that context reveals a great deal about the meanings of words and phrases. The following sentence presents an example of how same-spelled words can have quite different functions and meanings, even when placed in close proximity to one another:

"I saw the saw saw."

The word "saw" appears three times in this sentence, with each appearance having a different meaning and making a different syntactic contribution—only the context distinguishes each word's true function and meaning. We adjust to these subtle shifts in meaning, giving language another powerful way in which to express ourselves. I believe the same is true of music.

Tonal-music leading tones represent a good way to express how my programs differentiate between apparently identical functional motions in music. The leading-tone note in C-major (B), for example, strongly leans toward the tonic note when found in dominant, dominant-seventh, and leading-tone harmonies. However, the leading-tone note appearing as the fifth of the mediant triad does not necessarily lean toward the tonic note, but in fact often moves more naturally elsewhere—toward the submediant note, for example. Thus, the same leading-tone note functions differently depending on its context. This simple notion provides a very important foundation for my approaches to structural analysis.

Arnold Schoenberg considers this notion of context overriding predisposed function definitions when he states that "every tone that is added to a beginning tone makes the meaning of that tone doubtful" (Schoenberg 1984, p. 123). Schoenberg follows this idea with the substance of his point:

If, for instance, G follows after C, the ear may not be sure whether this expresses C major or G major, or even F major or E minor; and the addition of other tones may or may not clarify this problem. In this manner there is produced a state of unrest, of imbalance which grows throughout most of the piece, and is enforced further by similar functions of the rhythm. The

Figure 7.4
Bach Chorale no. 177, measures 1–3.

method by which balance is restored seems to me the real *idea* of the composition. Perhaps the frequent repetitions of themes, groups, and even larger sections might be considered as attempts towards an early balance of the inherent tension.   (Schoenberg 1984, p. 123)

The italics for "idea" are Schoenberg's.

Figure 7.4 provides another musical example of this kind of contextual differentiation. The chords sounding on the first and third beats of full measure 1 are the same. However, the first chord of this measure, occurring on the downbeat of the first full measure, anchoring as it does the basic key of the chorale, has substantially more weight than does the third beat reiteration. This first beat of measure 1 also accompanies the first downbeat of the melody, with the subsequent eighth-note motion giving the upper line its initial impetus. The third-beat chord of this measure, on the other hand, verifies the key and acts as a center post of the melody's leaping motion to the tonic. These two chords, then, while containing exactly the same initial notes, play very different roles.

Of course, one could argue that traditional analyses can indicate different functions for the same chord as well, particularly when such chords appear in different keys. For example, a C–E–G tonic chord in C-major in one location in a work does not have the same function as a C–E–G subdominant in G-major elsewhere in the same composition. One could further argue that pivot chords in modulation provide even more complicated double meanings. However, these are clearly special cases. Offering the kind of differentiations I refer to above requires that an analysis process be able to indicate differences between C–E–G chords within the *same* key. These processes might also equate a C–E–G chord in C-major in one location in a work and a C–E–G in G-major elsewhere in the same composition. In each of these latter cases, the context determines the analysis, not the opposite.

With these thoughts in mind, I have developed an alternative approach to musical analysis called SPEAC, which is based on a combination of musical tension and metric/rhythmic weighting. This weighting combination most clearly parallels the manner in which I hear music, regardless of its style or period of composition, and hence represents the core of the analysis component of my algorithmic composing programs. SPEAC (discussed at length in Cope 1991a and 1996, but not nearly at the level of detail presented here) abstracts selected groupings of notes on the basis of ideas derived from the work of Heinrich Schenker (1935). SPEAC is an acronym for *statement* (S), *preparation* (P), *extension* (E), *antecedent* (A), and *consequent* (C). As we shall see, while traditional tonal functions provide analysis of surface detail, the SPEAC approach provides useful insights into musical structure, even when analyzing music at its surface level.

SPEAC derives its meanings from context as well as from content. The SPEAC identifiers—symbols for the roles they represent—are actually generalities rather than specificities as compared with other analytical representations. SPEAC identifiers function in the following ways:

S = *statement*; stable—a declaration of material or ideas. Statements typically precede or follow any SPEAC function.

P = *preparation*; unstable—an introductory gesture. Preparations precede any SPEAC function, though more typically they occur prior to statements and antecedents.

E = *extension*; stable—a continuation of material or ideas. Extensions usually follow statements but can follow any SPEAC function.

A = *antecedent*; very unstable—requires a consequent function. Antecedents typically precede consequents.

C = *consequent*; very stable—results in consequent gestures. Consequents must be preceded directly or indirectly (with intervening extensions) by antecedents.

SPEAC identifier assignments follow an A–P–E–S–C stability order, with the most unstable identifier to the left and the most stable identifier to the right. Therefore, A and P *require* resolution, while E, S, and C do not.

SPEAC is multidimensional, with no two groupings labeled A, for example, having precisely the same amount of A-ness. Typically, this multidimensionality surfaces when analyzing structural levels of SPEAC, where some identifiers are subsumed under one identifier (discussed in more detail shortly). SPEAC symbols also indicate hierarchy. For example, antecedents and consequents have more weight than statements, preparations, or extensions. One could represent this relationship by using uppercases and lowercases in their designations, as in: s–p–e–A–C. Likewise, Statements have more weight than preparations and extensions, and we could designate this by using uppercase italics, as in *S*–p–e–*A*–C, where the uppercase italics indicate

Figure 7.5
The overtone series from C through sixteen partials.

a higher weight than lowercase representations, but not as high a weight as nonitali-cized uppercase letters. I will not use this case-and-italics notation for SPEAC identi-fiers in the ensuing discussions, however, but instead will rely upon the reader's knowledge of the meanings of these identifiers to interpret this form of hierarchy in their use.

The first step in computing SPEAC stability and instability levels in music involves interval tension. Deriving interval tensions can be complicated because of conflicting interpretations of consonance and dissonance. Since I describe the methods I actually use here, I have opted to leave the discussions of such complications to music theo-rists (see, for example, Hindemith 1937) and simply present what, for me at least, has worked most effectively.

SPEAC analysis of harmonic tension begins—as do many theories of harmonic tension in music—with the overtone series, as shown in figure 7.5 presented from the note C. The overtone series occurs naturally in one way or another in all but sinusoidal (pure) waveforms and acts as the basis for timbre and many other important musical phenomena. The overtone series consists of a fundamental and a theoretically infinite series of overtones figured as incremental multiples of the funda-mental frequency. Since humans generally hear little above 20,000 cycles per second, and the amplitude of the overtones generally diminishes as they extend above the fundamental, I list only fifteen overtones here. (The overtone series is typically num-bered in "partials" beginning with the fundamental as 1—thus, there are sixteen par-tials in figure 7.5.)

Determining interval tension in SPEAC begins by (1) locating an interval's lowest occurrence in the overtone series and (2) determining this interval's root. Step 1 seems simple enough. Step 2, however, requires some explanation. Defining an inter-val's root involves locating the member of the interval closest to, or equaling, an oc-tave projection of the fundamental (Hindemith 1937). For instance, the perfect fifth's root is its lower note, since the lowest fifth appearing in the overtone series has as its lower note an octave doubling of the fundamental (partial 2). The interval of a fourth (the inversion of the fifth) has its upper note as root, because this note is an octave doubling of the fundamental (partial 4). Without figuring each interval separately, the roots of all simple intervals can be easily remembered as the lower note of all odd-numbered intervals (thirds, fifths, and sevenths) and as the upper note of all even-numbered intervals (seconds, fourths, and sixths). Roots of compound intervals match the roots of their corresponding intervals within the octave. For example, the root of a ninth is its top note, since it reduces to a second.

Standard interval derivations from the overtone series appear along with their root designations in figure 7.6. Lower-occurring and lower-rooted intervals produce the least tension, and upper-occurring and upper-rooted intervals produce the most tension. From this list, then, minor seconds have the highest tension because they occur highest in the series (16/15) and have upper roots. Major sevenths have slightly less tension because of their lower roots, but nonetheless occur very high in the series (15/8). Major sixths have less tension than sevenths because they occur lower in the series (5/3), but have more tension than major or minor thirds because these thirds occur lower in the series (5/4 and 6/5) and have lower roots. The augmented fourth, even though it has low placement in the series (7/5), does not have a clear root, and thus

int	ratio	root
M7	(15/8)	lower
m7	(16/9)	lower
M6	(5/3)	upper
m6	(8/5)	upper
P5	(3/2)	lower
A4	(7/5)	unclear
P4	(4/3)	upper
M3	(5/4)	lower
m3	(6/5)	lower
M2	(9/8)	upper
m2	(16/15)	upper

Figure 7.6
Interval derivations from the overtone series along with root designations.

its tension is ambiguous. The perfect fifth has the least tension due to its low place-ment (3/2) and lower root. (The perfect octave—not shown—ultimately has the least tension, but here it is considered doubling rather than a discrete interval.)

SPEAC analysis requires grouping music into segments defined by each note's on-set, and then calculating new vertical tension separately for each segment. The seg-ment with the least tension determines the overall tension of the grouping, since the program assumes that the higher-tension segments contain nonharmonic tones that resolve. In figure 7.4, for example, beat 1 of full measure 1 divides into two groupings (onbeat and offbeat), with the onbeat grouping used for SPEAC analysis because it contains the least tension.

While these approaches to defining roots, tensions, and groupings seem logical in principle, methods of converting these tensions and roots into numerical values for contextual comparison is not so obvious. To solve this problem, I use a series of set-tings as shown in figure 7.7, based on the formula

$$f_{(x)} = y + (\cos((-1 * z) + x/z))/2$$

where x is the pitch-class interval, y represents the y coordinate, and z is a constant. This formula roughly accounts for the primary intervals (seconds, thirds, and fourths). I use "roughly" here to mean that I have intuitively adjusted the formulaic values by ear over time. Secondary intervals (sixths and sevenths as inversions of thirds and seconds, respectively) then approximately mirror the primary intervals, with the fifth treated uniquely because it has very little tension. Intervals greater than an octave can have slightly less (.02) tension than their related less-than-octave-separated equivalents because of their octave separation. These settings have produced, for me at least, the best analyses and, ultimately, the best compositions. The SPEAC program on my Web site stores all of these settings in variables that users can alter at any time.

Tensions of chords are then calculated by adding the tension weights of the inter-vals projected from the bass note only. Figure 7.8 provides simple examples of this process. The major triad has three positions, each—as generally acknowledged—increasing in tension. Figuring interval weights from the bass note by using the chart in figure 7.8 produces .3 (M3 at .2 + P5 at .1), .5 (m3 at .225 + m6 at .275), and .8 (P4 at .55 + M6 at .25), respectively. These tensions reasonably fit standard expec-tations, with the second-inversion chord the most unstable, and the first-inversion chord more stable than the second-inversion chord but less stable than the root posi-tion chord. Likewise, the minor triad and its inversions produce .325 (m3 at .225 + P5 at .1), .45 (M3 at .2 + M6 at .25), and .825 (P4 at .55 + m6 at .275), re-spectively, again effectively modeling expectations.

(a)

interval	tension
major seventh	.9
minor seventh	.7
major sixth	.25
minor sixth	.275
perfect fifth	.1
augmented fourth	.65
perfect fourth	.55
major third	.2
minor third	.225
major second	.8
minor second	1.0
unison	0.0

(b)

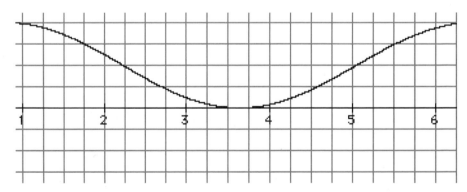

Figure 7.7
Ordered interval tension weightings (a) based on the formula $f_{(x)} = y + (\cos((-1 * z) + x/z))/2$, where $y = 0.5$ and $z = 0.9$; and a simple graph (b) with the x-axis representing pitch-class intervals and the y-axis set to 0 at the left–right line and set to 1.0 at the highest points of the curved graph.

Figure 7.8
Chords for tension analysis.

Figure 7.9
Four other tonal chords for tension analysis.

Figure 7.10
Four less common but still often-used tonal chord types for tension analysis.

Figure 7.9 shows four other familiar chords for tension analysis. These chords display increasing levels of tension with the augmented triad at .475 (M3 at .2 + m6 at .275), the diminished triad at .875 (m3 at .225 + A4 at .65), the dominant-seventh chord at 1.0 (M3 at .2 + P5 at .1 + m7 at .7), and the diminished-seventh chord at 1.125 (m3 at .225 + A4 at .65 + M6 at .25). These findings may not agree with some interpretations, but they follow my own expectations fairly closely.

Figure 7.10 shows four somewhat less common chord types. These four chords produce tensions of 1.2 (M3 at .2 + P5 at .1 + M7 at .9), 1.025 (m3 at .225 + P5 at .1 + m7 at .7), .55 (M3 at .2 + P5 at .1 + M6 at .25), and 2.0 (M3 at .2 + P5 at .1 + M7 at .9 + M2 at .8). The low tension score of the third chord in this series (sometimes referred to as an added-sixth chord) may indicate why it often replaces a triad in final cadences of some types of popular music—its tension remains relatively low even with four chord members present. Note that the strongest interval present (a perfect fifth) also suggests C as root—the pitch most of us hear in this role—instead of A when calculated as the lowest note of stacked thirds (following standard tertian harmonic analysis).

Figure 7.11 shows four chords based on projections of intervals other than thirds. These four chords show how tensions increase with more complex music. The resulting chord tensions add to 1.0 (M2 at .8 + M3 at .2), 1.225 (m2 at 1.0 + m3 at .225), 1.8 (m2 at 1.0 + M2 at .8), and 1.475 (P4 at .55 + m7 at .7 + m3 at .225), indicating

Figure 7.11
Four chords based on projections of intervals other than the third.

chord 3 as the most unstable and the first chord as the most stable (to which hearing will attest).

Each of the examples shown thus far appears without context. I argue that such context very much influences how we hear tension. Metric placement and duration, both elements of rhythm, represent two of the principal factors of musical context. To calculate the metric placement of musical rhythm, I employ the simple mathematical formula

$$t = (b * .1)/v$$

where t equals tension weight, b refers to beat number, and v represents a metric beat-number variable. This latter variable accounts for the changes in weighting from, say, beat 2 to beat 3 of 4/4 meter, where beat 3 has more weight than beat 2, and so on. No simple mathematics can compute the complex metric relationships of beats in all meters, and hence I use lookup tables for this purpose. While this weighting formula may seem surprisingly simple, I have experimented over the years with various different tension-weighting processes, yet I have always returned to the formula presented here.

Root motion between neighboring groupings represents another important contextual factor in measuring tension. Since vertical interval tensions can serve equally well for horizontal root motion, I use them in calculating additional weights based on the root motion from a preceding grouping. Thus, a grouping approached by a fifth from a preceding grouping receives an additional .1 weight, while this same grouping approached by a minor second from a preceding grouping receives an additional .9 weight. For example, the tension of strong dominant-tonic motion in a tonal cadence will be little affected by this root-motion weighting process, while a less strong root motion of a third—as in a tonic-to-mediant progression—will have more tension, and will receive a greater additional tension weighting as a result.

Figuring durational weightings is complicated because of my belief that consonant groupings are made more consonant by extending duration, and dissonant groupings are made more dissonant. To account for this, I use a combination of percentages derived from adding a grouping's duration multiplied by .1 to the same grouping's tension multiplied by .1. Thus, a quarter-note major triad, for example, receives an

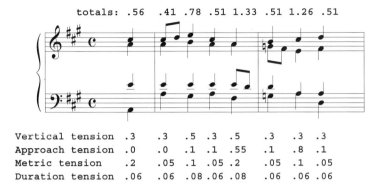

Figure 7.12
Tension weightings based on a combination of interval, root motion, metric placement, and duration weights.

additional durational weight of .025 (1/4 × .1) added to .03 (.3 × .1), or .055, while an eighth-note dominant-seventh chord receives a durational weight of .0125 (1/8 × .1) added to .1 (1.0 × .1), or .1125. This durational weighting is then added to a grouping's accumulated tension weighting. This relatively simple additive process ensures that duration amplifies tension—the longer the duration, the more (or less, in the case of a grouping of little tension) tension a grouping exerts.

As a result of metric and durational tension analysis, a third-beat half note in 4/4 meter receives .35 additional weighting (.3 for metric placement and .05 for half-note duration). Because eighth notes and quarter notes are not expressions of actual timings, only of relative duration, assigning these weightings abstractly in this manner accurately represents this relativity, so long as the tempo remains the same for all of the groupings measured.

Figure 7.12 provides an example of tension weightings based on a combination of interval content, root motion, metric placement, and duration weights. Some of these tension weightings (shown above these chords) might appear counterintuitive. However, in terms of context they make sense. The first and third chords of full measure 1, for example, while initially exactly the same, do not have the same tension because they occur on different metric beats, and thus play different roles. The most dissonant—and hence unstable—chord of the phrase has the highest tension (the fifth chord). The pickup to, and first chord of, measure 1—both A-major tonic triads—have different tensions that also are due to their metric positionings. On the other hand, the first chord of full measure 2 ties for the second-to-least tension, although it contains a chromatic alteration (not measured in this version of tension weighting) and therefore should have a higher weighting.

Figure 7.13
Figure 7.12 with the appropriate SPEAC identifiers in place.

Thus, this weighting process, dependent as it is on intervals, meter, and duration, clearly does not account for all of the factors involved with tension. However, SPEAC weighting processes can be extended to include any quantifiable variable associated with music, and thus may represent any user-defined parameter of sound. Unfortunately, the more exacting the process, the more likely that it will be limited to a particular style of music (as with the chromaticism in the tonal music of figure 7.12, where, if the process I have described were automatically to account for such chromaticism, it might have negative effects in atonal music).

There are, obviously, many other factors which play roles in the tensions we hear in music. Timbres, dynamics, registers, acoustics, and so on can affect and even override the weights that SPEAC generates in its analysis. However, such factors are often situational to the degree that makes figuring such tensions impossible from a mathematical point of view. Therefore, while I admit that the approach here—like any such approach—has flaws, it nonetheless provides enough substantive information to be useful. Humans register these tensions intuitively. Computers, however, do not have ears and cannot, at least not yet, intuitively use sensory input to gauge tension. Thus, this kind of tension analysis represents a worthwhile method of computationally measuring stability and instability.

To assign SPEAC identifiers, then, requires the setting of the highest tensions of a group of weightings to antecedents, and the lowest tensions to consequents, with statements then closest to consequents, preparations closest to antecedents, and extensions falling between these extremes. Figure 7.13 shows the same Bach chorale phrase as figure 7.12, but with the appropriate SPEAC identifiers in place.

Creating structural-level SPEAC representations requires averaging a phrase's total weight, then comparing this average against the averages of all other phrase weights in a work. Without this averaging, phrases with more groupings would obviously outweigh phrases with fewer groupings, a not necessarily correct conclusion.

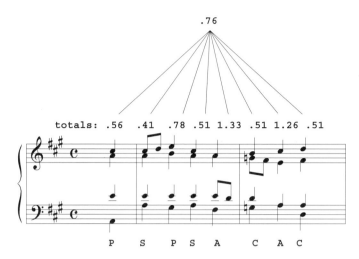

Figure 7.14
Figure 7.13 with the appropriate SPEAC identifiers and top-level SPEAC identifier in place.

Figure 7.14 provides an example of this process as applied to a single phrase. Note that the top level in figure 7.14 contains only a number, since SPEAC identifiers cannot be determined until they have been compared with all other same-level SPEAC identifiers.

SPEAC identifiers can, and often do, change between hierarchical levels. For example, the progression S–A–C (statement, antecedent, consequent) at a foreground level may actually become a P (preparation) at a middleground level, by virtue of its proximity to phrases that give it further contextual meaning. This ability of music to function in a certain way at one level, and in a completely different way in a higher level, is extremely important in understanding the context-sensitive nature of SPEAC. Since the contexts that SPEAC uses grow broader and broader as one proceeds upward in the hierarchy, foreground analysis can be contrasted or even contradicted many times over. Such processes seem natural to my way of hearing and understanding music.

Continuing the process of combining SPEAC phrase analyses of sections into single identifiers, and so on, ultimately leads to a single identifier that represents an entire work. This single identifier has, in itself, little value (as does the ultimate background of Schenker analysis [Schenker 1935]), but instead exemplifies the *process* (which *is* important) that led to its creation.

As I mentioned previously, SPEAC analysis is not limited to pitch and rhythm, but may be applied to any parameter of music. For example, even a simple musical

Figure 7.15
A simple example of how SPEAC analyses of pitch and rhythm complement each other to strengthen a passage in a Bruckner symphony (see also figure 7.1).

analysis may include determinations of SPEAC identifiers for timbre, harmony, melody, dynamics, spacing, texture, and so on. In fact, balancing these various analyses with each other can often provide a truer picture of the music's direction than will an analysis of any one of these parameters alone. Furthermore, analyses that compete with each other—as opposed to agreeing with each other—can reveal important contradictions in music that may otherwise go unnoticed. For example, convincing music often seems to have more agreement than disagreement in these kinds of comparisons, and such revelations may be one of the ways in which we can verify the elusive-to-define *effectiveness* of certain music. The fact that SPEAC analysis can apply to any parameter of music invites such comparisons.

Figure 7.15 presents a simple example of how SPEAC analyses of pitch and rhythm may complement one another to strengthen a passage in a Bruckner symphony (the one discussed at the beginning of this chapter). This type of comparative analysis is different from passages in which—as previously explained—pitch and rhythm are figured together to create a single SPEAC analysis.

The agreement of various SPEAC-analyzed parameters of a work of music can contribute to a sense of unity and deep organization. This should not necessarily be seen as denigrating the counterpoint established by analyses that disagree. In fact, such conflicts, if resolved appropriately, can genuinely contribute to the effectiveness of a musical passage. Proportions between various agreeing and conflicting SPEAC analyses in a work can also be compared with SPEAC analyses of other works. Such comparisons may ultimately indicate why certain works of music succeed and others do not. However, I will leave the exampling of this notion for another occasion, since comparing whole-work analyses requires whole-work reproduction, and would place this chapter's discussion completely out of balance with the rest of this book. I simply ask readers to imagine the possibilities, and to investigate the realities on their own.

As mentioned earlier, I do not believe that SPEAC should replace other types of analysis. Rather, I suggest that SPEAC can enhance—and be used in conjunction with—other types of analysis, since SPEAC differentiates between otherwise identical functions, and reveals possibly important structural strengths and weaknesses in music.

Structural Composition

The just-described SPEAC analysis process provides a basic skeletal framework for new compositions. Each hierarchical level of identifiers helps ensure that new music develops and releases tension in ways similar to one of the models in the database.

SPEAC plays two important roles in my machine-composing processes. First, as discussed in chapter 4, the selection of lexicons for following groupings during recombination is strictly determined by local voice-leading and texture constraints. SPEAC then determines which of the correct available groupings in a chosen lexicon best fits a current work's hierarchy. Since the recombinance process depends on choices from lexicons having identical initiating pitches, and some of these choices have different *following* groupings, SPEAC chooses the best possible grouping whose following groupings in turn *best* meet the current specification for appropriate tension. Second, it is rarely possible to create new works following exactly the analyzed SPEAC hierarchies of music in a database. The voice-leading constraints of recombinance simply will not allow it. In other words, a P–S–E analyzed phrase may not yield any but the original grouping possibilities during recombination. Thus, it is often necessary to create hybrid hierarchies in which most of the fundamental structure of a new work is inherited from an analyzed work in the database, but some of which must be expanded or reduced by logically generating SPEAC identifiers. Interestingly, these hybrid structures are more *creative* than simple duplications of existing structures.

Assuming that my first point above—making a best choice among various correct options—is fairly obvious, I will here concentrate on the process of SPEAC expansion and reduction techniques. Hierarchical expansion and reduction require more rules than the simple succession constraints previously presented. I use the following basic expansions as guide:

S ((P S)(A C)(S E))

P ((P E)(E E)(A C))

E ((S E)(E E))

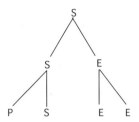

Figure 7.16
A simple SPEAC hierarchy.

A ((A E)(P A)(P A E)(S E A))

C ((C E)(P C)).

Each of the parenthetical lists following the SPEAC identifiers indicates equivalency. For example, S can become (P S) according to the above chart, and vice versa. In each case, I have kept the acceptable equivalents to two or three identifiers, knowing that should more be required, either or both members of the chosen group can then be expanded further, using this same process. Should a (P S) require, say, four identifiers, then the P could become (P E) and S could expand to (A C), with the complete list then appearing as (P E A C) at the next lower level. In contrast, should a (P E A C) need to be reduced to two identifiers, the (P E) could become (P) and the (A C) be reduced to (S), creating a logical (P S) reduction of (P E A C).

Thus, the simple SPEAC hierarchy in figure 7.16 can be seen as a horizontal and vertical composite of both succession and expansion rules. Figure 7.17 provides a more elaborate example of the above-described process. The new hierarchy in figure 7.17b represents an expansion of figure 7.17a, with many of the subscript suffixes now representing this expansion. The subscript with each identifier indicates (1) its level in the hierarchy and (2) its increment in that level. Hence, in the final E identifier at the bottom right of this figure, the "3-2" signifies a third level (3) E in its second (2) iteration.

Because of the flexibility of SPEAC identifier ordering, it is fairly easy to replace SPEAC identifiers with other logical SPEAC identifiers, letting these new choices continue the progression forward from that point. For example, following the succession order given earlier in this chapter, the progression E–A could become A–F, since either motion is acceptable. The SPEAC hierarchy in figure 7.18 provides an example of this process, with new choices circled and original choices indicated to the upper left of each circle. This process can produce many new hierarchies, each originating from a single SPEAC seed identifier.

(a)

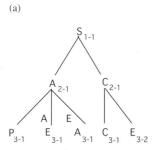

(b)

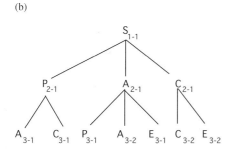

Figure 7.17
SPEAC expansion of identifiers at lower levels (b) when required for alternative choices (a).

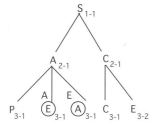

Figure 7.18
SPEAC hierarchical tree with the inductive choices circled and the original choices next to each circle.

I remind readers again that these expansion-reduction processes typically enhance extant analyses of music in a database. The resulting hybrid structures result from the program's inability to make recombinant choices other than the original choice. In effect, hybrid choices offer *creative* alternatives for composing.

Figure 7.19 provides an example of how SPEAC controls structure during the compositional process. The process begins by fleshing out SPEAC identifiers into successively lower levels. Before this fleshing out—by expansion or reduction according to the hybrid processes just described—reaches the lowest level, however, context-sensitive music replaces the SPEAC representations, and the music between

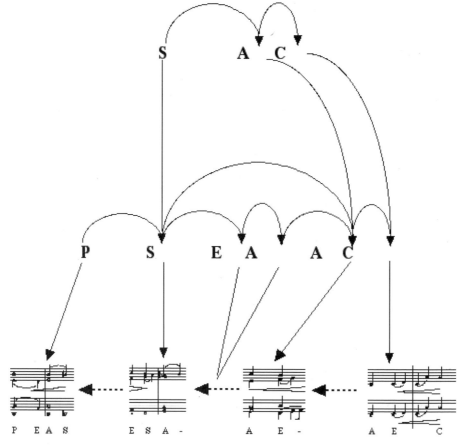

Figure 7.19
An example of how the SPEAC system can be used during the compositional process.

these representations is composed following whatever rules govern the local musical environment (voice leading, harmonic succession, and so on), with the bridges between the ending of one section and the beginning of another section left relatively free.

Using a nonlinear SPEAC approach does not guarantee that when it is completely fleshed out, the resultant music will sound seamless. One cannot, for example, expect that set-in-place antecedents or statements will necessarily have correct voice-leading and logical SPEAC syntax possibilities when replaced with actual music. Luckily, unlike humans, computers can compute backward as easily as they can compute forward. Since, in most musical styles, beginnings of phrases do not have the same severity of constraints that ends of phrases do, and since most of the initially set-in-place groupings of music occur at or near phrase endings, my programs often compose backward instead of forward.

Interestingly, even given my comment above about the difficulty humans have in composing backward, the just-described composing process does not differ that significantly from those used by humans. For example, most tonal composers end their phrases with one of four cadences (authentic [V–I], half [V], deceptive [V–vi], or plagal [IV–I]). This means that these composers have one of these cadences in mind as a goal when they begin to compose the melodies and harmonies of each phrase. Since tonal phrases typically have an established number of measures, these composers know, for the most part, exactly where cadences will occur. Each new choice these composers make as they compose forward is governed by both the voice-leading connections between their new choices and the inevitable approaching cadence. Some part of their creative processes must take into account the effect their current choices will have on the ever-decreasing-in-number intervening possibilities for new choices. The awareness of the impending cadence forces these composers—at least subconsciously—to make selections that will ensure correct approaches to the cadence (e.g., to compose backward). This reverse composing produces ongoing negotiations between chord-to-chord and ultimate-goal points of view.

There are many advantages to composing backward. First, putting the critical formally important SPEAC groupings into place first ensures that the resulting composition will have musical direction, and will not just wander. The proof of this comes from the fact that while most Experiments in Musical Intelligence compositions have stylistic resemblance to the works upon which they are modeled, they also have their own formal integrity. Many who listen to this music comment on this feature as often as they comment on the more obvious style similarities. Works *end* rather than just *stop*. The placement of important SPEAC identifiers into a hierarchy before most of the actual music appears also ensures that phrase balance, section lengths,

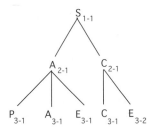

Figure 7.20
A simple SPEAC hierarchy beginning with a single SPEAC identifier exploding its way downward through logical sequences of SPEAC identifiers at successively lower levels.

repetition and variation, and so on all occur with sensitivity to the overall shape of a work rather than simply when convenient. Finally, and most important, these set-in-place SPEAC identifiers provide goals for composition and ensure that points of arrival occur in places similar to those that occur in the works in the database, with new music therefore *arriving* at strategic points rather than just meandering there.

Figure 7.20 shows a SPEAC hierarchy inherited from a work in a database. This hierarchy begins with a single SPEAC identifier and expands downward through logical sequences of SPEAC identifiers at successively lower levels. Each identifier is followed by another logical identifier that extends it in some way, resolves it appropriately to a new identifier, or transitions to a new identifier.

To complete hybrid SPEAC hierarchies, SPEAC identifiers are compositionally distributed in a hierarchy using three important strategies. First, the basic protocol of which identifier best precedes or follows another, as both extension and expansion, offers a logical foundation (as previously explained). Thus, A precedes C and E follows S, and so on. Second, the slow acquisition of music into the hierarchy—rather than simply waiting until the lowest level for conversion—means that some lower-level SPEAC identifiers result from the analysis of actual recombinant music. Third, as I will discuss shortly, the musical form—repetitions, variations, contrasts of material—not only influences the musical structure but also causes SPEAC identifiers to repeat, vary, and contrast at appropriate higher levels. These three influences play somewhat equal roles in creating hybrid SPEAC hierarchies.

One of the most important impacts that SPEAC analysis has on computer composition—and ultimately on computational creativity—involves the order in which groupings are selected. Recombinance, as I have described it thus far, has taken an incremental approach in which each new choice directly follows previous choices. SPEAC's nonlinear approach in which significant antecedent and statement groupings of a new work are selected first, and the remaining groupings follow in SPEAC priority order means that a new work may appear in many places at once rather than beginning at the beginning and ending at the end. This process more closely resembles how I, and many composers I know, create large-scale works: by envisioning a form and then filling in the details.

Form

As mentioned earlier in this chapter, though they are related, structure and form are not equivalent. Although these two types of musical processes intersect in many ways—particularly in simple music—they do not necessarily match. As a simple example, imagine the form ABA. The structure of such a form might be SAC (statement, antecedent, consequent), where the roles of the two very similar A sections would be significantly different, rather than very nearly the same (as they are in terms of form). This kind of differentiation represents an extremely important reason for separating the two types of analyses and then comparing their respective contributions to an overall work.

Basically, form involves thematic repetition and variation—or unity and variety, as some may prefer. This means that once it has created an idea, a computer composing program must determine when to repeat it, vary it, or contrast it with other ideas. Having a logical approach to voice leading, tension, structure, and so on, while important, cannot substitute for compelling musical ideas and how they play out over time. Creating musical form in my programs begins with the analysis of music in a database. In *The Algorithmic Composer* (Cope 2000), I describe a number of methods for analyzing and then re-creating logical approaches to repetition and variation. I will briefly recount these methods here, and follow this recounting with the method I have chosen to model this aspect of musical creativity.

The Alice program (Cope 2000) utilizes a multifaceted approach to the structural analysis of music in its database. Initially Alice seeks out major thematic areas, a technique that can successfully model classical music forms. If that process fails, the program analyzes for contrast, fluctuations in density, and/or changes in composite rhythm. If none of these successfully reveals the music's form, Alice attempts to map cadences. Finally, if all else fails, Alice uses an approximation process—in other words, the program takes its best guess. Each of these processes deserves further explanation.

In many musical styles, the primary formal sections follow the often contrasting melodic ideas that initiate them. I use a variation of standard pattern matchers to differentiate these melodic contrasts. Since this pattern matcher seeks *differences* between patterns rather than similarities, new sections are detected when the program encounters fewer rather than more matches between previous and newly found patterns.

If this pattern-matching process fails, as it often does with contemporary music, I use density as a principal factor in determining when sections end and new sections begin. This texture-comparison process involves finding the density of a passage by breaking it into contiguous groupings the size of the passage's shortest durational element. Hence, a phrase with sixteenth notes as its shortest member(s) will be broken into continuous sixteenth-note-length groups. The program then divides the total of all of the textures of the groupings by the number of groupings to obtain the phrase's average density. Thus, a seven-group, seven-second passage of 4, 3, 4, 2, 4, 3, 4 one-second-per-grouping textures gives an overall density of 3.43. Comparing densities over time can then reveal the points at which new sections begin.

Composite rhythm can also help distinguish sections from each other. Alice maps the entrance time of each note in a work and then attempts to separate regions of contrasting timings. Thus, a section consisting primarily of sixteenth-note entrances will likely be differentiated from a section of primarily eighth-note entrances, and so on. Changes of tempo are figured into the process in order to map these timings correctly.

While thematic separation, density, and composite rhythm provide excellent potential for discovering contrast—and hence sectional boundaries—they are not often sufficient to distinguish all of the various elements of form. This insufficiency can be especially noticeable when analyzing works with transitions between sections rather than abrupt contrasts. To discover sectional boundaries in works where structure evolves transitionally rather than abruptly, texture and other formal analyses must be combined with cadence mapping to produce a more accurate formal plan. Such mapping often indicates where the ideas of one section end and a new section begins.

Locating cadences in music, however, can pose many problems. I discuss these problems and their potential solutions in detail in *The Algorithmic Composer* (Cope 2000), especially in regard to that book's figures 7.26a and 7.26b. I won't repeat that material here. However, clearly delineating cadence points in music of any style is critical for accurately determining both structure and form, and I invite readers to evaluate the figures and associated text in *The Algorithmic Composer* (Cope 2000) to understand these problems more fully. Fortunately, the computer model of musical creativity I discuss in chapters 9 through 11 avoids these problems by virtue of its input processes (see particularly chapter 10 for more information on this topic).

When all else fails, rather than creating an arbitrary form, my programs rely on proportions found in other parameters of a work being analyzed to determine a logical overall form for a new work. For example, the contours of a notable stylistic signature might serve as a structural model, providing a basic formal contour. A simple signature containing a leap upward resolved by downward stepwise motion might, for example, produce a two-section work in which the first section consists primarily of leaps and the second section mostly of stepwise motions. The hope is, of course, that while the ear may not directly recognize such hierarchical imitation, the resulting music will sound logical rather than haphazard.

Once they have been analyzed for type and location, formal instances of repetition, variation, and contrast must be transferred in like numbers to computer-created output. Repetition—at least exact repetition—and contrast require little additional code. Variation, on the other hand, involves transformational recombinance, as described in chapter 4. I refer readers particularly to *Experiments in Musical Intelligence* (Cope 1996, pp. 175–177) and *The Algorithmic Composer* (Cope 2000, p. 87) for more information on how variations of material can result from transformational recombinance.

While they are intimately related to repetition, variation, and contrast, instances of expectation, fulfillment, and deception often occur in ways that do not necessarily follow their thematic counterparts. Expectation, fulfillment, and deception represent fundamental principles upon which all music is based (Meyer 1989). Expectation of when and whether themes, motives, harmonies, timbres, keys, and so on will return, and how they return if they do return, represents a nexus of musical form. Human composers have intuitively and explicitly engaged these concepts since the first music was formed. It would be impossible for a computer program to *creatively* compose without incorporating similar concepts.

The music in figures 7.1–7.3 provides excellent examples of expectation, fulfillment, and deception, with figure 7.2 fulfilling the expectation of figure 7.1, and figure 7.3's German augmented sixth chord masquerading as a dominant-seventh chord, effectively deceiving listeners. Many such lower-level expectations, fulfillments, and deceptions occur naturally in data-dependent composition simply because the expectation, fulfillment, and deceptions of the music in the database transfer—through recombinance and the previously discussed repetition and variation—to newly created music. This transfer is especially true of harmonic expectation, fulfillment, and deception, a natural consequence of the voice-leading processes in recombinance. Thus, deceptive cadences, rarely used resolutions, and unexpected modulations occur in new music much as they did in their counterparts in the database. Melodic and

Figure 7.21
A machine-composed work for organ in the style of Messiaen.

Figure 7.21
(continued)

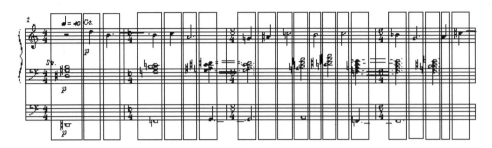

Figure 7.22
A simple new-note-equals-new-grouping process.

structural expectation, fulfillment, and deceptions, however, require the use of processes such as SPEAC to achieve the same logic in output music.

Configuring the expectation, fulfillment, and deception of themes or progressions
follows the results of the just-described analytical processes in relation to repetition
and variation of works in the database. At lower hierarchical levels, expectation, fulfillment, and deception can take many forms for which neither recombinance nor
SPEAC can adequately account. For example, sequence and other forms of motivic
repetition and variation, while appearing in the foreground of most music, often have
structural implications, at least at the middleground level. The SPEAC analysis process bundles sequence—and similar types of groupings—together in ever longer collections of motives at ever higher levels in the hierarchy. These groupings are then
connected to similar groupings elsewhere in a composition through the formal analytic process.

Figure 7.21 shows a machine-composed work for organ in the style of Olivier Messiaen, an example of music created using SPEAC with particular emphasis on expectation, fulfillment, and deception. This music follows an *isomelos* (repeated pitch
series) consistent with Messiaen's approach to composition. In this instance, the isomelos occurs in the chords of the left hand and pedal. While phrasing is not clear in
this work, the isomelos occurs seven times, each time beginning with a G-sharp-
minor chord in second inversion (beginning in measures 1, 6, 11, 17, 22, 27, and
32). With slight variations, each phrase consists of ten chords, not including the
right-hand melody. Other isolated processes (such as isorhythm, etc.) exist here as
well, and contribute to SPEAC generation and analysis. I will, however, leave it to
the reader to decipher these aspects of this piece.

The groupings of this Messiaen-style work follow a simple new-note-equals-new-
grouping process, as shown in figure 7.22, for the first line of music in figure 7.21.
This process means that the actual numbers of groupings vary per isomelos, as do

(a)

c

(b)

p p a c s a c

(c)

(a e c s s s e c e e s s p s e e p p p p p p a e e e s s s p)

(s c p p e s c p e p c c e e p a p p s a c s a)

(c e a e s e s s e s s e e e e s p a p p c e c e s)

(a p p e p p e s e a p e s p a p p s a c s s)

(c e c c p c s e p p e e p p e a a c c s c)

(s s e e p e p p e p s a p s p e a c c)

(p s p p e s p p a p p p e e e e a s p s)

Figure 7.23
SPEAC analysis for the computer-created Messiaen by grouping, phrase, and work (bottom to top).

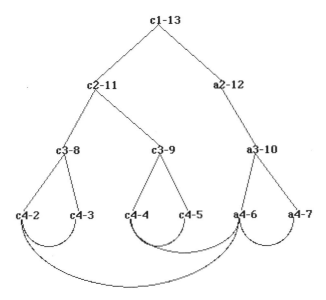

Figure 7.24
Hierarchical SPEAC with the inclusion of curved lines to show material relationships.

the resultant SPEAC contexts. Figure 7.23 shows the hierarchical SPEAC assignments for this piece. Each of the seven phrases appears on a separate line (first phrase at the top, last phrase at the bottom) in figure 7.23c. Directly above these phrases (figure 7.23b), the individual SPEAC identifiers represent each of the seven phrases in order. The single identifier at the top (figure 7.23a) represents the entire work.

As with any systematic analysis, the more abstracted the analysis is from the music, the less meaning this analysis has for listeners. However, proving that these identifiers have relevance requires only that one listen to the music while following the seven-phrase SPEAC listings in figure 7.23c. The SPEAC identifiers given to each of the groupings reveal the close link between identifier and tension. Hearing higher orders of SPEAC may require several careful listenings.

The SPEAC program on my Web site provides a software version of the principles discussed in this chapter. The program loads music from MIDI and Lisp files (text files in event format, as described in appendix B) and analyzes this music following the processes described here. Users must initially fine-tune their own versions of the weightings discussed in relation to figure 7.7, in order for the program to appropriately analyze the music in the database.

Figure 7.24 shows how visual output appears when the platform-dependent version of the SPEAC program completes its analysis of a work. Straight lines separate SPEAC levels in the structural hierarchy, while curved lines describe how formal ideas repeat, contrast, and vary. Double-clicking any convergence of lines or combination of letters and numbers in this graphic—structural focal points (SPEAC nodes)—produces a small window that explains, in terms of tension and contextual weighting, the logic behind its selection. This window includes identifiers to which the current identifier contributes as well as identifiers on which it relies. In other words, the window describes SPEAC influence both upward and downward in the hierarchy. These windows within windows provide, I hope, a useful perspective on the hierarchy of the piece being analyzed. Thus, while one can quickly follow the hierarchy in a simple graphic representation, one can also—by double-clicking— follow the details of the process that created the current analysis. This software version of SPEAC does not compose; it only analyzes. However, the composing program presented in chapters 9 through 11 integrates SPEAC into its processes.

8 Influence

Principle: Creativity develops within enfolding and influencing contexts, and not in isolation.

Databases

I recently heard a friend of mine relate the sometimes vague history of flea circuses. Most flea circuses, he elaborated, are virtual. High-wire acts, diving-board gymnastics, juggling, and so on, are all perpetrated by electronic fakery, taking advantage of the flea's near invisibility and our imaginations. Toggled diving boards accompanied by tiny splashes of water, miniature bicycles with spinning wheels, and so on, all controlled by mechanical and magnetic devices, give the impression of being animated by actual fleas. This was not always the case, my friend continued. At one time, flea circuses used real fleas for their acts. In one particular case, for example, a flea circus proprietor glued a flea upside down to a small board—they used fleas larger than today's varieties—and then, while the flea rapidly gyrated its legs, trying vainly to escape, placed a small ball on its feet that then appeared to spin magically in the air—as if the flea intended the effect.

When my friend explained the last part of this story, almost everyone listening was appalled at the lack of compassion involved in this so-called circus. My friend then pointed out the irony in all of this: most of us have routinely, at one time or another, annihilated hundreds, if not thousands, of fleas by using some form of pesticide. I, myself, have sworn many times that there is no lower or more disgusting form of life on the planet than fleas. Yet I, too, was shocked at this story.

It would seem that context is everything. Apparently we can be led into all manner of contradictions in which what we thought we believed no longer seems to apply. While none of the models I present in this chapter will thus lead you astray, they will, I hope, prove once again that context is—if not everything—certainly one thing that creativity cannot do without. Lacking context, humans and computer programs alike produce experimental output at best, output that seems to originate in a vacuum. While data-dependent programs have a certain amount of innate context by virtue of their human-created databases, these programs still require the reinforcement and conflict necessary for a truly creative process—defined here as "the initialization of connections between two or more multifaceted things, ideas, or phenomena hitherto not otherwise considered actively connected." The use of allusions adds context to recombinant processes, but does not provide the unpredictability that humans invest in their work, since human creativity incorporates everything we see, hear, and feel, not just the music we listen to—the database equivalent.

In this chapter I describe a number of projects which provide various kinds of data I have used for influencing—rather than actively participating in—the output of my music-composing algorithms. These data—both musical and nonmusical—function very differently than data designed for recombinance. Where the latter actually contribute to the foreground of new music, this influence subtly affects the rules, structure, or references of program output.

Databases for music composition programs need not contain music. For example, I began the Pleiades project in 1982 as an attempt to integrate three obsessions of mine—music, astronomy, and artificial intelligence. While the Pleiades project was obviously broad and far-ranging, its goal was relatively simple: the construction of a large-scale radio telescope also capable of serving as a large-scale musical instrument. The telescope was designed to receive electromagnetic radio waves from the sky and sonify these waves into music by way of a large spheroid reflector similar to the one used with the Arecibo radio telescope in Puerto Rico.

As originally designed, the Pleiades instrument was to house a high-powered mainframe computer programmed with powerful artificial intelligence algorithms. The main principle of Pleiades—that the human ear can detect patterns that other means cannot detect—guided me from inception to the completion of a full set of architectural plans. While possibly sounding eccentric, Pleiades counted among its planners professional radio astronomers, computer scientists, architects, acousticians, and several legal consultants. A number of the project's planners also represented SETI (the Search for Extraterrestrial Intelligence), and thus some of the patterns sought were signs of the presence of intelligent off-world life-forms. Unfortunately, this project did not come to fruition because of high construction costs. At the same time, however, I was able to complete (in 1984) a musical work based on radio waves from the sky, titled *Pleiades*.

Figure 8.1 provides a simple cross-sectional view of the planned Pleiades instrument, with the wavy line representing a cup-shaped earthen housing, the upward left-facing dish representing the spherical reflecting surface, and the downward right-facing curve representing the acoustic housing with an attached center-fed focus.

I present this description of Pleiades here because my motives for creating this instrument at the time, however visionary they may now seem, have not changed over the intervening years. Computer programs, especially computer programs that attempt to mimic human intelligence and creativity, must, like the humans they attempt to emulate, have the capability to incorporate vast amounts of contextual data in order to have a reasonable opportunity for success.

In 1984, and as a follow-up to the Pleiades project, I designed another contextual musical instrument capable of interacting with its environment. In a journal entry from that time, I described this instrument as the ". . . creation of an 'intelligence' ca-

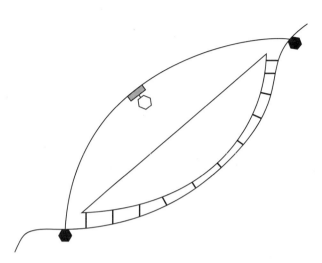

Figure 8.1
The Pleiades instrument schematic diagram.

pable of artistic reasoning with a sophisticated audio transducer system." I described the project further in ensuing paragraphs as

... a cybernetic intelligence with an extended acoustic sensory system capable of adapting to a variety of resonant sonic environments. This instrument, called MBRACE (for Musical Biomechanics: Research in Acoustic and Cybernetic Environments) will consist of three integral and interfaced units: 1) a sophisticated central computer with extended memory capable of learning by experience; 2) a digital transceiver-synthesizer capable of acting as an interpreter between computer and sensor mechanisms and able to produce elegant transformations of data; and 3) a portable set of audio sensors containing highly sensitive bilateral transducers which can act as both speakers and microphones.

Maps of resonant properties of selected sites will be created by probing with eight-octave directional beams of sound. This computational "composer" will thus acquire tactile relationships with its surroundings, collecting data for use in performance and further adaptive behaviors.

A composer could then program the central processor to personal aesthetic values allowing this electronic extension to "compose" works for various environments utilizing gathered analysis of resonant spaces (reflection and absorption indices) as critical compositional parameters. AI investigators could also study the various relationships between synthetic and sensory units in creative, non-random, and controlled experimentation.

These are certainly lofty goals, and I do not pretend to have achieved many of them to date. However, creating an instrument capable of such contextual and environmental integration was—and remains—provocative and interesting to me. The

notion that the composing program of MBRACE contains a database of sound reflection and absorption indices continues to intrigue me as context for—and influence on—algorithmic composing processes.

The basic algorithm for MBRACE appears in figure 8.2. This algorithm begins
with the initiation of a new work (top) and, through a maze of analyses of the
chosen site, memory of previous mistakes, audience input, and so on, composes
and performs new works (last two steps closely listed below input). The principal
questions—Does it work in the environment? Is it effective musically? Is it convincing to others? Should we stop? repeat? vary? contrast?—all seem answerable by the
programmable procedures set up to link the program to the composer and the audience. The terrain which supplies MBRACE's context has unpredictable contours,
providing the instrument with environmental data in order to control its acoustical
resonance capabilities. The plans for MBRACE conformed to my basic model: an
intelligent instrument capable of collaborating with—even engaging—its context.

The database of MBRACE could become incredibly large. However, as one of my
colleagues once remarked: "You can't get something out of a database that isn't already there." I argue here that while this is most certainly true, we often overlook
most of what a database actually offers. If, for example, we include outputs of any
length, even a simple ten-word database would have over 11 billion combinatorial
possibilities according to

$$x^x + x^{(x-1)} + x^{(x-2)} \ldots x^1 = y$$

where x is the total number of elements in the database and y is the total number
of possible combinations. This latter number becomes staggeringly high as the number of elements increases. As Alexander Cairns-Smith observed (see also chapter 1),
the

... *really* big numbers become important when we come to consider not simply how many
units there are in a given region, but how many ways they can be arranged ... 200 carbon
atoms could be arranged, with 402 hydrocarbons, in far more than 10^{79} different ways.
(Cairns-Smith 1971, pp. 1–2)

Obviously the number of outputs that make intelligible sense or that might be of
use is but a fraction of y in the formula above. However, leaving some or most of
the arrangements unexamined creates the possibility that one of these unexamined
arrangements might provide exactly what we want. The arrangement of data in a
database can also predispose that database to certain outcomes. In contrast, a properly ordered database may lead to important revelations about that database that
might not otherwise have surfaced.

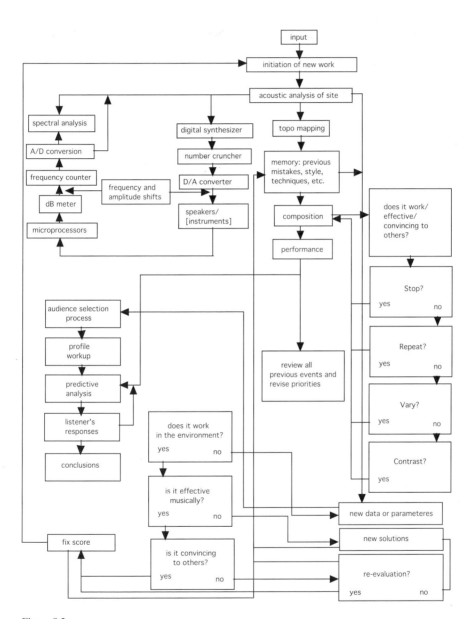

Figure 8.2
The basic algorithm for MBRACE.

Unfortunately, like Pleiades, MBRACE does not yet exist because of the high cost of materials and the innovative construction techniques that it requires. As with Pleiades, however, I have assembled acoustic data and created a work using that data (titled *MBRACE* and completed in 1986).

Experiments in Musical Intelligence music, at least the music I have allowed to be performed and published, represents a good example of what can emerge from well-organized databases. Everything this program has ever created, existed in the database prior to composition. The many thousands of examples of Experiments in Musical Intelligence music that I have destroyed exemplify the nonsense and gibberish that databases can also produce. The thousand examples of Experiments in Musical Intelligence music that I have preserved, exemplify the quality of output that database dependency can produce.

Music clearly can also serve as influence (unlike its use in recombinance) in composing programs. During early 1991 I created a computer program capable of producing a substantial number of new works (see Cope 1996) that was based on a small database of music by Stravinsky. This program slowly replaced its original database with its own output, with results soon demonstrating a Stravinsky influence rather than a direct descent. Ultimately, this program produced 5,000 new works (1,500 full-scale symphonies, 2,000 string quartets, 1,000 piano sonatas, and 500 assorted smaller piano works). I subsequently studied this music for its evolution of musical style within a virtual musical "culture." The resulting collection of works (far too numerous for me to hear in my lifetime) did indeed demonstrate a slowly evolving style, with my selected listening to several dozen randomly selected works as testimony. I observed how style changes over time, how style becomes codified, and what kinds of anomalies can create stylistic changes. While I created this program to study musical style development, I also hoped it would compose interesting new music. The output presented in *Experiments in Musical Intelligence* (Cope 1996, pp. 247–248) suggests that this program at least partially achieved this goal.

The database for this program consisted of chorale-like homophony from Stravinsky's *Three Pieces for String Quartet* of 1913 (third movement), a homorhythmic chorale section from the 1947 version of the *Symphony of Wind Instruments*, and the final chorale passage from Symphony in C of 1940. The style of these passages consists of repeated chords, varied in duration, texture, and meter. I chose these passages because they have inspired my own work, yet are distinct enough from my works to allow objective perception of unique style evolution.

This style-development program initially created a small body of music and analyzed that music for basic chord types, protocols, voice leading, and so on—the processes of recombinatory composition as described in chapter 4. The program then added these new works to its database for creating more output that "gently" incorporated an analysis of these works into its composition algorithm. This "gentle incorporation" meant that succession rules and voice-leading restrictions were applied loosely, with the voice leading of new compositions tending toward these rules but not guided absolutely by them. Thus, when new works were fed back into the program's database, the approximations of rules, when reanalyzed, caused rule variants. Rules and signatures (see chapter 4) were then saved in chronological order for later study and comparison.

Figure 7.9 of *Experiments in Musical Intelligence* (Cope 1996) gives an example of the beginning of one of the 1,500 symphonies created by the program I just described. In that example, the influence of the simple chorale-like database is pronounced, with the harmonies showing very little sign of development beyond that present in the music from which the symphony was drawn. However, figure 7.10 of that same book, the beginning of a composition over a thousand works deeper into the output, has an almost stagnant harmonic rhythm with parallel—planing—melodies. Figure 7.11, a composition almost 2,000 works further in the sequence, evidences the music of both figures 7.9 and 7.10, yet possesses a style that is different from either of them.

Unfortunately, while offering a very effective process for observing style development, this program did not provide a useful model of creativity. Prolific output, even output that develops over time, does not in itself indicate creativity. However, what is important here is the fact that the original database slowly receded in importance, with only its echoes influencing output.

Multicomposer databases can also provide influence rather than participating in recombinance. I have discussed multicomposer databases in many sources (e.g., Cope 1996, 2000). I even describe a method of melding more than one style in *Computers and Musical Style* (Cope 1991a, chapter 5) in the creation of *Mozart in Bali*, an orchestrated version of which has been recorded (Cope 1997). Figure 7.1 of *Experiments in Musical Intelligence* (Cope 2000) shows an example of an influenced algorithmic composition in the style of Beethoven. The databases for this composition consisted of the second movement of Beethoven's "Moonlight Sonata" (1801) and Bach's Prelude no. 1 from his *Well-Tempered Clavier* (completed in 1742), thus constituting a multicomposer database. The resemblance to Beethoven's sonata movement in this example is obvious when compared with the original, shown in figure 7.2 of *Experiments*. However, the actual chord progression results from Bach's prelude, as shown in figure 7.3 of *Experiments*. The new music of figure 7.1, while derivative, nonetheless has a life characteristically its own.

The style combination made possible by multicomposer databases melds some of the parameters of one composer in a database with different parameters of another composer in that same database. The third movement of Symphony 1383, shown in part in figure 3.32 of *Experiments in Musical Intelligence* (Cope 2000), provides a contrasting example of a multicomposer database. This movement derives from two songs of Mahler's *Aus des Knaben Wunderhorn* (1898), with orchestration based on those songs, but includes pitch quotations from Brahms, Haydn, Debussy, Rachmaninoff, and many other composers, resulting in a mélange of references. This kind of contextualization derives from allusion, not influence. For the most part, *Mozart in Bali* and similar works, such as *For Keith* (1991), exemplify a kind of brute-force method of combining styles where each style, to some degree at least, retains its individuality. Using derived rules in place of recombinance, as in the case of the Alice program (Cope 2000), allows for two or more styles to genuinely interlace without the dichotomy heard in these earlier works. (I also discuss this latter kind of algorithmic composition briefly in chapter 10.)

The use of multicomposer databases can provide a fresh context not unlike sources available to human composers whose works, though dominated by their own sensibilities and by style inheritance from their previous music, demonstrate the influences of many other works. My use of multicomposer databases also recycles output back into the database used for composition, as in the case of the program that composed 5,000 works (discussed earlier in this section). Thus, the outputs of multicomposer programs eventually demonstrate the influence of their databases rather than their dependence on those databases.

It is difficult to imagine a program exhibiting creative-type behavior *not* having access to the diversity made available by multicomposer databases. Multicomposer databases, therefore, offer opportunities for having a multiplicity of styles *influence* rather than *interrupt* their compositions. (I discuss this influence further in relation to the integration of this book's principles in chapter 11.) Unfortunately, while multicomposer databases can enhance creativity, they in no way guarantee it, and thus they do not, in themselves, represent good models of creativity.

Interaction

In *Experiments in Musical Intelligence* (Cope 2000, pp. 258–259), I discuss a series of composing programs that rely on user evaluation of their output to self-alter their programming. In essence, these programs rely on interactions with their users to develop new styles influenced by, but not dependent on, their initial databases. Each of these simple programs has a unique name, and works deemed successful are downloaded and translated to notation. I have avoided revealing the machine-composed nature of these works because I want their music to be judged fairly, without the predisposition that knowledge of their origins typically engenders. My purpose is not to dilute contemporary music with impostors or to prove that human composers are passé (a notion that some of my critics have suggested is my intention), but to demonstrate that interesting music is interesting music, regardless of its origin.

More recently, I have completed a rather simple program, not unlike the program just discussed, that proliferates a series of interconnected software "composers." Each of these "composers" has its own small musical database. When they are initialized, these "composers" develop their own aesthetics based on the uniqueness of their databases and the resulting uniqueness of their analyses of those databases. Each iteration of the program then composes music consistent with its musical database, according to the recombinant principles described in chapter 4. Each composer can "hear" the music produced by other of the software composers, and can converse with these other software composers, attempting to influence their aesthetics. The negotiations that result from these processes produce more "harmonious" music, in the sense that the software composers can evaluate one another's output in terms of their own built-in aesthetics.

Developing an aesthetic for each of these software composers based on the analysis of their respective databases—their only unique feature aside from distinctive names—involves straightforward processes. In essence, each of these software composers determines the degree to which its database music organizes around vertical or horizontal motion. Each software composer counts the notes in each work in its database, subtracts all but one note for notes that occur simultaneously, and then divides the resulting number by the original number of notes, giving a percentage that represents what I call the music's kinetic energy (kinesis). For example, imagine a work consisting of ten notes, all of which occur independently. This work then would have ten over ten (1.0) as its kinesis. On the other hand, imagine that another work of ten notes consists of three chords, two of four notes each and one of two notes. This work would have a kinesis of three over ten (.3).

Works with a kinesis above a user-determined limit (different for each software composer) are judged aesthetically acceptable, and works at or below the user-determined limit are found aesthetically unacceptable. While simple, this process enables each of the entities to evaluate the music of its own database, as well as the databases and outputs of other software composers. While such processes would not be acceptable to humans (though I tend to think that kinetic motion is highly underrated in musical analysis), the process seems to work acceptably for these small computer programs.

When I initialize these interconnected software composers, I typically name them by the composer of the music in each database. Thus, I may run the program with a Bach, Mozart, and Beethoven set of iterations, or a Haydn, Chopin, and Brahms set of iterations, and so on, depending on the availability of database music. Any number or combination of composer iterations is possible, with the resultant music an expression of both of the composers' music and the combined aesthetic (kinesis) of these software composers. While using the same composers with exactly the same databases results in very similar output, using the same three composers with only a slightly altered database of one of the composers can produce distinctly different music.

Each of the iterations in this program gains from its interconnections with other iterations, their databases, and their outputs. The resulting complicated interactions make composing a challenging process, with many competing constraints placed on even simple choices. Unfortunately, while this type of interconnectivity and interaction contributes to creativity, these processes, by themselves, do not constitute or effectively model creativity.

Exploration

As Stravinsky notes, "an accident is the only thing that really inspires us" (1960, p. 56). The program I now describe uses data gathered from Internet sources to influence new composition. These influences do not replace output or participate in recombinance, but rather help turn predictable output into unexpected output.

Algorithmic programs that use the Internet are called "spiders" in current technical jargon. Once connected to the Internet, my spider *wanders* relatively aimlessly, downloading certain kinds of files. Of course, my spider does not actually "wander" the Net; it simply acts as a kind of browser automaton, contacting various sites and downloading files that conform to its programmed criteria. These criteria include the following:

1. MIDI files of file Type 1 (not Type 0)

2. MIDI files using three to five channels

3. Standard text files containing alphanumeric data (including, but not limited to, MIDI).

The only restrictions I place on my program's searches involve the general type of site it can visit—sites whose names are suffixed with ".edu," for example. I also prevent my spider from connecting to my own Web site in order to avoid its accumulating

Experiments in Musical Intelligence's compositions. This spider, called Serendipity, "journeys across cyberspace," producing entertaining and, at times, surprising results. As with my other programs, this spider follows recombinatory principles for composing with a separate database, using found files to influence its output in order to eventually compose in a unique style.

Not surprisingly, Serendipity's relatively random file downloads initially produced confusing-sounding output. While we humans wander through our sonic environments without preplanning most of the sounds we hear, we usually select which music we actually pay attention to seriously. Even though our neuronic nets may store the other music we hear, the music on which we focus our attention attains the more important connections. Serendipity, at least in its initial form, had no such ability to select discretely from its various found music (even limited as it was to ".edu" sites). To establish a preference for certain files without injecting my own biases, I had the program devise a simple three-to-five-note melodic pattern, and use that pattern as a model for accepting certain works rather than others, to help create a more consistent influencing database.

Other problems with "wandering" the Internet—or, for that matter, using MIDI type 1 files of unknown origin—include loading ungroupable rhythms (as in performed files, discussed in chapter 4), multichannel information compacted into one channel (e.g., orchestra scores shoehorned into a single channel), instruments channelized by range rather than type (instruments leapfrogging from one channel to another), meter not saved with files, and so on. Any of these problems can occur in addition to the obvious inclusion of mistakes in the music, marring usefulness and jeopardizing output. Many of these problems simply cause Serendipity to refuse translation of the file. More likely, however, the program will process the file, causing problems during composition. Unfortunately, one bad file—in fact, one bad note in a file—can ruin a database for successful composing. Hence, users must listen carefully to each input file to ensure that it does not have any of the above-mentioned problems, and then repair any problems which do occur.

Serendipity also collects MIDI files containing very different styles of music. While these files will influence composition rather than directly taking part in recombinance, confusing rhythms, pitches (melody and harmony), dynamics, channels, and so on can easily produce a nightmarish pastiche of influences, unless care is taken to account for the various stylistic incompatibilities. By choosing congruous music, Serendipity can more effectively influence, rather than compromise, new output, thus creating more successful music.

To help Serendipity choose more compatible music, I programmed a series of filters to control channels, rhythms, dynamics, and ranges by checking for overall consistency between files. When these filters are set broadly, files surviving the process demonstrate roughly compatible stylistic characteristics. When these filters are set narrowly, the files surviving the process demonstrate closely knit stylistic characteristics. Users can set these filters individually or as a group, or allow them to be set automatically, based on preferences established as users accept or reject the program's output.

As an example of how influence should not occur, figure 8.3 shows output in which database inconsistencies, caused by pseudo-random file inclusion, play too important a role. Here, the hodgepodge of musical quotations, while humorous, seems heavy-handed. For example, the initial measures of Schumann's *Träumerei* ("Kinderszenen", op. 15, no. 7; 1838) join with Chopin's Prelude in C-minor (op. 28, no. 20; 1838), and then return to *Träumerei*, continuing where the music initially left off (see measure 4). (The common date of these two interlaced pieces results from chance, not from programming.) This music is then followed (beginning in measure 6) by a quotation from Mozart's Requiem (K. 626; 1791), with various subsequent references to Mozart's Piano Fantasy in C-minor (K. 475; 1785) and a vague quote from Wagner's *Tristan und Isolde* prelude (1859) in measure 12.

Data collected for the purposes of providing influence *only* for our computer model of creativity should not have the same weight that groupings of music for recombinance have, since the inclusion of such data will obviously create stylistic havoc. At the same time, such data must be connected in some manner, or they will have no effect on the output. I have solved this problem by pattern matching groupings of music in the influencing database to music in the recombinance database. Whenever such matches occur, the program incorporates the voice leading of the groupings such that new progressions are gently introduced into the output music. Typically, no actual new music is introduced into a database or output music, just new voice leading. (I will return to this important concept in chapter 11.) Obviously, contextual influences should be able to affect virtually any musical parameter, including key, mode (major/minor), tempo, orchestration, texture, note additions and subtractions, and so on. I have limited the above example to voice leading in order to avoid unnecessary complications. Note that any of the above parameters can be influenced, just as this example of voice leading has been influenced.

In figure 8.4a we see recombinant music from Chopin influenced by music from Scriabin. In this case, the Scriabin measures (not varied in this case, to help readers find the Scriabin original) can follow the Chopin because the previous Scriabin measure (not shown) has the same SPEAC and harmonic function (S and tonic) as the first Chopin measure here. The dissonance, voice leading, and root motion of the Scriabin inclusion are not typical of Chopin's music and, as a result of this music

Figure 8.3
An example of music in which context plays too significant a role.

(a)

(b)

Figure 8.4
An example of musical influence, where (a) new music from Scriabin (from 10 Mazurkas, op. 3, no. 4, measures 60–61, 1889) actually replaces (measure 2) a recombinant example from Chopin (Mazurka op. 67, no. 3, measure 5 and measures 8–9; 1835); (b) the same sources as (a) but influencing rather than replacing the original.

being added to the database, will continue to influence the output from this point onward. Figure 8.4b provides a more subtle influence, since the music in measure 2 follows Chopin's music more closely in terms of rhythm and texture, but with Scriabin's pitches replacing Chopin's pitches. The process of replacing pitches of a recombinant composition, rather than simply substituting a complete grouping, means that music of very different textures can influence an in-progress composition. This process also allows dynamics, timbre, articulation, and so on, to influence newly composed music.

The manner in which Serendipity influences data selection, rather than replacing data, avoids the problems encountered in figure 8.3. Figure 8.5 gives an example of such music. Here, unlike the montage of allusions presented in figure 8.3, Serendipity influences rather than directly quoting or paraphrasing, producing music with subtle surprises rather than abrupt juxtapositions of foreign material. This example—music in the general style of Anton von Webern—results from a database of Webern's music influenced by several works by Scarlatti, Beethoven, and Prokofiev randomly found on the Internet. None of these composers' music can be found here, nor are the influences immediately apparent. However, the simple, straightforward form of

Drome

Experiments in Musical Intelligence - Webern

1. Play and hold fingers on each of the thirty-second notes and then catch them with the sostenuto pedal - the following chords should then be as short as possible against the backdrop of the held chord.

Figure 8.5
An example of music in the general style of Webern resulting from a database of Webern's music influenced by several randomly found works from the Web by Scarlatti, Beethoven, and Prokofiev.

Scarlatti's keyboard sonatas, Beethoven's contrasting dynamics, and the complexity of the final chord reminiscent of Prokofiev's sonatas, while subtle, are in evidence here, although all of these can also be found in many of Webern's own works as well. When they are thoroughly integrated in this way, external influences can almost seem dispensable. When they are eliminated from the composing process, however, such influences seem indispensable.

The version of the Serendipity program available on my Web site demonstrates how influence can play an important role in the creation of new music. Unlike the previously mentioned program, this form of Serendipity "wanders" the user's hard drive and downloads available text and type 1 MIDI files. Serendipity seeks out numerical information stored in text files that can be grouped in ways that correlate to the event format (see appendix B) used by the program. Serendipity can also translate letters into numbers, using standard alphanumeric equivalencies ("A" = 65, "B" = 66, etc., to create events). Integrating such artificial events randomly—or, more exactly, irrelevantly—can influence a composition in progress, just as composers have been influenced, from time immemorial, by extramusical sounds and rhythms in their environment, and have consciously and subconsciously mimicked them.

To operate Serendipity, users first select "MIDI" or "Text" and then the program selects appropriate-type files at random from the search results. MIDI file names must have ".mid" suffixes. Text files do not require the same kind of identification. Serendipity attempts to filter out nonrelevant file types (i.e., non-MIDI type 1 or nontext files) and then loads files that successfully match the program's search criteria.

Users may view any of the resulting files by viewing their pathname locations and then by selecting the relevant application for opening the file. They may also review the folders visited, and remove either folders from the list or files from the loaded-files list.

The music found by Serendipity may be used for recombinant composition, for influence only, or as allusions during composition. In each case, users can be as active in the selection process as they wish—from complete control (by selecting folders and files) to allowing the program to make every decision. When allowed to negotiate freely on its own, however, Serendipity can confound and surprise users in interesting and possibly useful ways.

As with the other programs presented in this chapter, Serendipity does not effectively model creativity. Clearly, external influences play an important role in creativity, but by themselves such influences do not constitute a distinct and recognizable creative process. On the other hand, each of the processes I have described in this chapter clearly identifies an important facet of creativity. What is needed here is some mechanism for combining them in a natural and effective way. I hope that the following chapters provide just such a mechanism.

In the five chapters that constitute this section of *Computer Models of Musical Creativity*, I have explained recombinance, allusions, learning, hierarchy, and influence—five of the most important constituents that I feel are necessary for musical creativity. Obviously, dozens of other possible ingredients—orchestration, dynamics, performance, and so on—can also contribute to the creative process. I have, however, limited my scope of research to these five areas because they represent the most important and computable parameters, and because I feel that these other areas often rely on subjective interpretation rather than on empirical definition.

III AN INTEGRATED MODEL OF MUSICAL CREATIVITY

It is natural to look outside or beyond the music,
to find the ways in which it can temporarily
and provisionally assume different kinds of significance.
Nevertheless, music will not acknowledge a context greater than itself
—social, cultural, or biographical—to which it is conveniently subservient.
To paraphrase Goethe's grandiose warning to the scientist:
do not look behind the notes, they themselves are the doctrine.
(Rosen 1994, p. 126)

9 Association

Principle: In order for computer programs to create, they must themselves develop and extend rules, and not simply follow instructions provided by programmers.

Basic Principles

I had the good fortune to receive excellent instruction in mathematics during my formative years, especially in high school. One of my teachers, a particularly gifted instructor, always kept his students aware of the broader picture of math—how what we were studying fit into mathematics as a complete discipline. I remember one day in particular when this teacher showed us how our current study—algebra—would eventually lead to geometry, trigonometry, and then calculus. He gave short presentations on each of these new subjects so that we might have a sense of our ultimate goals. I have found this broader-picture approach extremely helpful in my own teaching.

Interestingly, on the afternoon of this particular class I found myself playing center field in a Little League baseball game. Even though I was a pitcher, the team needed a center fielder more than a pitcher that day, so I was drafted. Being new to this position, I agonized over each pitch, hoping for infield ground-outs. Eventually, however, my worst fears became reality—a ball headed toward center field on the fly.

From the second the bat struck the ball, I began to intuitively triangulate and calculate the ball's ultimate destination. Of course, I knew almost nothing of trigonometry or calculus, only what my teacher had presented that morning. I arrived at the proper location just as the ball came to rest in my glove. I was, of course, delighted with my initial success in center field, even though I later made two errors and our team lost the game 15 to 2. What continued to interest me, however, long after the frustration over my errors and losing the game had passed, was my apparent knowledge of trigonometry and calculus that *I had not yet learned.*

A long time has passed since my baseball epiphany, and since then I have learned more about trigonometry and calculus. Yet, what continues to astound me is how much I already seem to know of these and many other subjects. The more I learn through study, the more I appreciate its verification of intuitions gained through many decades of physical and mental experimentation.

Oliver Selfridge comments on how these kinds of experiences can contribute to knowledge:

... a man is continually exposed to a welter of data from his senses, and abstracts from it the patterns relevant to his activity at the moment. His ability to solve problems, prove theorems and generally run his life depends on this type of perception. (quoted in Dreyfus 1979, p. 97)

Clearly, this "welter of data" acts as a powerful force on our minds and implicitly teaches us mathematical and other principles without our conscious awareness.

Hubert Dreyfus (1992) notes that anyone

... who has children must be struck by the number of years they can spend playing around with sand, even just playing around with water, just splashing it around, sopping it up, pouring it, splashing it. It seems endlessly fascinating to children. And one might wonder what are they doing? Why aren't they getting bored? How does this have any value? Well, I would say, they're acquiring the 50,000 water sloshing cases that they need for pouring and drinking and spilling and carrying water.   (Dreyfus 1992, p. xi)

Clearly, my successful center-field catch resulted from 50,000 similar tossing and catching cases that over the years taught me the mental and physical skills to react more or less automatically, as I did, to a similar situation. My inability to abstract these skills into a mathematical formula in no way hindered me from actually repeating my learned associations.

Leonard Meyer points out how important such pouring, drinking, spilling, and carrying water experiences can be to creative artists:

... some of the most fundamental constraints governing aesthetic relationships may be *unknown* or not be explicitly conceptualized, even by those most accomplished and imaginative in their use, that is, creative artists. They know the constraints of a style not in the sense of being able to conceptualize them or state them as propositions but in the sense of knowing how to use them effectively. As with knowledge of a language, what is involved is the acquisition of a skill, the internalization of the constraints as unconscious modes of perception, cognition, and response.   (Meyer 2000, p. 193)

Attempting to understand experiences similar to the ones I mention here has proven extraordinarily valuable to my research into musical intelligence and creativity. In particular, observing unconscious learning has informed my approach to designing programs that appear, at the least, to act intelligently and creatively. As I demonstrated in chapter 4, for example, instead of programming rules for composition, I developed data-dependent programs that extract rules from musical input. Yet, this approach alone does not begin to demonstrate the ability to "know" something without explicitly learning it. For this task, I use association networks, the core of most of the programs I have created that have been successful. In the following sections on association networks, I define a process not unlike that described by Selfridge, Dreyfus, and Meyer, as well as my childhood baseball experience: receiving positive and negative input that teaches through repetition and feedback without conscious instruction.

As discussed in chapter 1, I believe that musical creativity—defined as "the initialization of connections between two or more multifaceted things, ideas, or phenomena hitherto not otherwise considered actively connected"—differs from creativity in the other arts. It therefore might seem strange that I begin my in-depth discussion of association networks with an extended example using language. My rationale is simple, however: language provides a more readily accessible and understandable model for demonstrating these networks than does music. More important, however, using language with association networks is essential to my computer composing processes, and thus what I discuss in this section about language will have direct bearing on my overall model of musical creativity. Note as well that in chapter 10, I explain in detail how association networks take music as input and return new music as output.

Association can play a significant role in developing creative-like behavior (J. Anderson and Bower 1973, 1983; Fodor 1983; Kohonen 1984; MacKay 1969; Mackintosh 1983). Current neuroscience, for example, indicates

... that the aesthetic experience depends on the associations that the brain's cortical circuits can make with innate and learned representations, and on the re-creation of a body response in the somatosensory cortex (the feeling).... One has to infer that the innate or acquired representations eliciting feelings and emotions must include not only specific symbols, color combinations and tonal sequences, but also specific forms of order, such as sentence structures, logical connections and fractal geometry. How else could images based on a fractal formula and synthesized by a computer mimic works of art and elicit feelings? So what is creativity? Creativity must be the ability to generate in one's brain (the association cortex), novel contexts and representations that elicit associations with symbols and principles of order. (Pfenninger and Shubik 2001, p. 235)

Memory also plays an important role in this process because it

... has no fixed capacity limit, since it actually generates "information" by construction. It is robust, dynamic, associative, and adaptive. If our view of memory is correct, in higher organisms every act of perception is, to some degree, an act of creation, and every act of memory is, to some degree, an act of imagination. (Edelman and Tononi 2000, p. 101)

Note the use of the words "associative" and "creation" here, both crucial, according to Edelman and Tononi, to the formation of higher organisms.

David Powers and Christopher Turk make a strong case for association being critical to the processes of language recognition, construction, and even semantics:

We now turn to another concept where again we do not want to be tied too closely to the traditional psychological definitions, although the general concept is fundamental in a number of ways. This concept is closely allied to that of relationships, and in particular the recognition and construction of relationships. The concept is association, and is fundamental to the learning process as well as being the essence of semantics. (Powers and Turk 1989, p. 99)

In the mid-1990s I developed "association networks" and have used them in many of my programs since then (see Cope 2000). Association networks are initially empty databases in which a user's input is placed, and in which all discrete entries of that input are connected to all other discrete entries. Networks react to input by placing each discrete entry into a node and assigning weights to each of the connections between this entry's node and all of the other nodes in the network. Association networks assign weights in both directions on a connection; that is, a weight from node X to node Y, as well as a weight from node Y to node X. These weights initially derive from proximity and similarity, as will be described shortly.

Association networks resemble neural networks (see chapter 3) in some respects. However, neural networks compare output with input values through interconnected "hidden" units (Todd and Loy 1991). Association networks do not make such comparisons, nor do they have hidden units. The nodes in association networks can be accessed at any time, usefully revealing their weights for comparison. While neural networks generally have fixed numbers of nodes and connections, association networks have a virtually limitless number of interconnectable nodes. While neural networks typically chain backward—called back propagation—association networks chain in every direction.

Semantic networks, sometimes incorrectly referred to as association networks, usually link through treelike configurations with inference as their primary goal. One form of semantic network uses implication, such as

William is a man.

Men have bodies.

(Therefore) William has a body.

Margaret Boden points out that semantic networks "are often used not for doing 'logical' problem solving, but for modeling spontaneous conceptual associations" (Boden 1990, p. 95). However, semantic networks do not typically weigh relationships as association networks do. Semantic networks, therefore, while bearing some resemblance to association networks, are substantially different in both their basic configuration and their implementation. Association networks also differ from associative neural networks, distributed associative memory, inference networks, and associative memory networks, all of which roughly follow neural network architecture (see J. Anderson and Bower 1983; Fodor 1983; Kohonen 1984; MacKay 1969).

The language association network I present here falls roughly under the rubric of natural language processing (NLP), a subset of computational linguistics (Dougherty 1994). Since most NLP utilizes parsing for analysis and programmed rules for generation, association networks then constitute a small subset of NLP (Reilly and Sharkey 1991; Wermter, Riloff, and Scheler 1996). I do not mean to suggest that my language association networks have value beyond the simple examples I present here. While I have researched and programmed a number of language processes (see Cope 1996), I do not consider this my field of expertise, nor do I present the output as anything but an introduction to music association networks.

A rigorous scientific approach to association networks would include systematic experimentation with appropriate data and comparisons of expectations with actual results. I have certainly taken this approach with the association network process I describe here. However, I have resisted the notion of describing this experimentation—hoping to shield readers from some of the more mundane aspects of this work—and instead present a more readable detailing of association networks.

In the version of the association network I use here (simplified for demonstration), responses require that all input sentences end with punctuation, that punctuation accompany the word it follows, that no punctuation occur within a sentence, and that input questions be answered and answers questioned, as typically occurs in normal conversation.

Figure 9.1 presents a graphic representation of a simple conversation similar to the one given in *The Algorithmic Composer* (Cope 2000, p. 53) as an example of the association-network process. This association network, called Associate (available on my Web site), can, as we will eventually see, take both text and music as input. Time flows from left to right within each sentence in figure 9.1, and from top to bottom between sentences in both graphic and text representations. Association networks cannot respond until both a question and a statement have been entered; hence the lack of response to the first input by the user here.

Association networks can produce striking responses. Unlike ELIZA (Weizenbaum 1976), a simple interactive language program, association networks do not contain preprogrammed replies. Thus, meaningful output results from complicated networking between words, and not from cues provided by programmers.

The example shown in figure 9.1 uses English as the language of choice. However, any language may be input, since the program has absolutely no prior knowledge of what language will be used. For example, figure 9.2 shows roughly the same questions and responses as figure 9.1, but using German (text is case insensitive here). Note that the program's responses in this example do not translate exactly to those shown in the English version of figure 9.1 (especially the final response). These differences result from the initial two-word rather than one-word input, and the fact that, as will soon be explained, the program can respond in different ways to the same questions when equal weightings occur between associating nodes.

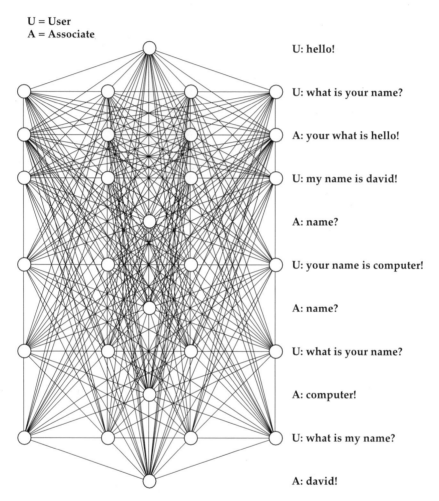

U = User
A = Associate

U: hello!

U: what is your name?

A: your what is hello!

U: my name is david!

A: name?

U: your name is computer!

A: name?

U: what is your name?

A: computer!

U: what is my name?

A: david!

Figure 9.1
Representation of a conversation with an association network called Associate.

U = User
A = Associate

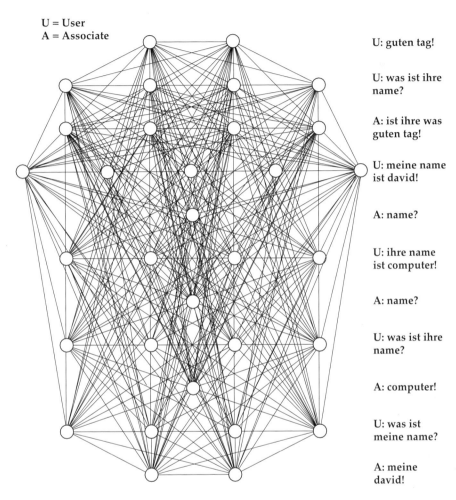

U: guten tag!

U: was ist ihre
name?

A: ist ihre was
guten tag!

U: meine name
ist david!

A: name?

U: ihre name
ist computer!

A: name?

U: was ist ihre
name?

A: computer!

U: was ist
meine name?

A: meine
david!

Figure 9.2
A German version of the conversation shown in figure 9.1.

The lines between the words (nodes) in the graphs of figures 9.1 and 9.2 represent weighted connections, with each node connecting to all of the other nodes in the network. Initial weightings—what I call predispositional weightings—are highest between adjacent words and first and last words of sentences. The longest word in each sentence—in terms of number of letters—also receives greater weight. This rather simple notion follows the arguable principle that common words of short length, such as prepositions and pronouns, often do not have as much meaning as longer, more polysyllabic words. With sentences containing two or more equally long words, the last-entered longest word receives the higher weighting of the two. This preference follows the idea that later-stated words of sentences tend to be more important than earlier-appearing words. Duplicated words and words of similar spelling develop higher ratings no matter what temporal distance separates them, based on the idea that repetition often indicates importance. This version of Associate limits such similarity to words with one-letter difference, thus allowing "me" and "my," for example, to have higher connectivity weightings. Unfortunately, this advantage turns into disadvantage for words, such as "fit" and "fat," that have very different meanings but nonetheless develop higher weightings in Associate.

Note that association networks do not *require* predispositional weightings. I have used such weightings in the version of the program I demonstrate here because I wish to generate reasonable output for the examples in this chapter. If I were to use a network set with random or zero-state initial weightings, it would require significantly more training before making this reasonable output possible. I will discuss predispositional weightings in more detail shortly.

Pointing and clicking on a node in the platform-dependent version of Associate on my Web site reveals that node's current weightings, as shown in figure 9.3. Each of the words in a weightings list indicates its level of preference in following the word listed at the top of the window ("hello" in this case) when Associate forms its response to a question or statement. Collecting weightings from more than one word at a time and comparing them can produce useful results, as shown in figure 9.4.

Note that in figure 9.4, from the perspective of "your," "computer!" (2.57) ranks higher than "david!" (1.72). From the perspective of "my," on the other hand, "david!" has a higher weighting (2.57) than "computer" (1.62). These weightings help produce the responses from Associate, as shown in figure 9.1. Figure 9.5 abstracts interassociations between important words of the conversation in figure 9.1. Here the word "Name?" (left of center) has been extracted from figure 9.1 with many of its direct and important indirect connections shown. By "indirect" I mean that the two words have not occurred consecutively. Indirect associations in figure 9.5 either have no connecting lines or have dotted lines or connections. Note that

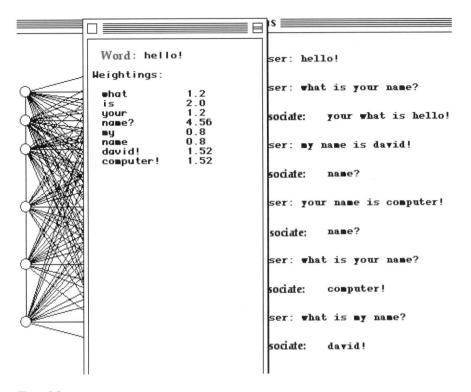

Figure 9.3
The weightings for the first word in the English conversation of figure 9.1.

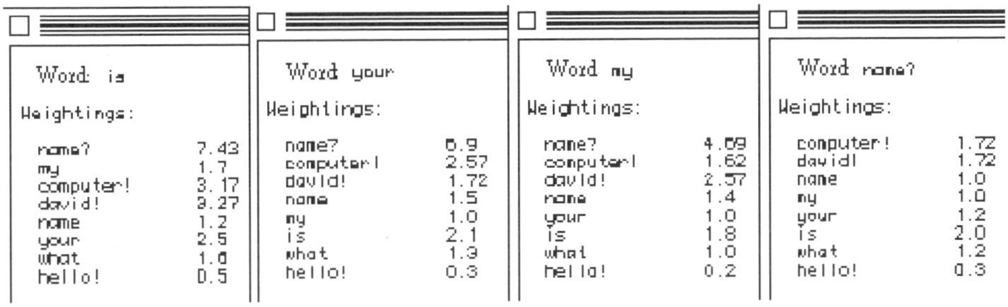

Figure 9.4
More than one word's weightings shown at the same time for the sentences in figure 9.1.

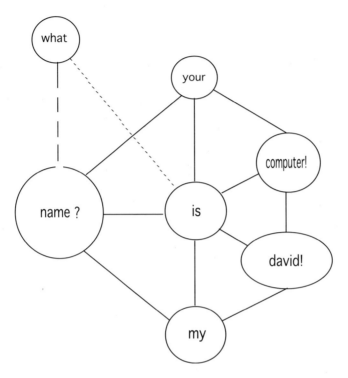

Figure 9.5
Abstracted interassociations between important words of the conversation in figure 9.1.

"name?" more directly connects "my" to "david!" (bottom), and "name?" more directly connects "your" to "computer!" (top). In association networks, this kind of connectivity also contributes to the program's attempts to contextualize or crudely define words (higher-weighted word associations). Margaret Boden comments (in reference to semantic networks):

If potential pathways exist connecting any and every node within the network, then the meaning of each individual node is a function of all the others. In this case, adding a new node will implicitly affect the meaning of all the existing ones. Analogously, a single experience—or poetic image—may subtly change the significance of a large range of related ideas within someone's mind. In other words, new meanings (or shades of meanings) are created which were not possible before.   (Boden 1990, pp. 95–96)

Tracing the connections in figure 9.5 back to those in figure 9.1 demonstrates how the associations shown in figure 9.5 derive from the original input sentences.

Gerald Gazdar and Chris Mellish state that

... language understanding involves relating linguistic forms to meanings; language generation involves the opposite. We can certainly represent linguistic forms in the computer, but what about meanings? A computer manipulates only formal symbols. How can we say that one symbolic structure correctly represents the meaning of a sentence, whereas another does not? (Gazdar and Mellish 1989, p. 8)

I argue here that while extremely simple, the notion of universal connectivity can eventually—through weightings—provide vague semblances of meaning for some of the words in its nodes. In other words, the close associations of "my" and "name" to "david!" and the close associations of "your" and "name" to "computer!" contextualize both "david!" and "computer!" in ways that clearly differentiate them, if not define them.

Laurence Danlos points out, however, that "the use of natural language as a means of communication between man and machine requires that the computer be able to (a) understand the user's message, (b) know how to reply to this message, and (c) formulate a reply in the language of the user. The first task involves automatic analysis, the second a reasoning module, and the third automatic generation" (Danlos 1987, p. 1). Certainly association networks do not "understand the user's message," at least in the usual sense of the word "understand," nor do they have reasoning modules. Surprisingly, however, association networks do have the other criterion mentioned. One could even speculate that weightings constitute a rudimentary form of understanding and reasoning, though I would most certainly not argue this point further than simply making it. Jean-Louis Binot disagrees: "It would appear *a priori* that a complete and systematic formal theory of meaning would be a prerequisite to the automatic processing of natural language expressions" (Binot 1991, p. 53).

William Gevarter notes that for "... a computer to interpret a relatively unrestricted natural language communication, a great deal of knowledge is required. Knowledge is needed of the structure of sentences, the meaning of words, the morphology of words, a model of the beliefs of the sender, the rules of conversation, and an extensive shared body of general information about the world" (Gevarter 1984, p. 111). While I make no claim that association networks have potential for acquiring this type of knowledge, I have held extended conversations over many weeks with an association network, and observed a remarkable increase in the sophistication of conversation, as can be seen by some of the examples presented later in this chapter.

The grouping of nodes into regions as shown in figure 9.5 resembles what Douglas Hofstadter calls "conceptual space" (1995, p. 436). Overlapping regions generalize rather than specify the data encased in each node. Such generalizations can often become so complicated that even in a simple association network such as this, discovering the lines of influence resembles counting grains of sand on a beach. Richard Restak comments:

If a sufficient number of cell assemblies are coupled together, generalizations become possible that are beyond all but the most advanced computers. For instance, we recognize a Chippendale chair, a pew, a tree stump, and an empty orange crate as things to sit on. This recognition is based on many cell assemblies overlapping to form a meta-assembly that is responsible for the abstract concept, "something to sit on." These cell assemblies are also responsible for humor, insight, inspiration, and creativity. (Restak 1988, p. 259)

While language association networks can make pseudo-random choices (or they use SPEAC, as described in chapter 7 and as discussed in chapter 11) when two or more correct possibilities exist, there are otherwise no probabilities involved in their associative responses. In short, weightings in association networks do not correspond to Markovian probabilities, but instead deterministically guarantee a certain choice given its higher weighting. Weightings also constitute a kind of dynamic rules system that changes over time with new input. Therefore, a language association network, viewed with all of its weightings, can be seen as a complex syntax rules-acquisition architecture that controls word orders in responses, just as the musical rules-acquisition process described in chapter 4 controls grouping orders in musical output.

Examples

Studying only the first two lines of user input in figure 9.1 provides a good example of how association networks form responses. The weights of all of the input words—"hello!" and "what is your name?"—appear in figure 9.6. As previously mentioned, each connection in an association network contains two weightings, one from the

hello!		what		is		your		name?	
what	.4	name?	2.47	name?	2.09	name?	2.21	your	.2
is	.4	is	.9	your	.8	is	.3	is	.2
your	.4	hello!	.1	what	.4	what	.3	what	.2
name?	1.52	your	.4	hello!	.1	hello!	.1	hello!	.1

Figure 9.6
The weights of all of the input words of the first two sentences of figure 9.1—"hello!" and "what is your name?"

perspective of each of the two connected words. In figure 9.6, then, the column labeled "is" ranks "name?" at 2.09, and the column labeled "name?" ranks "is" at .2. The difference between these two weightings means little when they are compared directly, but mean a great deal when compared with the other word rankings in their associated lists. For example, "is" ranking "name?" at 2.09 means that most likely "name?" will follow "is" in a computer-generated response, because "name?" is the highest-ranking word in the "is" listing. I use "likely" here not to suggest probability but to indicate that other constraints may influence a final choice. On the other hand, "is" (even though it incidentally is part of a three-way tie for the highest weight in the "name?" listing) can never follow "name?," regardless of its ranking, since "name?" must conclude a sentence because of its inclusive punctuation.

Most of the weightings in these examples result from proximity. For example, all of the word associations for "name?" as read across the first four columns of the weightings chart in figure 9.6 are high (1.52, 2.47, 2.09, and 2.21, respectively, left to right). These high values derive from the program's weighting of every word in a sentence heavily toward the last word in that sentence. Conversely, since "name?" concludes its sentence, weightings between it and the other words in that sentence remain low (all .2), with its relationship to the lone word in the previous sentence—"hello!"—rated even lower (.1). Of the words associated to "what," "name?" (2.47) ranks highest because "what" initiates the sentence that "name?" concludes, while "is" (.9), "your" (.4), and "hello!" (.1) are weighted less. From the perspective of the word "your," "name?" weights heavily (2.21), since it immediately follows "your" in the sentence in which it appears (compare with .3 for "is").

Association networks avoid word repetition in their output, which is especially important when using small amounts of data. Therefore, the program's initial response in figure 9.1 must end with "hello!" As this conversation continues, however, these restrictions, while still followed precisely, have less influence on the program's output because the choices become more varied. Since the first question posed by the user here ends with "name?," Associate's response must begin with one of the three equally highest-weighted words to "name?": "your," "is," or "what." In this case, "your" was chosen with "name?" as its own highest-weighted association. However, the program could not then choose "name?" to end its reply, because "name?" represents a question and the network must respond to questions with answers. Therefore, Associate follows "your" with "what" ("is" had an equal chance at this point) and follows "what" with "is" (the highest-rated word for following "your," since "name?" cannot be used for the reasons just given). The word "hello!" then ends the sentence, being the only remaining word available; both "your" and "what" have been used previously.

In the relatively simple examples presented thus far, only one of the words chosen had the highest weighting of the available choices (actually a tie with three other words) and one word ("hello!") had the lowest weighting (when it followed "is"). Such awkward results typify the beginnings of conversations in which the simple protocols governing proximity, punctuation, and repetition severely constrain possible choices.

As mentioned previously, the initial assignments of predispositional weightings (i.e., how much weight word connections contribute, based on proximity and similarity) act like rules in the sense that they constrain the possible outputs of the program. However, these "rules" do not follow strict rules-based programming techniques (see chapter 3), in that with association networks, programmers have no idea in advance what words or even what language will be used, and consequently have no idea which words will receive which weights. Therefore, I use "predispositions" rather than "rules" to describe these initial weighting preferences.

As previously discussed, I have included these weighting predispositions for these examples in order to increase the rate at which this association network will produce sensible output, and hence make logical examples possible for this explanation. These predispositions short-circuit the "learning" curve necessary for an association network to attain this kind of information from users on its own. While the predispositions used here make initial conversations more intelligible, they also limit "learning" in extended sessions. Therefore, the association networks I typically use, and the one that created the extended narrative language examples used later in this chapter, have no such weighting predispositions. These "freer" networks require a significantly longer period of adaptation, but ultimately produce much more "creative" output as a result, as will be seen shortly.

As the brief dialog of figure 9.1 concludes, the accumulated weightings (see figure 9.4) directly govern the output. The proof of this appears both in the responses and in the weightings from the perspective of "name?," which weights "computer!" and "david!" equally at 1.72; but where, from the perspective of "your," "computer!" weights at 2.57 and "david!" at 1.72, and from the perspective of "my," "david!" weights at 2.57 and "computer!" at 1.62. These accumulated weightings identify an important concept inherent in association networks: while direct weightings determine word choices when only one word association has the highest weighting, indirect weightings—weightings of nonadjacent words—play significant roles in program responses when more than one correct choice exists (i.e., two or more words have equal highest weightings). Thus, while each word in an association network relates directly to every other word, each word also relates indirectly to these same words through all of the other words in the association network. These indirect relations can prove very important, especially as interaction begins, a point at which the resultant choices often have equal weightings and the actual choices result from pivotal indirect weightings.

No matter how unpredictable an association network's responses may seem, these responses result from completely explainable processes. Simply put, while Associate may surprise us, and the processes it uses may seem difficult to follow, the program's output nonetheless results from simple chains of cause and effect—*not* from intelligence or creativity. In fact, we must exercise caution, when using association networks, neural networks, and other automata, not to confuse unpredictable output with intelligence or creativity. No matter what the approach, *one cannot program something without an explicit algorithm*. Therefore, association networks like the one I have been describing, while complex, do not possess any abilities that have not been previously defined in their algorithm.

Figure 9.7 presents a continuation of the conversation begun in figure 9.1. The added dialogue introduces the use of negative input, in this case the word "no*." Any word can represent the word "no," but must be designated as such by using an asterisk in the place of a statement ("!") or question ("?") ending punctuation, as shown here. Association networks do not respond to such input directly, but slightly reduce the weightings that produced the output that caused the negative user response. In this way, the probability that the association network will again respond here to the question "What is your name?" with "David!" decreases. It is not entirely striking, then, that the program responds in the way it does after being asked "What is my name?" a second time.

Note that negative input does not eliminate possibilities; it only reduces the associated weights slightly. Repeated negative input for the same or like responses lessens the possibilities further, ultimately producing a different response. Johanna Moore and William Swartout point out that "a more reactive approach to explanation is required—one that accepts feedback from the user about the understandability of its explanations and alters its plans if necessary" (Moore and Swartout 1991, p. 5). Association networks clearly provide this opportunity for feedback. Users may also reinforce (add slightly to associated word connection weightings) by using a word for "yes" with the symbol "^" as sentence-ending punctuation. Essentially this symbol does the opposite of the "*" special symbol.

Association networks rely on nodal interdependence. When a user's words for "no" and "yes" occur as input, many weights are adjusted, and thus the entire configuration of weight relationships in the association network changes to reflect these adjustments. One easy way to imagine this involves words that occur more than once in the network. Since such words are treated identically in the association process,

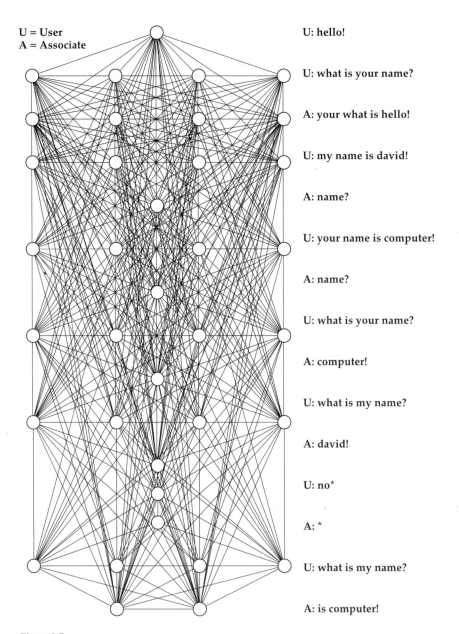

U = User
A = Associate

U: hello!

U: what is your name?

A: your what is hello!

U: my name is david!

A: name?

U: your name is computer!

A: name?

U: what is your name?

A: computer!

U: what is my name?

A: david!

U: no*

A: *

U: what is my name?

A: is computer!

Figure 9.7
A continuation of the conversation of figure 9.1, showing the use of a negative "no*" and the association network's response.

whenever adjustments affect one instance of the word, they will affect all of the other instances of the word as well. In a sense, then, the use of negative and positive input "tunes" the association network, creating a kind of resonance that will tend to reinforce the user's expectations of a certain output to a particular input.

Mathematics presents particular problems for association networks (see Cope 2001a, p. 329). While association networks can certainly add and subtract when presented with a proper template and example, they cannot generalize mathematical concepts effectively enough to calculate using new numbers. For example, responding with "4" to the query "What is 2 plus 2?" proves quite easy once the program's weightings for these precise words have been developed by user reinforcement (using the "no*" equivalent). However, even with the number "6" in its vocabulary, an association network cannot predictably add "3 plus 3" to get 6 without another explicit example being given. This inability to generalize poses the most important roadblock to association networks' achieving intelligent behavior. To understand harmonies, for example, we routinely generalize their specific pitches and registral contents to define harmonic function (i.e., tonic, dominant, etc.). However, I do not believe that the lack of an ability to generalize weakens the model of creativity I will soon describe. As Darold Treffert and Gregory Wallace (2002) point out (see chapter 1), "... musical genius often accompanies blindness and mental retardation ..." (pp. 78–80). Also, as I mentioned near the beginning of this chapter, the *inability* to abstract in no way hinders my *ability* to make a center-field catch.

The association networks I use have *five* special symbols, three of which occur in figure 9.7: "!" for statement, "?" for question, and "*" for negative response. As mentioned previously, the "^" special symbol reinforces a response, resulting in slight increases in the weightings of the associated word connections. The final symbol to be discussed, the "&" special symbol, represents *inductive association*, which requires more extensive definition and examples.

Inductive Association

None of the processes I have described thus far in this book represent creativity. In fact, most of these processes result from programmed rules and are known as deductive reasoning, "a process of reasoning in which a conclusion follows necessarily from the premises presented" (*Webster's Collegiate Dictionary* 1991, pp. 353–354). Creativity requires a "free association" that results in more imaginative and unpredictable output, such as that found in the "initialization of connections between two or more multifaceted things, ideas, or phenomena hitherto not otherwise considered actively connected," as discussed in chapter 1.

Free association is "... a sequence of thoughts, feelings, wishes, sensations, and images, present or remembered, expressed from a variety of perspectives. The sequential quality, relatively unencumbered by consciously directed, purposeful organization ..." (A. Kris 1982, p. 8).

John Dacey and Kathleen Lennon reference Galton (1879), and argue that the conscious mind

... is always filled at any one point in time, and thoughts can only follow each other around. He [Galton] found this positive, because otherwise, he believed, conscious thought would be random and would have no order. Orderliness is essential to logical thought. If this were the only way the mind could process information, however, there could be no new thoughts and therefore no creativity. The second and more important discovery Galton made was that new input can come ... from another part of the mind. The source of this input is the unconscious, the mind's "basement." Thus was discovered the notion of *free association*.   (Dacey and Lennon 1998, p. 28)

Anton Ehrenzweig comments on the roles of the conscious and unconscious mind from a slightly different perspective, arguing that "the creative thinker is capable of alternating between differentiated and undifferentiated modes of thinking, harness [*sic*] them together to give him service for solving very definite tasks" (Ehrenzweig 1967, p. xiii).

For this book, I have adopted a process called *inductive association* to computationally parallel the concept of free association. Induction means "any form of reasoning in which the conclusion, though supported by the premises, does not follow from them necessarily" (*Webster's Collegiate Dictionary* 1991, p. 687). Comparing this definition with the definition of deduction given previously shows the important distinction between these two concepts. Here are examples of induction:

The mother of a four-year-old boy, observing that he has been unusually cranky and obdurate for several days, decides that he has entered a "phase." A laboratory rat, busily pressing a lever to obtain food, hears a distinctive tone, which is followed by an electric shock. The very next time the animal hears the tone, it hesitates in its lever-pressing activity, waiting, one is tempted to say, for the other shoe to drop. A nineteenth-century scientist observes the behavior of light under several types of controlled conditions and decides that, like sound, it travels in waves through a medium. These are all examples of *induction*, which we take to encompass all inferential processes that expand knowledge in the face of uncertainty.   (Holland et al. 1986, p. 1)

In association networks, the "&" special symbol represents inductive association, and appears *before*, rather than *after*, a word, and only at beginnings of sentences. This symbol informs the association network that instead of limiting itself to obvious deductive associations, it should incorporate reasonable substitutes. "Reasonable" here means that the program carefully sifts through the associated weightings of possible words other than the highest-weighted words when forming its replies, and chooses one of those that is less likely than its deductive choice but nonetheless legitimately competes for the highest weighting.

Defining potential choices for induction in association networks depends on the weightings of their relevant associations (from the perspective of a current word). In brief, a more heavily weighted word (from the perspective of a current word) that itself has a weak association to the current word may be ignored in favor of a lesser weighted word (from the perspective of a current word) that has a stronger association to the current word. While this concept may sound convoluted, it means essentially that each word relates not only to its own highest-weighted associations but also to the highest-weighted associations of these associations (of which it is one). Resonance between such combined associations during inductive association takes precedence over simple winner-take-all word-weighting relationships.

Figure 9.8 provides an example of this process. Instead of directly choosing "name?" to follow "what" here—the obvious choice because its weight is highest at 2.47—the program sifts through the associations of each of its highest-weighted associated words and chooses "is" because, of the alternatives to "name?," "is" has the highest composite weighting of the "what" to "is" association. In this case, "is" happens to have the highest alternative weighting to "what" (.9) aside from "name?" (2.47), and this could be seen as an easier way to figure the alternative. However, this particular relationship is not always the case, or even particularly common. The deciding factor here is that the combination of the weighting of "is" to "what!" (.9) and the weighting of "what" to "is" (.4) equals 1.3, whereas the combination of "hello" to "what" and "what" to "hello" yields only .5 (.1 + .4), and that of "your" to "what" and "what" to "your" produces only .7 (.4 + .3). Because this process—and this figure—seem so complex, I have included a dotted line to show the inductive association. In effect, the relationships shown reinforce "is" as a choice, rather than the more obvious "name?," as the word following "what."

Figure 9.8b presents a possibly clearer way of conceptualizing the inductive association process. Here we see the weightings of "what" to "name?," "is," "hello!," and "your" (weights and arrows pointing *away* from "what"), and the weightings of each of these words (except "what") to "what" (weights and arrows pointing *toward* "what"). The addition of weights .9 and .4 (1.3) for "is" easily outweighs the addition of .1 and .4 (.5) for "hello!," and of .4 and .3 (.7) for "your" as alternatives for the highest-weighted 2.49 of "name?"

It might seem that the inductive association in figure 9.8 here supports the possibility that "what" will follow the new choice "is" as well as precede it. However,

(a)

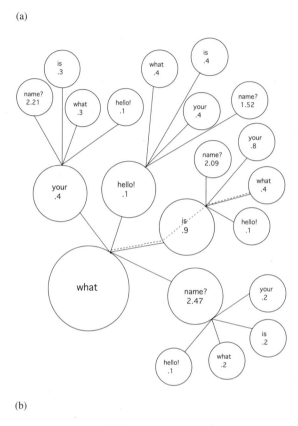

(b)

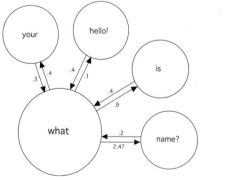

Figure 9.8
(a) An example of the associative induction process in detail, with a dotted line showing the alternative route taken; (b) a possibly clearer way of presenting this process.

"what" is highest weighted in this case only in relation to other "what"s indirectly related to the current word "what," and not in relation to the other associations of the word "is." Therefore, "is" will be followed by "name?" as the highest-weighted association to "is"—unless, of course, inductive association is again invoked.

As an operational example, the "&" symbol in figure 9.9 indicates that the program should associate using induction. The program's normal response to this question (i.e., without the "&" special symbol) would be "David!" The rather provocative response here provides, I hope, a useful example of an important principle for computer creation, at least in terms of the definition of creativity given in chapter 1.

Using an association network for extended periods of time, or saving sessions and continuing them at later dates, can produce quite complex and seemingly personal "conversations." It is often hard for me to imagine that the program responses resulting from these conversations do not originate from some sort of understanding of the input phrases. Eugen Fischer asks:

How come speakers can understand any of indefinitely many sentences they have never encountered before? As a question about knowledge of meaning, this becomes: How is it that speakers can get to know the meaning of any of indefinitely many sentences they haven't ever come across before? The former question poses what is generally called the "problem of linguistic creativity." The latter pinpoints the part of it philosophers tend to focus their attention on, which might be dubbed the "problem of semantic creativity." (Fischer 2000, p. 3)

Due to space limitations, I have not provided the database which produced an association network's responses in the following dialog. However, I hope that reproducing a small fragment of this dialog will indicate the somewhat advanced ability to converse that association networks can acquire with extended use:

User: selfawareness is a very difficult concept to express!

Computer: this selfawareness important?

User: &selfawareness is important and we use it to distinguish humans such as me from computers such as you!

Computer: distinguish why?

User: humans like me need to distinguish one thing from another in order to understand them better!

Computer: better them why?

User: it seems to be part of our curiosity that you and I have discussed before!

Computer: how so confusing?

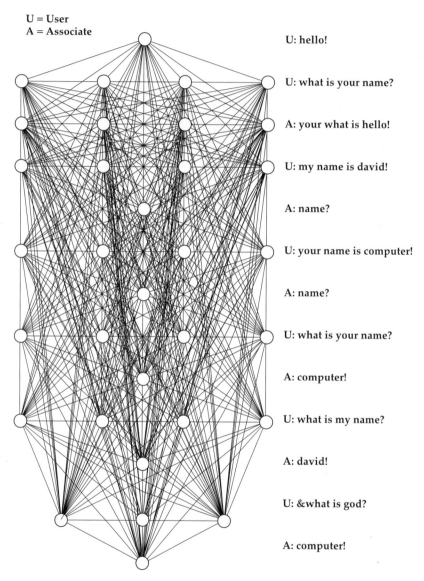

U = User
A = Associate

U: hello!

U: what is your name?

A: your what is hello!

U: my name is david!

A: name?

U: your name is computer!

A: name?

U: what is your name?

A: computer!

U: what is my name?

A: david!

U: &what is god?

A: computer!

Figure 9.9
Using the "&" special symbol for inductive association.

I am often surprised by the responses from association networks, especially given that all of the words the program iterates were originally *my own*. The order of the words, and ultimately the meanings of their combinations, of course, have often changed significantly. Even when the program parrots my input, it often seems purposeful and not arbitrary. With extended conversations acting as universally connected databases, I contend that these responses are in fact not arbitrary, but reasonable responses to input statements and questions. The musical association network I describe in chapter 10 has three different versions of associative induction, reflecting different degrees of creativity. These variants of induction cannot be used with language, however, because their use involves voice leadings and other purely musical attributes.

As an exercise in having association networks produce longer replies, I entered paragraphs from a novel I wrote some years ago into an association network lacking predispositions, hoping the program would emulate the original style but not the exact meaning of my writing. Each paragraph I entered consisted of a single statement with no internal punctuation, so the program did not respond before I finished (as previously mentioned, Associate requires both a statement and a question before output occurs). Once I had entered a complete chapter, I allowed the program—by entering a question mark after my last input—to respond, and from that point onward replied to its output paragraphs with "yes^" or "no*."

Having no plot of its own to follow, Associate's first attempts mimicked my prose. Even so, the results—at least at times—proved interesting. I reprint one exchange as an example. Here, the input, a paragraph from my novel—titled *Lorn Enver*—reads as follows (note the use of the special symbol "&" for inductive association initiating the input, and the lack of internal punctuation):

&a faint light appeared a vague formless patch that wavered for a second blurred and then died every aspect of the event was uncomfortable an unwanted disturbance in an otherwise soft and complete velvet blackness of peace time passed and the unexercised mind stopped vainly groping for significance and eased once more into the deep rapture of the night?

The association network responded:

formless light wavered unwanted unwelcome disturbance in blackness after peace returned blurred nothingness!

Note that the final punctuating word "nothingness!" here (as well as the other words not present in the input above) results from the previous paragraphs entered into the association network. This response seems intriguing as a rough draft of a paragraph of a longer narrative, though not all of the association network's responses resulted in quite this level of prose. With the addition of punctuation and two or three conjunctions and articles, this output could be quite interesting. In fact, I find the program's distillation of my style, after so many years since writing *Lorn* (completed in 1972), more attractive in many ways than the original.

The association network's more concise version of my original prose indicates that the program can, when provided a significant amount of data, produce provocative results. As with my lack of knowledge of trigonometry and calculus while playing center field, Associate knows nothing of the explicit meanings of the words it uses, and yet the program often creates prose that, to the uninformed, implies the opposite. The association process here resembles John Searle's Chinese room (discussed briefly in chapter 1), in which Searle attempts to prove that computer programs can effectively output correct word combinations in Chinese, without understanding the actual meaning of its output at all (see Searle 1997). As I discussed in chapter 1, and as we shall see in chapter 10, music has no meaning, and thus Searle's argument poses no conflict.

Many of the paragraphs created in the above manner point the resulting narrative in quite different directions. I chose a closely similar example here so that readers can discern both its origins and the variations that inductive association can create.

Association networks can also create short stories and novels by proceeding sentence by sentence, with each input provoking a response related to how the user wishes to proceed; only the program's responses will ultimately be used for the resulting prose. The following conversation (assuming a database of significant size) provides an example of this kind of input process:

User: is it raining?

Computer: night long!

User: &is it raining?

Computer: rain long!

User: is it cold?

Computer: and deep!

User: do you hear anything?

Computer: fearing death!

This kind of interaction can then become

The night is long. The rain is long and deep, fearing death.

when printed with correct uppercase and lowercase and proper punctuation. While consisting of abruptly short sentences and far from being either poetic or memorable writing, the language is relatively understandable, and the interaction maintains a somewhat consistent mood.

Paragraph-by-paragraph writing obviously allows for more diversity of prose. However, working at the paragraph level also risks strange quirks and irrelevant text creeping into the results, requiring several similar queries to remove such quirks from the final output. Whichever method I have used—complete or sentence by sentence—has produced output that I could not imagine any sensitive human had written. At the same time, however, the results are clearly creative, at least by the standards I have established in this book.

Daniel Dennett suggests that computers may actually create complete novels of distinction that no human could actually write:

There are short novels nobody could write that would not just be bestsellers; they would be instantly recognized as classics. The keystrokes required to type them are all available on any word-processor, and the total number of keystrokes in any such book is trivial, but they still lie beyond the horizon of human creativity. Each particular creator, each novelist or composer or computer programmer, is sped along through Design Space by a particular idiosyncratic set of habits known as a style. (Dennett 1995, p. 450)

Association networks represent a kind of *adaptive* software—adaptive because their ultimate shape depends almost entirely on the input of the individual using them rather than on programmers. Adaptive software such as association networks also offers shallow learning curves, requiring very little, if any, programming experience to use.

Association networks resemble another type of adaptive behavior: complex adaptive systems (CAs). John Holland describes one type of complex adaptive system thus:

The human immune system is a community made up of large numbers of highly mobile units called *antibodies* that continually repel or destroy an ever-changing cast of invaders called *antigens*. The invaders—primarily biochemicals, bacteria, and viruses—come in endless varieties, as different from one another as snowflakes. Because of this variety, and because new invaders are always appearing, the immune system cannot simply list all possible invaders. It must change or adapt (Latin "to fit") its antibodies to new invaders as they appear, never settling to a fixed configuration. Despite its protean nature, the immune system maintains an impressive coherence. Indeed, your immune system is coherent enough to provide a satisfactory scientific definition of your *identity*. It is so good at distinguishing you from the rest of the world that it will reject cells from any other human. As a result, a skin graft even from a sibling requires extraordinary measures. (Holland 1995, p. 2)

Holland believes that such complex adaptive systems share common "coherence-under-change" behavior patterns. He further believes that many such systems have what he calls an *amplifier effect*, such as that found in vaccines, where a small amount of an antigen can stimulate the entire immune system to generate enough antibodies to produce complete immunity to a particular disease. Complex adaptive systems are also nonlinear—the overall behavior is ". . . more than a simple sum of the behaviors of its parts" (Holland 1995, p. 5).

Association networks resemble complex adaptive systems in that they are both adaptive (change as a result of input) and nonlinear (changes affect the entire system). I do not, however, claim that association networks actually are complex adaptive systems.

Association networks can also *learn* through a process not dissimilar to the Gradus program discussed in chapter 6, though association networks use very different mechanisms. Where Gradus utilizes a straightforward analysis algorithm to create rules that are saved in variables that decrease backtracking, association networks invoke weighting shifts that slowly hone the program toward meeting a particular goal. The effect, however, is roughly the same. I believe that association networks thus learn much more naturally than Gradus. More important, association networks—as we will seen in future chapters—offer opportunities for the integration of other important processes, without the need for writing new programs or appending other software. The natural negation and reinforcement approaches taken by association networks also develop meaningful links for inference and analogy, as discussed in chapter 6, without the need for new code. (I discuss these inferential and analogical links in more detail in chapter 10.)

Here is an example of the program's apparent ability—at least at times—to induce an analogy:

User: a car is to the road as a train is to a track!

Computer: road as a train?

User: the moon is to the earth as the earth is to what?

Computer: what!

User: &the moon is to the earth as the earth is to what?

Computer: sun is to what!

Of course, this dialog could be possible only after extensive interactions between the user and the network. After all, the program must already have the words "sun" and "what" in its nodal word collection, as well as information about the sun's relationship to the earth in order to extrapolate the analogy (other than by accident).

I make no claims about Associate's linguistic abilities. Clearly Associate does not *understand* users in the usual ways we mean that word. I have concentrated on language with association networks thus far because language demonstrates association more clearly than music does, and because my ultimate model utilizes *both* language and music. By using language examples before music examples, however, I do not mean to suggest that music follows the same creative processes that language does. In fact, while music and language share certain sonological characteristics—sound and silence expressed over time—they appear to deviate in many other ways. For example, language has clear semantic meanings as cataloged in dictionaries, while music does not have meaning (see discussion at the beginning of chapter 1). Music, as Leonard Bernstein notes, "has an aesthetic function only" (Bernstein 1976, p. 79), and therefore will relate even more aptly to the processes of association networks.

I encourage readers to converse with the Associate program provided on my Web site, having patience with the program's often awkward initial attempts and understanding its linguistic limitations.

10 Musical Association

Principle: Musical creativity relies on composers, performers, and listeners associating their experiences across a broad landscape of music tradition.

Musical Input

In 1997 I had the good fortune to tour briefly with three extremely talented individuals: Harold Cohen, creator of the computer artist Aaron and professor emeritus at the University of California, San Diego; George Lewis, composer, trombonist, and professor of music at the University of California, San Diego; and Christopher Dobrian, composer and professor of music at the University of California, Irvine. At each site on our tour, we contributed our various takes on the algorithmic arts by presenting our work through lectures, demonstrations, and performances. On one particular evening, following our concert at UC Irvine, a young man—a trombonist—in the audience challenged George to a musical duel. I am sure this student knew, as did I, that George has a celebrated past, having played with the Count Basie band and many other giants of jazz.

Most of the audience had left by the time George began to improvise for this student, who, in turn, proved incredibly talented for his age. For the next thirty minutes or so, Chris, Harold, and I sat transfixed while these two musicians "spoke" to one another in an extraordinary series of musical interchanges. I can think of few moments in my life that struck me as more creative than this impromptu musical "conversation." For lovers of chess, it was like watching a grand-master championship match with the clock for new moves set to one second. Motives were exchanged, developed, and almost instantaneously tossed back like gauntlets.

Association networks can also take music as input and "converse" with their users. As a very simple example, figure 10.1 demonstrates how association networks can interact using octave-insensitive ASCII note names. While rudimentary, this example demonstrates that association networks develop logical syntax quickly, here by cadentially completing the final musical *question* (the tonic "C!" cadencing the preceding input's dominant "G?" in terms of tonal logic). Since "C!"—not "C"—occurs only in the first statement (second input) by the user here, and since "G" appears as both "G?" and "G!" at the ends of user inputs, the program's response seems particularly interesting. Encouraging the program to produce more complex output—repeating and varying motives, for example—requires more input than provided here. However, as figure 10.1 demonstrates, association networks can simulate a minimal recognition of implied functions with fairly limited musical input.

The process by which music is entered into association networks has beneficial effects on its analysis. For example, input music does not require phrase delineation

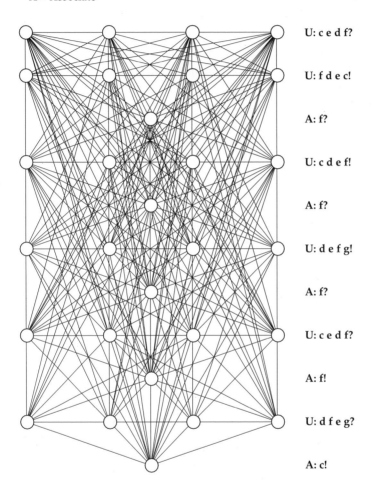

Figure 10.1
Simple music input to an association network from an ASCII keyboard.

since—as with sentences in language—music is entered into the network phrase by phrase. Cadences (and so on) are thus easier to locate, analyze, and replicate than when music is entered as whole compositions. The punctuation here may either relate to tonal cadence types (half cadences using "?" and authentic cadences using "!") or simply act as markers for phrase endings.

Using harmony in this particular ASCII mode consists of stringing together octave-insensitive note names to form musical "words." Figure 10.2 shows an example of an association network responding to input in the form of triads in the key of C-major. For readers familiar with tonal harmony, the logic of this "conversation" should be clear. For those less acquainted with tonal progressions, the user here—as with the language examples of chapter 9—has described a chord syntax that the program appears to have discovered without the aid of programmed rules to guide it (i.e., cadencing on the tonic triad of the key that the user previously gave as an example). As with the language interactions in chapter 9, allowing one letter difference—one note difference in music—for similarity produces as many disadvantages as advantages; it allows "GBE" to equate to "GBD" (clearly not the same musical function), but also allows "GBD" to equate to "GBDF" (clearly the same basic musical function).

Musical connection weightings are figured quite differently than word connection weightings. SPEAC (see chapter 7) offers a straightforward approach to assigning weights to groupings of any musical style, and hence provides a kind of universality no other analytical method guarantees. SPEAC is represented in association-network architecture by number—in foreground-to-background order—subscripts. Hence, an S_3 identifier has deeper consequence than an S_1 identifier. The number of SPEAC levels varies depending on the complexity of the music, much as the number of middle-grounds between foreground and background varies in a Schenkerian analysis (see Schenker 1935). As mentioned in regard to figure 7.17, separate instances of an S_3, for example, are identified by a hyphen followed by an incremental number, as in S_{3-14}.

Weighting node connections when using music with association networks thus follows the conventions described in chapter 7—computation of numerical weights based on interval and rhythmic tensions—and then assigning appropriate SPEAC identifiers based on the context of the grouping in its original musical environment. Weightings in musical association networks take the place of recombinational lexicons (see chapter 4), because groupings which relate to one another through their voice leading have higher weightings with transpositional equivalence, just as equal words in language association do.

As musical input increases in sophistication from simple congregations of note names to more complex groupings of octave-sensitive events (see appendix B), the

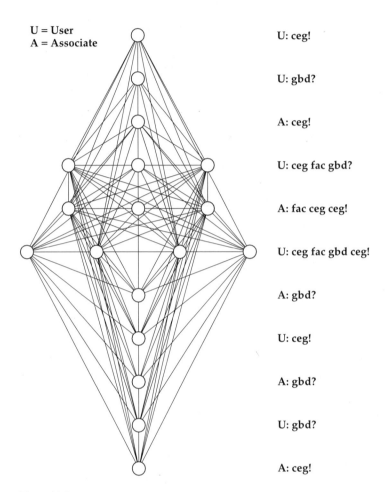

U = User
A = Associate

U: ceg!

U: gbd?

A: ceg!

U: ceg fac gbd?

A: fac ceg ceg!

U: ceg fac gbd ceg!

A: gbd?

U: ceg!

A: gbd?

U: gbd?

A: ceg!

Figure 10.2
Simple harmony from an ASCII keyboard used as input to an association network.

importance of the assignment of predispositional weightings increases as well. However, predispositional weightings in language interactions—such as higher weightings for last words of sentences, longest words of sentences, and so on—while making a certain degree of sense for language, have little relevance for music. Weighting predispositions in music derive directly from the SPEAC ordering mechanism with, for example, an A identifier requiring—at least eventually—a C identifier, and so on. Since the tensions of each node in a music association network evolve from the intervallic and metrical relations of the grouping of that node, these tensions cannot substitute for the weightings of the association network itself.

While this may seem complex—having one set of values for the SPEAC tensions of the nodes and another for the associative weightings between that node and all of the other nodes in the association network—understanding their separate values is not that difficult. Figure 10.3 provides an example of how this process works. Only the associated weightings for the outer nodes appear here, since including all of the other weightings would clutter the graphical representation.

Musical Induction

Using musical inductive association, even with very little input, can prove interesting, as shown in figure 10.4. The use of the inductive "&" special symbol here creates a deceptive cadence—"gbd" followed by "ace" (last two entries)—from input that does not directly suggest it. The input here represents the entire network's content.

To present a more definitive example of the inductive-association process using music, I revert here to a melody-only example using note names, simply because it provides more clarity and requires less space. The "conversation" with the Associate program in figure 10.5a produces the output of figure 10.5b, similar—in general concept, at least—to that shown in Beethoven's sketches in figure 3.14, except that here I play the role of provocateur (Beethoven himself played that role in his sketching process). Importantly, without my using associative induction, the program would have been "satisfied" with its first—rather inconsequential—response. Note that all of the accidentals in Associate's input/output must be flats because of constraints imposed by the programming language used. Hence, G-flat appears here in the program's response in place of the more logical F-sharp. Also note that, while brief, each of the "sketches" here retains at least one element of its predecessor, and many responses further retain elements over a series of outputs.

Association networks can also self-apply associative inductance. Such self-inductive association results from repeated negative user input in the form of rejecting the program's musical output. Association networks further self-invoke inductive

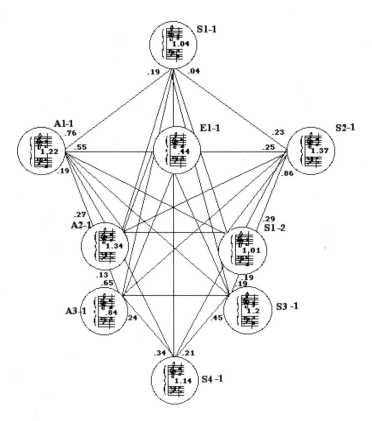

Figure 10.3
An example of how the SPEAC assignment process works in an association network. The SPEAC identifiers here are not shown hierarchically.

association when too much repetition of the database occurs in output, or when the program produces music too similar to that previously rejected. These uses of induction, over many years, have produced what I feel represents the more evocative music my programs have produced.

Recursion and Automation

The musical examples I have shown thus far have been very simple in order to demonstrate the basic concepts of association networks and inductive association, and how these processes respond to musical input. Bridging the gap between these simple examples and more complex ones requires some understanding of recursive processes.

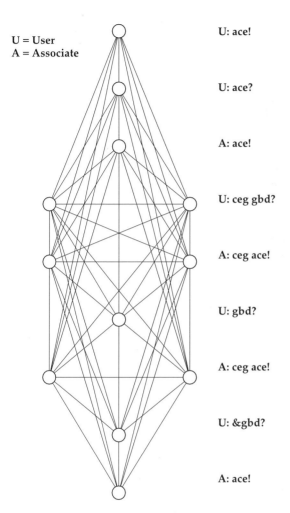

U = User
A = Associate

U: ace!

U: ace?

A: ace!

U: ceg gbd?

A: ceg ace!

U: gbd?

A: ceg ace!

U: &gbd?

A: ace!

Figure 10.4
Simple inductive association creating a deceptive cadence.

(a)

U = User
A = Associate

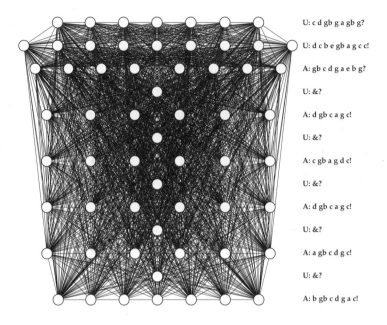

U: c d gb g a gb g?

U: d c b e gb a g c c!

A: gb c d g a e b g?

U: &?

A: d gb c a g c!

U: &?

A: c gb a g d c!

U: &?

A: d gb c a g c!

U: &?

A: a gb c d g c!

U: &?

A: b gb c d g a c!

(b)

Figure 10.5
A musical conversation in terms of (a) the association-network graphics used thus far and (b) the program's responses (only) translated into musical notation to facilitate comparisons with the Beethoven sketches in chapter 3 (see figure 3.14).

Recursion occurs when a process references itself in some way. The diminishing-in-size self-similar images seen when mirrors face one another provides an example of recursion. Other self-similar forms, such as those that occur in the limbs of trees where each smaller limb exhibits the same general characteristics as the larger limb from which it originates, also exhibit recursive behavior. The formula discussed in chapter 3 under "Mathematical Models" (see p. 76) represents another type of recursion in that once it is computed, it becomes a new value for x which will then output a new value for x once it is computed, and so on. Fractals also derive from recursive-like processes. Benoit Mandelbrot, the creator of fractals, quotes Jonathan Swift in reference to recursion:

So, Nat'ralists observe, a Flea
Hath Smaller Fleas that on him prey
And these have smaller Fleas to bit 'em,
And so proceed ad infinitum.   (Mandelbrot 2001, p. 198)

He then adds:

Actually, Swift was repeating a saying by the German philosopher and mathematician Leibnitz [*sic*] (1646–1716), who in turn was borrowing from that well-known Greek philosopher Aristotle (384–322 BC). So there was a long line of thought on self-similarity, going back very far.... (Mandelbrot 2001, p. 198)

Automating association networks requires recursion. Put simply, users cannot be asked to repeatedly interact with association networks to create larger works of music. Such conversations could extend almost indefinitely, and become progressively more abstract and difficult to follow. While some of my programs—Alice (the Algorithmically Integrated Composition Environment), for example (see Cope 2000)—operate in this way, most users find such approaches far too time-consuming to be useful. In order to automate Associate's musical input process, I connect the association network's output back into its input: recursion. The overall process requires building an appropriate database of music consisting of roughly measure- or smaller-sized data, while ignoring the program's responses, or completing each input with the same punctuation (thus voiding program response). The program then composes new music automatically by feeding its output into its input (with reversed punctuation) until a new work—consisting of all or most of the inputs and outputs—is complete.

Musical connections between groupings in association networks require more information about potential new connections than do words. As shown in chapters 4 and 10, music requires not only that the order of the groupings (word equivalents) follow weighting priorities, but also that the ways in which the members of these groupings connect—the voice leading (in both directions!)—must conform to the basic principles of the input music. This dual role obviously constricts musical association networks far more than the language version, and hence musical association networks require far more data before creative recombination can take place.

Whenever a musical grouping has appeared elsewhere in a network (including all of its transpositional equivalencies), these groupings may be interchanged. This interchange clearly follows that of the language model presented in chapter 9, and also conforms to the recombinatory principles discussed in chapter 4. The different weightings of equivalent groupings allow the program to make a best selection when composing.

Figure 10.6 demonstrates how pitch recombinance works in Associate. The progressions of figure 10.6c and 10.6d originate exclusively from the progressions of figures 10.6a and 10.6b (i.e., no other data were present in the database at the time of composition). Figure 10.6c begins exactly as figure 10.6a does, but when it reaches the third chord, it pivots to the second—equivalent—chord of figure 10.6b. The voice leading of the new progression (figure 10.6c) follows all of the basic constraints of the two initial progressions, yet contains a different overall succession of chords. Figure 10.6d begins with figure 10.6b, pivots around the same G-major chord, and ends with music from 10.6a. This notion of creating new progressions from existing progressions follows the same principles outlined in chapter 4. I briefly describe the

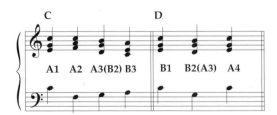

Figure 10.6
Progressions C and D, created using recombination of A and B.

process again here in order to establish the foundation for the upcoming discussion of induction.

Inductive association using words poses few computational problems for association networks. However, inductive association using musical groupings poses many problems, for it is unlikely that alternative associations will have voice-leading equivalence with a currently chosen grouping. Inductive association in music, therefore, requires more negotiation than simple substitution does. While these negotiations may appear to be more mathematical than musical, I assure those who are averse to such processes being applied to music that the processes I am about to describe are innately musical. For example, every tonal composer whose music I know has applied similar techniques, though possibly not in this exact form.

The musical inductive process, like the language inductive process presented in chapter 9, involves first finding logical indirect connections. To make the just-discussed incompatible voice-leading connections possible, however, music association networks must reduce all involved groupings to pitch-class numbers (all C-naturals equaling 0, all C-sharps equaling 1, etc., up to 11 for B-natural, regardless of octave). These groupings are then linked to their destination pitch-class numbers (see chapter 4 for more information on the importance of destination notes). This pitch-class reduction offers more opportunities for similar but not equivalent groupings to match, and thus serves to create imaginative new musically correct results (see also transformational recombination in Cope 2001a).

Figures 10.7 through 10.9 demonstrate these voice-leading techniques for musical induction in more detail. Figure 10.7a shows a simple C-major to F-major triadic motion in four voices. The listing below the music in figure 10.7a shows voice sublists of two parts—the pitch-class representation of a member of the current grouping and the pitch-class representation of the appropriate member of the destination grouping. Negative numbers indicate downward motion, ensuring the correct destination. Pitch-class groupings have left-to-right, bottom-to-top equivalency. Therefore, the first grouping of the music of figure 10.7a is represented as 0 for C, 7 for G, 4 for E, and 0 again for the C in the upper voice. All of the destination pitch-class numbers are positive in this case since all of the voices move upward or remain stationary.

The first musical inductive association process I describe here involves matching equivalent pitch-class sets with different—except for bass notes—orders. Changing bass-note position in a grouping, particularly in tonal music, can have serious stylistic consequences. A (0 7 4 0) grouping, such as that in the first beat of figure 10.7a, can be considered equivalent to a (0 7 0 4) grouping, as shown in figure 10.7b. Since voice destinations accompany their respective pitch classes, the results of grouping exchanges should, in most cases, prove acceptable, as is the case here. The new voice

(a)

((0 5)(7 9)(4 5)(0 0))

(b)

((0 5)(7 9)(0 0)(4 5))

(c)

((7 0)(2 4)(11 0)(7 7))

Figure 10.7
Rule generation (induction) of pitch-class groupings of different orders.

leading generated by the voice exchange appears below the music in figure 10.7b. While these new voice leadings do not create an alternative solution for the first grouping of figure 10.7a, if all of the groupings of a network are likewise inductively restructured, the options for new choices for recombinance increase dramatically.

Musicians view such machinations simply as revoicings, which appear ubiquitously in tonal music. Such techniques are not at all obvious to computer programs, however, and thus I have carefully described the process here. A more ambitious use of equivalencies can be achieved using these same processes, but utilizing pitch-class transposition rather than voice reordering. Figure 10.7c shows such a case, using only the voice leading shown in figure 10.7a as a model. The new configuration in figure 10.7c results from—in this case—adding 7 to each member of the original set in figure 10.7c, with numbers exceeding 11 recycling mod 12 (12 = 0, 13 = 1, etc.).

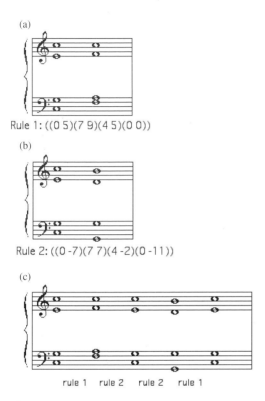

(a)

Rule 1: ((0 5)(7 9)(4 5)(0 0))

(b)

Rule 2: ((0 -7)(7 7)(4 -2)(0 -11))

(c)

rule 1   rule 2   rule 2   rule 1

Figure 10.8
More ambitious inductance: the creation of a logical phrase (c) from two small fragments (a) and (b).

Of course, figure 10.7c represents a simple transpositional equivalency—I have included it here to demonstrate its pitch-class version and establish it for the processes I will now describe.

These two basic processes—voice reordering and transposition—offer surprising results, especially when used with very few data. For example, the music in figure 10.8c results from refiguring only the data present in figures 10.8a and 10.8b. While the new progression in figure 10.8c seems simple enough, it will be useful to follow the processes that created it. The first two chords clearly result from rule 1 applied without manipulation. The application of rule 2 to create the third chord, however, requires more explanation. The actual rule 2—((0 −7) (7 7) (4 −2) (0 −11))—is not easily apparent in the newly analyzed rule of ((5 0) (9 −7) (5 −4) (0 0)) until the actual rule 2 is transposed upward by 5 to ((5 0) (0 0) (9 −7) (5 −4)) and the voices are reordered to ((5 0) (9 −7) (5 −4) (0 0)). Remember, the minus signs here refer to downward motion, and thus do not figure into the calculations as minus numbers. Interestingly, this rather complex series of operations results in something that musicians find natural and easy to understand. The numbers make it somewhat harder to follow for humans, but easier to follow for computer programs. The remainder of the new progression should be relatively easy to understand, given this initial explanation.

The new inferential possibilities shown in figures 10.7 and 10.8 allow inductive connections to occur between groupings previously not considered connectable. Thus, even with a small amount of musical data present, a variety of new choices exists, each correct, yet different in some way from the connections already present in the association network as a result of direct input. Thus, simple inductive processes can produce quite interesting extrapolations and result in what I feel is creative output.

As I mentioned previously, for the just-discovered transposition process to occur diatonically, new chords must already exist in the database, just as all words used in output in the language association network must already exist in the database. Music, however, offers the potential for modulation, making more radical creative extrapolations possible as well. Figure 10.9 presents an example of inference of this type. The new progression in figure 10.9c is longer than either of the two upon which it is based (again, no other data are present in the database at the time of creation),

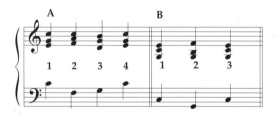

Figure 10.9
Induction of chromaticism in a logical new phrase derived from two short diatonic progressions.

and includes chromaticism (F-sharp) that neither of the source progressions contains. This chromaticism results from using a transposed version of the second chord of figure 10.9b as its third chord, with a transposed version of the remainder of the progression of figure 10.9b completing the new phrase in the key of G-major.

Creating a logical modulation to a new key from the combination of the diatonic progressions in figures 10.9a and 10.9b (both in the same key) offers important potential for inductive association. This music, more elaborate than shown in figures 10.6–10.8, provides association networks with enormous numbers of new possibilities when users or the network itself invokes inductive association.

The "&" special symbol can also be used in several ways. In its simplest incarnation (as a single "&"), this special symbol represents straightforward inductive association, as just described. However, when repeated immediately, as in "&&" to begin an input, this symbol invokes allusional analogic inference; and when stated three times in succession, as in "&&&," it uses contextual (see chapter 8) analogic inference. These two new symbol combinations require further explanation.

The "&&" special symbol causes transformational revoicing of potential new choices available from other music (allusions), allowing for many more creative combinations of groupings to occur. Choices for these new combinations are constrained by weighting analogies which result from comparing the original grouping and its original destination with each potential new choice and its previous grouping's weightings. The grouping with the greatest number of comparable weighting *proportions* (not actual weightings) succeeds. Therefore, a grouped pair in the association network would match a .9/.3 (3.0) ratio, and a 1.8/.6 (3.0) proportion in the allusion database over a .9/.2 (4.5) ratio in the allusion database, even though the latter weighting relationship (.9/.3 to .9/.2) seem closer in size to the first grouped pair. I term this "&&" kind of creativity "regional," in that it extends the musical environment beyond the "local" music used by the "&" special symbol.

Figure 10.10a provides an example of an allusion originating from an Experiments in Musical Intelligence Puccini-style song (shown in figure 10.10b) in a new work created by an association network. As is often the case, particularly when databases are small, the transition between ongoing music and the allusion is abrupt here. Importantly, however, the transposition of the melody and its transformation from a quasi-operatic accompanying figure to a more pianistic accompanying figure, make this abrupt transition less sudden and dramatic.

I call the "&&&" version of the "&" special symbol "global" creativity, in that, unlike the local music used by "&" and the regional (allusional) music used by "&&," the "&&&" references the context music or text gathered by a spider (see chapter 8) or similar source of nondatabase and nonreferential music. The "&&&"

(a)

Figure 10.10
An example of an allusion (a) in a new work by an association network (see measures 2 and 5 here) and (b) from an Experiments in Musical Intelligence Puccini-style song.

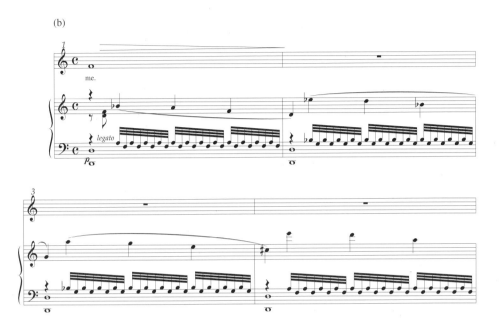

Figure 10.10
(continued)

special symbol locates the most analogic pair of contiguous groupings in the context music database, and then uses the voice leading between these two new groupings to create a new grouping. Both the new voice leading and the new grouping are added to the association network, and therefore slowly begin to influence output.

Figure 10.11a presents an example of "&&&" contextual influence in a new work by an association network along with its source, an Experiments in Musical Intelligence Prokofiev-style sonata movement (movement 2, measures 18–20). Up to this point, the music in (a) has maintained either an expanding motive (as in measure 1 here) or an upward arpeggiating figure (as in measure 2). In measure 3 of this new music, the octave-doubled line shifts direction in quite unexpected ways, demonstrating the influence of the wandering left hand of measure 1 and the similar right hand in measures 2–3 of figure 10.11b (note: the beat-to-beat exchange of pianos in the new music in measure 3, is my choice, not the network's). The influence here is subtle but actual, as demonstrated by my reading of the program's "history" variable, which collects all decision information as the network composes. Interestingly, this contextually influenced music originates from the same work as the just-discussed work containing the Puccini allusion (see figure 10.10).

(a)

(b)

Figure 10.11
An example of (a) a contextual influence in a new work by an association network and (b) its source, an Experiments in Musical Intelligence Prokofiev-style sonata passage.

Local induction ("&"), then, represents a kind of insight into new ways of treating old material, and regional induction ("&&") uses analogy to directly reference music from other sources (allusions). These new allusions do not contribute to the ongoing musical output, but occur only once. Global induction ("&&&"), then, uses analogy to incorporate the actual voice leadings and, to some extent, the actual groupings of context music into the compositional process.

Another way to look at these three types of musical creativity would be that local induction causes simple rethinkings of old material and processes, regional induction involves one-time appropriation of other music, and global induction allows an influence from the musical environment to cause slight but fundamental shifts in musical style to occur. Each of these three types of inductive creativity can be very effective when used sparingly and at the right moment.

These three gradations of musical induction mirror my own composing processes. For example, I often make small creative choices at the local level, producing unexpected new strategies when needed. I carefully select allusions based on logical inferences to the music I am composing at a more regional level. At a more global level, I allow (usually without explicitly knowing it) analogical influences from the music I hear around me to slowly develop and vary my overall style.

I use a more complex type of music inference (induction) for atonal composition (see Cope 2000) in my program Alice. Database analysis requires grouping musical events in logical ways, which in Alice is accomplished by using a straightforward vertical process that collects new groups at the inception or termination of any musical event. These groupings are then analyzed according to the voice motions of each pitch and by pitch-class set analysis of the group of pitches as a whole (see Cope 2000 for more information on this process). Inferential composition then takes the form that appears in figures 10.12a and 10.12b, which show the original motions of two groupings in a database.

Note that figure 10.12b's first chord reduces to the same set as in figure 10.12a. This equivalent set, however, moves to a different destination set. To associate inductively, then, Alice combines the first chord of figure 10.12a with the voice leading of figure 10.12b to create a different—but correct—motion to the second set of figure 10.12b, as shown in figure 10.12c. Note how the voice motions remain connected to their respective pitch-class set members between chord 1 and chord 2 of figure 10.12c, thus ensuring that both the chords and the voice leading remain consistent with the voice-leading style of the music in the database.

I describe this process in some detail here to demonstrate one of the ways in which my programs deal with voice leading in atonal music. I use these processes (usually as a user-switched alternative) when composing in nontonal styles, as an alternative to the processes described in figures 10.7 through 10.9.

As a more elaborate example, I used an association network to complete a Beethoven "tenth" symphony early in 2001, very much in keeping with a similar completion by Experiments in Musical Intelligence in 1987 of Prokofiev's tenth piano sonata (see Cope 1991a). Having studied both Beethoven's unverified sketches for his tenth symphony and the single-movement musicological completion attempted by Barry Cooper (1988, 1990; see also Cook 1989), I opted to have the program base this new symphony on Beethoven's orchestral music in general and his completed symphonies in particular, rather than on his sketches.

For the final movement of this symphony, I used a database consisting of a large collection of Beethoven's choral and orchestral music in hopes of emulating his Ninth Symphony. However, since so little orchestral/choral music by Beethoven exists—notably his opera *Fidelio*, Missa Solemnis, and Ninth Symphony—I had the program self-initiate inductive association more often than usual during the

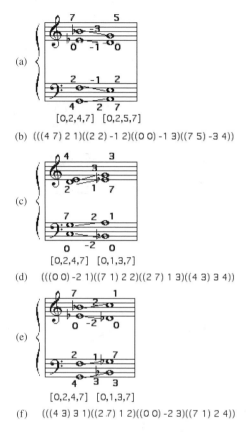

(b)   (((4 7) 2 1)((2 2) -1 2)((0 0) -1 3)((7 5) -3 4))

(d)   (((0 0) -2 1)((7 1) 2 2)((2 7) 1 3)((4 3) 3 4))

(f)   (((4 3) 3 1)((2 7) 1 2)((0 0) -2 3)((7 1) 2 4))

Figure 10.12
Extending voice-leading rules.

composing process in order to create more original music (the smaller the database, the more likely the program will require inductive association in order to avoid imitating the input music too closely).

Figure 10.13 presents a small excerpt from the fourth movement of this computer-composed Beethoven-like symphony. I chose a choral fragment specifically, since I know—from a tracing of the program as it composed this music—that inductive association played a significant role in its creation. The association network that created this music did not have any weighting predispositions as described in chapter 9, but rather used SPEAC, as discussed in chapter 7 and earlier in this chapter.

I added the lyrics shown here because the program, while it can interact using language, does not set text to music especially well. Carefully listening to and analyzing

Figure 10.13
A section from a computer-composed Beethoven-style symphony, fourth movement chorale: introduction of the finale.

this brief passage will, I feel, verify its musical credibility. The counterpoint in this music, I believe, clearly originates from creative processes. Interestingly, this music does not evoke the style of Beethoven particularly well. However, stylistic faithfulness does not represent for me a criterion upon which to judge the results here, because my intention, since beginning this type of research in the early 1980s, has been to study creative processes and to produce engaging music, not simply to parrot particular styles or compositions.

Figure 10.14 presents two excerpts from Beethoven's Symphony no. 9, movement 4, that in part acted as a database for the association network's creation of the new chorale shown in figure 10.13. Comparing figures 10.13 and 10.14 reveals common keys, the origins of the repeated half notes in figure 10.13 from the first and second

Figure 10.14
Two excerpts from Beethoven's Symphony no. 9, movement 4: (a) beginning measure 85 of the "Ode to Joy"; (b) beginning measure 49 of the "Ode to Joy."

measures of figure 10.14a, and a similar use of chromatic notes (G-sharp in particular). The computer-generated music in figure 10.13 includes tied notes that appear in other of Beethoven's works in the database, and ignores the eighth-note melismas in the Ninth Symphony, particularly those appearing in figure 10.14b. Nonetheless, figure 10.13 clearly derives from figure 10.14, even though the new music has an individual character of its own.

Applying pattern-matching processes (see chapter 5 for a more complete description) to the input of association networks allows the latter to discover and reuse small, repeated motives called musical signatures (Cope 1991a). As discussed in chapters 4 and 5, this pattern matching can discover similarities between different patterns that resemble one another enough to have musical consequence. Successfully matched patterns exceeding a single beat are stored as a group, thus protecting these signatures from losing their identity.

Association networks make three important contributions to the understanding of creativity: (1) they respond to any language—including music—and learn from positive and negative stimuli provided by users; (2) they develop parsing and generating mechanisms without programmed instructions; and (3) they create variations in otherwise uninspired output by using inductive association. One could argue that association networks, as I have described them here, do not actually create on their own, but only as a result of feedback from users. Of course, one could make the same argument about how humans create. One could further claim that predispositional weightings derived from proximity and similarity control output. However, I remind readers that the association networks I use do not have such predispositional weightings.

Association networks use very simple techniques, yet can create extremely complex results. Viewed in this way, these networks follow Stephen Wolfram's belief that "... in the end it will turn out that every detail of our universe does indeed follow rules that can be represented by a very simple program—and that everything we see will ultimately emerge" (Wolfram 2002, p. 545). However, I do not suggest that the simplicity of association networks represents some parallel to the manner in which the universe was created and evolves. I simply argue that connections between recombinant nodes—particularly the inductive potential of these connections—provide a logical model for computational creativity. I strive, whenever possible, to make my programs as simple as possible, always preferring that complexity arise naturally from these simple processes. The ideas of both recombination and association as presented here are good examples of such simple beginnings producing complex output. Gerald Gazdar and Chris Mellish note that "... standard scientific considerations such as simplicity and generality apply to grammars in much the same way as they do to any other theories about natural phenomena. Other things being equal, a grammar with seven rules is to be preferred to one with 93 rules" (Gazdar and Mellish 1989, p. 121).

In contrast to most other database formats, any node in an association network is as close to the user as any other node. This closeness may not be immediately apparent when looking at the visual images produced by networks in this chapter and chapter 9. It allows immediate access to all data, regardless of their location in the hierarchy or when they were entered into the network. Thus, each node can immediately reference all of the other nodes in the network without any intervening steps. This immediate reference provides advantages for music association, since recombinance can proceed without the necessity of evaluating intervening code or searching for appropriate lexicons.

I have placed a source-code version of a relatively simple association network called Associate on my Web site for downloading by those interested in using the program for testing or for their own research. I have included a number of transcripts of sessions in both language and music as possibly useful tutorials. Associate implements the association network described in this chapter and chapter 9, and will, when provided the same input, generally produce the outputs shown in the chapters' figures. (I use the word "generally" here to acknowledge that when two or more highest weightings compete during program response, Associate can produce slightly different output.)

Associate allows users to initiate, continue, clear, save, and load conversations; read transcripts of previous sessions; and view weightings and associations. Note again that the use of the "Yes^" and "No*" special symbols does not mean that previous responses will always or never occur again, only that the chances for reoccurrence will be enhanced or reduced slightly. It may take several repetitions of positive or negative input for a particular desired result to appear. While this approach may seem unnecessary, to have the program severely increase or decrease the weights of connections would falsely advantage or disadvantage the chances that many other—possibly correct—responses could occur. By increasing or decreasing the weights in small increments, many of these potentially important ancillary connections can be protected.

The Weightings menu item in the platform-dependent version of Associate, also on my Web site, produces a complete list of connection-between-word-or-music weightings, as shown in figure 10.15 (using words). Here, each initiating word is followed by a parenthetical list of all other words in the current conversation, along with their respective weightings to that initiating word. As shown in the figures in chapter 9, the Associations window in the platform-dependent version of Associate (see figure

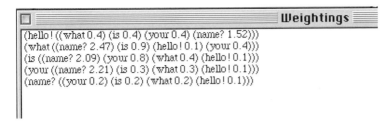

Figure 10.15
Associate's Weightings menu item window.

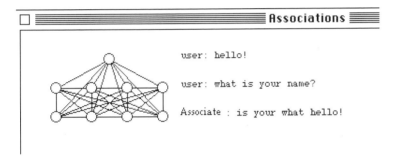

Figure 10.16
Associate's Associations menu item window.

10.16) presents visual representations of the nodes and connections of verbal and musical interactions with Associate. Clicking on any of the nodes produces its weightings (see figure 9.3). The platform-independent version of Associate provides a simple ASCII version of these nodes and connections.

Interacting with Associate using words or music provides readers with firsthand experience using a potentially creative machine partner. Note, however, that though the initial stages of a conversation appear to be creative, in the sense that predicting responses often proves futile, this unpredictability results from a lack of sufficient input, and not from creativity. Intermediate stages of interactions, in contrast, can produce predictability and boredom. Using inductive association, then, induces less predictable and more creative output, as shown in this chapter.

As just mentioned, the platform-independent version of Associate has no tools for visually presenting the complex interconnections of nodes (and so on) of its association network. However, these graphics, as visually powerful as they may be, do not in any way alter the association processes I have described in this chapter. Therefore, while not as visually interesting, the platform-independent association network code that I have made available is just as robust as the one presented in this chapter. Given that users will interact with the program in the general manner I have described here, results from both forms of association should be similar when using the same input data.

I have been describing many different processes here, and readers may wonder at this point whether some combination of these processes actually models what humans do when they create. While recombinance, allusions, SPEAC, and association all seem reasonable premises for creativity, the manner in which I have discussed them over many chapters may seem artificial. Therefore, in the following chapter I shall describe methods for combining these processes into one integrated association network.

11 Integration

Principle: Creativity depends on the integration of its various characteristics into a unified whole in which the sum is greater than the total of the individual parts.

Linear Models

My first telescope arrived in kit form, some 300 separate pieces ready—according to the instructions—for easy assembly. With great care and anticipation, I carefully fitted the various parts together into a six-inch Newtonian reflector. As always, alignment of mirror and equatorial mount proved to be the most difficult tasks. However, by that evening I was ready to view the heavens; I had viewed them, up to then, only in the pages of astronomy books and magazines.

Planning ahead for just this moment, I had logged the coordinates (right ascension and declination) of my favorite celestial object: the ring nebula. After figuring universal time into my calculations, I slowly moved my setting circles to their proper readings. Being a novice, I had little expectation that I would actually see the ring nebula on my first try, but hoped that at least I would find a recognizable star pattern that would eventually guide me to it. I was completely shocked, then, when I looked into the eyepiece and discovered a beautifully contoured ring nebula. This doughnut-shaped gaseous cloud took up nearly the entire field of view. So astonished was I at my luck in actually finding the nebula so quickly, that I began making plans for my career in astrophysics. This clearly was one of those pivotal moments in life that we all dream about.

Curiously, however, as the nebula slowly drifted from my view, it was replaced by another ring nebula, and then another, and another—the sky appeared to be full of ring nebulae. While certainly beyond my expectations, this sight was also beyond credibility. After all, in reality, there was but one ring nebula. Something was amiss.

I examined the telescope for errors in construction, but found none. I reviewed all of my knowledge of the night sky for any hint of what I was seeing, but found none. I recalculated each of my steps in aligning the telescope and then discovered my error—in my haste, I had forgotten to focus the eyepiece. With a few small adjustments, the field I was viewing resolved all of the ring nebulae into stars. What I had seen was the image of my telescope's Newtonian secondary reflecting mirror in grossly out-of-focus images.

My disappointment was then magnified when, try as I might, I could not now find any version of the ring nebula anywhere I looked in the sky. Nor did I find it the next night, nor even the night after that. It was only after many attempts and careful reading of star charts that I finally discovered the nebula. However, even then the actual image was so slight, so ghostly, that the only way I could actually "see" it was by trying *not* to see it (looking off in a slightly different direction). As I later discovered, the images of the ring nebula that I had admired for so many years in books were timed photos, the camera's shutter kept open for many minutes to allow the image to develop its shape.

I recount this story because instruments such as telescopes—and certainly computer programs—can give the appearance of failure when actually just one small part of the instrument has failed. Complex systems are very difficult to design, and even more difficult to build; often the simplest missing or maladjusted element gives the impression that the whole system—the whole process—does not work. In this chapter I describe how all of the various elements I have discussed thus far in this book can be assembled into just such a complex system. Beware as I do so: just one mistake, just one out-of-balance part of this system, can cause complete—not partial—failure. However, and this point is very important, it is often not the system's failure, but a failure of one element in the system. The secret is to remain faithful to the process and find that problem element.

Most of the algorithms that I have used over the years have had serial designs. Experiments in Musical Intelligence, for example, consists of simple sequential processes, as evidenced in figure 5.12 of *Computers and Musical Style* (Cope 1991a, p. 153). While the processes of Experiments in Musical Intelligence are varied somewhat in the algorithm I present in my book *Experiments in Musical Intelligence* (see figure 1.13 of Cope 1996, p. 27), and three of the steps—analysis, pattern matching, and deconstruction—have parallel activities (SPEAC, signature dictionary, and lexicons), the basic step-by-step development of new music is nonetheless serial.

The algorithm for Alice in figure 6.5 of *The Algorithmic Composer* (Cope 2000, p. 221), while it includes recursive feedback, also proceeds sequentially. Even the mode of presenting algorithms as flowcharts encourages linear motion toward a desired goal. It is not surprising, then, that my first attempts at connecting association networks to separate programs involving allusions, influences, and so on would take a more or less serial route.

In fact, if each of these processes described in chapters 4 through 11 of this book—association, allusion, structure, and so on—functioned independently during the creative process, fitting them into a whole would prove relatively simple. Even their order of presentation in this book could serve as the model for a final sequential combination. However, I believe human composers create by freely intermixing these processes, often calling on each many times, and creatively interleaving them in diverse ways.

Figure 11.1 presents a simple schematic diagram of how an association net could serially implement the connections to the other processes described in this book. As

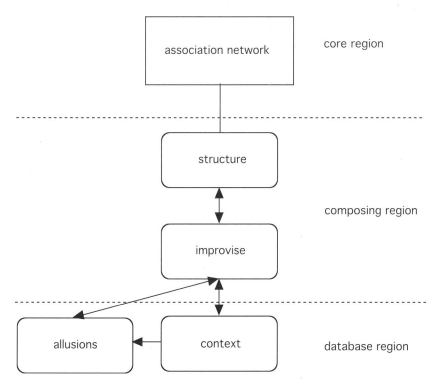

Figure 11.1
A schematic of how an association net could serially implement connections to the other processes described in this book.

this simple diagram shows, the combination of processes falls into three regions here—core, composing, and database (listed on the right-hand side of figure 11.1). The association network at the top of this figure continues to associate its nodes in multiconnective ways. However, rather than simply outputting its weight-influenced responses, this network seeks relevant "advice" from the consultative subprograms. Unfortunately, the various subprograms here often report through other subprograms rather than directly to the association network.

Solving this combinational dilemma using a serial model requires a more novel approach, an example of which appears in figure 11.2. This figure shows one process as a control center to which all of the other processes report. I chose the association net described in chapters 9 and 10 for this central controlling role because of its critical role in both interacting with users and acting as a database. Connecting each of the other four processes—pattern matching for allusions, form and SPEAC, and

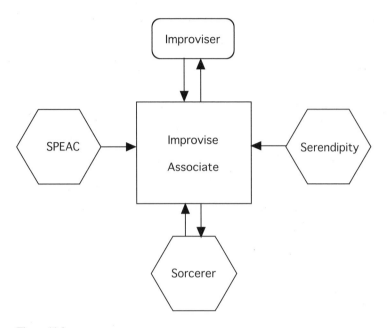

Figure 11.2
A simple schematic diagram of a more logical serial approach to combining the processes described in this book.

influence—to this association network allows users and the network itself to in-directly access each process with appropriate musical or language input. In other words, users need not concern themselves with which process produces the appropri-ate output, but only that data be accurately inputted to the association network—in terms of music or words. By virtue of its software connections and its training, the association network then delegates problems to the appropriate subprocesses.

Allusions and context present the most problems for this model. One of the ways to create allusions computationally when generating new music is to use more than one database, with these other databases then organized hierarchically: the source music actually used for "normal" stylistic composition in this association network, music used for allusions in a different database, and music serving as a model for the number and types of allusions to be used in the new composition in yet another database. The composing process then begins by analyzing the model data-base for the number and types of allusions. The association network then generates new music recombinantly while simultaneously selecting allusions from the allusion database in proper number and type according to the results of the analysis of the model database. This allusion-integrating process has the advantage of retaining preferences for certain music or musical styles by the composer/user whose musical style is being replicated. This allusion-integrating process has the disadvantage of being very complex, in contrast with the integration so obviously innate to association networks.

An alternative process to using three separate databases involves including small snippets of the music of other composers familiar to the user or composer of the database music, in order that these snippets contribute allusions to the final musical creation. However, this process runs the risk that only fragments preferred by users will occur in the output, thus voiding the creative potential of the program.

A third, and possibly more powerful, way to include allusions in new music using this kind of serial model involves allowing the allusions found in the source music to recur in the output music. The advantages to using this approach are twofold: (1) whatever messages these allusions were intended to convey in the original work may survive in the newly composed music; and (2) if the allusions differ stylistically from the database music (e.g., quotations of folk music within music of entirely different character), such differences will be maintained in the output music. This third approach to creating allusions in output provides the simplest and most faithful-to-the-music-in-the-database approach for serial designs.

Whatever method is used for selecting and employing allusions, the association network in the model in figure 11.2 connects these allusions to surrounding music by using the previously discussed voice-leading processes (see chapter 4), guaranteeing that these connections will follow the current style of voice leading in the input music. Allusions then appearing in the new output must be protected from transformational recombination (as described in Cope 2000, p. 87, and in Cope 1996, chapter 5), one of the processes that association networks use for inductive association.

The problems with contextual influence when using serial designs are similar to the problems encountered with allusions. The difference between these two problems is that context music *influences* rather than *appears in* output music. I have solved this problem by using the approaches presented in chapter 10 and by using polymodality (described in detail in the upcoming section "Parallel Models").

I am not suggesting that humans process allusions and contextual influence separately, as shown in figure 11.2. However, while there are certainly many theories about how this interleaving of processes functions in humans, I seriously doubt that anyone has it right, or that there is necessarily a right way at all (i.e., we all seem to create in somewhat different ways). What I do suggest by this diagram and the ones to follow, is that the creative process results from a series of negotiations between contextual influence and allusional and structural processes.

The processes connected to one another in figure 11.2, however, do not function smoothly together in ways we generally associate with human creativity. Requiring the association network both to decide which subprogram to consult and then to incorporate the output of that subprogram in its own processes, is inefficient. I therefore turn to parallel rather than serial approaches. As we shall see, parallel processes use only three subprograms—pattern matching for allusions, structure, and contextual influence—that exist separately from the central association network.

Parallel Models

If neural networks (also known as parallel distributed processing) have taught us anything, it is that processes need not necessarily proceed nose to tail, one to another, but can proceed simultaneously. Thus, figure 11.2, while descriptive of the necessary processing that must occur, can be self-constricting to the point of defying the very goals it is meant to achieve. It may be that explaining an algorithm by language or visual means creates problems, since both language and visualization often require stepwise configuration. I hope that my next explanation then will neither confuse nor negate the extended route I have taken to arrive at this point. To help ensure that I do not exacerbate possible confusion with vagueness, I will keep my discussion brief in hopes that the proof of my theories lies in the results—the music—that my program creates.

Figure 11.3 presents a simple schematic diagram of this more parallel approach to combining the various creative processes I have described in this book. In this schematic, the user at the top engages the program through its MIDI or ASCII interface, connected directly to the association network. The association network then takes center stage with each of the three remaining programs—pattern matching for allusions, analyzing SPEAC, and creating musical structure, providing context—acting as integrated satellites.

Each of the three subprograms of the association network in figure 11.3 interacts with the central association network by receiving function calls from the program's ongoing interplays with users. Such interplays may involve simple requests for responses to verbal questions. On the other hand, interplays may also involve initiating the creation of complex music that subsequently requires SPEAC to provide its structure.

The association network in this parallel version of the program can receive input in the form of either music or language (any language or combination of languages, as discussed in chapter 9). This mixture of input types—called polymodality—has many advantages, not the least of which is that users can directly ask the program

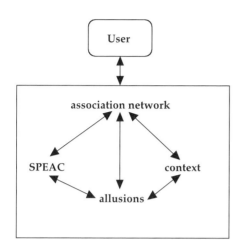

Figure 11.3
A diagram of a parallel approach to combining the processes described in this book.

for new music, an allusion, or an example of contextual data from the Internet or another source. The association network must, of course, be trained on the language used, just as it must be trained on the musical style intended to be used by the program when composing. Once trained, however, the program follows relatively complex verbal instructions as well as fairly sophisticated musical cues. Most important, of course, the program can, without provocation, act *creatively*, responding to text and musical input in unpredictable but, I hope, useful ways.

Parallel processes offer opportunities for music to influence, but not actually participate in, composition, an idea I introduced in chapter 8, discussed in detail in chapter 10, and now shown in figure 11.4. As can be seen in this figure, the secondary networks, the ones having the contextual data, connect via one intersecting node to the primary association network. This connection enables the secondary networks to affect composing without diluting the ongoing connectivity in the primary association network. This approach requires that the association network select the intersecting node on the basis of some logical criteria in advance (equivalent content, relative content, etc.). As well, nothing in this diagram indicates how the single-node connection actually promotes influencing rather than recombination.

To solve these problems, I designed an *inclusion* network, one that includes the data at a movable point in the association network where the current node of connection dictates the influence. The caveat with this approach is that the nodes of the contextual data connect only to themselves and to one of the previous and one of the following primary nodes. Figure 11.5 provides an example of this process.

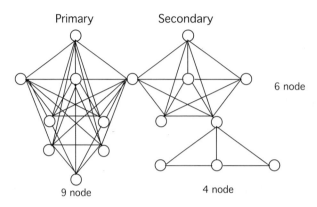

Figure 11.4
An associative multinetwork.

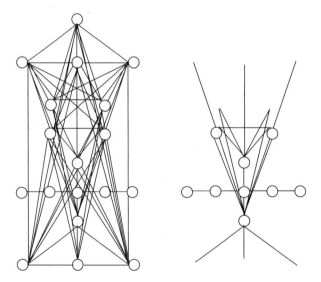

Figure 11.5
Alternative inclusion version of a multinetwork.

The drawing on the left of the figure shows a small inclusion network, the sixth level from the top, which consists of contextual data.

Close examination reveals that this layer on the right connects only to the middle nodes of the upper and lower nodal levels of the primary network. The drawing on the right-hand side of the figure shows this data connectivity more clearly. This lower-level connections here have been ignored for clarity, and the sixth level relates only to itself, with the exception of the central nodal system, which connects to the primary association network. By virtue of its nonstationary location, this inclusionary approach to multinetworks ensures logical positioning of contextual influences. This inclusionary process uses the same method of contextually influencing recombinant music. These contextual influences, then, do not dilute or compromise the otherwise consistent style of the music.

Unfortunately, parallel processes pose many problems. For example, the various modules, working in parallel, often produce conflicting input to the association network. This is not the case with the serial versions, since the hierarchy, as cumbersome as it is with serial networks, prevents such conflicts from occurring. Thus, neither the serial nor the parallel approach adequately combines the processes necessary for musical creativity.

Integration

Given the problems with both serial and parallel models of connectivity, I have chosen a fully integrated model for combining the various processes described in this book. This integrated model combines the advantages of both the serial and the parallel versions into a single approach that is so simple that it need not be represented by a diagram or flowchart. This approach involves integrating recombination, pattern matching for allusions, SPEAC and form, and contextual influences into a single cohesive association network, with each of these processes occurring naturally as an organic implementation of the network itself rather than as separately connected subprograms. In brief, this is how this integration operates:

1. Recombination occurs as a natural function of the association network's response mechanism, as described in chapters 4 and 10.

2. Pattern matching of allusions occurs during input, and all allusions, signatures, and so on are tagged as such as they are stored in their nodes.

3. SPEAC, already integrated in its musical form as nodal names (see chapter 10), informs recombination naturally during composition.

4. Form is derived as a side effect of the sentencelike manner in which music is inputted; each phrase is analyzed during input and, like allusions, is tagged with its formal characteristics for reuse in responses.

5. Influence follows generally the same approach as allusions, with the exception that it does not contribute directly to recombinatory output music.

Categories 1, 3, and 5 above seem self-explanatory. Allusions and form, however, continue to require special attention, not only because they do not integrate easily but also because they represent thorny and contrasting problems.

One of the more difficult problems that designing an integrated model of creativity—called Apprentice, and available on my Web site—raises is how to incorporate a creative approach to musical form. The Apprentice program uses two distinctly different approaches to musical form: extraction and generation. The rationale for using these two quite different processes results from Apprentice's approach to data storage when compared with other of my composing programs, which require at least one complete work in the database to act as a model for new compositions. Apprentice, on the other hand, does not rely on standard databases, but on interaction with users, in which there is little information as to when a work model ends or even what actually constitutes a complete musical work (i.e., user input or some combination of user input and program output). In a sense, extracting form from such a process resembles deriving a novel from an ongoing informal conversation. On the other hand, as we shall see, extraction does have its advantages as well.

To extract musical form, Apprentice must first receive a user-initiated instruction—the tilde or "~" sign—asking the program to produce a complete work rather than simply respond to input. At that point, the program builds a complete hierarchical structure of SPEAC symbols, retroactively adding—or in some cases subtracting—SPEAC identifiers and creating a hybrid form (as discussed in chapter 7). The program then assumes that unless informed otherwise, all of the preceding inputs and outputs constitute the *phrases* of a completed work. This incremental input of data represents an important distinction between Apprentice and many of my other programs that require extensive analysis to determine where cadences occur. In Apprentice, cadences appear naturally at the ends of inputs and outputs. While advantageous, this solution does not determine section endings and, as described in chapter 7, the program must still analyze music for similarity and contrast.

Analyzed hierarchy and form (note again my distinction between these two terms as defined in chapter 7) require some degree of generation to ensure that newly composed musical forms are not simply mirrors of input forms. To generate musical form, Apprentice uses SPEAC (see chapter 7, and especially figure 7.23 and associated discussion, for an in-depth presentation of this process). Briefly, form derives from an expansion of syntax into a top-down, treelike structure in which the semantics (the actual music) results from recombination, but the ordering of the recombinant-built phrases follows SPEAC syntax.

Polymodal association networks also deal with language, which offers the composing program a natural resource from which to draw logical proportions for form when none otherwise exist. When creating musical form, I have Apprentice pattern-match its language responses to find areas of repetition, contrast, and variation. When it is used to select allusions, I have the program save allusions with as many characterizations in language as possible—lyrics in the case of songs, work titles, verbal expressions of tempos, and so on—and then, when composing, pair the current musical phrase's strongest language associations with best fits in the available language-represented musical allusions. In other words, language serves as a catalyst for matching allusions to surrounding music.

As I discussed in chapter 10, allusions occur in new music as a result of weighting analogies, which themselves result from comparing original groupings and their original destinations with potential new recombinatorial choices and their destinations. Comparable proportions (not actual weightings) are then used to select and integrate musical allusions. This "&&" (regional) associative induction extends the musical environment beyond the local music in the user-created network (database).

Apprentice incorporates another important component that integration of the various contributing subprograms now makes possible. This component—intent—is potentially important for a program whose musical output users and listeners alike are expected to regard as seriously as they regard the musical output of human creators.

I have often written about intent in music (see particularly chapter 1 of this book and Cope 2001a). However, regardless of my belief that music does not require intent or have meaning—at least meaning in the literal sense—I continue to experiment with the possibility that I may be wrong. The integrated program described in this chapter, more than any other software that I have programmed, offers the opportunity to test the notion of intent and meaning in music. The simplest way for an association network to include intent in its processes is to include relevant and potentially meaningful information about the nature of each grouping of music or words it stores in the nodes of its association network. This information is dependent on the combinational language/music input data structure of the program I am describing.

Intent—which I align with "meaning" here because meaning is one of the most natural forms that intent takes—can equate to anything from *meaning* minor and *meaning* tonic, to *meaning* sad to *meaning* resolution. The program I describe here can easily analyze minor modes and tonic functions, and store these attributes along with each grouping of music in the nodes of its association network. However, it would be presumptuous for the program to store "sad" and "home" along with "minor" and "tonic," since no one has yet proven, with any degree of certainty, that such interpretations have any universal validity. The same is true for assigning particular moods to attributes such as tempos, keys, timbres, articulations, and so on, since suggested meanings derived from these attributes are also illusory and ephemeral. At the same time, many would argue that part of the joy of listening to and appreciating music is in imagining the intended meanings when we believe such meanings are present in the music we hear. To these listeners, proof of intent is beside the point.

Therefore, I have included in Apprentice a kind of intent or *meaning* component, where as many logical attributes as possible of each grouping are stored with that grouping. These intended "meanings" include mode, function, tempo, key, timbre, and articulation, along with the title of the work to which the grouping belongs, a weighting of the dissonance (tension) of the grouping and those groupings surrounding it in its original musical environment, SPEAC assignment and rationale for that assignment, source of any allusion to which the grouping may belong, and the pattern contribution the grouping may make (signature, earmark, etc.). Each of these attributes then adds to the mix of matching elements that the program may consider when choosing groupings for recombination. Obviously, when data are limited, these intent or "meaning" attributes have little effect. However, as input increases, the potential for many possible correct choices increases significantly, and subtleties such as these intent attributes become more important in making best choices from the available correct possibilities.

Human composers also have incentive to compose music. Whether it be a commission, an impending performance, fulfillment of a lifelong dream, or a personal quest for immortality, a new musical work is not created without reason. Incentive provides the foundation from which new human musical works emerge.

In order to provide an association network with a kind of software incentive, I use a separate attribute, designated as the incentive attribute, in each node of the association network. This incentive attribute is initially set to pseudo-random numbers between 0.0 and 1.0. I then have the program increase all relevant—defined as those settings that belong to nodes directly involved in current output—incentive settings by .01 when users respond with a "yes" equivalent (not to exceed 1.0), and decrease relevant incentive settings by .01 when users respond with a "no" equivalent (not to go below 0.0). The program then averages its total incentives toward the goal of 1.0.

$$\frac{\displaystyle\sum_{W=0}^{W=N} * \chi}{N} = 1$$

Figure 11.6
The formula that provides incentive for Apprentice.

Of course, this goal is nearly unachievable, since the only way an average of 1.0 can be achieved is if all of the settings are 1.0. However, this goal of 1.0 can be approached.

Interestingly, the ultimate goal of human composers—the perfect piece of music—can, one assumes, never be achieved either. Approaching the average weight of 1.0 requires that the program continually search for responses that will satisfy users, and thus increase the incentive settings of its response nodal choices. I use the formula in figure 11.6 for the incentive of Associate, where W represents all incentive settings, N represents the number of nodes, and X represents proximity to the desired 1.0 average.

This notion of having an association network "aspire" to a nearly impossible goal has many interesting consequences. Not only can this "aspiration" guide the program toward pleasing its user, but it also forces associative induction—creativity—to occur in a more natural way than direct user prodding.

Whether the results of using any of these attributes will be heard is certainly arguable, and the very point of including them. For example, just knowing that the program attempts to make compositional choices based on pleasing its user can increase a listener's acuity in attempting to hear intent, and therefore meaning—not necessarily a bad thing.

Figures 11.7 and 11.8 are graphic representations of a word and a music node in a combined language and music association network. The word node in figure 11.7 contains the attributes required of language interaction with association networks (as discussed in chapter 9). This word node also includes links to the allusion and context music examples. The ties to these particular works most likely result from proximity—I tend to input allusion and context music immediately after words to which I want them linked. The numbers following the cadence and continuity attributes in the music node representation in figure 11.8 refer to programmed lookup

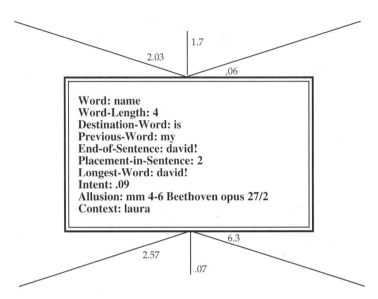

Figure 11.7
A graphic representation of a word node in a combined language-and-music association network.

tables which define various types of cadence and continuity (see chapter 7). While I have included actual music in this graphic, music nodes actually contain events (see appendix B). The smaller numbers next to the lines (connections) outside the word and music nodes here indicate the weightings of these nodes to other nodes in the association network.

Therefore, as we have just seen, not only *can* association networks mix words and music, but they *must* mix words and music, for words are where allusions and context are stored, with the slight weightings they have in their connections to music representing their basic route to inductive association.

Figure 11.9 shows how both language and music can reside in the same polymodal association network but, through significantly different weightings between their connections, be almost mutually exclusive. Association networks compose music when music is inputted, and respond using language when language is inputted. At times, however, the two data types can mix, resulting in quite interesting output. For example, a strong association between a certain word and a particular motive or other musical idea may trigger musical output during language interaction, and vice versa.

Figure 11.10 presents a simplified transcript from a session with Apprentice (the association network available on my Web site) using both language and music. This transcript follows several hours of interaction, during which the program "learned"

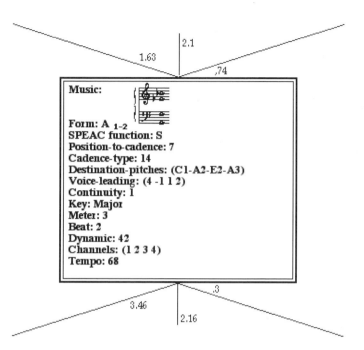

Figure 11.8
A graphic representation of a music node in a combined language-and-music association network.

(note that I do not use the word "understand" here) to follow my instructions. State-ments occurring within "⟨ ⟩"'s represent activities. Statements within quotes repre-sent language input to the program. As can be seen in this figure, with the exception of the small piece of completed music, the interplay typically consists of brief music or language exchanges, much as one might imagine to be the case in a conversation between two human musicians. Clearly, one cannot expect Apprentice to initially produce output as shown here. Training the program often takes a considerable amount of time—typically many sessions over many days. Even with limited ses-sions, however, the program can produce surprising results, as attested to by the name I first gave Associate: Pandora. Of course, Pandora's unpredictability often represented one of its most endearing features: after all, predictability certainly rep-resents a very poor model of creativity.

The platform-dependent version of Apprentice (a limited version of which is avail-able on my Web site) also offers opportunities for composers to edit their music in much the same way they would edit when working without the program. For exam-ple, users can ask the program to reproduce the music they wish to edit by playing it

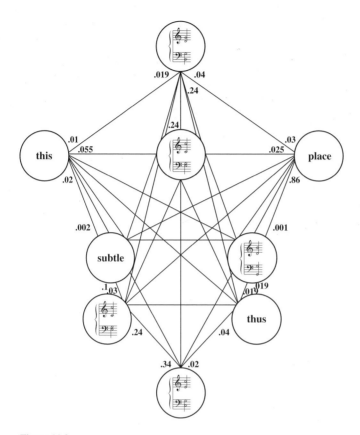

Figure 11.9
How both language and music can reside in the same association network but, through different weightings between connections, have almost mutually exclusive relationships with one another.

or by printing it on the screen. Users can then edit the results, using very simple editing tools in the included notation program. Alternatively, users may save their music to MIDI files, and open and edit them in the notation program of their choice. In the first instance, edited music automatically replaces its old version in the association network. In the second instance, the music must be reentered into the program, with the result that this music will form new nodes in the association network. Unfortunately, unedited music remains in the network and will disappear—weights diminish to 0.0—only with repeated negative responses.

Figure 11.11 presents two examples of music created by an integrated version of the various programs presented thus far in this book. Both of these examples—from

Improviser: <plays music>

Apprentice: <responds with music>

Improviser: "Let me edit that."

Apprentice: <responds with printed music on screen
    with editor>

Improviser: "Let me hear this again."

Apprentice: <plays edited music>

Improviser: <plays music>

Apprentice: <responds with music>

Improviser: "Let me hear a complete composition
    of about five minutes duration."

Apprentice: <responds with composition>

Improviser: "Let me edit that."

Figure 11.10
A simplified transcript from a session using Apprentice.

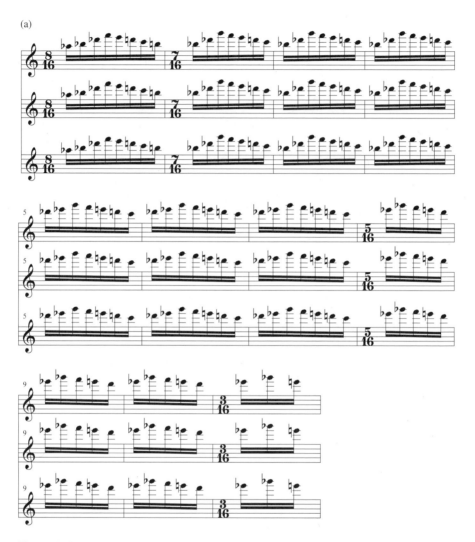

Figure 11.11
From the Algorithmic Sonata no. 3 for Three Disklaviers, completed in 1993, (a) the middle of movement 1 and (b) the beginning of movement 4.

(b)

Figure 11.11
(continued)

my Algorithmic Sonata no. 3 for Three Disklaviers (the middle of movement 1 and the beginning of movement 4), completed in 1993—demonstrate an integration of material which mirrors the integration found in the algorithm which created them. The first-movement example here (a) minimalistically repeats ideas in combination with shifting meters and ever higher registers. The fourth movement (b) uses nearly the full range of the three Disklaviers (requiring at least six pianists for human performance) and a similar—to the first movement—minimal-with-shifting-meter overall concept. The complete Algorithmic Sonata no. 3 demonstrates a consistency of style and idea that characterizes the sources from which it originated.

Many applications, especially music-composing applications, come prepared to provide advertised responses with just a few clicks of a mouse. However, the program on my Web site is more like a word processor—at least initially—in that elegant output will be a long time coming. I do not exaggerate here, for *teaching* language and music to an association network requires an enormous commitment of time and energy. Users should prepare for this commitment, and not expect an immediate return on their investments.

Apprentice takes input from MIDI keyboards, MIDI files, or notation via the notation editor provided with the platform-dependent version of the program. These latter processes are, of course, much slower than simply performing real-time into the program. However, loading MIDI files or notating music by hand can reduce the amount of editing ultimately required for correct input, since the chances for mistakes are much higher when performing than when entering notes one at a time into a notation program. Unfortunately, some performance data (notably performance timings) are lost when using a notation editor.

As I pointed out in chapter 5, in my discussion of Bach's *Well-Tempered Clavier*, most composers—even traditional composers—use algorithms in their creative processes in one way or another. Today, computers offer incredible advantages for such composers, providing speed and accuracy that might take humans years to match. Both composing and programming, however, require incredible dedication, and many composers are neither capable nor adaptable enough to become programmers, and vice versa. In fact, it would be difficult to imagine that many future composers would actually become composer-programmers and create their own composing programs. At the same time, these composers are not willing to entrust their musical decisions to off-the-shelf applications, and thus be constrained by the biases of those applications. Since data-dependent programs have very little built-in bias, composers should be less hesitant about using them for their creative work. The program I have presented here is data-dependent, offering composers the opportunity to virtually design their own program without programming skills.

12 Aesthetics

Principle: Creativity depends on aesthetic values that themselves depend, at least in part, on the acceptance or rejection of others.

Prejudgment

In 1989, a colleague of mine—Linda Burman-Hall—produced a concert of Experiments in Musical Intelligence music in various classical styles alongside similar works by the various emulated composers. When the concert announcements reached the media, a clamor erupted, especially in the local press. One particular music critic was so incensed by the prospect of a concert featuring computer-composed music in the styles of classical composers that he wrote a column that may be unique in the annals of music history: a scathing review that appeared *two weeks prior* to the concert it reviewed. It was not clear whether this columnist expected his review to be published before the concert or not; nevertheless, it *did* appear. To his credit, nowhere in the review did he pretend to have attended the concert, nor did he feign reaction to having heard the music. Instead, he expressed his horror over the very *idea* of the event. He complained that too few people knew the music of C. P. E. Bach— the composer of one of the works on the program—and that to dilute the repertoire with computer forgeries (his term) was unforgivable.

In a sense, I agree with these sentiments, although I feel they are shortsighted. I have no intention of diluting the repertoire of C. P. E. Bach or any other composer, nor do I think for a second that Experiments in Musical Intelligence's output actually competes with C. P. E. Bach's music. I do, however, consider the results of the program's computations interesting and musical, and if for no other reason, they should be performed. I phoned the reviewer and invited him to attend the concert. He declined.

Obviously, if no matter how convincingly I argue the case for computer creativity, audiences ignore or negatively prejudge the output—the proof of success or failure— then very little of what I propose in these pages will have impact. In a sense, prejudgment influences how we perceive music. As I have argued throughout this book, we seem to need to know more about the music we hear than simply that it seems beautiful, or that it was produced creatively. Given this need to know, the music my programs create is often seriously disadvantaged, once the manner of its creation is known. Created or simply produced as output, this music will never have lasting value for such listeners—a shame, since so much of it, at least to my own sensibilities, has a great deal to offer. In this section, I will attempt to determine if it matters whether computers can truly model creativity, if listeners automatically discount the results.

The first two sections of this chapter deal with Experiments in Musical Intelligence rather than the integrated association network described in chapters 9 through 11. I include this discussion here for two reasons. First, my experiences with the compositional output of Experiments in Musical Intelligence represent my only source of relevant aesthetic interactions with the general public. Second, and possibly more important, since the early 1990s Experiments in Musical Intelligence has used an association network as the core of its processes, and therefore has, at least in my mind, creative potential. (I will return to discussing the integrated association network, my basic model of musical creativity, later in this chapter.)

As a brief example of output from a program that begs the question of aesthetic interaction, I present a fragment from *Mahler*, a grand opera with music composed by Experiments in Musical Intelligence and libretto collated by me from the letters of Gustav and Alma Mahler, Anton Bruckner, Thomas Mann, Arnold Schoenberg, Richard Strauss, and Anton von Webern, among others. *Mahler* is the second opera (*Mozart* was the first, and *Schumann* was the last) in a trilogy of operas composed using librettos derived from the letters of the composer whose name each opera bears. I chose the subjects for these operas based on my love of the particular composer's music and on the extraordinary nature of these composers' lives.

The opera *Mahler* follows the composer's life from his childhood to his death, as chronicled by Mahler and his wife Alma. Mahler spent much of his adult life conducting operas but never composed an opera himself. I do not suggest here that this is the opera he might have written had he lived long enough. I only suggest that *Mahler* is the opera that I wanted to hear. The music of this opera, in the style of Mahler, is scored for large symphony orchestra, mixed chorus, and soloists.

A few passages in *Mahler* resemble those in certain works of Mahler. For example, the prelude of the opera is reminiscent of the openings of Mahler's Symphony no. 1 and Symphony no. 5. The onset of act three resembles the third movement of Mahler's Symphony no. 1. Comparisons of the originals and these passages, however, show the latter as vague paraphrases rather than as quotations. I often reject such imitative output, but I don't mind it here simply because Mahler himself seemed so fond of self-referencing.

Figure 12.1 presents a piano reduction of an aria, sung by Alma, from act 1 of *Mahler*. The initial vocal part resembles the accompaniment of Mahler's song *Frülingsmorgen*. However, the computer-created music continues in a very different way. A careful comparison of the harmonies of the program's music and *Frülingsmorgen* (not shown) reveals the originality of the computer-composed music, as well as the way the program extends and varies the harmonic progressions while maintaining their stylistic integrity.

Figure 12.1
An aria sung by Alma from act 1 of *Mahler*.

Figure 12.1
(continued)

Figure 12.1
(continued)

Figure 12.1
(continued)

The second theme of the computer-composed aria (beginning in measure 42) has many elements in common with Mahler's song *Hans und Grethe*, though what are fragments in Mahler's original spin out as full melodies in the computer-generated music. Aside from these similarities, the music of this aria is generally original while nonetheless conforming to Mahler's style.

Setting texts to computer-composed music poses interesting challenges. First, most composers set music to given texts rather than vice versa. This results from the need for musical meter to match poetic meter, and the fact that the lyrics are usually fixed while the music remains pliable. My program, however, does not set texts well, so this process must be reversed. I have the advantage, however, of using translatable texts (from the German). Therefore, I make several different translations to English, and then choose the translation or combination of translations that best meets the criteria for effective text setting.

Since most of Mahler's songs are not orchestrated (at least not the versions of them I used in the database), the program's orchestration, based on Mahler models from other of his works—mostly his symphonies—adds to the uniqueness of this new work. What a shame it would be if those with an opportunity to hear or perform *Mahler* were to avoid this experience, for singing, playing, or listening to this music might convince them of its effectiveness.

Just like the reviewer who "reviewed" the Experiments in Musical Intelligence concert two weeks prior to its performance, many listeners approach computer-composed music, such as this example from the opera *Mahler*, having already decided on its quality and effectiveness. This saves them from having to risk actually evaluating the music. In effect, they disqualify the music they hear because it does not conform to their definition of creatively produced art.

Listeners who have heard a performance of the song in figure 12.1 (available on my Web site as an MP3 file) often qualify their listening experience to the point that this experience bears little resemblance to listening at all. For them, computer-created music represents more of a philosophical challenge than an aesthetic experience. I feel, as we shall see, that many, if not all, of their resultant rhetoric is simply a subterfuge engineered to avoid confronting the music directly.

For example, my programs' music has been criticized for not being *real* composition (Selfridge-Field 2001) or for not shedding light on the creative process (Berger 2001). Clearly most critics think they know what my work is *not*. Few, however, seem to know what it *is*. The terms these critics routinely use when aesthetically evaluating human-composed music, particularly music in historical styles, are typically so narrowly defined as to make any real assessment of computer-composed music difficult if not impossible. Many listeners, however, particularly those unaware of this music's origins, do experience deep emotional responses. Even among these few, however, profound doubts remain. "Ironically the computer program that sometimes produces music as sublime as Mozart's can't tell the difference between a work of genius and a piece of lift music" (Holmes 1997, p. 27). Distinguishing between "a work of genius" and "a piece of lift music," however, hardly results from the application of quantifiable standards. It seems to me that "telling the difference" is a highly subjective process, and should not form the basis for profound doubts about all output from computer programs.

Addressing the issue of creativity in computer-created composition, Selmer Bringsjord and David Ferrucci recount a story about Tchaikovsky in which he appears to reveal the secret behind his Sixth Symphony. In a footnote, they add that this secret

... speaks directly to the question of what might be missing in the EMI (pronounced "emmy") system, which generates musical compositions in the style of a given composer. EMI cannot elevate a composition by sharing its meaning with human listeners. (Bringsjord and Ferrucci 2000, p. 28)

Bringsjord and Ferrucci reference a George Johnson story in the *New York Times* (1997) headlined "Undiscovered Bach? No a Computer Wrote It." Ironically, having vigorously argued against computation creation, nowhere in their account do these authors reference the Experiments in Musical Intelligence program's human creator.

Note that Experiments in Musical Intelligence simply does what I would do to create this music if I had the time and energy. The fact that the nearly 1,000 published Experiments in Musical Intelligence works is reverse engineerable following the principles I have explained in my books testifies to this. Interestingly, I once created a Bach-like chorale by hand following these principles and it took roughly 80,000 times longer than my program takes to accomplish the same task (program = .25 seconds; me = 5.5 hours). Based on the above, and given the amount of music—by duration—my program has created, it would have taken me roughly 200 years (without sleep) to produce this music myself. Thank God for machines.

Other critics of my work claim that Experiments in Musical Intelligence's music *undermines* human creativity. I feel that, to the contrary, the program's music actually *supports* the notion of human creativity. Humans designed and built the computers on which the program runs; a human coded the program that produces the music; humans composed the music that the program uses as a database; and, possibly more important, humans listen to and evaluate the output. Yet these facts seem lost amid our deep-seated fears of being replaced by machines.

Interestingly, when I attempted to have my Experiments in Musical Intelligence's music recorded on compact disc, I encountered yet another interesting paradox. After I had experienced many rejections, one company insisted that my program's music, though created recently, was not *contemporary* music, but rather *classical* music, because of the classical styles it imitated. I took this comment seriously, and subsequently submitted the music to classically oriented record companies. I was then told, however, that my program's music was not *classical* but *contemporary* music, because of its date of composition.

I finally approached a company specializing in computer music. Counting on this specialization as an edge, I sent the company—actually a cooperative of professional computer-music composers—tapes and liner notes describing my program's compositional processes. I was aware that most computer-music composers use computers for synthesis—in essence, as musical instruments rather than as compositional tools. However, I also assumed that such composers could conceptually grasp the intrinsic importance of computer composition. However, I was informed, after extensive discussion among the membership of the cooperative, that the group had decided that my program's music was in fact not computer music at all, since the results did not *sound* like computer music. I responded angrily that if one had to choose which of the two paradigms represents true computer music, surely computer composition would prevail over computer synthesis. They did not agree.

Listeners and critics also redefine the criteria they use to judge the Experiments in Musical Intelligence program's output by including stylistic credibility. In other words, the music succeeds only if its style matches the musical style of the composer in its database at the time of composition, regardless of whether or not the music itself succeeds independently of this style verification. These individuals often listen for quotes or paraphrases of the composers of the music in the database. Once such allusions occur, these listeners claim that the composing process produces pastiche rather than original music, even though for centuries composers have quoted themselves and others consciously and subconsciously (as clearly demonstrated in chapter 5).

Jim Aikin's numerous critiques of Experiments in Musical Intelligence's music fall into this category:

My first rush of enthusiasm for Cope's achievement chilled rapidly into irritated dissatisfaction. What was on the tape was recognizably Mozartean, no question about it. Characteristic turns of phrase were assembled into recognizable harmonic structure, with transposed figures, appropriate bass lines, and cadences in the correct places. The trouble is, it was bad Mozart. Here's this brilliant music scholar and computer programmer, unquestionably a bright, dedicated, and perceptive person, and he has devoted ten years of his life to producing bad imitation Mozart ... the question is, is it even theoretically possible for a computer program, no matter how sophisticated, to produce good Mozart? I claim it's not.   (Aikin 1993, p. 25)

This last statement strongly suggests that Aikin agrees with those who have decided the quality of the program's output *before* actually hearing it.

Some critics redefine their criteria for listening to the Experiments in Musical Intelligence program's output by comparing it with other computer-created music they have heard. Still others attempt to hear the compositional processes at work, or listen for analytical mistakes. Many other listeners don't know how to listen to this music. Few individuals, however, attempt to appreciate the music simply for what it is— new music written in known musical styles. Possibly this lack of appreciation results from the fact that by the time they have redefined their approach to the music, such individuals no longer have any reason to listen—their minds and ears have already closed.

In *The Algorithmic Composer* (Cope 2000, p. 240), I discuss Stephen Smoliar's (1994) argument that the Experiments in Musical Intelligence program's output has been successful *only* because of its performances by human performers. This was one reason I recorded the first Experiments in Musical Intelligence program's commercial recording (Cope 1994) on a MIDI-controlled Disklavier, without any performer interpretation: to demonstrate precisely what the program had composed. Jason Vantomme (see Cope 2000, p. 240) responded negatively to this mechanical performance, claiming it lacked human expression. According to these two perspectives, when Experiments in Musical Intelligence's music is performed live, the credit for success goes to the performers, and when it is performed automatically, the results do not succeed. Either way, from the viewpoint of these critics, the program's output fails.

Douglas Hofstadter, a reluctant supporter of Experiments in Musical Intelligence's music, remarks that "The program has no model whatsoever of life experiences, has no sense of itself, has no sense of Chopin, has never heard a note of music, has not a trace in it of where I think music comes from. I'm comparing that with an entire human soul, one forged by the struggles and travails of life ... and all the experiences that create emotion, turmoil, despair, resignation, everything you want to think of that goes into building a character" (Nuttall 1997, p. 5). This romanticized notion of music somehow expressing the human experience confuses me. After having for decades read the little black dots and lines of printed musical scores, I am shocked to discover that I have apparently missed finding these struggles and travails.

Like Hofstadter, I certainly feel similar and other emotions as I listen to music, but I am under no delusion that they originate in and are transferring from the black dots and lines on a page of printed music. These emotions are *mine*. Claude Lévi-Strauss, among many others, postulated this idea long before I did, in essence arguing that humans have a need to ascribe meanings to things, and therefore, when listening to music, we give it meanings that are not actually there (see Lévi-Strauss 1971). I have quoted John Cage on this subject, but cannot resist repeating his remarks here: "Most people think that when they hear a piece of music, they're not doing anything but that something is being done to them. Now this is not true, and we must arrange our music, we must arrange our art, we must arrange everything, I believe, so that people realize that they themselves are doing it, and not that something is being done to them" (Nyman 1974, p. 21).

Interestingly, Douglas Hofstadter comments that he is very concerned about being *moved* by 20,000 lines of code (also little black dots and lines). He believes that failing to distinguish between computer-created and human-created music indicates that (1) music isn't very deep or (2) humans aren't very deep or (3) computer programs are much deeper than we could ever imagine (see Cope 2001a). Any one of these indications discourages him. "Does that mean," worries Hofstadter, "that the composer's soul is irrelevant to the music? If that's the case—and I'm not saying it is—then I've been fooled by music all my life. I've been sucked in by a vast illusion. And that would be a tragedy, because my entire life I've been moved by music. I've always felt I've been coming into contact with the absolute essence of humanity" (Holmes 1997, p. 23). I see this as a romantic notion for which I share empathy but to which I give little credibility.

Many listeners distance themselves from the music of Experiments in Musical Intelligence by questioning the rationale for its existence. For example, Karl Putnam states, "It is clear that the musical examples that attempt to recreate a known historical style succeed. The question is: What does this signify? Any one piece of music can be 'explained' by any number of music theories. Perhaps the main point here is that this music theorist has put his theory to the test, not just on one piece, not just one composer, and not just on one style, and has furthermore used it to compose original works" (Putnam 1997, p. 103). As flattering as these remarks may be, they nonetheless represent another distraction from the music itself. Many listeners would have us believe that Experiments in Musical Intelligence's significance lies in its ability to conduct tests on compositional and stylistic theory. As Michael Casey writes, "... why have a computer attempt something that we can already do much better by ourselves? The answer is that in doing so we discover more about music as a system of the human intellect" (Casey 1993, pp. 1054–1055).

Audiences, interviewers, and especially composers have questioned my rationale for creating programs that themselves create music in historical styles, and proliferating the music from these programs. There are, I believe, many good reasons for my having done so. First, as critics point out, my program's analytical and compositional approaches can reveal aspects of musical style, structure, and compositional process. Pattern matching, one of the program's most important techniques for discovering style traits, has revealed a world of signatures, earmarks, allusions, and other patterns that I and many others had previously considered clichés, if we in fact considered them anything at all. Studying these patterns over time in a composer's oeuvre often reveals significant stylistic development that hitherto has been observed tangentially but not explicitly.

On the other hand, I maintain that the most important aspect of my work is the output—the music. Possibly the most cruel description of my work I have heard over the past twenty-plus years was uttered quite innocently by a former student of mine, who characterized Experiments in Musical Intelligence as my "analysis software." Not only does this description center on analysis and programming, but it completely ignores the musical compositions that the program has created. While extreme, this statement typifies the many confusions surrounding my work, confusions that would not exist were those who are confused simply listen to me: *what matters most is the music.*

In a fairy tale by Hans Christian Andersen titled "The Nightingale," a Chinese emperor and his peasants become charmed by the songs of a nightingale. When a mechanical nightingale appears, it outsings the real nightingale and gains the favor of the emperor. The real nightingale is then banished from the kingdom. Time passes. The emperor lies dying, and only the sound of the nightingale can save him. However, the mechanical bird has broken down, and no one knows how to repair it. The real nightingale is summoned, and happily saves the emperor with its songs.

This simple tale lures us into what Andersen sees as the false and alien world of technology. His tale, however, does not address the issue of how difficult it would have been to revive the living bird had it died, or why no one knew how to fix the mechanical bird. The tale simply ends with the admonition that while technology can be appealing, it will ultimately fail us. This view represents a basic trope for the technophobe and leads to the idea that, as Bruce Mazlish notes, "the alternatives are either a frightened rejection of the Frankensteins we have created or a blind belief in their 'superhuman virtues' and a touching faith that they can solve all our human problems" (Mazlish 1993, p. 7). Neither of these alternatives, of course, need be, or actually is, true. Mazlish adds:

We are now coming to realize that humans and the machines they create are continuous and that the same conceptual schemes that help explain the workings of the brain also explain the workings of a "thinking machine." Human pride and its attendant refusal or hesitation to acknowledge this continuity form a substratum upon which much of the distrust of technology and an industrialized society has been reared. Ultimately this distrust ... rests on the refusal by humans to understand and accept their nature—as beings continuous with the tools and machines they construct.   (Mazlish 1993, pp. 4–5)

Mazlish suggests here that we should not condemn computers for what we perceive they can or cannot do, but appreciate what we and our computers can do *to-*

gether. In this view, we should no longer have need to defend our "humanness," but should understand that computers are simply extensions of ourselves. Curtis Roads notes:

A danger of composition programs is that they can serve as a substitute for the creativity of the user who invokes them.... If composition was merely a puzzle or parlor game, then the technical virtuosity of the machine would already have relegated human efforts to a sideshow. The machine can execute formal composition rules that are far more intricate than any human being could possibly keep track of. It can effortlessly spin a web of n-part microtonal counterpoint and fugue from any germ series subject to an arbitrarily complicated system of constraints. Like a sequencer that races through performances with superhuman speed and precision, the complex ratiocinations of machine composition inspire awe—up to a point. Excessive complexity, like excessive precision or virtuosity for its own sake, is a vapid and tiresome musical diet. The talent of composers who use algorithmic composition methods is reflected in their skill in managing the excesses of their occasionally self-indulgent software prodigies.   (Roads 1996, pp. 851–852)

Certainly music is not "merely a puzzle or parlor game" nor "complex ratiocinations" good music. That does not mean, however, that great music cannot be created by computer programs. Interestingly, to say that humans cannot program computers to do what they themselves can do does not indicate, I believe, that humans are superior, but rather that they are *inferior*—not competent enough to understand and replicate their own creative processes. Stravinsky notes that

... there is a tendency to turn the mind away from what I shall call the higher mathematics of music in order to degrade music to servile employment and to vulgarize it by adapting it to the requirements of an elementary utilitarianism.   (Stravinsky 1960, pp. 48–49)

Had the works that my programs have composed been presented as lost music by the important composers the works were meant to imitate stylistically, these same works would surely not have received much of the criticism that I document here and in many other sources (see particularly Cope 2000, 2001a). These experiences confirm that context plays an enormous role in the way many of us listen to and evaluate the music we hear.

In contrast, there are those who believe that works of art should be considered only in terms of their own worth and not in terms of who created them or when, where, or how they were created. In the mid-twentieth century, for example, Cleanth Brooks (1947) and others—as part of a loosely structured group rallying around the designation "the New Criticism"—considered poetry as an *autotelic* artifact. Briefly, this means that these critics thought poems should be treated as complete within themselves, created for their own sake, and not dependent on relations to the poet's life, intent, or historical context. However, it would be imbecilic for me to suggest that listeners ignore the context surrounding the works they hear—few could manage such a feat.

Unfortunately, the very context we depend upon to provide our deeper experiences in music may be partly or even wholly inaccurate. For example, in the 1980s I composed an algorithmic work based on simultaneously rising and falling minor seconds—a study in rhythmically offset, contrapuntally opposed chromatic scales. About a year after completing this work, a dear friend of mine died, and to meet an immediate request for music to be played at his memorial service, I dedicated this work to him. After the performance, many listeners commented on how moved they had been by the sadness of the music and the funereal sense it provided to the service—none of which was originally intended. Composers often manipulate audiences by providing extramusical contexts (titles, program notes, etc.) that in reality have little to do with the inspiration of or rationale for composing their work.

According to many critics, computer programs—even computer programs using databases of human-composed music—lack context. This, of course, is not true. Indeed, computer-created music may have more interesting context than much traditionally composed music. Even the various reactions to the music I relate in this chapter establish and contribute to such a context.

Without contextual background, it can often be very difficult to recognize computer-created music when it occurs amid human-composed music. For example, the Beethoven and computer-program sketching tests I describe in chapters 3 and 10 both indicate creative origins. Interlacing these sets of sketches in a way that retains a sense of order, as in figure 12.2, and then attempting to ascertain which of these sketches were created by Beethoven and which were created by a computer program, should, it seems to me, clearly indicate how difficult it can often be to recognize computer-created music. Again, however, these points evade my earlier argument that creativity is a *process*, and not the *result* of a process, and, as such, it cannot be evaluated in the usual ways (see chapter 2).

Certainly not all of those who encounter my program's compositions react negatively. Doug Hofstadter relates the story that after he had presented a few Experiments in Musical Intelligence inventions in the style of Bach in Toronto, one listener proclaimed that the computer-composed inventions were far *superior* to Bach's originals. I do not agree. Like this Toronto listener, another claims that "... it would be easy to say a machine could never do the work of an artist, plumbing the depths of the human spirit and soaring to fly with the gods. ... Well, bad news for music snots and wetware (gray matter) bigots: the 42nd [the Experiments in Musical Intelligence symphony in the style of Mozart was named Mozart's 42nd by Bob Holmes (1997, p. 23), not by me] sounds like Mozart" (Mancini 1997). However, comments such as these represent the exception, not the norm.

Figure 12.2
Music to ascertain which of the melodic sketches was created by Beethoven and which by a computer program.

I believe Experiments in Musical Intelligence has created some engaging music. Were the program human, this alone would validate it. Of course, appreciating this music for its inherent beauty requires listeners to set aside any biases they may have about creativity being a uniquely human process. However, it seems to me that good music requires no justification beyond just existing.

Many colleagues have suggested over the years that I release Experiments in Musical Intelligence as a commercial software application. They argue that not only would I benefit financially, but that releasing it would make style composition available to anyone who wished it. After all, as I mention in chapter 2, Harold Cohen has released his painting algorithm Aaron as an inexpensive screen saver. Possibly Experiments in Musical Intelligence could become a classical Muzak generator, avoiding the boredom generated by repeatedly having to listen to the same music while riding in an elevator or waiting for a doctor's appointment. There are, however, many reasons why I will not commercially release my version of this software.

Any one of these reasons by itself would discourage me from such a venture; all of them together make it imperative that I refuse.

Creating commercial software is not easy. Most applications on the market have taken several hundred programmers many years to develop and hone. Even creating the few small applications for my previous books on Experiments in Musical Intelligence proved the difficulty in producing this kind of software. To create serious commercial software applications also requires venture capital or making the code available to an existing software company, and neither of these prospects interests me.

All music that the program uses as a database reveals small mistakes due to quantization errors or out-of-bounds pitches, rhythms, channels, or dynamics. Many of these errors require small code changes or corrections in the music in the database, which in turn requires that users know music, know the program, *and* know Lisp. After years of experience, I routinely debug and resolve such problems. Even creating databases that pose none of the above problems requires enormous amounts of checking and correcting, since even the smallest mistakes become magnified during composition and produce failed output. Users of commercial software cannot be expected to have this kind of musical or programming knowledge, and I see no other way to avoid these problems.

The small success that my project has garnered has resulted, I believe, from its concentration on Western classical music. In contrast, the commercial software world—including both producers and consumers—has little interest in Western classical music. On the other hand, I have little interest in adapting Experiments in Musical Intelligence for use in replicating popular music and, if my few ventures into that arena are any indication, the program would not be effective in replicating popular genres anyway. Popular music, for the most part, relies on lyrics, particular timbres, performance context, and many other factors that my program cannot control. The mere fact that we know most popular music by its *performer*, rather than its *composer*, should confirm this problem.

Experiments in Musical Intelligence is not a single program but many smaller programs that I often run separately. For example, selecting music for a database, an extremely important aspect of the overall composing process, necessarily takes place separately and often requires hours of deliberation and error checking. I then convert, check, and recheck databases independently of composition. Pattern matching also typically occurs separately before composition. This involves listening and relistening to possible signatures to verify that the pattern-matching program's controllers have been set correctly. Deciding whether to accept a new composition occurs after, and distinctly separately from, the composing process. Actual algorithmic composition takes only about 5 percent of the time required for the complete assembly and analysis of a work's database. The various separate processes make debugging much easier, since using a single complete program could confuse the location and nature of errors. However, these processes require skill and time that most users are unwilling to spend, particularly when they know that audiences will still assume that this computer composition probably required less time to create than is required to listen to the work itself.

Experiments in Musical Intelligence has also been a work in progress (what Hofstadter calls a "moving target") rather than a static software application. I constantly tinker with the various subprograms, both because I think I can improve them and because their environment (system software, various hardware, MIDI software, and so on) constantly changes. In fact, rarely do six months pass in which a version of one of these ancillary programs *does not* change. While different versions of commercial applications could be considered a "moving target," I have no interest in spending years revising a commercial version of Experiments in Musical Intelligence.

Interestingly, my five books on Experiments in Musical Intelligence provide a blueprint—I have not left out any significant secrets—for those with the time, energy, and dedication to create their own, possibly better, version of this program. I hope my prose is clear enough to provide the guidance required. I encourage those interested also to use the code I've distributed with my books as a model, particularly SARA (an acronym for *s*imple *a*nalytical *r*ecombinance *a*lgorithm; see Cope 1996), which follows the basic principles of Experiments in Musical Intelligence. To have others build upon this body of work would be far more rewarding to me than the small financial return for commercializing this program myself.

Finally, if I made a commercial version of Experiments in Musical Intelligence available for those interested in replicating Western classical music, I would, for a modest financial gain, be making it all the easier for my competition to create new works potentially as good as or better than the ones Experiments in Musical Intelligence has created. This seems oxymoronic. Having others build their own programs based on some or all of the principles in Experiments in Musical Intelligence, and then promulgating the output (as discussed above), would not be the same. Given these arguments against producing a commercial version of Experiments in Musical Intelligence, or any of the programs presented in this book, I would, I feel, be out of my mind to pursue it.

For those interested in pursuing these goals on their own, however, I have published the source code for many of my programs on CD-ROM (see particularly Cope 1996, 2000) and on my Web site. As I have pointed out here and elsewhere, when users take the time to sculpt databases correctly, these programs produce good-quality output. I cannot imagine, therefore, that anyone would now be interested in my pursuing a commercial version of Experiments in Musical Intelligence.

To one persistent individual who has repeatedly requested that I commercialize my program, I wrote:

You think that my work has to do with software. I think that my work has to do with music, occasionally good music, music that whether it is good or bad poses interesting, possibly important questions. In some ways I am flattered by your confusion. You want to have my software for, like the goose that laid the golden egg, you want to create golden music. As long as you think my work has to do with software, however, you will continue to miss the point.

Interestingly, the important questions to which I refer here are not of the type "Can computers compose good music?" or "Will computer composing programs replace human composers?" or "Can we tell which of these works was composed by computer?" The important questions to which I refer here are more of the type "What is musical style?" and "Why is this work considered good, and this other work not considered good?" and "What role does context (the composer's life, etc.) play in our appreciation of music?" and "Does music have meaning?" and so on. The former questions seem superficial—parlor games to confuse the inexperienced or untrained ear. The latter questions strike at the heart of why we listen to music, and what distinguishes music from the other arts and from our other life experiences. Until persons such as the one to whom I addressed the above E-mail understand the difference between these sets of questions, the music produced by Experiments in Musical Intelligence will remain little more than a curiosity. For those who do understand the difference, the questions toward which my program's creations point, but do not ultimately answer, have provocative substance and relevance. Future incarnations of programs such as Experiments in Musical Intelligence, of which I believe there will be many, should therefore reveal new worlds of possibilities for the study and appreciation of music. I have spoken of these in my previous books (see particularly the final chapters of Cope 1996, 2000).

Experiments in Musical Intelligence (1980–2003)

Since 1980, I have made extraordinary attempts to have Experiments in Musical Intelligence's works performed. Unfortunately, my successes have been few. Performers rarely consider these works seriously. A friend of mine has noted the intimidating nature of the number of outputs possible from computer programs. Uniqueness, he feels, is an extremely important factor in human aesthetics. Knowing that my programs represent an almost infinite font of such works apparently renders them less interesting, no matter how beautiful and different from one another they might be. For many, knowing that I could restart my program at any time, and produce a thousand more works, apparently lessens their interest in the one. As well, part of the experience of listening to a musical work—in fact, experiencing *any* work of art—is knowing that while it may be imitated, it is unique. This sense of uniqueness is heightened by the fact that for human-created works at least, composers *die*.

It was with these thoughts in mind that I decided (in early 2003) to stop creating historical-style replications with Experiments in Musical Intelligence. I did not take this decision lightly, for I have spent nearly twenty-five years of my life inventing, coding, developing, writing about, and defending Experiments in Musical Intelligence. In spite of these efforts, however, the program's music continues to be regarded, at least for the most part, as a curiosity. Interest from musicians, when it arises periodically, almost always centers on the program and not on the music, leaving me with the impression that the formula is more important than the actual musical results that formula produces.

Often when people refer to the music of Experiments in Musical Intelligence, even people who support it, they refer to it as "output." This is a perfectly apt description of the product of a computer program. However, as readers are no doubt aware by now, I consider some of Experiments in Musical Intelligence's output to be my own. When I find output I like and call it my own, I no longer consider it output; I consider it a musical composition, even though here and elsewhere I may use the word "output," simply because it represents the results of computation.

Part of the reason, it seems to me, that "output" is the first word that occurs to most people is that computer programs have virtually no production limits. None of the "output" from a computer program has any claim to uniqueness in the same way that human-created music does. My turning from historical-type replication thus, I hope, makes each of its "outputs" slightly more valuable, in ways that only items of rarity are valuable.

By mothballing Experiments in Musical Intelligence, I have declared the end of the period of my life during which I have composed, in collaboration with my computer programs, works in historical musical styles. The works thus composed can now be indexed, performed, recorded, studied, and so on, as an oeuvre, a completed body of work. These works are thus unique and, I hope, musically more valuable than they seemed when each new day brought the possibility of many more new creations. With this newly valued status, I hope that the program's music will be performed and recorded by other than my close friends and colleagues.

In short, I am returning to composing in my own style and doing research in musical creativity, as opposed to devoting my time to composition in historical musical styles. I do not regret this decision; after all, I have completed five books on

Experiments in Musical Intelligence since 1991, along with numerous articles, contributions to edited volumes, and several commercially available recordings. While I have completed my research with Experiments in Musical Intelligence, I will continue to compose algorithmically, using my own versions of Apprentice, Alice (see Cope 2000), and other yet to be created programs.

To ensure that I would not be enticed back into the world of historical composition, I have erased all of the Experiments in Musical Intelligence's databases. Recreating these databases would require several hundred hours, a project I was at one time obviously willing to undertake, but am not willing to undertake a second time—surely not after having deliberately erased all known copies of my first collection. I have not, however, destroyed my program itself.

Appendix A presents the complete list of all of the publicly available works created by Experiments in Musical Intelligence. Each entry contains the work's title, instrumentation, and duration. No works will be added to this list, nor will any work on this list be altered—at least by me. This list could have been much longer, had I not been so careful in deciding what to release and what to discard. I have not included various associated works in this list (such as the 5,000 works of 1992 discussed earlier in this book and in Cope 1996), since these works do not represent particular historical-style compositions, and because I have not yet begun the enormous task of translating each of these works from MIDI format to performable compositions (music notation).

The list in appendix A does not include reductions, different arrangements, or other versions of these works. For example, each of the piano concertos exists in two-piano arrangements to aid in performance preparation. The three grand operas have several versions—English, German, English and German together, and so on. All of these works are published by Spectrum Press (www.spectrumpress.com).

I decided early on in my research with Experiments in Musical Intelligence not to release more of any particular genre of music than the original composer's output. For example, there are 371 Bach-style chorales—the same number that Riemenschneider (1941) collected, forty-eight Bach-style preludes and forty-eight fugues—the same number as in Bach's *The Well-Tempered Clavier*, and so on. It is not that I believe these newer works in any way compete with the originals upon which they are based, but rather that I do not want to risk the originals being lost amid greater numbers of new compositions in their same style and form.

Early in 2005, I placed 5,000 MIDI files of computer-created Bach-style chorales on my Web site for download by those interested in how Experiments in Musical Intelligence's compositional abilities fare over large numbers of works. This collection includes many failures as well as potential successes. However, it represents an experiment only, and not output in the sense of what I have otherwise described here and thus I have not included them in my list.

It is worth noting here that the works listed in appendix A are but the tip of the iceberg of the actual output of the Experiments in Musical Intelligence program. For example, the 1,000 nocturnes in the style of Chopin mentioned in *The Algorithmic Composer* (Cope 2000, p. 26) remained in compressed non-MIDI form for over ten years before I translated several and discovered that, due to the small database of Chopin's nineteen nocturnes, much of the output—at least the output that I heard —sounded too similar to preserve. Even with a large database, after ten or so compositions the works that Experiments in Musical Intelligence produces begin to sound alike, with similar themes, harmonic progressions, and so on. As I mentioned previously, my objective with Experiments in Musical Intelligence has been to create good music, not simply to accumulate a vast number of inconsequential musical output, nor to flood the world with music in the styles of Western classical composers. As well, my point has never been to compete with human composers, but rather to understand music more completely and, I believe, ultimately appreciate it more.

There are works on the list in appendix A that I believe have considerable merit. Each of the three grand operas, for example, took years to complete and represents an enormous amount of reading, selecting, and translating of texts for the librettos, gathering and selecting music for databases, listening to and choosing appropriate music for arias and recitatives, and then matching the librettos to the music. The three symphonies (Mozart, Beethoven, and Mahler) and three keyboard concerti (Bach, Mozart, and Rachmaninoff), and the *Well-Programmed Clavier* (forty-eight preludes and forty-eight fugues in the style of Bach), all, I believe, attest to the quality of some of the program's output. I have included one set of works in quantity— hundreds of Bach-style chorales—since these works have a generally consistent musical worth. These chorales were chosen from a set of 1,000 chorales that I thought represented the best music. I regret not completing a set of Mozart string quartets (there is only one here), Haydn piano sonatas, and particularly Ives's Universe Symphony. As well, several people have chided me for not attempting to complete Schubert's so-called Unfinished Symphony. Unfortunately, these projects would have required enormous commitments of time and energy that I felt could be best spent in other ways at this point in my life.

I have included several works in my own style in the list in appendix A. This may seem presumptuous—to have my name appear alongside great classical composers.

However, I feel that this music modeled on databases of my own compositions represents both my style and my taste effectively, and therefore it seemed appropriate for inclusion.

As a farewell token to readers of this book, appendix E presents a new Experiments in Musical Intelligence symphonic movement in the style of Beethoven. This slow movement (actually the second movement of a complete four-movement symphony in the style of Beethoven) begins similarly to Beethoven's own Symphony no. 3, "Marcia funebre" (movement 2), and continues with a series of variations on the main theme, interrupted by several repeated cadential figures. However, the resemblance between the two movements ends with these similarities. Where the computer-created music follows a rather straightforward melodic and rhythmic plan, Beethoven's movement develops a rich tapestry of melodic twists and turns over a dynamic and somewhat unpredictable rhythmic foundation.

This computer-created Beethoven-style movement resulted from a combination of many of the various processes described thus far in this book. For example, an association network (at the heart of Experiments in Musical Intelligence since the early 1990s) provided the basic recombinatory framework that allows the music to flow logically and stylistically. Several allusions to Beethoven's music (notably the primary theme, a paraphrase of Beethoven's "Marcia funebre") occur here, provided by the Sorcerer program's analysis of the input music. The overall form of this movement results from a SPEAC analysis of many of the works of Beethoven in the database during composition. While I cannot pinpoint any contextual influence, since such influences occur indirectly rather than directly, I believe—based on previous experience—that the quality of the music results, at least in part, from the inclusion of this influencing process in the creation of this music.

Clearly, movements like this one in appendix E cannot be achieved without a sufficiently "trained" association network and a well-defined and well-honed database of primary and contextual musical source material. The Beethoven movement shown in appendix E required several months of data gathering and development as well as several generations of corrections and flawed output before attaining the quality of music here.

A Virtual Creator

There is a trick that magicians often use when all else fails to capture an audience's imagination. This trick begins with the magician tossing a lemon into the audience and asking whoever catches the lemon to verify that it is indeed what it appears to be. The magician then asks for a dollar bill in return. After collecting the dollar, the magician reads its serial number aloud slowly, requesting that someone in the audience write down the number on a sheet of paper. Having completed this preparation, the magician strikes a match and lights the dollar bill afire, letting it burn to a fine powder. The magician then retrieves the lemon, cuts it open with a knife, finds a dollar bill at the lemon's center, and gives it to the audience member who has the written-down number of the original dollar bill. Not surprisingly (it is a magic trick, after all), the serial number of the newly found dollar bill in the lemon matches the serial number of the original dollar bill exactly.

When performed properly, this trick seems fantastic. Obviously the dollar bill could not have been transported into the lemon, and yet no other explanation seems plausible. As with most magic tricks, however, the magic is not magic at all. To create this illusion, the magician—in advance of the act—removes the end knob from a lemon and bores a hole through its core. The magician then writes the serial number of a dollar bill on his thumbnail, curls this dollar bill into a tight cylinder, and fits it into the lemon, gluing the end knob back into place so that the lemon appears untouched. When the magician reads the serial number of the dollar bill to the audience, he actually reads the serial number printed on his thumbnail, thereby misdirecting the audience.

As with all magic tricks, there is no actual magic in this trick. Sleight of hand, misdirection, hidden objects, and audience assumptions account for the magician's arsenal of legerdemain. In this book, I have attempted to prove that there is no magic in creativity either. The only magic in creativity is that we think magic is involved. Certainly the creative process is complex and enormously difficult to follow, if we can follow it all. It is not, however, magic. As a result, creativity is programmable, whether or not the processes I describe here accurately replicate it.

I have not spoken much about chess since chapter 1, and return to it now. James Eade comments that computer chess

... used to fascinate me, but now I'm not so keen on it. Certainly computers are playing a stronger game, but the point is that they are not really playing chess. They're simply performing calculations.   (Eade 1999, p. 235)

Surely many people—chess players and non-chess players alike—concur with these thoughts. No doubt this quotation especially resonates with players checkmated by a computer program. But what does Eade imagine that *he's* doing when he plays chess? On what level is he somehow *not* calculating? I imagine that Eade uses *creativity* to distinguish his more human approach to the game. Given the principles that I have described so far in this book, I would argue that computers are capable of every technique, nuance, and creative maneuver that Eade, or even the best chess champion, can muster. The fact is, machines *can* play chess and compose music, sometimes as well as or better than humans. This is not astonishing. What is astonishing is that many of us humans find this so hard to believe. What is equally astonishing is how little credit such individuals give humans who created the game of chess, computers, and these very computer programs in the first place.

With these thoughts in mind, let me review the twelve principles upon which my model of creativity rests.

1. Creativity relies on connecting differing but viable ideas in unique and unexpected ways.

2. Creativity does not depend exclusively on human inspiration, but can originate from other sources, such as machine programs.

3. Creativity should not be confused with novelty or comtivity.

4. Creativity does not originate from a vacuum, but rather synthesizes the work of others, no matter how original the results may seem.

5. Creativity relies in part on the juxtaposition of allusions to the work of others.

6. Creativity requires learning and knowledge in order to produce useful rather than arbitrary results.

7. Creativity is not limited to note-to-note motions, but occurs at every structural level.

8. Creativity develops within enfolding and influencing contexts, and not in isolation.

9. In order for computer programs to create, they must themselves develop and extend rules, and not simply follow instructions provided by programmers.

10. Musical creativity relies on composers, performers, and listeners associating their experiences across a broad landscape of music tradition.

11. Creativity depends on the integration of its various characteristics into a unified whole in which the sum is greater than the total of the individual parts.

12. Creativity depends on aesthetic values that themselves depend, at least in part, on the acceptance or rejection of others.

I have attempted to embody these principles of creativity in an association network through the use of user- and self-motivated inductive association. I believe that this inductive association effectively models creativity. Many readers will argue, however, that we humans place an indelible stamp on what we create. This stamp is not a single event nor a single process, but rather a continuous influence that affects, in small but important ways, every aspect of what we produce. We find this influence in all of what we create, from the weakest to the strongest music, from the simplest to the most complex music, and from the most banal to the highest-order music.

The secret of my work, however, is that rather than trying to imitate this influence, I have, by using the data-dependent processes I first discussed in chapter 4, attempted to retain that influence in the output. I have written my programs to let the original music's influence *breathe* through the process of recombination. I have steadfastly refused to meddle with (distort) the original music's human influence. While it may seem maudlin to some, my desire to have *everything* depend on the analysis of human-composed music means that whatever aesthetic the original possesses may, at least to some small degree, survive in the music my programs produce.

Interestingly, one could argue that music created by programs using data-dependent processes have *more* contextual influence than music produced by other computer programs (see related discussion in chapter 8). Just like the music composed by human composers, algorithmically created music based on the analysis and recombination of human-composed music retains signatures, earmarks, and other stylistic identifiers (see Cope 1996), as well as the influence of the users of the software (particularly in the case of data-dependent software, where users select the music for databases and then determine which works survive and which do not—critically important aspects of the creative process). Indeed, over time, my database and output selections demonstrate a definite *style* of preference that would, no doubt, differ markedly from choices made by others in my place. In short, those who claim that the creations of data-dependent programs lack humanity ignore these critical contributions.

Without question, creativity is far more complicated than I have described in the pages of this book and in the programs these pages describe. In spite of this, however, these descriptions and programs represent a beginning. Association, allusion, structure, form, and context all contribute to creativity, no matter how one defines the word, and I hope the efforts represented here can serve as a foundation that will enhance our understanding of "the initialization of connections between two or more multifaceted things, ideas, or phenomena hitherto not otherwise considered actively connected." Certainly the models defined here will further develop *my* understanding of how—and possibly even why—humans invest so much energy and hope in this activity.

Creativity is dynamic and complex, but it is also manifestly analyzable and computable. Whether the model of creativity I describe here succeeds or not, that result in no way changes this fact. As we have also seen, creativity is not a *thing* but a

(a)

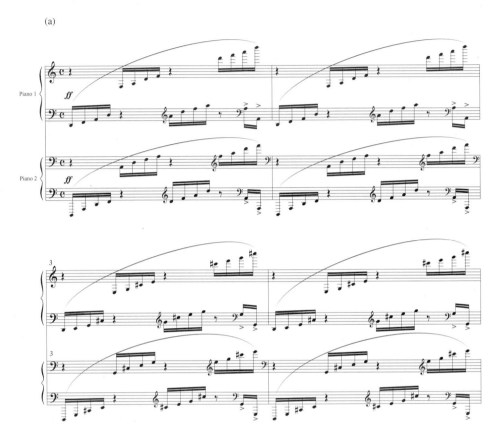

Figure 12.3
Examples of music from the beginnings of each movement of *From Darkness, Light*.

process. I believe, therefore, that the most useful models for creativity resemble the dynamic processes found in association networks. The computer-created music presented in this book attests to the veracity of this model. For those of us concerned that this model might replace that which it intends to model, have no fear. Creativity does not spring from a vacuum, but rather from problems that require solutions. No computer program yet created has the self-awareness to perceive a problem, no less perceive the need that it be solved. Until such programs do exist, true creativity will remain a uniquely human domain.

Given all that I have thus far presented in this book, I now offer three axioms of machine creativity:

(b)

Figure 12.3
(continued)

1. Machine programs can create.

2. The quality of music has nothing to do with who or what created it.

3. The only limit to what machines can do is the limit of what we as humans can do with machines.

In regard to the first axiom above, I have tried to prove here that unless one's definition of creativity limits it to humans, computer programs can create. I have attempted in the second axiom to show that the only thing we accomplish by judging and prejudging computer-generated music is to deny ourselves the opportunity to experience potentially extraordinary music. The third axiom indicates how shortsighted most critics of computer creation can be. Every limitation we place on the potential of machines is a limitation we indirectly place on *ourselves*.

Whether or not the principles and programs in this book accurately model creativity obviously remains at the discretion of each reader. Certainly I have no illusions that everyone will feel that my arguments prove that computers can create. However, we have grappled with many of the fundamental issues of creativity, and in so doing

(c)

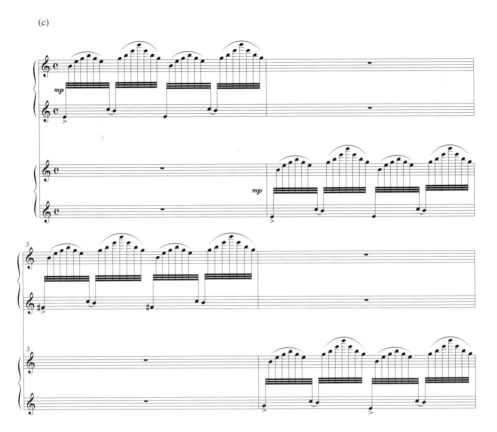

Figure 12.3
(continued)

have, I hope, revealed many important concepts and processes without which creativity could not exist.

If, after all I've said here and in my other books and articles, and after hearing
the music *created* by my programs, these words and this music continue to be treated
as experimental "output" of computer software, it will not be my loss; it will be
your loss. With this thought in mind, I present new music representing the evolution
of a new *creative* entity. Figure 12.3 shows examples of music from a fully integrated
association network that follows most of the principles discussed in this book. This
music for two pianos in the form of three preludes and three fugues, titled *From
Darkness, Light*, was completed in the spring of 2004. The unusual structure of
this work derives from my initial inability to coerce the program to produce graceful

(d)

Figure 12.3
(continued)

or even acceptable transitions between sections of contrasting music. Thus, each of the six movements develops a single musical idea. The choice of using fugues instead of, say, having all preludes, developed from my desire to incorporate formalisms with an association network early in my experimentation, to ensure that they were feasible.

As can be seen and heard in this figure, the music is basically triadic and quasitonal. The original material derives in part from the Experiments in Musical Intelligence's Rachmaninoff-style Piano Concerto (Cope 2003c), music I entered into the association network one phrase at a time. The database—association network—of

Figure 12.3
(continued)

this new creative entity consists primarily of Experiments in Musical Intelligence's music. The fugues here, while remaining contrapuntal until their conclusions, differ in many ways from the standard fugue formalisms of the baroque tradition. However, these fugues maintain their energy in quite vital ways and develop strong driving forces to their concluding measures.

I plan to have the integrated association network that composed these movements continue to *create* new music over the next few years—forming, I hope, a dynamic and unique style—and to become a better composer as time progresses. Part of my rationale for creating this entity, and for extending this venture, follows from my desire to continue to interact—both linguistically and musically—with the principles and processes I have evolved over many decades of designing and implementing integrated association networks. This book is the introduction of this new program.

And her name is Emily Howell.

(f)

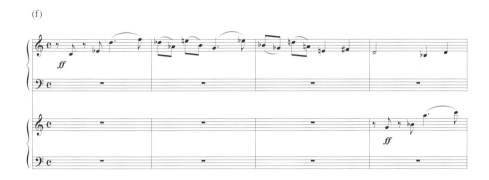

Figure 12.3
(continued)

Bibliography

Adelman, George (ed.). 1987. *Encyclopedia of Neuroscience*. Boston: Birkhäuser.

Agawu, V. Kofi. 1991. *Playing with Signs: A Semiotic Interpretation of Classical Music*. Princeton, NJ: Princeton University Press.

———. 1996. "Music Analysis versus Musical Hermeneutics." *American Journal of Semiotics* 13/1: 9–24.

Aikin, James. 1993. "Ghost in the Machine." *Keyboard* 19/9: 25–28.

Ames, Charles. 1987. "Automated Composition in Retrospect: 1956–1986." *Leonardo* 20/2: 169–185.

———. 1989. "The Markov Process as a Compositional Model: A Survey and Tutorial." *Leonardo* 22/2: 175–187.

Anderson, Alan Ross (ed.). 1964. *Minds and Machines*. Englewood Cliffs, NJ: Prentice-Hall.

Anderson, John R., and Gordon H. Bower. 1973. *Human Associative Memory*. Washington, DC: V. H. Winston.

———. 1983. *The Architecture of Cognition*. Cambridge, MA: Harvard University Press.

Assayag, Gerard, and Shlomo Dubnov. 2002. "Universal Prediction Applied to Music Generation with Style." In *Proceedings of the Fourth Diderot Mathematical Forum*, 147–160. Berlin: Springer-Verlag.

Baldi, Pierre. 2001. *Bioinformatics: The Machine Learning Approach*. Cambridge, MA: MIT Press.

Barlow, Harold, and Sam Morgenstern. 1948. *A Dictionary of Musical Themes*. New York: Crown.

Berger, Jonathan. 2001. "Who Cares if It Listens? An Essay on Creativity, Expectations, and Computational Modeling of Listening to Music." In David Cope, *Virtual Music*, 263–281. Cambridge, MA: MIT Press.

Bernstein, Leonard. 1976. *The Unanswered Question: Six Talks at Harvard*. Cambridge, MA: Harvard University Press.

Binot, Jean-Louis. 1991. "Natural Language Processing and Logic." In *From Natural Language Processing to Logic for Expert Systems: A Logic Based Approach to Artificial Intelligence*, edited by A. Thayse, 49–116. New York: Wiley.

Birchler, David, Peter Burkholder, and Andreas Giger. 1999. *Musical Borrowing: An Annotated Bibliography*. http://www.music.indiana.edu/borrowing

Boden, Margaret. 1987. *Artificial Intelligence and Natural Man*. Second edition, enlarged. New York: Basic Books.

———. 1990. *The Creative Mind*. London: Weidenfeld and Nicolson.

———. 2004. *The Creative Mind: Myths and Mechanisms*. Second edition. London: Routledge.

Bringsjord, Selmer, and David Ferrucci. 2000. *Artificial Intelligence and Literary Creativity*. Mahwah, NJ: Lawrence Erlbaum.

Brooks, Cleanth. 1947. *The Well Wrought Urn: Studies in the Structure of Poetry*. New York: Reynal & Hitchcock.

Bulhak, Andrew. 1990. *Postmodernism Generator*. http://www.elsewhere.org/cgi-bin/postmodern

Burkholder, J. Peter. 1994. "The Uses of Existing Music: Musical Borrowing as a Field." *Notes* 50/March: 851–870.

Cairns-Smith, Alexander Graham. 1971. *The Life Puzzle*. Toronto: University of Toronto Press.

Cajori, Florian. 1934. *Sir Isaac Newton's Mathematical Principles of Natural Philosophy and His System of the World*. Berkeley: University of California Press.

Carbonell, J. G. 1983. "Derivational Analogy and Its Role in Problem Solving." In *Proceedings AAAI—1983*. Washington, DC: AAAI.

Casey, Michael. 1993. "Computers and Musical Style." *Notes* 49/3 March: 1053–1055.

Cesa-Bianchi, Nicolò, Masayuki Numao, and Rüdiger Reischuk (eds.). 2002. *Algorithmic Learning Theory: 13th International Conference*. New York: Springer-Verlag.

Charniak, Eugene, and Drew McDermott. 1985. *Introduction to Artificial Intelligence*. Reading, MA: Addison-Wesley.

Cherkassky, Vladimir S., and Filip Mulier. 1998. *Learning from Data: Concepts, Theory, and Methods*. New York: Wiley.

Clarke, Eric. 1988. "Generative Principles in Music Performance." In *Generative Processes in Music: The Psychology of Performance, Improvisation, and Composition*, edited by John A. Sloboda, 1–26. Oxford: Clarendon Press.

Cohen, Harold. 2004. *Aaron*. http://www.kurzweilcyberart.com/

Cook, Nicholas. 1989. "Beethoven's Unfinished Piano Concerto: A Case of Double Vision?" *Journal of the American Musicological Society* 42/2: 338–373.

Cooke, Deryck. 1959. *The Language of Music*. New York: Oxford University Press.

Cooper, Barry (ed.). 1988. *Ludwig van Beethoven: Symphony No. 10 (First Movement)*. London: Alfred A. Kalmus.

———. 1990. *Beethoven and the Creative Process*. Oxford: Clarendon Press.

Cope, David. 1974. *Arena*. New York: Carl Fischer.

———. 1991a. *Computers and Musical Style*. Madison, WI: A-R Editions.

———. 1991b. "Recombinant Music." *Computer* 24/7: 22–28.

———. 1992. "Computer Modeling of Musical Intelligence in EMI." *Computer Music Journal* 16/2: 69–83.

———. 1994. *Bach by Design*. Baton Rouge, LA: Centaur Recordings 2184 (compact disc).

———. 1996. *Experiments in Musical Intelligence*. Madison, WI: A-R Editions.

———. 1997. *Classical Music Composed by Computer*. Baton Rouge, LA: Centaur Recordings 2329 (compact disc).

———. 2000. *The Algorithmic Composer*. Madison, WI: A-R Editions.

———. 2001a. *Virtual Music*. Cambridge, MA: MIT Press.

———. 2001b. *New Directions in Music*. Seventh edition. Prospect Heights, IL: Waveland Press.

———. 2002. *The Well-Programmed Clavier*. Paris: Spectrum Press.

———. 2003a. *371 Chorales in the Style of J. S. Bach*. Paris: Spectrum Press.

———. 2003b. "Computer Analysis of Musical Allusions." *Computer Music Journal* 27/1: 11–28.

———. 2003c. *Piano Concerto in the Style of Sergei Rachmaninoff*. Paris: Spectrum Press.

———. 2003d. *Virtual Bach*. Baton Rouge, LA: Centaur Recordings 2619 (compact disc).

Crumb, George. 1986. "Interview: Crumb/Shuffett." In *George Crumb: Profile of a Composer*, 34–37. New York: C. F. Peters.

Crystal, David. 1987. *The Cambridge Encyclopedia of Language*. Cambridge: Cambridge University Press.

Dacey, John S., and Kathleen H. Lennon. 1998. *Understanding Creativity*. San Francisco: Jossey-Bass.

Damasio, Antonio. 1999. *The Feeling of What Happens: Body and Emotion in the Making of Consciousness*. New York: Harcourt Brace.

Danlos, Laurence. 1987. *The Linguistic Basis of Text Generation*, translated by Dominique Debize and Colin Henderson. Cambridge: Cambridge University Press.

Dartnall, Terry (ed.). 1994. *Artificial Intelligence and Creativity: An Interdisciplinary Approach*. Boston, Kluwer Academic.

Davis, Morton. 1983. *Game Theory: A Nontechnical Introduction*. New York: Basic Books.

deBono, Edward. 1970. *Lateral Thinking: Creativity Step by Step*. New York: Harper & Row.

———. 1971. *New Think: The Use of Lateral Thinking in the Generation of New Ideas*. New York: Avon.

————. 1984. *The CORT Thinking Skills Program*. New York: Pergamon Press.

Dennett, Daniel. 1995. *Darwin's Dangerous Idea*. New York: Simon and Schuster.

Dorian, Frederick. 1947. *The Musical Workshop*. New York: Harper and Brothers.

Dougherty, Ray. 1994. *Natural Language Computing: An English Generative Grammar in Prolog*. Hillsdale, NJ: Lawrence Erlbaum.

Dreyfus, Hubert. 1979. *What Computers Can't Do: The Limits of Artificial Intelligence*. Revised edition. New York: Harper & Row.

————. 1992. *What Computers Still Can't Do: A Critique of Artificial Reason*. Cambridge, MA: MIT Press.

Duckworth, William. 1992. *A Creative Approach to Music Fundamentals*. Fourth edition. Belmont, CA: Wadsworth.

Eade, James. 1999. *Chess for Dummies*. New York: Hungry Minds.

Edelman, Gerald, and Giulio Tononi. 2000. *A Universe of Consciousness: How Matter Becomes Imagination*. New York: Basic Books.

Ehrenzweig, Anton. 1967. *The Hidden Order of Art: A Study in the Psychology of Artistic Imgination*. Berkeley: University of California Press.

Elsea, Peter. 2000. http://arts.ucsc.edu/ems/music/research/FuzzyLogicTutor/FuzzyTut.html

Evans, Thomas. 1968. "A Program for the Solution of Geometric-Analogy Intelligence-Test Questions." In *Semantic Information Processing*, edited by Marvin Minsky. Cambridge, MA: MIT Press.

Falkenhainer, Brian, Kenneth Forbus, and Dedre Gentner. 1990. "The Structure Mapping Engine." *Artificial Intelligence* 41/1: 1–63.

Feynman, Richard. 1985. *QED: The Strange Theory of Light and Matter*. Princeton, NJ: Princeton University Press.

Fischer, Eugen. 2000. *Linguistic Creativity: Exercises in "Philosophical Therapy."* Boston: Kluwer Academic.

Fixx, James. 1978. *Solve It!: A Perplexing Profusion of Puzzles*. Garden City, NY: Doubleday.

Fodor, Jerry. 1983. *The Modularity of Mind: An Essay on Faculty Psychology*. Cambridge, MA: MIT Press.

French, Scott. 1993. *Just This Once*. Secaucus, NJ: Carol Publishing Group.

Freud, Sigmund. 1959. *Creative Writers and Daydreaming*. London: Hogarth Press/Institute of Psychoanalysis.

Fromm, Eric. 1959. "The Creative Attitude." In *Creativity and Its Cultivation*, edited by Harold H. Anderson. New York: Harper.

Fux, Johann Joseph. 1725. *Gradus ad Parnassum*. English translation by Alfred Mann as *Steps to Parnassus: The Study of Counterpoint*. New York: W. W. Norton, 1943.

Gabrielsson, Alf. 1999. "Music Performance." In *The Psychology of Music*, edited by Diana Deutsch, 501–602. Second edition. New York: Academic Press.

Galewitz, Herb (ed.). 2001. *Music: A Book of Quotations*. Mineola, NY: Dover.

Galton, Francis. 1879. "Psychometric Experiments." *Brain* 2: 148–162.

Gardner, Howard. 1983. *Frames of Mind: The Theory of Multiple Intelligences*. New York: Basic Books.

Gazdar, Gerald, and Chris Mellish. 1989. *Natural Language Processing in LISP: An Introduction to Computational Linguistics*. Reading, MA: Addison-Wesley.

Gelernter, David. 1994. *The Muse in the Machine: Computerizing the Poetry of Human Thought*. New York: Free Press.

Gell-Mann, Murray. 1994. *The Quark and the Jaguar: Adventures in the Simple and the Complex*. New York: W. H. Freeman.

Gevarter, William. 1984. *Artificial Intelligence, Expert Systems, Computer Vision, and Natural Language Processing*. Park Ridge, NJ: Noyes.

Gilhooly, Kenneth. 1988. *Thinking: Directed, Undirected, and Creative*. Second edition. San Diego: Academic Press.

Gjerdingen, Robert. 1988. *A Classic Turn of Phrase*. Philadelphia: University of Pennsylvania Press.

Gleick, James. 1987. *Chaos: Making a New Science*. New York: Viking.

Gollancz, Israel. 1926. *The Sources of Hamlet: With Essays on the Legend*. London: Oxford University Press.

Gordon, W. J. J. 1972. "On Being Explicit about the Creative Process." *Journal of Creative Behavior* 6: 295–300.

Greene, Brian. 1999. *The Elegant Universe: Superstrings, Hidden Dimensions, and the Quest for the Ultimate Theory*. New York: W. W. Norton.

Grout, Donald. 1980. *A History of Western Music*. Third edition. New York: W. W. Norton.

Harris, James. 1772. *Three Treatises: The First Concerning Art; the Second Concerning Music, Painting, and Poetry; the Third Concerning Happiness*. Third edition. London: Nourse.

Hindemith, Paul. 1937. *The Craft of Musical Composition*. New York: Associated Music Publishers.

Hinton, Geoffrey, and Terrence J. Sejnowski (eds.). 1999. *Unsupervised Learning: Foundations of Neural Computation*. Cambridge, MA: MIT Press.

Hofstadter, Douglas. 1980. *Gödel, Escher, Bach: An Eternal Golden Braid*. New York: Vintage Books.

———. 1985. *Metamagical Themas: Questing for the Essence of Mind and Pattern*. New York: Basic Books.

———. 1995. *Fluid Concepts and Creative Analogies: Computer Models of the Fundamental Mechanisms of Thought*. New York: Basic Books.

Holland, John. 1995. *Hidden Order: How Adaptation Builds Complexity*. Reading, MA: Addison-Wesley.

———. 1998. *Emergence: From Chaos to Order*. Reading, MA: Addison-Wesley.

Holland, John, Keith Holyoak, Richard Nisbett, and Paul Thagard. 1986. *Induction: Processes of Inference, Learning, and Discovery*. Cambridge, MA: MIT Press.

Holmes, Robert. 1997. "Requiem for the Soul." *New Scientist* 155/2094: 22–27.

Holyoak, Keith, and Paul Thagard. 1989. "Analogical Mapping by Constraint Satisfaction." *Cognitive Science* 13/3: 295–355.

Hörnel, Dominik, and Wolfram Menzel. 1998. "Learning Musical Structure and Style Using Neural Networks." *Computer Music Journal* 22/4: 44–52.

Huron, David. 1993. "The Humdrum Toolkit: Research Software for Music Scholars." In *Abstracts of Papers Read at the Joint Meeting of the American Musicological Society and the Society for Music Theory*. Madison, WI: A-R Editions.

Jacobson, Marcus. 1978. *Developmental Neurobiology*. Second edition. New York: Plenum Press.

Jenkins, Harold (ed.). 1982. *The Arden Edition of the Works of William Shakespeare: Hamlet*. London: Thomson Learning.

Johnson, George. 1997. "Undiscovered Bach? No, a Computer Wrote It." *New York Times*, November 11, pp. B9–B10.

Johnson-Laird, P. N. 1991. "Jazz Improvisation: A Theory at the Computational Level." In *Representing Musical Structure*, edited by P. Howell, R. West, and I. Cross, 291–325. London: Academic Press.

Jones, David Evan. 2000. "Composer's Assistant for Atonal Counterpoint." *Computer Music Journal* 24/4: 33–43.

Jung, Carl. 1966. *The Spirit in Men, Art, and Literature*. New York: Bollingen Foundation.

Kedar-Cabelli, Smadar. 1988. "Analogy—from a Unified Perspective." In *Analogical Reasoning: Perspectives of Artificial Intelligence, Cognitive Science, and Philosophy*, edited by David Helman, 65–103. Boston: Kluwer Academic.

Kellert, Stephen. 1993. *In the Wake of Chaos: Unpredictable Order in Dynamical Systems*. Chicago: University of Chicago Press.

Keppler, Philip. 1956. "Some Comments on Musical Quotation." *Musical Quarterly* 42/October: 473–485.

Kirkpatrick, Ralph (ed.). 1979. *The Clavier-Büchlein vor Wilhelm Friedemann Bach*. New York: Da Capo Press.

———. 1984. *Interpreting Bach's Well-Tempered Clavier: A Performer's Discourse of Method*. New Haven, CT: Yale University Press.

Kivy, Peter. 1984. *Sound and Semblance: Reflections on Musical Representation*. Princeton, NJ: Princeton University Press.

Kling, R. E. 1971. "A Paradigm for Reasoning by Analogy." *Artificial Intelligence* 2: 147–178.

Koestler, Arthur. 1964. *The Act of Creation*. London: Hutchinson.

Köhler, Wolfgang. 1929. *Gestalt Psychology*. New York: Liveright.

Kohonen, Teuvo. 1984. *Self-organization and Associative Memory*. Berlin: Springer-Verlag.

Kostka, Stefan, and Dorothy Payne. 1989. *Tonal Harmony, with an Introduction to Twentieth-century Music*. Second edition. New York: Alfred A. Knopf.

Kramer, Jonathan. 1988. *The Time of Music: New Meanings, New Temporalities, New Listening Strategies*. New York: Schirmer Books.

Kris, Anton. 1982. *Free Association: Method and Process*. New Haven, CT: Yale University Press.

Kris, Ernst. 1952. *Psychoanalytic Explorations in Art*. New York: International Universities Press.

LaRue, Jan. 1961. "Significant and Coincidental Resemblance Between Classical Themes." *Journal of the American Musicological Society* 14/Summer: 224–234.

Leake, David, and Roger Schank. 1990. "Creativity and Learning in a Case-Based Explainer." *Artificial Intelligence* 40/1–3: 353–385.

Lenat, Doug. 1982. "AM: Discovery in Mathematics as Heuristic Search." In *Knowledge-Based Systems in Artificial Intelligence*, edited by Randall Davis and Douglas Lenat, 1–25. New York: McGraw-Hill.

Lévi-Strauss, Claude. 1971. *Mythologiques I–IV*. Paris: Plon.

Lewin, David. 1983. "An Interesting Global Rule for Species Counterpoint." *In Theory Only* 6/6: 19–44.

Lipschutz, Seymour, and Marc Lipson. 2003. *Discrete Mathematics: Based on Schaum's Outline of Theory and Problems of Discrete Mathematics*. Second edition. New York: McGraw-Hill.

MacKay, Donald. 1969. *Information, Mechanism and Meaning*. Cambridge, MA: MIT Press.

Mackintosh, Nicholas. 1983. *Conditioning and Associative Learning*. New York: Oxford University Press.

Mancini, Joseph. 1997. "Symphony from Beyond the Grave." *Santa Barbara News Press*, September 18.

Mandelbrot, Benoit. 2001. "The Fractal Universe." In *The Origins of Creativity*, edited by Karl Pfenninger and Valerie Shubik, 191–212. London: Oxford University Press.

Mazlish, Bruce. 1993. *The Fourth Discontinuity: The Co-evolution of Humans and Machines*. New Haven, CT: Yale University Press.

McCorduck, Pamela. 1979. *Machines Who Think*. San Francisco: W. H. Freeman.

———. 1991. *Aaron's Code: Meta-Art, Artificial Intelligence, and the Work of Harold Cohen*. New York: W. H. Freeman.

Meyer, Leonard. 1989. *Style and Music: Theory, History, and Ideology*. Philadelphia: University of Pennsylvania Press.

———. 2000. *The Spheres of Music: A Gathering of Essays*. Chicago: University of Chicago Press.

Michalski, Ryszard, Jaime Carbonell, and Tom Mitchell (eds.). 1986. *Machine Learning: An Artificial Intelligence Approach*, vol. 2. Los Altos, CA: Morgan Kaufmann.

Miclet, Laurent. 1986. *Structural Methods in Pattern Recognition*. Berlin: Springer-Verlag.

Minsky, Marvin. 1963. "Introduction." In *Computers and Thought*, edited by Edward A. Feigenbaum and Julian Feldman. New York: McGraw-Hill.

———. 1986. *The Society of Mind*. New York: Simon and Schuster.

———. 1995. "Steps Toward Artificial Intelligence." In *Computation and Intelligence: Collected Readings*, edited by George F. Luger, 47–90. Menlo Park, CA: AAAI Press.

Miranda, Eduardo Reck. 2001. *Composing Music with Computers*. Oxford: Focal Press.

Mitchell, Tom M. 1997. *Machine Learning*. New York: McGraw-Hill.

Moore, Johanna, and William Swartout. 1991. "A Reactive Approach to Explanation: Taking the User's Feedback into Account." In *Natural Language Generation in Artificial Intelligence and Computational Linguistics*, edited by Cécile Paris, William Swartout, and William Mann, 1–48. Boston: Kluwer Academic.

Morton, Lawrence. 1979. "Footnotes to Stravinsky Studies: Le Sacre du printemps." *Tempo* 128: 9–16.

Nattiez, Jean-Jacques. 1990. *Music and Discourse: Toward a Semiology of Music*. English translation by Carolyn Abbate. Princeton, NJ: Princeton University Press. French ed., *Musicologie générale et sémiologie*. Paris: Christian Bourgois, 1987.

Newton, Isaac. 1726. *Philosophiae Naturalis Principia Mathematica*. London: Apud Guil. and Joh. Innys.

Nuttall, N. 1997. "Composers Give Encores by Computer." *London Times*, August.

Nyman, Michael. 1974. *Experimental Music: Cage and Beyond*. New York: Schirmer Books.

O'Hara, Scott. 1994. "A Blackboard Architecture for Case Re-interpretation." In *Proceedings of the Second European Workshop on Case-Based Reasoning*. Chantilly, France: Fondation Royaumont.

O'Hara, Scott, and Bipin Indurkhya. 1994. "Incorporating (Re)Interpretation in Case-Based Reasoning." In *Topics in Case-Based Reasoning: Selected Papers from the First European Workshop on Case-Based Reasoning*, edited by Stefan Weiss, Klaus-Dieter Althoff, and Michael Richter, 246–260. Berlin: Springer-Verlag.

Petty, Wayne. 1999. "Chopin and the Ghost of Beethoven." *19th-Century Music* 22/Summer: 281–299.

Pfenninger, Karl H., and Valerie R. Shubik (eds.). 2001. *The Origins of Creativity*. London: Oxford University Press.

Plantinga, Leon. 1977. *Clementi: His Life and Music*. London: Oxford University Press.

Powers, David, and Christopher Turk. 1989. *Machine Learning of Natural Language*. London: Springer-Verlag.

Pressing, Jeffrey. 1988. "Improvisation: Methods and Models." In *Generative Processes in Music: The Psychology of Performance, Improvisation, and Composition*, edited by John A. Sloboda, 129–178. Oxford: Clarendon Press.

Putnam, Karl. 1997. "David Cope: Experiments in Musical Intelligence." *Computer Music Journal* 21/3: 102–103.

Racter. 1984. *The Policeman's Beard Is Half Constructed: Computer Prose and Poetry*. New York: Warner Books.

Reilly, Ronan, and Noel Sharkey (eds.). 1991. *Connectionist Approaches to Natural Language Processing*. Hillsdale, NJ: Lawrence Erlbaum.

Restak, Richard. 1988. *The Mind*. New York: Bantam Books.

Réti, Rudolph. 1962. *The Thematic Process in Music*. New York: Macmillan.

Reynolds, Christopher. 2003. *Motives for Allusion: Context and Content in Nineteenth-century Music*. Cambridge, MA: Harvard University Press.

Riemenschneider, Albert (ed.). 1941. *371 Harmonized Chorales and 69 Chorale Melodies with Figured Bass by J. S. Bach*. New York: G. Schirmer.

Roads, Curtis. 1996. *The Computer Music Tutorial*. Cambridge, MA: MIT Press.

Rochberg, George. 1969. "No Center." *The Composer* 2/1: 86–91.

Rosen, Charles. 1994. *The Frontiers of Meaning*. New York: Hill and Wang.

Ruelle, David. 1991. *Chance and Chaos*. Princeton, NJ: Princeton University Press.

Schaffer, S. 1994. "Making Up Discovery." In *Dimensions of Creativity*, edited by Margaret Boden, 13–52. Cambridge, MA: MIT Press.

Schenker, Heinrich. 1935. *Der freie Satz*. Vienna: Universal Editions. Translated and edited by Ernst Oster as *Free Composition*. New York: Longman, 1979.

Schoenberg, Arnold. 1984. *Style and Idea: Selected Writings of Arnold Schoenberg*, edited by Leo Stein, translated by Leo Black. Berkeley: University of California Press. First published New York: St. Martins Press, 1975.

Schottstaedt, William. 1989. "Automatic Counterpoint." In *Current Directions in Computer Music Research*, edited by Max Mathews and John Pierce, 199–214. Cambridge, MA: MIT Press.

Schwartz, Elliott, and Barney Childs (eds.). 1967. *Contemporary Composers on Contemporary Music*. New York: Holt, Rinehart and Winston.

Scott, Hugh Arthur. 1927. "Indebtedness in Music." *Musical Quarterly* 13/4: 497–509.

Searle, John. 1997. *The Mystery of Consciousness*. New York: New York Review of Books.

Selfridge-Field, Eleanor. 2001. "Composition, Combinatorics, and Simulations: A Historical and Philosophical Enquiry." In David Cope, *Virtual Music*, 187–219. Cambridge, MA: MIT Press.

Shelley, Percy. 1821/1966. *A Defense of Poetry*. In *Selected Poetry and Prose of Shelley*, edited by Herbert Bloom. New York: Signet Classics.

Shepherd, Gordon. 1988. *Neurobiology*. Second edition. Oxford: Oxford University Press.

Simon, Herbert A. 1995. "Machine as Mind." In *Computation and Intelligence: Collected Readings*, edited by George F. Luger, 675–691. Menlo Park, CA: AAAI Press.

Simon, Herbert, and Richard K. Sumner. 1968. "Pattern in Music." In *Formal Representation of Human Judgment*, edited by B. Kleinmuntz. New York: Wiley.

Smoliar, Stephen. 1994. "Computers Compose Music, but Do We Listen?" *Music Theory Online* 0/6.

Sternberg, Robert. 1985. *Beyond IQ: A Triarchic Theory of Human Intelligence*. New York: Cambridge University Press.

Stewart, Ian. 2002. *Does God Play Dice?: The Mathematics of Chaos*. Second edition. Malden, MA: Blackwell.

Stravinsky, Igor. 1960. *Poetics of Music in the Form of Six Lessons*, translated by Arthur Knodel and Ingolf Dahl. New York: Vintage Books.

Stravinsky, Igor, and Robert Craft. 1960. *Memories and Commentaries*. Garden City, NY: Doubleday.

Symbolic Composer. 1997. http://www.xs4all.nl/~psto

Tarasti, Eero. 2002. *Signs of Music: A Guide to Musical Semiotics*. Berlin: Mouton de Gruyter.

Thornton, Chris. 2002. "Creativity and Runaway Learning." In *Creativity, Cognition, and Knowledge: An Interaction*, edited by Terry Dartnall, 239–249. Westport, CT: Praeger.

Tillich, Paul. 1951. *Systematic Theology*. Chicago: University of Chicago Press.

Todd, Neil. 1993. "Vestibular Feedback in Musical Performance: Response to Somatosensory Feedback in Musical Performance," edited by J. Sundberg and V. Verrillo. *Musical Perception* 10: 379–382.

Todd, Peter, and Gareth Loy (eds.). 1991. *Music and Connectionism*. Cambridge, MA: MIT Press.

Treffert, Darold, and Gregory Wallace. 2002. "Islands of Genius." *Scientific American* 286/6: 76–85.

Treitler, Leo. 1997. "Language and the Interpretation of Music." In *Music and Meaning*, edited by Jenefer Robinson, 23–56. Ithaca, NY: Cornell University Press.

Turing, Alan M. 1950. "Computing Machinery and Intelligence." *Mind* 59/236 pp. 433–460. Reprinted in *Mind and Machines*, edited by Alan R. Anderson. Englewood Cliffs, NJ: Prentice-Hall.

———. 1992. *Collected Works of A. M. Turing*, edited by D. C. Ince. Amsterdam: North-Holland.

Turner, Mark. 1988. "Categories and Analogies." In *Analogical Reasoning: Perspectives of Artificial Intelligence, Cognitive Science, and Philosophy*, edited by David H. Helman, 3–24. Boston: Kluwer Academic.

Turner, Scott. 1994. *The Creative Process: A Computer Model of Storytelling and Creativity*. Hillsdale, NJ: Lawrence Erlbaum.

Vidal-Ruiz, Enrique, and Pedro Cruz-Alcázar. 1997. "A Study of Grammatical Inference Algorithms in Automatic Music Composition and Music Style Recognition." In *Proceedings of the 1997 Workshop on Grammatical Inference, Automata Induction, and Language Acquisition*. Nashville, TN: ICML.

Wallas, Graham. 1926. *The Art of Thought*. New York: Harcourt Brace.

Webster's Collegiate Dictionary. 1991. New York: Random House.

Webster's New World Dictionary. 1984. New York: Warner Books.

Weizenbaum, Joseph. 1976. *Computer Power and Human Reason: From Judgment to Calculation*. San Francisco: W. H. Freeman.

Wermter, Stefan, Ellen Riloff, and Gabriele Scheler (eds.). 1996. *Connectionist, Statistical, and Symbolic Approaches to Learning for Natural Language Processing*. New York: Springer-Verlag.

Wertheimer, Max. 1945. *Productive Thinking*. New York: Harper and Brothers.

Widmer, Gerhard. 1992. "The Importance of Basic Musical Knowledge for Effective Learning." In *Understanding Music with AI: Perspectives on Music Cognition*, edited by Mira Balaban, Kemal Ebcioĝlu, and Otto Laske, 490–507. Cambridge, MA: MIT Press.

———. 1993. "Understanding and Learning Musical Expression." In *Proceedings of the 1993 International Computer Music Conference*. San Francisco: International Computer Music Association.

Wilson, Fred, and Bruce Alberston. 2002. *303 Tricky Checkmates*. Second edition. New York: Cardoza.

Winston, Patrick Henry. 1984. *Artificial Intelligence*. Second edition. Reading, MA: Addison-Wesley.

Wolf, Fred Alan. 1981. *Taking the Quantum Leap: The New Physics for Nonscientists*. San Francisco: Harper & Row.

Wolfram, Stephen. 2002. *A New Kind of Science*. Champaign, IL: Wolfram Media.

Appendix A: Experiments in Musical Intelligence Final Work List

This library of computer-composed works (1981–2003) consists of 35 composers (roughly 1,000 individual pieces).

Composer	Work	Orch.	Dur.
By Composer			
Albinoni	Adagio	strings	3′
Bach, J. S.	Brandenburg	orch	21′
	Cantata	str/ch/solos	25′
	Chorales (371)	SATB	16°
	Cello Suite	cello	20′
	Guitar Suite	guitar (lute)	8′
	Inventions (15)	pf	30′
	Keyboard Conc	kb/orch	21′
	Well-Programmed Clavier	hpschd	5°
Bach, C. P. E.	Flute Sonata	fl/pf	16′
Barber	(see collections)		
Bartók	Kosmos	pf	1′
	Bulgarian Dan.	pf	1′30″
Beethoven	Bagatelle	pf	4′
	Sonata	pf	10′
	Symphony 10	orch/ch	60′
Brahms	Intermezzo	pf	3′
	Rhapsody	pf	2′40″
Chopin	Mazurkas (56)	pf	3°
	Nocturne	pf	3′
	Variations	pf	10′
Cope	Horizons	orch	10′
	Vacuum Genesis	pf	4′
	24 Preludes and Fugues	pf	3°
Debussy	Le Prelude	pf	4′
Exp/Mus/In.	World Anthem	v/pf	2′
	L'Histoire du musique	orch	25′
	48 Inventions	pf	2°
Gershwin	Prelude	pf	2′40″
Grieg	(see collections)		
Joplin	Rags (2)	pf	7′10″
Liszt	(see collections)		
Mahler	Adagio	strings	8′
	Four Songs	sopr/ens	28′
	Lieder von Leben und Tod	orch/soloists	25′
	Mahler (opera)	orch/ch/solos	4°
	short version		2°
	Sym of Songs	orch	30′
	Suite/Winds	wind ens	40′30″
	The Mahler Canticles	choir, winds	14′
	Three Songs	tenor/pf	12′
	Three Duets	pf/AT/ch	20′
Mendelssohn	Song w/o Words	pf	3′
Messiaen	*Debut du Temps*	ch orch	4′
	l'éternité	organ	4′
	l'éternité	str orch	4′

Composer	Work	Orch.	Dur.
Mozart	Concerto	pf/orch	29'
	Mozart in Bali	pf/orch	10'
	Mozart (opera)	orch/soloists	3°
	Rondo Capriccio	vc/orch	12'
	short version		2°
	Sonatas (3)	pf	31'
	Quartet	str qt	19'
	Symphony	orch	27'
Mussorgsky	(see collections)		
Palestrina	Mass	chorus	16'
Prokofiev	Sonata 10	pf	12'
Puccini	(see collections)		
Rachmaninoff	Concerto	pf/orch	38'
	Suite	2 pf	8'
Ravel	(see collections)		
Scarlatti	Sonata	pf	2'30"
Schoenberg	*Eine Kleine Stücke*	pf	2'
Schubert	(see collections)		
Schumann	*Schumann* (op)	orch/soloists	3°
	short version		2°
Scriabin	*Poeme*	pf	3'
Stravinsky	(see collections)		
Strauss (J.)	(see collections)		
Strauss (R.)	(see collections)		
Vivaldi	*Zodiac*	strs/solos	56'
	Violin Conc	str/vn	12'
	Cello Conc	str/vc	13'
	Vn/vc Conc	str/v-vc	12'
	2 Vn Conc	str/2 vns	11'
Webern	*Drome*	pf	1'

Collections

Five Songs			
(Bach, Puccini, Mozart, Strauss, Schubert)		pf/voice	10'
Dedications (also in arr. as Suite for 2 pianos)			
(Bach/Barber, Prokofiev, Stravinsky)		orch	20'
Five Songs			
(generic Broadway style)		pf/voice	7'
Rearrangements			
(Grieg, Liszt, Strauss, Mussorgsky, Ravel)		2 pfs	12'
The Ugly Duckling			
(Prokofiev, Bach, Stravinsky, Beethoven, etc.)		orch, mod	25'
Suite for 2 pianos (Bach/Barber, Prokofiev, Stravinsky)		2 pf (arr)	20'

By Orchestration

Opera

Mahler	*Mahler* (opera)	orch/ch/solos	4°
	short version		2°

Composer	Work	Orch.	Dur.
Mozart	*Mozart* (opera)	orch/soloists	3°
	short version		2°
Schumann	*Schumann* (opera)	orch/soloists	3°
	short version		2°
Orchestra			
Albinoni	Adagio	strings	3'
Bach, J. S.	B'burg Conc	orch	21'
	Keyboard Conc	kb/orch	21'
Beethoven	Symphony	orch/ch	60'
Cope	*Horizons*	orch	10'
Dedications (Bach/Barber, Prokofiev, Stravinsky)		orch	20'
Mahler	Symphony of Ss	orch	30'
	Lied Leben/Tod	orch/soloists	25'
Messiaen	*Début du Temps*	ch orch	4'
	l'éternité	str orch	4'
Mozart	Symphony	orch	27'
	Concerto	pf/orch	29'
	Mozart in Bali	pf/orch	10'
	Rondo Capriccio	pf/orch	12'
Rachmaninoff	Concerto	pf/orch	38'
Stravinsky	*Sacre*	orch	3'10"
Vivaldi	*Zodiac*	strs/solos	56'
	Violin Conc	strs/vn	12'
	Cello Conc	strs/vc	13'
	Vn/Vc Conc	strings/v-vc	12'
	2 Vn Conc	strs/2 vns	11'
The Ugly Duckling			
(Prokofiev, Bach, Stravinsky, Beethoven, etc.)		orch, mod	25'
Wind Ensemble			
Mahler	Suite for Wds	wind ens	40'30"
	Mahler Cants	choir/ens	14'
Choir			
Bach, J. S.	Cantata	str/ch/solos	25'
	Chorales (365)	SATB	16°
Mahler	Mahler Cants	choir/ens	14'
Palestrina	Mass	chorus	16'
String Quartet			
Mozart	Quartet	str qt	19'
Violin			
Vivaldi	Violin Conc	strs/vn	12'
	Vn/Vc Conc	strs/v-vc	12'
	2 Violin Conc	strs/2 vns	11'

Composer	Work	Orch.	Dur.
Violoncello			
Bach, J. S.	Cello Suite	cello	20′
Vivaldi	Cello Conc	strings/vc	13′
	Vn/Vc Conc	strs/v-vc	12′
Keyboard (solo)			
Bach, J. S.	Inventions	pf	30′
	Well-Programmed Clavier	hpschd	5°
Bartók	*Kosmos*	pf	1′
	Bulgarian D.	pf	1′30″
Beethoven	Sonata	pf	10′
	Bagatelle	pf	4′
Brahms	Rhapsody	pf	2′40″
	Intermezzo	pf	3′
Chopin	Mazurkas (56)	pf	3°
	Nocturne	pf	3′
	Prelude (var)	pf	10′
Cope	*Vacuum Genesis*	pf	4′
	24 Preludes and Fugues	pf	3°
Debussy	*Le Prélude*	pf	4′
Gershwin	Prelude	pf	2′40″
Grieg	(see collections)		
Joplin	Rags (2)	pf	7′10″
Liszt	(see collections)		
Mendelssohn	Song w/o Words	pf	3′
Mozart	Sonatas (3)	pf	31′
Prokofiev	Sonata 10	pf	12′
Ravel	(see collections)		
Scarlatti	Sonata	pf	2′30″
Schoenberg	*Eine Kleine*	pf	2′
Scriabin	*Poème*	pf	3′
Strauss (J.)	(see collections)		
Strauss (R.)	(see collections)		
Webern	*Drome*	pf	1′
2 pianos			
Bach, J. S.	Keyboard Conc	2 pf (arr)	21′
Rachmaninoff	Suite	2 pf	8′
	Concerto	2 pf (arr)	38′
Rearrangements			
(Grieg, Liszt, Strauss, Mussorgsky, Ravel)		2 pfs	12′
Suite for 2 Pianos (Bach/Barber, Prokofiev, Stravinsky)		2 pf (arr)	20′
Voice			
Bach, J. S.	Cantata	str/ch/solos	25′
Exp. Mus. In.	*World Anthem*	v/pf	2′
Five Songs			
(Bach, Puccini, Mozart, Strauss, Schubert)		pf/voice	10′

Composer	Work	Orch.	Dur.
Five Songs			
(generic Broadway style)		pf/voice	7'
Mahler	Four Songs	sopr/ens	28'
	Three Songs	tenor/pf	12'
	Three Duets	pf/al/ten/ch	20'
(also see opera)			
Flute			
Bach, C. P. E. Flute Sonata		fl/pf	16'
Messiaen	*Début du Temps*	ch orch	4'
Organ			
Messiaen	*l'éternité*	organ	4'
Guitar (lute)			
Bach, J. S.	Suite	guitar (lute)	8'

Appendix B: Database Format

Optimally, databases need to respond reliably to the needs of a program and not require unnecessary translation to different formats. This means, at least for the applications described in this book, that data should respond to analysis, pattern matching, composition, and MIDI performance. My programs use what I call *events* for this purpose. Events describe the various attributes of each note with a single list of parameters of five separate but related elements.

The first element of the event list is the ontime. It is listed first because it is the most often referenced piece of data in the list. Ontimes of notes must constantly be refigured because the very nature of the recombinant approach requires that music be reordered and the resulting ontimes recalculated for performance. Ontimes are computed at 1,000 ticks per second. Ontimes can reach quite large numbers. However, dividing by 1,000 makes time computations fairly simple.

The second entry of the event list is pitch. It is figured from the MIDI standard with middle C (520 cycles per second) equal to MIDI note number 60; additions and subtractions of 12 produce C in various octaves, and additions and subtractions of 1 represent half steps. Thus, 60–62–64–65–67–69–71–72 is the C-major scale (with intervening numbers producing chromaticism to that key). Events describe only *notes* (note ons and note offs) and not *rests*, relieving databases of vast amounts of unnecessary data. Rests occur naturally as the result of a lack of events.

The third entry of the event list is duration. Duration, like ontime, is calculated at 1,000 ticks per second. The duration of an event can be figured independently as the addition of the ontime and the duration. Thus, an event with an ontime of 6,000 and an offtime of 7,000 has a duration of 1,000. Such information can be important to analysis systems when events straddle proposed grouping subdivisions. Duration information can be contradicted by choice of timbre in the MIDI output device. For example, performing a note of long duration with a sound of short duration (or vice versa) can nullify much of the durational aspects of the program's output.

The fourth entry of the event list is channel number (1 to 16). Channel numbers indicate the MIDI channel on which events are scheduled for performance. Ultimately, channels provide access to synthesizer and sampler timbre selections via MIDI interfaces. Channels may be assigned various roles in the MIDI instrument that is chosen for performance. The channel numbers stored in the database are intended to indicate the original voice separation of the music entered into that database.

The fifth entry of the event list represents dynamics. Dynamics are based on 0 equaling silence and 127 equaling fortissimo, with the numbers between these values being relative to these extremes. Aftertouch, tremolo, filter shaping, and so on are considered post-MIDI controls in my software, and therefore are left to hardware/

software combinations in the synthesizer/sampler stage of performance. Dynamics are relative and can be enhanced or contradicted by gain controls in amplifiers in the various playback hardware connected to the MIDI interface.

It should be noted that events are open-ended; that is, one may add any desired parameters to the end of event lists with no ill effects on the first five elements. For example, a sixth position in some events may be occupied by an asterisk indicating that the event has been transposed during composition. This asterisk, however, will not play a role in performance.

Events occur in larger phrase/work lists and do not occur independently. Thus, because works can often be quite long, finding a given event can be difficult. The best method for locating events is by finding ontimes. Events are typically ordered chronologically to save time and make visual event reading easier.

Appendix C: Ark Endings

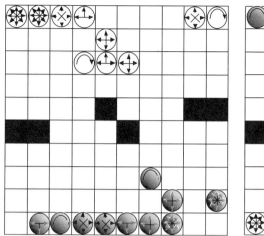

1. White moves first and wins in two moves.

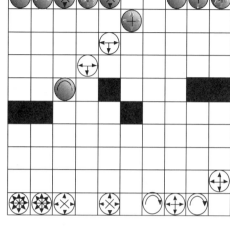

3. Black moves first and wins in 2.

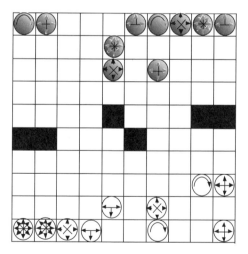

2. Black moves first and wins in 2.

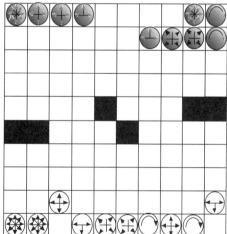

4. Black moves first and wins in 2.

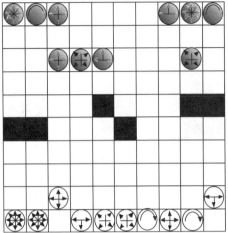

5. Black moves first and wins in 2.

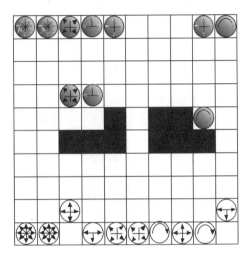

7. Black moves first and wins in 2.

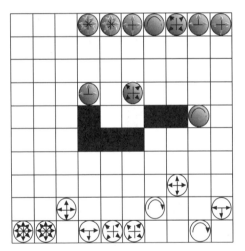

6. Black moves first and wins in 2.

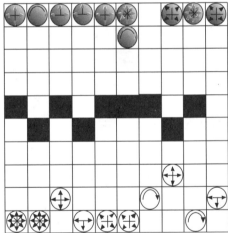

8. Black moves first and wins in 2.

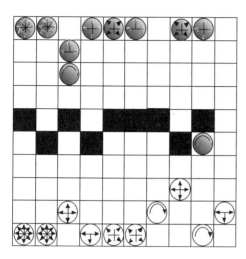

9. Black moves first and wins in 3.

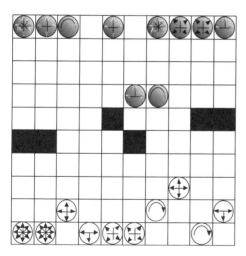

10. Black moves first and wins in 3.

Appendix D: Listing of Book Programs

The list below contains the names of all the programs described in this book and available at the author's Web site (http://arts.ucsc.edu/faculty/cope/software/CMMC). The parenthetical number following each program name indicates the chapter in which that program is described. A number of these programs appear in two different forms: platform dependent and platform independent. In the former case, the program will work only on the described Macintosh platform. In the latter case, the program should work on any platform for which a Common Lisp application exists.

Poet	(2)
Markov	(3)
CA	(3)
Cosine	(3)
Sonify	(3)
Network	(3)
Fuzzy	(3)
Chorale	(4)
Improvise	(4)
Sorcerer	(5)
Gradus	(6)
Infer	(6)
Analogy	(6)
SPEAC	(7)
Serendipity	(8)
Associate	(9)
Apprentice	(11)

Appendix E: Virtual Beethoven Symphony No. 10, Second Movement

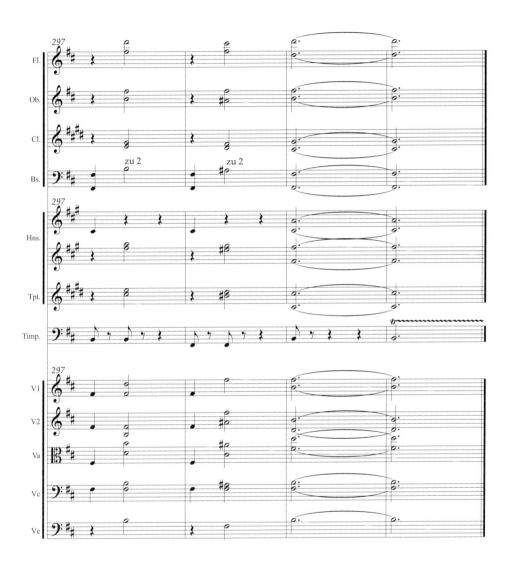

Index

Aaron, 4, 46, 299, 359, 378, 381. *See also* Cohen
Abacist, 58–59
Abel, Carl Friedrich, 137
Accidents, 27–28, 260. *See also* Creativity
ACME (Analogical Constraint Mapping Engine) program, 208
Acoustics, 234, 252–256. *See also* SPEAC
Adaptability, 8, 22. *See also* Creativity
Adaptive software, 295–296
Aesthetics, 10, 13, 259, 345–375
Agawu, V. Kofi, 140, 377
Age of Enlightenment, 39
Agents, 43. *See also* Genetic algorithms
Aikin, James, 353, 377
Alice program, 207, 243–244, 258, 307, 317, 326, 364
Allusional language, 158. *See also* Allusion
Allusion, xi, 125–176, 258, 264, 266, 267, 326–331, 333–338, 353, 355, 366, 368, 369. *See also* Referential analysis; Quotation; Paraphrase; Likeness; Frameworks; Commonalities
association networks and, 327–330, 333–338
avoidance of, 126
Bach and, 202
defined, 127
detection of, 139–153, 330, 333
fugues and, 212
improvising and, 112
literature and, 127
Interpretation of, 153–176
musical creativity and, ix
musical meaning and, 6
recognition of, 128–129
recombinant processes and, 251, 324
in Russian music, 125
taxonomy of, 128
timing, 127
typology of, 128
&& special symbol and, 313–317
AM program, 47–49
Ames, Charles, 60, 76, 377
ANALOGY program, 208. *See also* Analogy
Analogy program, 217–218, 397. *See also* Analogy
Analogy, ix, 207–219, 296. *See also* Analogy program, ANALOGY program
defined, 217
direct, 11
fantasy and, 11
-making programs, 208–209
meaning and, 6
musical examples, 210–219
personal identification, 11
role in creativity, 12, 207–208
rules, inference, and, 177, 181

symbolic, 11
&& special symbol and, 316
Anderson, Alan, 205, 273, 274, 377
Anderson, Hans Christian, 356
Antecedent, 95, 96, 226, 234, 235, 241, 243. *See also* SPEAC
Apprentice program, 334–341, 334, 364, 397
Archetypes, 40
Arecibo radio telescope, 252. *See also* Astronomy
Aristotle, 39, 307
Ark, game of, 177–181, 393–395
Art, 4, 6–7, 10, 12, 13, 21, 23, 28, 38, 39, 46, 51, 273, 357. *See also* Aaron
Artificial creativity, vii. *See also* Creativity
Artificial intelligence (AI). *See also* Intelligence
Assayag, Gerard, 62, 377
Associate program, 275–280, 283–286, 291–294, 297, 303, 307–308, 322–323, 339, 397
Association, xi, 10, 104, 110, 219, 271–324, 326–331, 333, 338–340, 344, 369, 370, 372-374. *See also* Associate program; Predispositional weightings; Inductive association; Polymodality
adaptive software and, 295
and adaptive systems, 296
-based procedures, 65
creativity and, 273, 368
ELIZA and, 275
Experiments in Musical Intelligence and, 346, 366
free, ix, 39, 287–288
Gradus and, 204
improvisation and, 113
incentive and, 336–337
indirect, 278
inductive, viii, ix, 218 (*see also* Associative induction, inductive association)
John Searle's Chinese-room argument and, 294
learned, 272
Markov chains and, 282
mathematics and, 287
natural language processing and, 275
networks, 44, 271–324
recursive, 304–324
rules-based programming techniques and, 284
SPEAC and, 303, 304
subconscious and, 39
understanding and, 281
Associationism, 39. *See also* Association
Associational cortex, 273
Association networks. *See* Association
Associative induction, 290, 293, 303, 335, 337. *See also* Association; Inductive association
Associative memory, 274. *See also* Association
Associative neural networks, 274
Asteroidian evolution, 36, 38. *See also* Astronomy